The Last Country Houses

The Last Country Houses

CLIVE ASLET

YALE UNIVERSITY PRESS
NEW HAVEN AND LONDON
1982

For Naomi

Designed by Faith Brabenec Hart
Line drawings by Russell Barnett
Filmset in Monophoto Baskerville by
BAS Printers Limited, Over Wallop, Hampshire
Printed in Belgium by
Brepols S.A., Turnhout

Library of Congress Cataloging in Publication Data

Aslet, Clive, 1955–
   The last country houses.

   Includes bibliographical references and index.
      1. Manors—England.   2. Architecture, Edwardian—
England.   3. Architecture, Modern—20th Century—England.
I. Title.
NA7620.A8   1982   728.8′3′0942   82-50439
ISBN 0-300-02904-7

(includes some Scottish!)

(frontispiece) The man-of-war garden at Sedgwick Park, Sussex

Preface

WHEN I began working on this book, it was my intention that it should conclude the English Country Houses series originally published by Country Life in the 1950s and 1960s and particularly associated with the late Christopher Hussey. The dates 1890 to 1939 were chosen to follow on from Mark Girouard's *The Victorian Country House*, which, although first published by Oxford University Press and reprinted in a new edition by Yale, had initially been intended as one of these volumes. However, the book as it now appears has changed so much since the first conception that it can only claim distant kinship with these predecessors.

Intially, I had meant to write thirty-five or so chapters on individual houses, in the manner of the previous books, but it soon became apparent that this method would not be appropriate to the period I was describing. Comparatively few of the houses, at most a dozen, were of sufficient complexity or decorative interest to justify extended analysis and illustration. The largest buildings were not always the most attractive, and many of the most impressive had already been demolished or turned into institutions, with the loss of internal features and consequent problems in obtaining present-day photographs. Therefore, I decided to tackle the subject thematically, in a limited number of long chapters rather than what could have been a multitude of disjointed ones; although if, having said all this, it is still possible to perceive something of a continuing purpose, no one could be more pleased than the author.

Much of the research for this book was undertaken in connection with articles I have published as an architectural writer for *Country Life*. I am immensely grateful to Michael Wright, editor of *Country Life*, for giving me the opportunity to do this work. Although rewritten, corrected, pruned and sometimes altered out of all recognition, some passages of the book were based on articles which have appeared in the magazine, and I am grateful to IPC Magazines Ltd for permission to make use of this copyright material. I would also like to thank other friends and colleagues on *Country Life* for their help, especially Marcus Binney and John Cornforth, who gave me invaluable advice and encouragement; the photographers Alex Starkey and Jonathan M. Gibson, who accompanied me on numerous trips and produced many of the illustrations; and the art editor, Reginald Thompson, who helped organise material from *Country Life*'s remarkable photographic archive.

In addition, I have profitted greatly from the comments of those who saw the manuscript either in whole or in part before publication, in particular those of Mark Girouard. The chapter on servants was read by Andrew Saint, the one on the Arts and Crafts movement by Alan Crawford, that on gardens by Tony Venison and several of the others by Alan Powers, all of whom I would like to thank for generously having given me the benefit of their special knowledge. Of the numerous people who have helped me in other ways, I would particularly like to express my gratitude to Baron Astor of Hever, Edward Barnsley, Countess Beauchamp, the Earl of Bessborough, Andrew Best, Major and Mrs A. Biddulph, Simon Blow, Robert Boutwood, Thomas Cook, Miss Kittie Cruft, Christopher Dalton, Baron Digby, Adam Faith, G. H. Ferriman, Roderick Gradidge, Charles Hall, Christopher Hartley, Peter Howell, Stephen Jones, Lionel Lambourne, David Learmont, Mary Lutyens, Susan Moore, Mr and Mrs Adrian Palmer, Mrs G. F. Pettit, Miss Elsie Seatter, Peyton Skipwith, Gavin Stamp, Clive Wainwright, David Walker and David Watkin. I would also like to thank the staffs of the Royal Institute of British Architects' drawings collection, the London Library, the British Library and numerous record offices throughout the country, especially the Surrey County Record Office at Kingston, for their ready assistance.

Finally, I would like to thank Faith Hart and John Nicoll, without whose energy and experience this book could never have been produced as it has; and also my wife, Naomi, without whose understanding and patience it could not have been produced at all.

PHOTOGRAPHIC CREDITS

British Library 204–5, 207–8; British Transport Commission 131; *Country Life* frontispiece, 1, 2, 12, 25, 27–31, 35, 45, 47–8, 50–1, 53, 57, 64–6, 73–7, 79, 81, 91, 94–5, 102, 110–14, 117, 128, 130, 136, 149, 151, 166, 172–7, 185–8, 190, 196, 198–200, 202–3, 206, 211–12, 216–18, 220–2, 225, 229–30, 232, 236, 238, 240, 244 (photographer Christopher Dalton) 46, 194–5 (photographer Jonathan M. Gibson) IV, XII, XXXIII, XXXIV, 6, 13, 19–21, 26, 40, 84–9, 105–7, 121–7, 134–5, 137–8, 152–6, 178–81, 191, 214–15, 237, 243 (photographer Alex Starkey) XVI, XVII, 3, 7, 11, 13, 42–3, 72, 93, 96–101, 140–5, 157, 160–5, 167–9, 209; Christopher Dalton 109; Howletts and Port Lympne Estates Ltd VI; O. G. Jarman 22, 34, 182, 226; Kent Archives Office 24, 183; National Monuments Record 4, 5, 23, 197, 223; National Monuments Record for Scotland 129, 132–3, 219; National Trust II, XIII, XIX, XXII, XXIII, XXXVI, XXXVII, 78; National Trust for Scotland XI; Adrian Palmer X; Royal Institute of British Architects drawings collection 49, 59, 104, 150,233–5; University Art Collection, Hull 60; Victoria and Albert Museum 52; specially commissioned photographs: Christopher Dalton, Charles Hall, Pat Macdonald, Reg Thompson.

Contents

1. *The Smart Set and the Romantics*

'Such are the follies of untrained minds, who are unable to read experience or to interpret figures. They cannot apprehend the astonishing facts of "super-wealth" as accumulated in this country; as accumulated in the past thirty years.' So wrote the Liberal politician C. F. G. Masterman in *The Condition of England*, published in 1909. Queen Victoria's reign had ended in a blaze of economic activity, which carried exports to a total of £354 million in 1900. Although trade slumped slightly in 1904 and 1909, even this figure had been almost doubled by 1913, when it rose to £635 million—all but £110 million of which was accounted for by home-produced goods.[1] The successful were rich, sometimes very, very rich. Like most of his contemporaries, Masterman was by turns astounded, appalled, and a little fascinated by the gargantuan incomes of the Edwardian plutocracy. Andrew Carnegie, 'the Scoto-American Plutus of Pittsburg', when he sold his Homestead steelworks in 1901, secured an annual return from that source alone of three and a quarter million pounds.[2] Sir Ernest Cassel, the financier, did not think a man rich unless his yearly income was well above two hundred thousand pounds.[3] These and similar statistics, thought Masterman, presented 'the reader with incredible arrays of increase'—increase that was perhaps to some degree an illusion 'fostered by the newspapers';[4] increase that did little to alleviate the poverty that was still the shame of the nation; but increase that left some individuals with unprecedented resources of disposable income.

Where did it all go? asked Masterman. How was it consumed, and what asset of permanent value would be left behind as evidence of the super-wealth of the twentieth century? As a low churchman, Masterman suspected that most of the money was simply wasted. More was spent on sport—largely hunting, shooting and racing—than on the whole British navy. Steam yachts and the baccarat table, not to mention 'motors along all the main roads, golf-courses, game-keepers, gardeners, armies of industrious servants, excursionists, hospitable entertainment of country-house parties', created a façade of 'feverish prosperity'. And Masterman, who wrote his jeremiad as his colleague the Liberal chancellor David Lloyd George was preparing to lay his controversial People's Budget before the Commons, was correct in saying that most of this would vanish without trace.

But there was one area of domestic expenditure whose results would prove lasting: this was the building of country houses. 'Turning to the present time,' wrote E. Guy Dawber,

1

1. Romantic approach to the land: Detmar Blow's farm seen from the front door of his house, Hilles, Gloucestershire

2. The ballroom at Mar Lodge, Aberdeenshire. The taste for shooting sometimes got out of hand.

future president of the Royal Institute of British Architects, in 1908, 'probably more country houses are being built and more money and thought expended on them, than perhaps at any time since the days of the Stuarts'.[5] If, as Masterman lamented (not quite accurately), his generation could not build a cathedral, it could still give rise to castles— witness the fact that only months after *The Condition of England* appeared in 1909, the grocery store owner Julius Drewe commissioned Edwin Lutyens to build him the granite fastness in Devon which became Castle Drogo. Millionaires possessed the means to realise their dreams of chivalry in stone.

This book is about what seem certain to have been the last country houses constructed in Britain. The buildings, erected in the period 1890 to 1939, are country houses rather than houses in the country, in the sense that they to some degree functioned—or gave the illusion that they functioned—as the centres of landed estates, and had attached to them an estate or at least a home farm, and also the offices, outbuildings and lodges associated

3. Country house, garden, lake and land: Sennowe Park, Norfolk, seen from the water-tower

with a substantial house. They are more than simply farmhouses or week-end homes. Although a number of comparatively large houses have been built on estates since the end of the Second World War,[6] it cannot be said that they represent a continuing or coherent tradition, and it is significant that most of them have been built to replace existing country houses which had come to seem too unwieldy for late twentieth-century requirements. Modern social priorities as much as the economic arguments make it impossible to imagine that country houses of Edwardian dimensions will be built in Britain again.

As it is, some of the country houses built between 1890 and 1939 were patently ill-equipped for survival. Born late in the evolutionary chain, they were nevertheless great mammoths of domestic architecture and were frequently unable to adapt to the change in habitat that followed the two World Wars. Inflexible in their service arrangements, they grazed in a savannah of cheap labour and cheap fuel, they basked beneath a sky in which the filmy clouds of income tax and death duties had only just begun to appear. They were

3

badly prepared for the chill. Some late Victorian and Edwardian country houses—Bryanston (Plate 4), Kildonan—fulfilled the purpose for which they were built for not much more than thirty years;[7] in the case of those few country houses built as late as the 1930s, the period of domestic use was not infrequently little more than a decade. Charters, built in 1938, was bought by the aircraft company Vickers in 1950; the Guinness family did not return to Bailiffscourt, finished in 1933, after the Second World War and it is now an hotel. Although not all country houses have done so badly as private homes, some fared worse. Sadly, a large number have been demolished. However, those that survive—whether as borstals or banks, schools, apartments or furniture stores, whether privately occupied or turned into hotels—offer tangible evidence of how super-wealth was spent, of how an age lived and perhaps why it died.

If a man built a country house after 1890, the chances were that his motives were rather narrower than they would have been in the mid-nineteenth century. Then it was expected—although of course it was not inevitable—that the colliery owners, railway magnates and cotton barons who had made their own fortunes would wish to consolidate their economic and social position by investing in land. That probably also meant building a country house. But by the end of the century it was impossible to see setting up in the country as even remotely profitable. Agriculture was depressed, and the life of the house had to be financed by investments elsewhere.

The buildings listed in the catalogue at the back of this book were designed for a semblance of landed life, but the estates were rarely much more than a thousand acres, and even then they were often bought for sport rather than farming. Virtually none was big enough or profitable enough to justify the size of the house it was apparently designed to support. In many cases, it was the form rather than the reality of land ownership that appealed to the generally self-made men who built new country houses; and the myth was not cheap to keep going. The poor state of agriculture also had the effect of providing a less expensive—and perhaps also a more prestigious—alternative to building from new. Malone, the Irish-American millionaire in George Bernard Shaw's *Man and Superman* who was 'coming back to buy England', could boast of having 'the refusal of two of the oldest family mansions' in the kingdom—one historic owner was not able to keep all the rooms dusted, the other was hard up after death duties. Owners who were in less desperate straits, but nevertheless felt the pinch, were coming to rent out their houses by the season. Be he a democrat or a snob, a new man could find a considerable attraction in finding somewhere with a long family history, even if that family was not his own. The German-born diamond magnate Sir Julius Wernher bought Luton Hoo, Cecil Rhodes bought Dalham Hall, the soap-boiler Joseph Watson bought Compton Verney, the newspaper magnate Lord Northcliffe rented Sutton Place, later the home of J. Paul Getty. Consequently, the act of building a new country house was of itself evidence that the owner was strongly committed (or keenly aspired) to a particular way of life; and the role he saw for himself in the country was in turn going to determine the style of his house and the type of architect who built it.

There were essentially two types of owner. There were those who wanted much the same as before, but wanted it smarter, glossier, equipped with the most up-to-date evidences of scientific wizardry (such as telephones, vacuum cleaners and garages for the motor cars), the most up-to-date decorations from a fashionable London firm, and

4

4. The hall at Bryanston, Dorset. Built in 1889–94, it became a school in 1928.

5. The winter garden at Hursley Park, Hampshire

7. The Romantic house: the kitchen court at Rodmarton Manor, Gloucestershire

probably also a winter garden and living hall—the latter representing the most decisive development in country-house planning in the two decades before the First World War. Marble was a favourite material. These owners tended to have what had become a rather old-fashioned attitude to land ownership as a means to social advance.

The other type of owner wanted a country house either because the country embodied a social order they saw disappearing; or because of their concern for the dying rural crafts and traditions; or because they enjoyed the historical fantasy of living in a castle or a building that appeared to be Tudor; or because they did not like the first type of owner or their houses and wanted to get as far away as they could. They were likely to own a farm because it expressed their romantic identification with the land as a way of life. In form, there was naturally some overlap between the houses which embodied these desires—few of the second sort of owner actually went without the benefits of modern technology, although there were some; and both liked to have living halls, if for rather different reasons. But it is not difficult to spot the difference in tone between Manderston (Plate 6) and Rodmarton Manor (Plate 7), or between Eltham Palace and Bailiffscourt.

7

6. The Smart house: the garden front of Manderston, Berwickshire

Punch's Almanack for 1907.

8. Life in a Smart country house, as seen by *Punch* in 1907

The purpose of the smart country house was principally social, and the pace was set by the hosts and hostesses vying to entertain the Prince of Wales (Edward VII). Their houses were conceived as the setting for that governing class, remorseless in the opulence of its tastes, which Hilaire Belloc characterised in his lines 'On a General Election':

> The accursèd power which stands on Privilege
> (And goes with Women, and Champagne and Bridge)
> Broke—and Democracy resumed her reign:
> (Which goes with Bridge, and Women and Champagne.)

The masculine element of a house party ventured into the country to kill pheasants or grouse or the odd stag, but could be sure that it would find champagne and an 'impromptu' meal—a typical one consisted of broth, hashed venison, stewed mutton, game pies, Irish stew, plum pudding and apple fard[8]—in a luncheon tent (possibly provided with floorboards, windows and heating)[9] erected nearby; the hamper would have been carried out by menservants in livery.

The other type of house was not designed for such ostentatious entertaining—although that is not to say that the owners were necessarily neither titled nor rich. The aristocratic intellectual elite known as the Souls generally despised the smart set that eddied around Edward VII. The 'romantic' country houses designed for them, and for bankers, industrialists and company directors who shared their outlook, were intended for what seemed a less artificial, a more genuinely rural, or possibly a more artistic or literary existence. Rather than the glamour of modernity, there was a solid feeling of simple, old-fashioned, even old world Englishness. Their furniture was probably of oak and rather

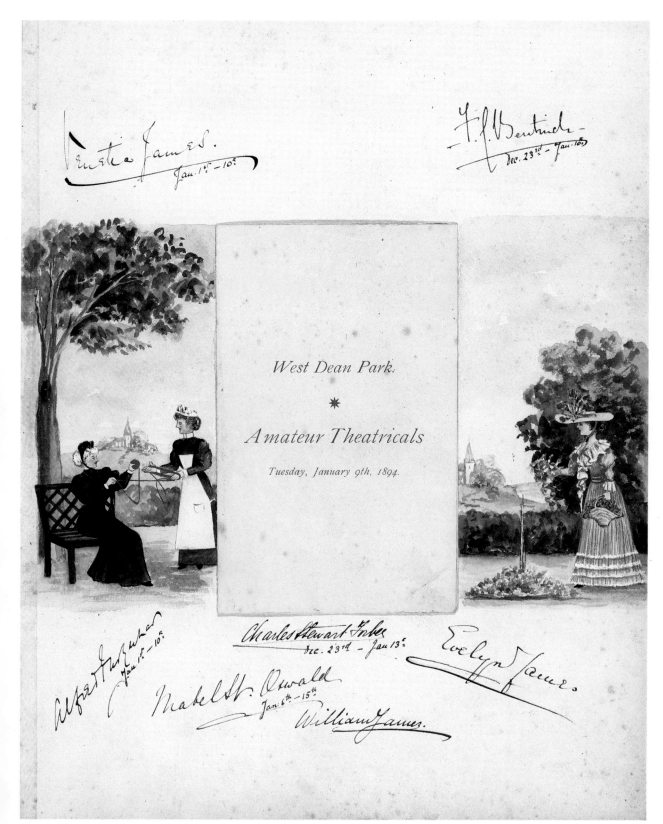

I. Page from the Jameses' guest book at West Dean Park, Sussex, with a programme for amateur theatricals

II. (following pages) Lindisfarne Castle, Northumberland

III. Nashdom, Buckinghamshire

IV. Tylney Hall, Hampshire

9. The range fronting the entrance court at Eastwell Park, Kent, 1926

10. Aerial view of Clover Top Farm, Hertfordshire

spartan, and they slept with plenty of fresh air in the bedrooms. They preferred folk songs and country dancing to bands brought from London to play selections from the light classics. Such houses were designed 'for the comfort of those who live most of the day out of doors in the muddy fields'.[10] Philip Webb expected J. S. Beale, the builder of Standen (Plate 12), to wear hobnailed boots in the country and consequently laid plain red rather than encaustic tiles in the conservatory.[11]

The romanticism of these houses also depended on a sense of the past. Arts and Crafts architects like Webb venerated old buildings: the roots of the movement lay in an ideal of the medieval craftsman, and its nucleus was the Society for the Protection of Ancient Buildings, founded by William Morris in 1877. They believed themselves to be 'rational' and abjured copying historical styles. But other architects accepted only the first part of the creed. After 1909, shaken by suffrage agitation, strikes, changes in the system of government and the threat of war, an increasing number of owners chose to build houses which did not look in any way modern, but literally reproduced the appearance of sixteenth-century buildings, by using old materials and materials faked to seem old— even by moving old buildings *en bloc* to new locations. It was an idyll that suited the nostalgic mood of the age, realised on a larger scale—especially by American millionaires—in the building and remodelling of castles.

It would be tempting to think that a formal style of architecture denoted a formal way of life, but that was not always so. Many Classical houses were informally planned (although symmetry became increasingly common after 1900), and most have the wide corridors and ample staircase halls or living halls that suggest an Edwardian rather than eighteenth-century sense of space. Instead, the difference between the social and the romantic country house lay in the kind of things you did and the type of architect you went to. There were some architects who saw architecture as a profession, employed large numbers of assistants, and enticed clients by drawing attractive perspective sketches. They were probably accommodating on the question of materials in relation to cost, and ran large practices designing not only country houses but probably public buildings as well. Then there were those who saw architecture as an art: on the one hand, the professionally trained architects who nevertheless thought building more important than design, who worked on a small number of buildings at any one time, did much of the work in the office themselves, and would not compromise when they thought their clients were wrong; on the other, the antiquarians who had no architectural training, designed entirely by eye, and had a generally hit or miss approach to construction.

Style of itself was no longer a matter of burning contention, and most architects— unlike their Gothic Revival predecessors—were equally happy using a wide range of styles. However, there was still lingering a conflict between formal and informal values, between Classical planning and the use of romantically weathered materials. Its ideal resolution was found not in the house itself but in the Edwardian garden—whether geometrically planned but with a self-conscious hint of desuetude, or wistfully evoking the Roman Campagna on misty English hills.

The Arts and Crafts country house—embodying such noble but impractical aims— never quite realised the hopes in which the builders set out. But the simpler way of life it expressed, with more sunshine, more time in the open air, less social ritual and probably a smaller size of house, was the one young people increasingly turned to, especially after the

11. The drawing room at Polesden Lacey, Surrey, the ideal setting for Mrs Greville's rich and glittering guests

12. The hall at Standen, Sussex, designed for an entirely different approach to life in the country

First World War. It had to be. Beneath even the luxury of the social country house it was evident that the upper classes were not as secure as they had been; changing tastes and changing habits often reflected a changing economic reality. The easy, opulent way of life associated with King Edward 'the Peacemaker' and seen in the social country house passed away with the outbreak of war four years after his death. The domestic crisis brought about by the shortage of servants had been much discussed in the 1890s and early 1900s, but the First World War made it acute. The vacuum cleaners and other labour-saving inventions that had themselves seemed something of a luxury before 1914 became essentials after the war. Owners tried a way of life that did not require so much cossetting, and sometimes found that they liked it; but it was a way of life which probably required a house in the country rather than a country house. The end of the country-house building tradition can be seen in the increasingly extreme and eccentric houses and estate buildings built in the 1920s and 1930s (Plates 9–10): virtually no common ground was shared between Charters (Plate 53) and Nymans (Plate 117).

Before the First World War, the clients most typical of the different worlds represented by the social and the romantic country houses were probably William Dodge James, the heir to two American fortunes (railways and metal broking), and Edward Hudson, founder of the magazine *Country Life*. According to T. H. S. Escott in 1907, James's house, West Dean Park, in Sussex, was 'socially so characteristic of the Edwardian age that it might have seemed the sudden growth of a single season'[12]—a compliment that not everyone would have welcomed. The Jameses themselves equally expressed the mood of the time. Of all the hosts who entertained Edward VII, James was 'not only the most favoured but the most typical'.[13] The house was not new, but—originally built by James Wyatt in 1804–8—it was replanned, re-equipped, remodelled and redecorated in 1891–3 by Ernest George and Peto, probably the biggest firm of country-house architects at work in the 1890s and early 1900s. The tone of the house was very smart indeed.

It was not easy for a new man to rocket himself into the universe that revolved round the monarch, but it was easier than it would have been fifty years earlier. Money was admired with a frankness which mid-Victorians would have called vulgar. An industrialist building his country house in the 1850s or 1860s was not likely to be warmly received by his county neighbours, and certainly not by those who regarded themselves as the best families or as Society with a capital *S*. His town manners, lack of familiarity with the countryside, and his flashy, *nouveau riche* palace would have been subject to equal ridicule. By 1900, however, parts of Society were turning their eyes towards the main chance. A gentleman's traditional source of income, the land, had become a good deal less dependable; but his equally traditional appreciation of comfort and country pleasures and sports had not abated. Social barriers were lowered, at least in certain directions, and millionaires prepared to suppress the worst signs, if there were any, of eccentricity or boorishness could expect to go almost anywhere.

The lowering of social barriers came from the top. Both as Prince of Wales and as King, Edward VII, whose tastes forever ran ahead of his income, lived in the centre of a mixed group of friends. Many, certainly, were of ancient lineage—the Dukes and Duchesses who would by virtue of birth have been on familiar terms with any monarch—but others were not merely new, but so conspicuously *arriviste* that Society shuddered to read the court circular. 'Rather strange' was how the last Tzar of all the Russias found the house party to

16

13. West Dean Park, Sussex, as remodelled by George and Peto in 1891–3

which he was invited at Sandringham in the early 1890s. 'Most of them were horse dealers,' he wrote to his mother, the Tzarina, 'amongst others a Baron Hirsch.'[14] For a week-end in 1895, the Prince of Wales entertained Colonel North, the 'Nitrate King' of South America, and J. B. Robinson, a millionaire fresh from the South African gold fields, neither of whom would have been received by his mother, Queen Victoria; and— little better—there was also William Waldorf Astor, the somewhat tactless millionaire son of the American Astor family, who had recently settled in Britain.[15]

Baron Hirsch was in fact a Hungarian railway tycoon, and he was able in turn to entertain the Prince on his vast estates in Hungary; but most of the other new friends, including North and Astor, decided to acquire or build country houses in Britain that were on a scale and of a comfort to satisfy royal expectations. Such a house was West Dean. Willie James bought the house shortly after his marriage, which took place in Knightsbridge in 1889. The list of wedding presents already gave a hint of what the flavour of the place would be. The Prince and Princess of Wales gave a sapphire and diamond brooch, while other jewellery included diamond necklaces, diamond pendants, diamond brooches, diamond earrings, diamond bracelets, diamond aigrettes, diamond combs, diamond tiaras and diamond crescents, with a sprinkling of other stones.[16] They equipped Mrs James to hold her own in (literally) the most glittering society—the society in which to wear a crescent instead of a tiara would infallibly have brought down a rebuke from the Prince of Wales; a society in which a blaze of diamonds was the natural accompaniment of décolletage. At Edward VII's coronation, the peeresses had successfully insisted that they should be allowed to show off their diamonds by wearing tiaras on top of their coronets; the effect, commented one courtier, was the equivalent of a man wearing two hats.[17]

But on the whole it is the smaller wedding presents that bring to mind a picture of West Dean. The high degree of personal cossetting the Jameses and their guests enjoyed was prefigured by the way wealth and ingenuity were expended on the most mundane objects. Looking down the numerous columns of print that fashionable papers gave over to the long catalogue of the gifts, one notices two silver button-hooks, a gold-mounted walking stick, a silver string-box, an easel (an adjunct of nearly every smart drawing room, and used for displaying pictures rather than painting at), a paper cutter, menu holders, a

17

14. Polar bear and big-game trophies at West Dean

silver crumb-scraper, two silver moustache brushes, and a polar bear. The polar bear, which was stuffed, held a lamp in one paw and a tray for visiting cards in the other, and was put in the entrance hall (Plate 14).

Willie James was the very image of a 'good fellow'. He was erect, steady-eyed, immaculately groomed, and wore curling moustaches. Much of his youth had been spent exploring and big-game hunting with his brother, Frank. According to his entry in *Who's Who*, he travelled in the Sudan, Abyssinia, Somaliland, Arabia, Afghanistan, the West Coast of Africa and the Arctic. He had been a member of the party that made the first European ascent of mount Tchad-Amba, in Abyssinia, beneath a hail of rocks from the monks in the monastery at the top. He helped map the upper reaches of the Khor Baraka, and spent the winter of 1882–3 in an exploratory expedition along the Somali coast in an Arab dhow. There was also sport. The game book for December 1881 to April 1882 records a total of thirty-five beasts, including a lion, two buffalo and ten gazelle. Lions, when they were shot, were stuffed and put in bamboo and glass cases in the entrance hall at West Dean. The fun ended only when Frank James was killed by the wounded elephant he was attempting to bag in Gabon.

Willie James inherited Frank's yacht, the *Lancashire Witch*, and became a member of the exclusive Royal Yacht Squadron at Cowes, where even Sir Thomas Lipton, the millionaire grocery store owner and friend of Edward VII, had been unable to gain entry. In memory of his brother, he built a row of Elizabethan style almshouses for aged seamen, designed by F. Risbee, overlooking Cowes harbour. Nearness to Cowes was one of the three reasons for the Jameses choosing West Dean; the others were the racing at Goodwood and what was authoritatively said to be the best covert shooting in England.

Mrs Willie James was the eldest daughter of a Scottish baronet, Sir Charles Forbes, and a neice of the Countess of Dudley. While *Vanity Fair*, in an article on 'Beauties of Today', would have called Lady De Grey magnificent, Lady Helen Vincent ethereal, the Duchess of Devonshire stately and Lady Eden 'Madonna-ish', Mrs James was unquestionably witty.[18] She was petite, clever and lovely, but extremely myopic, which forced her to wear spectacles. The architect Edwin Lutyens, who visited West Dean when he built Monkton in 1902, recorded an unflattering first impression: 'Roundabout bar maid,' he wrote to his wife, Lady Emily, 'quizzy, cynical and conceited . . . *Very* short-sighted. Strong pince nez. Hair done in *horrid* Batten way, not suited to a round cherubby face. Nose tipped and very tilted.' But even he was won over. 'Gay thoughtless extravagant as she has rights to be; beautifully dressed lovely rings: makes all the noises and squeaks that only a little woman may dare make.'[19] She was celebrated for amateur theatricals in which house guests were expected to take parts. The local paper praised her own performance as Polly Eccles in *Caste*—a play about the son of a nobleman who married a chorus girl (something that was becoming increasingly frequent).[20] Once, when the Jameses were staying with Baron Hirsch in Hungary, she dressed up as a peasant woman begging for alms and apparently fooled the whole party.

This kind of jape would have made Edward VII roar with laughter. Mrs James was one of a succession of beautiful women—Mrs Paget, Mrs Greville, the Duchess of Marlborough, Lady Londonderry, Mrs Arthur Sassoon, Lady Troubridge, Lady Lonsdale, Mrs Cornwallis-West and, above all, Mrs Keppel—in whose company the elderly monarch took pleasure not just because of their beauty, but because they knew how to keep him amused. Mrs James was probably also his mistress—at least that was the talk—but equally, as the fashionable papers stressed just a little too often, she was a friend of Queen Alexandra. In 1896, while still Princess of Wales, Alexandra actually stayed at West Dean. It was the first time she had spent the night in the house of a commoner, and the magazine *World* hailed the event as a social landmark.

> Until this surprising 'end of the century' not even a Prince had stayed in any but the most important houses. At one time the visit of a monarch or an heir-apparent made the greatest of great ladies, great statesmen or great courtiers, greater. But by degrees the line has been drawn lower and still lower, until at last of very few rich people it can be said that they have never had Royalty under their roofs . . . Mrs James fulfils the conditions of her time—she is amusing.[21]

The typical Edwardian gentleman was no longer a Duke; he could come, as *Vanity Fair* remarked with accustomed asperity, from the ranks of 'very new and unknown people'.

In 1899 the Prince of Wales snubbed the sixth Duke of Richmond by staying at West Dean rather than Goodwood House for the Goodwood week races. The episode says a lot about the new age. The eighty-year-old Duke was a Victorian through and through, held in particular regard by the Queen. He had refused to invite two ladies 'à la présence

15. (left) Mrs Willie James with her son, Edward, in about 1910

16. (right) Lutyens's thumbnail sketch of Willie James, 1902 (reproduced larger than actual size, RIBA)

desquelles le prince tenait beaucoup', as a French paper tactfully put it[22]—and it was no use telling him that they had already been received at court. As for the heir to the throne, his reaction was summed up in the headline to the *Cleveland Plain Dealer*: 'Prince of Wales Sassy'. He informed the Jameses (Mr and Mrs Villie-James as the French report rather endearingly called them) that he wanted to stay with them, and they immediately invited 'les deux dames en question'. Afterwards, he pointedly declared that it had been the best Goodwood he could remember—all of which gives an edge to Belloc's scurrilous lines:

> And there it is that when the dryads grope
> Their young enchanted arms to grace the spring,
> There comes a coroneted envelope,
> And Mrs James will entertain the King!
>
> There will be bridge and booze till after three,
> And, after that, a lot of them will grope
> Along the corridors in Robes de nuit
> Pyjamas, or some other kind of dope.

There is a certain irony in Willie James's punning family motto: 'J'aime à jamais'—I love for always.

West Dean stood on an eight thousand acre estate which James had bought for £200,000 in 1891. Although long and low, the Wyatt house was in the castle style, faced in knapped flint, with an ecclesiastical window over the porch. The architects who renovated it for the Jameses, Ernest George and Peto, had a very large practice building very large houses. A former pupil, Darcy Braddell, remembered how he had plucked up courage to ask if he could look at the drawing on George's desk as he left his first interview:

'Certainly, to be sure, yes,' came the reply. What I saw was the ground plan of what, even if it had been a complete building in itself, would have constituted an enormous house, but it was obviously not complete, for in beautiful lettering across the top of the drawing ran this legend: 'Welbeck Abbey. His Grace the Duke of Portland. The Oxford Wing.' 'Is this only one *wing* of a house?' I gasped. 'Yes, to be sure, yes,' replied George, and, presumably seeing no need for any further explanation, left it at that.[23]

George did most of the designing; his partner, Harold Peto, who was the son of the financier Sir Morton Peto, and later became a great garden designer, was not often seen in the office, but was understood to spend most of his time charming the clients.[23]

George and Peto substantially altered the south façade—replacing the porch with a *porte-cochère*, building a tower, raising the low link wing to the east, constructing a new service court and adding a wing full of bachelor bedrooms. 'So bad, I think,' moaned Lutyens, when he saw the result. Only four years before work on the remodelling of West Dean had begun in 1891, Lutyens had spent six months in the office of George and Peto— it constituted almost his only formal training, but even so it was not a time he looked back on with great affection. He had a low opinion of George—a shy, sensitive man, well known as a skilful watercolourist who would beguile clients with his perspectives.

But the major work of remodelling was done inside. An oak hall—thirty-four feet by thirty and a half—was created by knocking two existing rooms into one and removing the ceiling, so that it went up through two storeys (Plate 17). Next to it a new staircase was put in with solid oak treads. A billiard room, with the table lit from above, was added next to the smoking room, and the rooms on the south front were redecorated and made to open into each other to form an enfilade, which had advantages for entertaining. Marble replaced stone in the entrance hall, and all the damask and much of the panelling was renewed. Old masters—mostly Flemish and Dutch, with paintings by Cuyp, Rembrandt, Ruysdael and Steen—were bought at London salerooms to hang on the walls.

It must have been the oak hall that prompted the *Studio* to remark that for West Dean's 'progenitors one has not to turn to old France, nor to Lombardy, but to England, and to "Merrie England" at that'.[24] Merrie England seems strangely old-fashioned for the 1890s—Ernest George, whether with Harold Peto or his subsequent partner, Alfred Yeates, was never a progressive architect. But the oak hall represented a more advanced form than the *Studio* might have us believe: it was not a great hall, such as might be found in a mid-Victorian house, but—square in proportions, comfortably furnished, overlooked by the bedroom corridor—a move towards the open, relaxed living halls of the turn of the century. There was still a minstrels' gallery, however—the minstrels coming in the form of Cassano's orchestra, which was hired from London for big house parties.[25]

Despite his low view of the architecture, Lutyens found the tone of the interior 'very smart and luxurious and lots of beautiful things—and a ping pong table etc. etc. No

23

17. The oak hall, West Dean

untoward evidences of Royal favours by way of photos.' West Dean was opulent, easy, discreet. That subtle combination was achieved only by an enormous expenditure of money.

The atmosphere of West Dean was in marked contrast to the faded gentility of some more ancient seats, and Edward VII, with his eye for the comforts of life, must have known it. The house was equipped with every form of modern technology. Electric light was installed, and there were three hundred and sixty-four incandescent bulbs—or 'burners' as they were called—throughout the building, some of them attached to hideous brass lanterns. Pounding away in the engine house behind the stables were two single cylinder steam engines which gave off up to twenty-one brake horsepower at one hundred and seventy revolutions per minute. An extra engine and dynamo were kept in readiness in case additional power was required. Strictly speaking, three batteries would have been sufficient to store the necessary current, but the battery house contained five, since—out of consideration for the boiler man—it was decided not to run the engines on Sundays.

It was said that West Dean perfectly fulfilled that desideratum of royal entertaining in the Edwardian age: that servants should magically materialise at your elbow when they were needed and be invisible when they were not. Equally, guests did not see many of the other domestic arrangements, like the hydraulic dinner lift from the kitchen (installed by the American Elevator Company) or the automated steam laundry, one of the first in the country. As a precaution against fire, there was an electric pump capable of discharging fifteen hundred gallons of water an hour from a reservoir constructed in the hills above West Dean, and hydrants were constructed all through the house. A fire did break out in 1899, and it was largely thanks to the 'splendid equipment of fire-extinguishing apparatus', wrote the *Sussex Daily News*, that it had been brought under control by the time Chichester Fire Brigade arrived on the scene, some three hours after the alarm had been raised.

A marble niche in the entrance hall emphasises the note of sophistication of the house, and the excitement caused by the advances in science. The niche (Plate 20) is in many ways a symbol of everything West Dean stood for, since it is also evidence of an intimate connection with royalty. It commemorates the spot from which an 'electric spark' was transmitted to Canada by Edward VII. The occasion was the opening in Montreal of a sister institution to the King Edward VII Sanatorium at Midhurst, which Edward VII visited on each of his many trips to West Dean, and of which Willie James, typically, was executive chairman. The King could not cross the Atlantic in person, so it was decided to perform the ceremony by remote control. Wrote the *Daily Telegraph*'s correspondent:

Over land and under ocean the current, despatched on its way by his Majesty, travelled at an inconceivable pace. Arrived at Montreal, it operated the special machinery installed there, and, influenced by the invisible power, the doors flew open for the guests to enter, the electric lights were turned on throughout the building, and, as the culminating event, the Union Jack was run up the mast and broken. The swiftness and silence of the whole proceeding must have been deeply impressive to those who witnessed it, and demonstrated in most dramatic manner how electrical science, in its latest developments, has annihilated both time and space.[26]

18. Mrs James's boudoir, West Dean

19. The library, West Dean

FROM·THIS·SPOT
ON·OCTOBER·21·1909
HIS·MAJESTY·KING·EDWARD·VII
TRANSMITTED·ACROSS·THE·SEAS·TO·CANADA

THE·ELECTRIC·SPARK·WHICH·OPENED·THE·DOORS·OF
THE·ROYAL·EDWARD·INSTITVTE·FOR·TVBERCVLOSIS·AT·MONTREAL
COMPLETING·BY·THE·MAGICAL·AID·OF·SCIENCE
A·NOBLE·HANDIWORK·OF·MERCY

By contrast, the ceremony at West Dean was rather an anticlimax: the King simply walked out of the dining room and put his finger on something that looked like a bell-push.

In terms of habits and technology, West Dean was thoroughly sophisticated; in terms of its size it soon seemed hopelessly out of date. Almost symbolically, the pace of life in this most Edwardian of houses began to slow up after the King's death in 1910. About that time, Mrs James began to suffer badly from heart trouble, then Willie James died in 1912. As a result the house was let from 1914 to 1932, although Mrs James lived until 1927. There was a brief recrudescence during the period that Willie James's son, Edward, was married to the dancer Tilly Losch (Plate 21). The house was full of artists and poets, and a whole *corps de ballet* stayed there for the summer of 1933. But the marriage broke down, and West Dean ceased to be used as a house.

21. Carpet at West Dean woven with the footprints of the dancer Tilly Losch

20. (left) Niche at West Dean commemorating the opening of the King Edward VII Sanatorium at Montreal by remote control

22. The winter garden at Sir Ernest Cassel's house, Moulton Paddocks, Suffolk

Even in the smart set it was not strictly necessary to own or build a large country house. It was a sign of the times that those 'coroneted envelopes' could arrive at houses that were not in fact absolutely vast. The millionaire financier Sir Ernest Cassel, who could have afforded a palace if he had wanted one, made do with Moulton Paddocks (Plate 22), a medium-sized house on a horse-breeding stud (not an agricultural estate) in Suffolk, and the King regularly stayed there. The secret was that it had a croquet lawn, excellent partridge shooting, and was near to Newmarket, whence the Jockey Club's housekeeper was brought by dog cart every morning to cook bloaters or kippers for the King's breakfast.

Nevertheless, the Jameses were certainly not the only friends of the King who felt it necessary to build on a large scale. The racehorse owner and Viceroy of Ireland, the fifth Earl of Cadogan—'a bluish-faced gentleman' who habitually wore an expression somewhere 'between a simper and a sneer'—enlarged Culford Hall (Plate 226), in Suffolk, from twenty bedrooms to fifty. His architect, Clyde Young, was a popular choice for the smart set, with its special liking for glacial rooms lined with marble. The Prince of Wales attended Culford's house-warming luncheon in 1894, and ten years later stayed at

28

v. Kildonan House, Ayrshire

VI. The Moorish court at Port Lympne, Kent

the house. On that occasion, an equerry made a preliminary trip to reconnoitre the plumbing, and apparently insisted on modifications.[27]

Sometimes the King motored over to Culford from Elveden, home of the Guinness brewery peer, Lord Iveagh. There Clyde Young—taking over on the death of his father, William Young—had again been at work, more than doubling the size of the house previously occupied by the usurped Indian potentate, Prince Duleep Singh. In Surrey, the financier Lord d'Abernon and his wife, Helen, one of the great Edwardian beauties, built Esher Place, a large, French Renaissance style house—although this was more or less in the town of Esher and did not have an estate: the position was determined by the proximity of the Sandown Park racetrack, recently established by Hwfa Williams, himself very much smart set material.

The social country house was, par excellence, the house of the millionaire. There were still numerous routes to wealth, but the surest and most tempting now lay overseas. American dollars were already maintaining some ancient seats, following a series of spectacular marriages in the mid-1880s. 'An English Peer of very old title is desirous of marrying at once a very wealthy lady,' read an advertisement in the *Daily Telegraph* of 1901:

> her age and looks are immaterial, character must be irreproachable; she must be a widow or a spinster—not a divorcée. If among your clients you know such a lady, who is willing to purchase the rank of a peeress for £25,000 sterling, paid in cash to her future husband, and who has sufficient wealth besides to keep up the rank of a peeress, I shall be pleased if you will communicate with me in the first instance by letter when a meeting can be arranged in your office.[8]

The interest that American girls took in titles, and that titles took in American fortunes (even at an exchange rate of five dollars to the pound), is shown by the book *Titled Americans* by Chauncey M. Depew, which gave advice on how heiresses could enter the European aristocracy, and impressively long lists of those who had already done so.

Heiresses obviously married men who already possessed old country seats, and it may seem that there was little incentive for rich American males, who did not have so ready an entrée to British society, to settle and build ones from new. But, despite the United States' reputation as the land of freedom, they could well have thought that English society was less repressive than the one they knew at home, and by 1900 it was—perhaps unexpectedly—more accessible to straight money. 'It may seem a paradox to observe that a millionaire has a better and easier social career open to him in England than in America,' wrote Lord Bryce in *The American Commonwealth*. '. . . In America, if his private character be bad, if he be mean or openly immoral, or personally vulgar, or dishonest, the best society may keep its doors closed against him. In England great wealth, skilfully employed, will more readily force these doors open.'[29] Whether or not immoral, vulgar and dishonest are adjectives that applied to William Waldorf Astor, Andrew Carnegie or William Randolph Hearst, they did not always find it easy to blend in. 'Norfolk suits of patterns loud enough to be heard a good league into the Atlantic, shooting-coats of plaid tweed, chequered on so large a scale as to do duty for chess-boards, coaching attire that might have taken away the elder Weller's breath, with mother-of-pearl buttons the size of saucers, like those once affected by our own Mr. Cherry Angell. These articles,' wrote

31

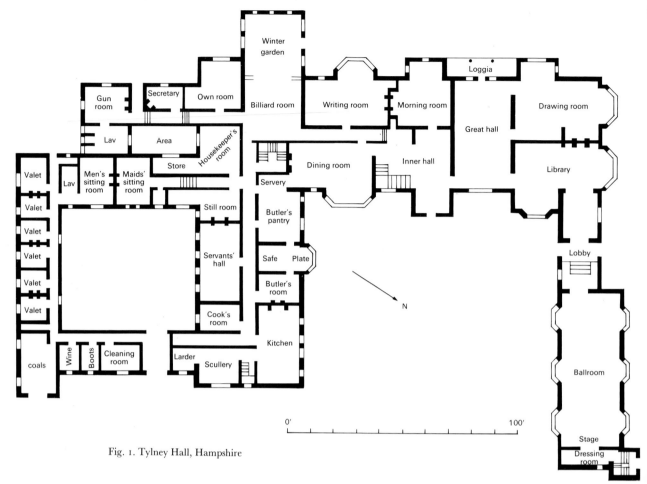

Fig. 1. Tylney Hall, Hampshire

T. H. S. Escott of Andrew Carnegie, 'in season are the outward and visible signs of the pursuits dear to the lord of Skibo Castle.'[30]

The group most conspicuous as builders of large country houses were the Randlords, as the gold and diamond millionaires of the South African Rand came to be called. They were the twentieth-century nabobs. They would have gone to India had they been born a hundred and fifty years earlier, but by 1900 it was South Africa that held out the greatest prospect of immediate wealth to the adventurous. 'There's no house in the country would take you in except as a common clerk,' David Crawfurd's uncle told him in *Prester John*, 'and you would never earn much more than a hundred pounds a year all your days. If you want to better your fortune you must go abroad where white men are at a premium.'[31] John Buchan, who had himself been to South Africa as one of Lord Milner's idealistic young civil servants working in the effort of reconstruction after the Boer War, dedicated *Prester John* to Lionel Phillips.

Phillips was the Randlord at his boldest.[32] The son of an Aldgate pawnbroker, he had left for Kimberley in 1875, aged twenty, and was managing a diamond mine two years later. He made a fortune before he was thirty, but lost half of it when De Beers shares fell while he was on holiday in England. He started again, became general manager of Wernher Beit and Co., left diamonds, went into gold and made a second pile out of the 1888–9 boom. Having taken a prominent part in Dr Leander Starr Jameson's abortive raid on the Transvaal in 1895, he left South Africa hurriedly. On returning to England,

32

he bought Tylney Hall, in Hampshire (Colour Plate IV), at first remodelling, then virtually rebuilding it, with a wing of six valets' rooms for the personal servants his millionaire friends were expected to bring with them. Even after the raid, however, he found the lure of South Africa irresistible. He went back there, became a politician—as which he survived an assassination attempt—and came to use Tylney less and less, eventually selling it in 1916. But even during his short time there, Phillips was able to establish himself as a pillar of county respectability—far quicker than would have been the case in the mid-Victorian period—becoming deputy lieutenant and high sheriff, as well as a J.P.

The social style of the Randlords was parodied in a popular music-hall song, 'The Diamond Queen'. The Queen in question was the daughter of a Cockney who had gone to South Africa, become 'a glorious millionaire', and was now to be seen

> Driving his coach and pair
> With a Barney Barnato air

and 'walking down Piccadilly with his chum the Prince of Wales'. (Barnato, the financial genius, was born in the Whitechapel slums, became Cecil Rhodes's adversary as a diamond producer, and committed suicide leaving an estate of over three million pounds.) Sir Julius Wernher, the self-effacing principal of Werner Beit and Co. (he enjoyed the popular misapprehension that Wernher was Beit's Christian name), was on equally amicable terms with Edward VII, who lunched with him at Luton Hoo, Wernher's Adam mansion in Hertfordshire.

On the whole, however, Randlords did not feel at home in the country, and many—the famous Barnato included—did not buy a country house. Wernher rarely went to Luton Hoo, except for shooting in the autumn and occasionally on Sundays, but it was remodelled expensively by Mewès and Davis, the architects of the Ritz Hotel, and throughout the year Wernher maintained a full staff of fifty-four gardeners, ten electricians, twenty to thirty house servants and a horde of labourers, whom Sidney and Beatrice Webb—when they stayed in a small house on the estate to write, of all things, their minority report for the Royal Commission on the Poor Law—were apparently unable to count.[33]

Nevertheless, when Randlords did set up in the country, they did so on a larger scale than most home-grown plutocrats: Ottershaw Park, in Surrey, originally quite a modest eighteenth-century villa, was almost completely rebuilt by Friedrich Eckstein, Wernher Beit's man in Johannesberg, with the obligatory marble-lined vestibule, Louis XVI drawing room, winter garden and billiard room filled with big game trophies, including a complete collection of South African horns. There was also a swimming pool and an aviary of exotic birds.[34]

The prominence of overseas wealth—whether American, South African or occasionally Australian (Wickham Hall (Plate 24), Witley Park)[35]—in country-house building reflected some disquieting facts about the British economy. Although in popular estimation Britain seemed to be riding a tide of prosperity, and although the trade figures showed astounding rates of increase, by 1890 it was only the dividends on her foreign investment that prevented the country's current account from falling into the red. In 1909, the year Masterman published his diatribe against accumulated wealth, the American journalist Price Collier brought out a cooler assessment of Britain's prospects in

England and the English from an American Point of View. England was spending over a billion and a quarter dollars on drink, sport, the navy, paupers and interest on the national debt—all objects that were in no sense productive. Indeed, he was certain that national expenditure would rise even further if the State continued to see itself as, in his words, 'the grandmotherly guardian of the people'. Between 1892 and 1905, income increased by only 15 per cent in Great Britain—a rise in line with the population; but in Germany it rose by 60 per cent over the same period. The 50 per cent by which Britain increased her manufactured exports between 1890 and 1907 looked encouraging until put beside Germany's 124 per cent, and the United States' 320 per cent. Collier interpreted the massive income from foreign investments and shipping, estimated at nine hundred million dollars, as a bad rather than a good sign, since it meant that English capital was drifting away from use in England, to assist the development of rival industries in foreign lands. Employment figures collected in the 1901 census showed, for the first time, a drop in the factory production of textiles, symbol of mid-Victorian prosperity (although the industry picked up after 1905). Iron founders and steel barons were proportionately less likely to become millionaires than the purveyors of food, drink and tobacco.[36]

Country-house building was quite an accurate index of the economy. Probably the largest groups of new houses were those built by the traditional sources of country-house wealth, beer (Polesden Lacey, Elveden, Bailiffscourt, Pyrford Court) and banking (Lambay Castle, Halnaker Park, Port Lympne, Rodmarton Manor). But in the financial community, what were still thought of as the rogue professions of stockbroking and company promotion made an appearance, with Marsh Court, Formakin and Witley Park. The last house was built by the eccentric Whitaker Wright, and had an underwater billiard room as well as a ballroom that a later owner tried to sell to a seaside resort. By some, Wright was at one time thought to have been the richest man in the kingdom,[37] so his suicide at the Law Courts after his London and Globe Society collapsed and he was convicted of fraud caused a sensation.

The great industrial fortunes of Victorian England had largely been made by 1890, and their possessors had already set themselves up in the country. Textiles were no longer financing country houses, and would not do so again until the development of synthetics after the First World War (Eltham Palace, Gledstone Hall). Ashby St Ledgers seems to have been the only house in the period built from a steel fortune, though even there at least part of the money came from banking and an inherited estate. Shipping and shipbuilding were more active (Pangbourne Towers, Coldharbour, Abbey House);[38] and so was the new chemical industry through the Tennant family (Great Maytham, Lympne Castle, Wilsford Hall). The Nobles (Ardkinglas, Besford Court, Wretham Hall) also had interests in chemicals, although the bulk of their fortune came from Sir Andrew's connection with the armaments firm of Armstrong Whitworth and Co. Other new industries, such as tobacco (Harcombe Chudleigh, Ednaston Manor) and motor cars (Nuffield Place), financed country houses, although generally small ones.

The most striking factor revealed by a run around some of the other big country houses of the 1890s and early 1900s is the impact of new methods of selling and distribution. The Victorian shop, as H. G. Wells knew it, was a genteel place, where ostentation was discouraged as lacking in manners, and an almost sacred distinction existed between retail and wholesale. Fortunes were being made by those—the Vesteys, the

34

24. The nursery at Wickham Hall, Kent, built for Gustav Mellin, Australian baby food manufacturer

Leverhulmes—who bought in bulk, sold direct and advertised. The working-class inhabitants of the towns were now sufficiently well off to afford at least the essentials of life, and they bought from the cheapest. The not-so-essentials, sold to the middle classes, had already made fortunes for Thomas Cook, the travel agent, and W. H. Smith, the newsagent, and their sons or grandsons built country houses. Altogether, distribution industries financed North Bovey Manor, Castle Drogo, Thornton Manor (Plate 23), Whittington, Sennowe Park and Barnett Hill.

Lawyers were also doing well: the Bar provided by far the greatest number of new peers in the Edwardian decade. Some lawyers built country houses (Standen, Friar Park, Spiddal House), but most were too shrewd to set themselves up as old-fashioned gentlemen with the costly responsibilities of estates. Soames Forsyte, in John Galsworthy's novel *The Man of Property*, published in 1906 (the first volume of the trilogy *The Forsyte Saga*), was the paradigm of a successful solicitor. The dream house he built at Robin Hill was close enough to London for him to commute to the City and, despite the uninterrupted country views, had no more than a couple of acres and a copse. The fictional Robin Hill was near Pangbourne, in Berkshire, where in fact several large and comfortable houses of the Robin Hill type had recently been built, notably one for D. H. Evans of the Oxford Street store. The *Builder* or the *Architectural Review* would have described the house at Robin Hill as a 'small' or 'smaller country house'—a form that seemed both socially and architecturally progressive, but which takes the term 'country house' beyond the sense in which it is used in this book.

C. F. A. Voysey specialised in the smaller country house, and on the whole designed for

36

the artistic middle classes—professional people, vicars, maiden ladies, writers, artists and publishers—not generally the kind of self-made people who would want a country house for big house parties. The logic of his style was that, by designing without unnecessary ornament, houses and furniture of wholesome solidity became accessible to people of relatively modest means. The publisher Walter W. Blackie, for whom C. R. Mackintosh built The Hill House in the suburbs of Helensburgh, was very much the liberal literary client you might expect to employ an advanced Art Nouveau architect. Perrycroft, built for J. W. Wilson, M.P. and Financial Secretary to the Miners' Union, was among Voysey's larger houses, but still cost only £4,000.

But Voysey's two biggest houses, Broadleys (Colour Plate IX) and Moorcrag, both of which were summer homes on a few acres of land on the edge of Lake Windermere, were designed for industrialists—a colliery owner from Leeds and a mill owner from Altrincham, near Manchester. Other industrialists who might have built country houses in the mid-century now found themselves happy with a small country house. M. H. Baillie Scott's largest house in Britain, Blackwell, another Windermere holiday house, was built for the Prestwich brewer, paper manufacturer and Conservative party activist Sir Edward Holt. Again, the two biggest houses built by C. E. Mallows—both smaller country houses—were for industrialists. Tirley Garth, which had a substantial number of main rooms (business room, drawing room, hall, study, dining room and billiard room), was built on a forty acre site chosen for its spectacular views. It was begun by a director of the chemicals firm Brunner Mond, one of the original companies amalgamated into ICI in 1927, but finished by R. H. Prestwich, whose firm produced the waterproof yarn for Burberrys' raincoats. Craig-y-Parc outside Cardiff was slightly smaller and was built for the colliery owner Thomas Evans.

These smaller country houses often expressed an ideal of life in the country which was rather different from the life going on there already. Irene Prestwich, one of R. H. Prestwich's three daughters, remembered that, in Manchester, the family had been used to 'a society that had retained good manners and thought for others, and had musical and artistic interests'. In the country, however, 'we found ourselves among people absorbed in hunting, bridge parties, race meetings and beautiful gardens, with little time for the obligations and amenities of a quieter social life'.[39] Similar social tensions were analysed by E. M. Forster in *Howard's End*. The fear that the landless middle classes were creating, in Forster's phrase, a 'civilization of luggage' gave new relevance to the country-house ideal.

Middle-class interest in country houses was the key to the success of Edward Hudson's magazine *Country Life*, the first issue of which appeared in 1897. Hudson's principal interest for us is through his close association with Lutyens. The fact that he commissioned three of the architect's best houses—Deanery Garden (Plate 25), Lindisfarne Castle (Colour Plate II) and Plumpton Place (Colour Plate XXXIV)—as well as his first important office building would make him a patron of some importance by itself. But by founding *Country Life*, which quickly crystalised a popular English ideal of life and home based on a romantic view of the country, and which almost at once began to give Lutyens's work an exposure far greater than that enjoyed by any other architect in the country, he became a vital figure in the history of the country house.

It was not a role that could have been predicted from his appearance. He was a kindly man, but extremely inarticulate and exceptionally plain. He dressed conventionally and looked so lugubrious that his devoted, if almost certainly platonic, *grande passion* for the world-famous cellist Madame Suggia seems a touching case of Beauty and the Beast. A devastating description came from Lytton Strachey, who spent an uncomfortable weekend on Lindisfarne, off the Northumbrian coast, in the sixteenth-century castle Lutyens converted to a holiday house. The tide was rising as Strachey was bumped over the causeway in a dog-cart, and he arrived to find everyone already tucking into lobster and champagne. Under these circumstances, Hudson seemed 'a pathetically dreary figure . . . a fish gliding under water, and star-struck—looking up with his adoring eyes through his own dreadful element . . . a kind of bourgeois gentilhomme also'. The 'adoring eyes' were of course for the lovely Suggia.

Lutyens, ceaselessly inventive, had been practising architecture for slightly over a decade before he met Hudson. His career—helped first by a web of personal contact, then by association with a wide-circulation magazine—was almost a metaphor for the society that employed him, still close-knit but increasingly affected by new mass-market techniques of selling and distribution. Lutyens was a personality in marked contrast to Ernest George, his former master. Although similarly a man of few words, those he did utter came forth in a spangled stream of puns, witticisms and jokes, some of them banal but most of them engagingly childish and very funny. Staying with the Sitwells, he once seized a few strands of horsehair stuffing from a broken sofa, screwed them up in a scrap of paper, wrote on it and put it in a drawer of a desk—Osbert Sitwell came on the little package many years later and found it bore the legend: 'A lock from Marie Antoinette's hair, cut from her head ten minutes after execution'. He won the support of Lady Hardinge, wife of the Viceroy of India for whom he was building Government House at New Delhi, by offering to wash her feet with his hair—'It is true,' he said, 'that I have very little hair, but you have very little feet.'[40] Such constant, compulsive quipping sometimes made people say he was frivolous, but the jokes often reveal a magical, romantic imagination; and a similar combination of wit and romanticism—the romanticism being that of William Morris and the Arts and Crafts movement—can be seen in his Surrey vernacular buildings.

It was not a combination that appealed to the more doctrinaire Arts and Crafts architects like Weir Schultz (whom he met during his training in Ernest George's office), who disparagingly called him a 'society architect'[41]—perhaps because of his ambitious marriage to Lady Emily Lytton, daughter of the former Viceroy of India. Lutyens did design the small house Homewood for his mother-in-law, but otherwise his new relations-in-law, who had been left very badly off at the first Earl's death, were not greatly influential in shaping the young man's career. Nor, with four exceptions, were his patrons aristocrats: the only house he designed which might possibly be described as a country seat was one of his last, Middleton Park, built for the ninth Earl of Jersey in 1935. Indeed, comparatively few of his houses were built on estates, and some of his most famous are among those that were not: they include Tigbourne Court (for the chairman of the Prudential Assurance Company), Great Dixter (for the managing director of the Star Bleaching Company, turned antiquarian), Heathcote (for a cotton broker) and Middlefield (for a university don). They perhaps look bigger than they are, especially in the contemporary photographs, but then it was one of Lutyens's architectural jokes to dress a house in robes that were, intentionally, one size too large.

38

25. Deanery Garden, Berkshire, the first of three houses by Edwin Lutyens for Edward Hudson, founder of *Country Life*

26. Alabaster relief of Princess Alexis Dolgorouki from Nashdom, Buckinghamshire

Lutyens managed to keep a foot in a number of camps. He is thought of as a country-house architect, but not that many of his houses can really be called country houses. He could design a social country house at its most extreme in Nashdom, which was intended to look like a country house but was in fact built on only thirteen acres. This 'mad house' was for the Jameses' friend Princess Alexis Dolgorouki (Plate 26), a Lancashire heiress born plain Fanny Wilson who married a Russian prince. (She tried to get the house as cheaply as she could and said it did not matter if parts only stood for twenty years.[42] The plan was wonderfully modern, with a winter garden, a small drawing room, a big room for entertaining, and a smoking room opening into the dining room, but what looked like mahogany was in fact stained deal—not something Lutyens could have been proud of.) Yet the architect's real sympathies were for the romantic country house, and he approved of the Barings, who used Lambay Castle off the Irish coast as a retreat from London and the oppressive social world, and spent the evenings reading Homer in Greek. 'I feel so for Mrs B.,' wrote Lutyens to his wife, 'through you, for her antipathy to the big house and all it means from one point of view.'[43]

The speed at which Lutyens's career developed was meteoric, thanks partly to his astoundingly early development, and partly to the championing of Gertrude Jekyll. By 1889, the year he met her at a Surrey tea party, she was a daunting, myopic woman, aged forty-six and shaped like a cottage loaf. She had been an artist and craftswoman, had known William Morris, and possessed strong ideas about architecture, some of which she instilled into her protégé when he built Munstead Wood for her. She began to introduce the young architect to her wide circle of garden-loving friends, some of whom wanted

40

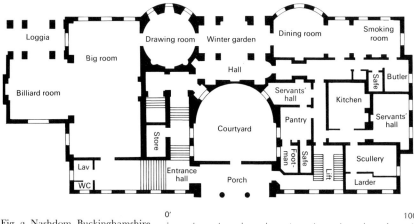

Fig. 2. Nashdom, Buckinghamshire

houses. It was through Miss Jekyll that Lutyens, still very much a country boy, met Princess Louise, a granddaughter of Queen Victoria; she commissioned him to work on the Ferry Inn at Roseneath in Scotland. Miss Jekyll also saw to it that Sir William and Lady Chance, who first espied her perched on a ladder outside Munstead Wood giving directions to workmen, should dismiss Halsey Ricardo, who had already prepared the foundations of their new country house, Orchards, and replace him with Lutyens. Soon after, it seemed natural that Miss Jekyll's brother, Colonel Sir Herbert Jekyll, when he was Commissioner for the British Section of the International Exhibition to be held in Paris in 1900, should ask Lutyens to design the British Pavilion. It was a small commission, but one that was to be seen by thousands of people. The next year, 1901, Miss Jekyll introduced Ned, as she and everyone else called him, to Mark Fenwick of Abbotswood, and later probably also to Ernest Blackburn, the skilful amateur gardener who built Little Thakeham.

Consequently, when Reginald McKenna, who married Herbert Jekyll's daughter, Pamela, in 1908, contemplated building a house in Smith Square, he found that his relatives by marriage had firm views on the subject of who should design it. Heavy lobbying was at work. Lutyens wrote to Lady Emily: 'Reginald McKenna has bought a site in London and I *do* hope he asks me to build for him. Pamela is for me—and the whole Jekyll family.'[44] The result was almost a foregone conclusion, but thankfully happy, since the architect was soon able to report that 'McKenna thinks my staircase is a miracle.'[45] The success of 36 Smith Square not only led to Halnaker Park, the country house built at the late date of 1936; but in 1919 McKenna became chairman of the Midland Bank, and raised the architectural consciousness of the boardroom to the pitch at which employing Lutyens was more or less inevitable. Three major bank buildings, including the Poultry Head Office, went up as a result.

Gertrude Jekyll had introduced Lutyens to Hudson, for whose magazine she was writing, in about 1899, and Hudson gave him the commission for Deanery Garden, a beautiful but quite small house in the village of Sonning, the same year. Already, recording and even—through his presentation of Lutyens—shaping the culture of the country house through *Country Life*, founded in 1897, had become his life's work.

Country Life was a shrewd cocktail of idealism and business sense, liberally laced with sentiment, which appeared to catch the flavour of the old country-house world, but in reality appealed as much to the new. The idea of it was first proposed by Hudson's

41

solicitor, G. A. (later Lord) Riddell, who became chairman of *News of the World*.[46] He was struck by the high quality block-making techniques for the reproduction of photographs that had been developed in the United States. Hudson and Kearns,[47] the family printing firm, were already publishing periodicals in association with Sir George Newnes, the man who revolutionised the popular press by publishing *Tit-Bits*, the first magazine devoted exclusively to gossip. Hudson changed the name of a not very profitable paper called *Racing Illustrated* to *Country Life Illustrated*, and introduced articles on golf, the dying rural crafts, field sports, farming, motor cars, fashion, furniture, society figures and— above all—on country houses. Largely because it instantaneously became the natural place for estate agents to advertise at a time when more and more big estates were going onto the market, *Country Life* soon became a financial success—as Hudson's own succession of houses bears witness.

In part, the magazine appealed to people who already owned country houses—after all, it was agreeably novel that surroundings which they had taken for granted should have become the focus of admiring interest. Equally, it was read by people who—like Hudson himself—were looking into this world from outside. Before he acquired his fortune or title, Lord Lee of Fareham leafed his way longingly through the pages, dreaming of an ideal country existence which he was not yet able to realise; he later bought Chequers (Plate 224). On the other hand, the nostalgia of the magazine— conveyed in watery photographs of fishermen and other country folk—caused at least one officer in the First World War to have *Country Life* sent out to the trenches as the symbol of what he was fighting for.[48]

Lutyens regarded Hudson as a friend, a helpful friend—a 'brick' or 'an angel' as he put it. Hudson quite simply thought Lutyens was a genius. When Lady Emily, having been neglected in the course of the architect's long site visits in the country, strayed into the 'vasty mists' of Theosophy and left Lutyens as the only meat-eater in the household, Hudson sent her a letter to say that she had a supreme architect in her care and that looking after him should be her sole work in life.[49] Hudson was the least demonstrative of men, so the gesture must have been difficult—although, inevitably, it did no good and left Lady Emily feeling deeply resentful. Lutyens used to lunch regularly with Hudson at his house in Queen Anne's Gate, and in 1910 moved his office into the building next door.

As well as his own three houses, Hudson commissioned Lutyens in 1904 to build the Country Life offices on the south side of Covent Garden market. It was Lutyens's first important work in the capital. Lutyens's name appeared in the magazine with telling persistence, not simply in the country-house articles, some of which were written by Gertrude Jekyll, but in a whole range of little references to keep his name before the public: as a designer of model pubs; for his work to a wooden bridge at Sonning; in a letter (written by Lutyens himself under the guise of a passing cyclist) to accompany a photograph of a lytch-gate he designed. 'Do get Country Life this week,' he wrote to Lady Emily in 1911. 'There is Temple Dinsley in it, and some baths mantels etc. in the supplement by me.'[50] Then the same year: 'Riddle [*sic*] Hudson etc want me to prepare anonymously a King Edward Memorial scheme at once and they are going to boom it like anything.'[51]

Hudson's booming of Lutyens brought him three of his biggest and most important country houses. He was introduced to Mrs Belville, whose husband Frank, the maker of

27. Aerial view of Lindisfarne Castle, Northumberland

Robinson's Barley Water, commissioned the 'butterfly-plan' house Papillon Hall, at a week-end party at Deanery Garden; Herbert Johnston went to Lutyens for Marsh Court after seeing Crooksbury, Lutyens's first house, in *Country Life*;[52] and when Julius Drewe wrote to Hudson, as proprietor of *Country Life*, about whom he should ask to design Castle Drogo, Lutyens was of course recommended as 'the only possible choice'.[53] To complete the picture, Lord Riddell, the man who suggested the idea of *Country Life* in the first place, employed Lutyens in 1906 to design the Dormy House, a golf clubhouse on Walton Heath.

But Hudson himself remains an enigma. Although he vetted photographs with the eye of an artist, he never acquired a detailed historical knowledge of the subjects covered in his magazine; and although Deanery Garden was described as 'the house of a man with a hobby—viz., rose-growing and wall-gardening'—he gave the impression of hardly knowing a chrysanthemum from a dahlia.[54] The greatest irony of all is that he was never really at home in the country. At Lindisfarne in 1918 he had a correspondence with W. J. Bolam, agent of the island's owner, Laurence Morley Crossman, which would have appalled a true countryman. Hudson was deeply distressed to find the gamekeeper trapping the rabbits in a field he rented. 'These rabbits I take it belong to me—anyway the rent I pay for the field would include rabbits,' he wrote to Bolam. 'I propose to cultivate these rabbits, and I should be glad if you will kindly instruct the gamekeeper that he is not to interfere with them.' Bolam had to point out that, not only did Hudson not have a right to the rabbits, but the rabbits were destroying the crops. 'I do not think that Major

43

Crossman would like you to "cultivate" rabbits on Castle Field, in fact I feel certain that both he and the tenants would object, and I doubt if the War Agricultural Committee would allow it.'[55] Hudson's approach to land management was essentially romantic.

Lindisfarne (Colour Plate II) was at the opposite extreme from West Dean. Lytton Strachey hated the inconvenience, the cold, and the dawn fishing expedition he was forced to go on with George Reeves, Suggia's accompanist. Lutyens loved it. 'Ramparts and three miles from land!' he wrote enthusiastically when he first heard the description.[56] He delighted in the provision made on the causeway for travellers caught by the tide: '½ barrels on posts up into which you can get by means of ladders there!' The idea that, before restoration had even begun, Hudson planned to invite thirty guests (he thought there were thirty bedrooms) to 'picnic' in the castle over Christmas he found enchanting. When he went on a site visit in 1906, he entered into the spirit of the place by taking a raven up on the train (its beak made 'a noise like castanets' all the way), and Lady Emily and the children—suffering the smoking fires and probably a north-east wind—spent a ten week holiday there the same year (Plate 28).

There could not have been a clearer contrast made between the different worlds of the social and the romantic country house than when the Prince and Princess of Wales (George V and Queen Mary), who were regular guests at shooting week-ends at West Dean, visited Lindisfarne in 1908.[57] The visit began at the far end of the island with a lecture by an archaeologist, during which the Prince could not conceal his boredom and looked at his watch every two minutes. Finally the party rolled towards the castle in six coaches and pairs. Lutyens managed to amuse the Prince as they clambered up to the castle. He overheard the equerry saying, 'You know, Sir, this place has been rebuilt by E. Lutyens . . .', and shouted out, 'Hi, stop! I'm here', at which the Prince, wrote Lutyens, 'nearly had a fit of laughter'. On the whole the visit was not a great success, since the royal party failed to see any charm in discomfort. The Princess could not bear the cobbles because they hurt her feet, though Lutyens told her he was very proud of them. The only thing she admired going round the castle was some fleurs-de-lys on a fireback. 'Oh yes, drains, of course, drains,' said the Prince when Lutyens enthusiastically told him he wanted to use gun barrels instead of pipes. He was very anxious to get away and, for a sailor, expressed surprising concern about the tide. Meanwhile the Duke of Northumberland seemed 'very demure and quiet and a good deal bored'. Poor Hudson was in a terrible state of nerves, and both Hudson and Lutyens had to lie down to recover when they had all gone.

But it was the Prince and Princess of Wales and their world who were beginning to look out of date. The austerer, simpler values of Lutyens and Hudson were bound to become increasingly adopted as the servant shortage—and the shortage of so many things—made itself felt after the First World War. Although social country houses were built until 1910, the romantic country house lasted much longer. It is an index of Lutyens's modernity that even the Jameses could turn to him when they sought an architect for their new summer lodge at West Dean.

Nine years after the remodelling of West Dean the owners were finding it a little *too* opulent, at least for family life. Mrs James was pregnant when Lutyens arrived in 1902; she wanted to bring her children up in more healthy surroundings, with plenty of fresh air and exercise.[58] They employed Lutyens to build Monkton (Plate 31), a small retreat in a

45

28. Edwin Lutyens's daughter, Barbara, at Lindisfarne

29. The dining room at Lindisfarne

30. The entry hall at Lindisfarne

remote corner of the estate about five miles from West Dean itself, higher up on the foothills of the Downs and surrounded by beech, heather, gorse and thorn. It had views over Chichester and to the Channel. In comparison to the big house, it was by no means grand—and the planning had none of the *jeu d'esprit* of other Lutyens houses of comparable size. White panelling replaced red damask for the walls; there was painted wood instead of mahogany; and the furniture—if not the scrubbed oak you would expect in an Arts and Crafts house—was Sheraton, Chippendale and Hepplewhite, with no Louis XV or XVI. There were special balconies for sleeping in the open air, and a loggia for dining outside.

Monkton was really for the children, and it ended up as somewhere they were sent when the big house parties were going on. West Dean itself was just the same as ever—if anything, more so, because at almost exactly the time the Jameses employed Lutyens, they also called in Mellier and Co. to create a new drawing room in the *style Louis Seize* (Plate 19). Nevertheless, they must have liked Monkton, since they bought another house by Lutyens, Grey Walls, Gullane, on the east coast of Scotland in 1906.

Romanticism, remoteness, a certain simplicity, even a sense of the past—these values were becoming increasingly appreciated, and were even making their way into the luxurious, if somewhat airless rooms at West Dean. Ernest George had arrived at West Dean by train; Lutyens was jolted up the rough track to Monkton in the Jameses' glossy new motor car. The tastes of Lutyens's world, for all its romanticism, would come to be seen as the more modern and would survive longer.

31. Loggias and sleeping balcony at Monkton, on the West Dean estate, Sussex

2. *Changes in the Country House*

'Glorious, stirring sight! The poetry of motion! The *real* way to travel! The *only* way to travel! Here to-day—in next week tomorrow! Villages skipped, towns and cities jumped—always somebody else's horizon! O bliss! O poop-poop! O my! O my!'[1] So Mr Toad saluted the first motor car he had seen, then disappearing at speed after having overturned his canary-coloured caravan. *The Wind in the Willows* was published in 1908. The next year C. F. G. Masterman lamented the 'action of a section of the motoring classes', which, 'in their annexation of the highways and their indifference to the common traditions, stands almost alone as an example of wealth's intolerable arrogances'.[2] Motoring was the very symbol of self-assertive opulence, and 'Toad once more, Toad at his best and highest, Toad the terror, the traffic-queller, the Lord of the lone trail', was a familiar figure.

Toad, however, was also 'that well-known and popular Mr Toad, a landed proprietor'. Although what happened at Toad Hall during the course of the book cannot be said to be true of the changes taking place in British country houses beyond the river bank (even if some owners might have begun to feel that the invasion of Toad Hall by stoats and weasels could have proved an uncomfortable allegory),[3] motoring was a new and important element in the country-house world. It did not of itself create the new landscape made up of smaller estates, visited for shorter periods of time; but it fitted in so well that, if only as expensive toys, the presence of a 'motor' or two was an expected ingredient of smart country-house life—the life of the Saturday-to-Monday and that cosmopolitan world whose members did not want to be stuck with dim gentry as their only country society— by about 1905. Owners of canary-coloured caravans and horse-drawn conveyances generally were finding themselves again and again in the ditch. A *Punch* cartoon of 1907 shows an irate farmer answering the motorist offering to settle damages to his cart with the words: 'What d'ye *usually* pay?'[4]

Motoring, for all its unreliability (and partly because of it), made a deep impression on country-house habits. Victorian house parties had been characterised by their agreeable seclusion. 'Comings and goings were slower and more ponderous affairs, only undertaken deliberately and after a careful study of Bradshaw (generally by proxy).' Bradshaw, of course, was the great railway timetable, and the job of consulting it often fell to the butler.

49

32. Part of Walter Crane's frieze on the theme of locomotion at Paddockhurst, Sussex

1.—THE VILLAGE. OLD STYLE.

33. The Village Old Style and the Village New Style: a cartoon from *Punch*, 1907

The house-party, shut off from the outside world, sang and danced and flirted and shot and hunted and fished in a little self-contained Kingdom, of which the host and hostess were the undisputed King and Queen, and which, from purely physical causes, was immune from unheralded invasion from outside, for—by the grace of God—neighbouring Kingdoms were, as a rule, beyond the compass of a carriage and pair.[5]

Visits by carriage were confined to a radius generally defined as about ten miles, and single riders could only go slightly further. In *Memoirs of a Fox-Hunting Man*, Aunt Evelyn lived about twelve miles from Dumborough Park, and was therefore fully two miles beyond the range of Lady Dumborough's round of calls—those were the days, wrote Sassoon, in which 'twelve miles meant a lot, from a social point of view'.[6]

The bicycle began the revolution, and was more democratic than the car. Even the aptly named Mr Hoopdriver, a shop assistant in the H. G. Wells' story 'The Wheels of Chance', could afford to spend his annual holiday pedalling across the South Downs. Evidence that the bicycling craze thrived at country houses is provided by the sheds built to store the machines at Elveden and Crathorne Hall. Among its other attractions was the possibility of physical contact with the opposite sex, especially if the lady was learning and prone to fall off.[6] But not everyone was well-adapted to bicycling. Had it not been for the car, Edward VII would not have thought of going from Buckingham Palace to Luton Hoo—a distance of twenty-eight miles—for luncheon with his friend Sir Julius Wernher and returning to Buckingham Palace the same evening.[7]

The ease of travel had an unsettling effect on country-house life. Lord Ernest Hamilton remembered with nostalgia the 'certain contented group spirit' of the week-long house party of the mid-1800s, which had been destroyed by motor cars. They 'make *ex tempore* radiations during the visit too easy,' he wrote in *The Halcyon Era*.

50

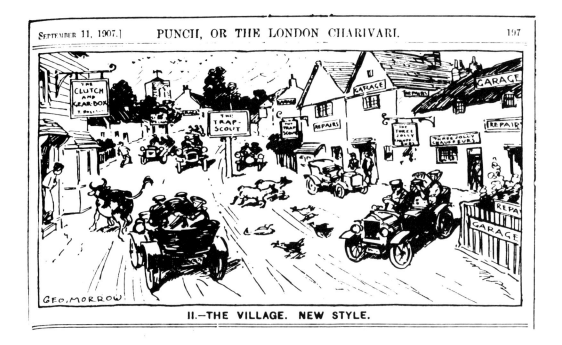

II.—THE VILLAGE. NEW STYLE.

The party is in a ceaseless state of metabolic flux. You come down to breakfast to find that your charming neighbour at dinner the night before has gone off in her car to some other country house 200 miles away. Somebody else—probably a complete stranger—arrives during breakfast and introduces a discordant note that does not, perhaps, even begin to blend in with the general harmony for two or three days. It is upsetting.[8]

Despite the antiquated twelve-mile-an-hour speed limit in force until 1903, motor cars had the advantage of speed. Speed traps (policemen hiding in hedges) were set, but they proved ineffective, especially in the face of 'trap scouts' provided by organisations like the Automobile Association, which was initially founded to provide anti–speed trap patrols on the London to Brighton road.[9] But there was something very tiresome about the un-predictability of motoring, especially from the point of view of the hostess. The Luton Hoo trip was by chance one of the very few on which the King himself, who always travelled with his 'personal motor expert', C. W. Stamper, dressed in a blue reefer suit, arrived late.[10] A large house party involved a high degree of organisation, and punctuality had formerly been expected, particularly for meals. Queen Alexandra was notoriously forgetful of time, but even for her to be ten minutes late for dinner was 'remarkable', quarter of an hour 'beyond the pale'.[11] But hostesses came to expect as inevitable the telegram to announce the late appearance of guests arriving by motor. George V, with eleven cars at his disposal, invariably drove with a second car behind his own (Plate 34); Queen Mary, who did not, occasionally had to flag down a passing motorist for help.[12]

When guests did arrive, they were unlikely to be in their usual state of immaculate grooming. The heroine of *A Waif's Progress*, the coquettish Bonnybell, knew that to motor any distance would mean arriving 'touzled and stained', which would devastate her chance of a successful flirtation.[13] 'Porty', the eccentric Earl of Portsmouth who built

Hurstbourne Park, used to put his long red beard in a sponge-bag to protect it from dust.[14] Appalled at seeing a photograph of the Prince of Wales in an open car, his silk hat blown onto his nose, Queen Victoria expressed the hope that the Duke of Portland, her master of horse, would never allow any of 'those horrible machines' to be used in her stables.[15] There was more than one way in which the motor car, when it became popular, helped encourage the informality that was an outstanding characteristic of even the smartest Edwardian country houses.

Early motor houses—as the first garages were called—were more than somewhere to put cars under shelter. The one at Manderston, for instance, built in 1903, incorporated an engineer's shop in the basement, where a car could be virtually rebuilt if required; a lift bay in the floor would take the car down.[16] This motor house was in the service court, since the need to provide one had not been foreseen when Manderston's stables were built in 1895. Other motoring owners preferred to have their garages built into a free-standing cottage, with the chauffeur's flat above (Plate 38). Like the power house containing the electricity plant, this kind of building was often tricked out in half-timbering and thatch.[17] At first this was probably the result of architectural embarrassment; later, when the motor car had opened up the deepest glades of the countryside to the week-ender, it became part of a rustic fantasy. 'Some of the half-timbered garages that I have seen,' wrote P. A. Barron, 'are works of art.'[18]

Motoring, as bicycling had been, was a craze, and some of the most unlikely people succumbed to the excitement. Lady Digby, the delightful but rather unadventurous mistress of Minterne Magna in Dorset, had her first motor ride in 1902, the year the rebuilding of the house was begun. Even though she found that 'going round corners at

34. Lord Iveagh leaving Elveden Hall, Suffolk, with the future George V, and a spare car in case of breakdowns behind

35. Carriages in the stable court at Manderston, Berwickshire, built in 1895 before the need for a motor house had been envisaged

36. Mrs Greville's motor cars at Polesden Lacey, Surrey

37. The garage at Grey Walls, Gullane, East Lothian

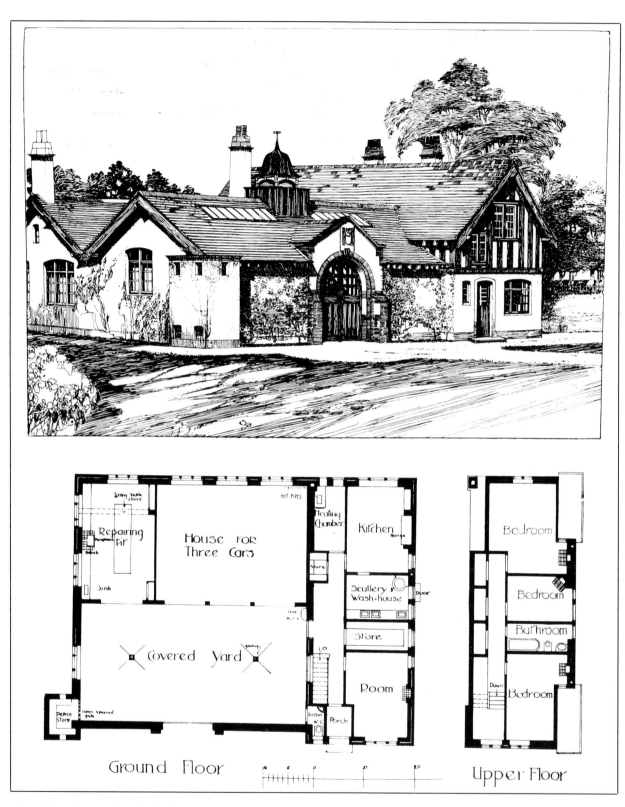

Ground Floor

Upper Floor

38. Architects' perspective and plan for a 'motor car house' with chauffeur's flat attached, Gallowhill, Renfrewshire, by James Salmon and Gillespie (*Architectural Review*, 1903).

such a pace is anything but pleasant,' the Digbys ordered a car of their own to be ready in June. On 19 August 1908 the garden party to celebrate the completion of the house took place. 'It was a lovely day,' she wrote, 'and all went off well—about 300 people turned up and my brother counted 58 motors.'[20] It was a sign of things to come that oil was financing country houses: H. W. Deterding, the director general of Royal Dutch Petroleum, built Kelling Hall.

The advantage of motoring was that it made it easier to get to the country just at the time that the country was becoming somewhere to go rather than somewhere to live. 'Country life, or rather short spells of it, has now become a sort of luxury of the rich,' wrote Lady Dorothy Nevill;[21] 'but few of any considerable means care to reside for long periods in the country, as was the case in the old days when people regularly settled down there.' This reflected an economic reality. As early as 1873 a House of Lords committee reported that 'the improvement of land . . . as an investment is not sufficiently lucrative to offer much attraction to capital'.[22] That was before the run of bad winters in the late 1870s, and when the influx of cheap foreign wheat, first from American prairies, then from Canada, India, Australia and the Argentine, was only just beginning. The price of wheat still stood at over fifty shillings a quarter; by 1894 it had fallen by over fifty per cent, to a low point of twenty-two shillings and ten pence. In 1885 Joseph Chamberlain consoled an Ipswich audience with the thought that 'almost universally throughout England and Scotland agriculture has become a ruinous occupation'; and in the same year the Duke of Marlborough prophetically declared that 'half the land in England' was ripe to go on the market when land prices rose.

Arable farmers were the worst affected by the great agricultural depression. Livestock farmers, and those who could turn part of their land over to horn rather than corn, experienced the benefit of a fall in the cost of feed.[23] But livestock, too, was soon to suffer from cheap imports as refrigeration improved. Thirty thousand tons of foreign mutton entered the country in 1886, a quarter of a million tons in 1914. Ironically, importers like Gustav Mellin and the Vesteys built country houses out of the profits.[24]

Since the days of the Tudors, economic, social and even perhaps military considerations had combined to make buying an estate seem the safest investment that could be had. Other enterprises might have offered a higher return, but they would almost certainly have involved a greater degree of risk. Land spelt security, in every sense of the word. That fundamental assumption could not be made in the last quarter of the nineteenth century. The most eloquent indication of a change in attitude was the provisions of the Settled Land Act of 1882, which affected most of the great estates in the country. The object of settling an estate, which was usually done by a grandfather on his grandson, was to ensure that it would pass intact from one generation to the next, its apparent owner in reality only enjoying a life interest in his possessions, because a settled estate could not be sold. Now the law was amended to make it possible to sell the land and invest the resulting capital, which still could not be touched. The notion that shares might be a better bet than land turned accepted maxims on their heads.

Slowly the structure of government was changing to accommodate the declining power of the landed interest. A network of county and parish councils run by elected members was set up under the Local Government Acts of 1888 and 1894. The financial and residential qualifications for justices of the peace were abolished in 1906. Following the

39. Coats of arms of Lords Cowdray, Astor and Leverhulme, with supporters indicating the sources of their wealth

creation of the first industrial peer (Lord Belper, 1856), the complexion of the House of Lords began little by little to change, as financiers, newspaper owners, newspaper vendors, store owners and even a non-Caucasian (Lord Sinha of Raipur, 1919) found their way onto the benches. 'In a word,' wrote Price Collier, somewhat disingenuously, 'the present House of Lords is conspicuously and predominantly a democratic body, chosen from the successful of the land.'[25] Anyone who leafed through the pages of Debrett's would have seen that the coats of arms of the traditional aristocracy, heraldically supported by the beasts of myth and romance, were being jostled by creatures from a strange, new world (Plate 39)—like the deep-sea diver and Mexican peasant which supported the arms of Lord Cowdray, the government contractor who built the Blackwall Tunnel under the Thames and had extensive oil interests in Mexico; or the Red Indian and Davy Crockett–like frontiersman of Lord Astor, whose wealth derived from his great-grandfather's furtrading business; or the two elephants rampant of Lord Leverhulme, which represented Lever Brothers' Congolese plantations.[26]

It was perhaps to be expected that the prestige of land would fall proportionately. This was shown in the numbers of new rich who chose not to go into the country. If Randlords often preferred not to stray far from Park Lane, department store owners like William Edgar, of Swan and Edgar, James Marshall, of Marshall and Snelgrove, and the second Peter Robinson, did not venture beyond the suburbs—Clapham Common, Mill Hill and Esher, respectively.[27] Even a socially ambitious man like Sir Thomas Lipton could content himself with Osidge, in New Southgate; and Edward VII could visit him there for luncheon. Those of Edward VII's self-made friends who did buy large estates did not do so as an investment—they were too canny. Lord Iveagh, a Guinness raised to the peerage in 1891, may have been bidding for social position through his purchase of fifteen thousand acres in Suffolk, but he never thought of running the estate at a profit. Two-thirds of it was devoted to scrub and woodland for raising an annual total of over twenty thousand pheasants. Only five thousand acres were cultivated, and the yearly wage bill, excluding indoor servants, was £20,000—the game department alone employed seventy men. However, there was a gradual change in tastes and habits, noted by the *Estates Gazette* in 1910, which made this kind of profligacy unattractive, even for those who could afford it: 'many who used to shoot in England now take a shoot in Scotland, and go

56

abroad much earlier than they used to, often in October and November . . . and many now prefer golf'.[28] As a result, although 'farms and small holdings sell well, residential and sporting estates as a whole are difficult to realise. This causes certain owners to break up their estates in order to sell at all. Consequently many country houses are empty.'[29]

The traditional element in society was looking for less traditional forms of income. By 1896 one hundred and sixty-seven peers and peeresses, over a quarter of the nobility, had picked up directorships, many of them in a scramble for positions that had begun in the previous decade; the figure was two hundred and thirty-two in 1920, although some of that number were newly created industrial and commercial peers, like Lords Cowdray, Leverhulme and Devonport.[36] The dangers were illustrated fictionally by E. F. Benson's novel *Mammon and Co.*,[31] in which the crash of an Australian mining company severely compromised Lord Conybeare. In real life, Whitaker Wright's bankruptcy involved Lord Dufferin, a former Viceroy of India, and the Duke of Connaught, brother of Edward VII. 'There are many young men of your class who should never go east of Temple Bar,' was Sir Ernest Cassel's crushing advice to the enthusiastic young George Cornwallis-West. 'Perhaps you are one of them.' Ignoring the verdict, Cornwallis-West went into the City, and his firm foundered at the outbreak of the First World War.[32] To his credit, Cornwallis-West wanted something more than the figurehead directorships which he had been offered; but temperament, training and tradition made him peculiarly unsuited to the ruthlessness of commercial life.

The crisis which the Duke of Marlborough had predicted in 1886 came in the last years of Edward VII's reign. Although income tax and death duties (the latter introduced by Lord Harcourt in 1894) took their toll, and produced varying degrees of outrage from the landed classes, neither was in fact particularly onerous before the First World War, and neither specifically penalised owners of land. But with Lloyd George's Budget of 1909, which proposed an Increment Value Duty and Undeveloped Land Duty, and made provision for a valuation of all the land in the kingdom, landowners felt that they were experiencing a frontal attack. That was not wholly so. Both Duties were aimed principally at urban rather than agricultural landlords, in an attempt to redress the inequitable balance between rates and rents. However, Conservative politicians did not scruple to call the Budget 'a revolution', and Sir Edward Carson believed that it spelt 'the beginning of the end of all rights of property'.[33] The Duke of Buccleuch claimed that he was now so poor that he could not afford a guinea subscription to the Dumfriesshire football club.[34] The political result was the constitutional crisis in which, after the Lords had rejected the Budget, a general election had been fought on the issue, and Asquith and Lloyd George had been returned with a majority (albeit modest) to enact the legislation, the Lords— 'five hundred men, ordinary men chosen accidentally from among the unemployed', as Lloyd George called them[35]—lost the power to veto money bills, under the threat of a mass creation of new peers. The result as it affected the country house was a loss of confidence in land. Triggered by the Duke of Bedford who sold about half his estates without being under any financial necessity to do so, unprecedented volumes of land started to roll onto the market: one hundred and four thousand acres in 1910, one hundred and seventy-four thousand acres in 1911, even higher figures in 1912 and 1913. Sales decreased during the First World War, when the land market was barely active; but immediately after the war, under the threat of the taxes that would be needed to pay for it, the landslide at once turned into an avalanche, as half a million acres were rushed onto the market in 1918. When the eighth Earl of Bessborough, who had prudently removed the family pictures and furniture from Bessborough House, Co. Kilkenny, before it was burnt during the Troubles, was looking for a large house in 1920, he was able to consider sixty-five possible seats before choosing Stansted Park, near Portsmouth. The property market subsided in 1921; but by then a new breed of owner walked over much of what had been thought of as the traditional landscape of England, made up of great estates. The *Estates Gazette* calculated that, over the previous four years, a quarter of England changed hands. The result, wrote F. M. L. Thompson in his classic study *English Landed Society in the Nineteenth Century*,[36] was the 'formation of a new race of yeoman'. It was a suggestive coincidence that *Country Life* started its series of articles on the smaller country house in 1909.

Socially, the effect of the changing status of land was that, for many people, the country was enjoyed in shorter bursts. Men and women brought up in an earlier, more stable age, like Mr Longdon in Henry James's *The Awkward Age*, were shocked to see the younger generation letting its own country houses and renting other people's, to live surrounded by another family's furniture, portraits and servants. 'Formerly country-house life was very quiet, perhaps even humdrum,' wrote Lady Dorothy Nevill in 1907,

> but within the last thirty or forty years it has undergone a complete transformation . . . The modern practice of letting one's country house would have appalled the landed proprietors of other days when such a thing was yet undreamt of. There was then, of course, a real bond of connection (very often one of respectful sympathy) between a landlord and his tenants, which, except on a very few estates, has now quite ceased to exist.[37]

One cannot fully subscribe to Lady Dorothy's ideal view of the Victorian countryside; the bond of sympathy may have been broken, but the 'rich city men and American millionaires' who owned large estates often did more by way of improvements than their impoverished neighbours. But it was quite possible that they had a different attitude to entertaining: 'The modern standpoint as regards country life is well demonstrated by the remark of a lady whose husband had bought a country house, and was told that some pleasant people lived in the country-side near by. "Pleasant or not, it matters little to us," was the retort; "we shan't see anything of them,—we shall get our friends down from London with the fish." '[38]

In 1917, when the future Lord Lee of Fareham established a trust to make Chequers (Plate 224), then his home, the official residence of the prime ministers of Britain, the day was envisaged when the premier himself would have no country house of his own and no private income; indeed, it had already arrived. In addition, he hoped, as he wrote to the prime minister, Lloyd George, that the 'residential allowance' he provided would 'encourage regular week-end visits'.[39] This is a statement that could not have been made before the First World War. As an institution, the week-end became an established fact of country-house life in the 1890s, but it was regarded as dreadfully middle-class to call it anything other than a 'Saturday-to-Monday'. This maintained the polite fiction that there was really no difference, since everyone had time on his hands, between Saturdays and Sundays and any other day of the week, except perhaps (and this was becoming

58

increasingly optional) for the need to turn out to church. A Saturday-to-Monday meant just that: it would have been rude in the extreme for a young man, anxious to hurry back to his City office, to have left on Sunday night—even if not to do so meant that he would have had to leave at dawn on Monday.[40]

Week-ends suited the new, not-so-leisured upper-class male, who could not leave London during the week. After a time, hosts found that they had to hold shoots on Sundays in order to get guns.[41] But the 'week-end habit', as it was called, lent fuel to the fashionable complaint that country houses had become like hotels. People dropped in and out as they liked, and meals—at least breakfast—could be at any time. According to T. H. S. Escott, the Murrietta brothers—Spaniards, bankers and, until their rapid disappearance from English society after the Baring crash of 1894, friends of the Prince of Wales—were the first to run their house as 'a residential club for non-paying guests'.[42] Most people at Wadhurst Park, Escott noted censoriously, had breakfast some time between eleven and twelve in a room 'which daily, till noon, looked like the coffee room at a Metropole Hotel'. A similar order prevailed at Surrenden Court in Ouida's novel *A House Party*, written in 1887. 'It's too much like an hotel,' grumbled Lord Usk, its owner, who was out of temper after having sold his grouse moor to an American; 'and an hotel where the *table d'hôte* rings to deaf ears.'[43]

The architectural expression of this more informal life, appropriate to men and women who had less inclination and often, because of business commitments, less possibility of spending so much time in the country, was the hall. Medieval-style great halls had been familiar in Gothic Revival houses since the 1820s. Their principal use—or this was the excuse for them—was for the great organised occasions expected of the Victorian landowner and gentleman who took his responsibilities seriously. These included tenants' dinners, hunt meets, and, as Sir Gilbert Scott suggested, 'meetings of scientific societies, agricultural meetings, consecrations and reopenings of churches'.[44] On the medieval pattern, great halls were usually separate from the entrance hall; they were entered by a screens passage and went up through two storeys, with all the possibilities of an elaborately timbered roof that that afforded. But in about 1890 the great hall started to go out in favour of something less forbidding. The oak hall at West Dean would not have held large assemblies of tenantry; instead, it provided a place for guests to mingle away from the more formal atmosphere of the drawing room.

The de luxe hotel, which encouraged the much-remarked habit of dining out rather than eating with your own friends in your own house, had its role to play in the break up of the old, cohesive society of the Victorian age (at the Ritz, mothers even let their daughters dine out unchaperoned).[45] Perhaps it is significant, therefore, that the living hall, as the new type of hall came to be called, functioned very much like an hotel lounge—in fact the terms 'lounge' and 'lounge hall' were used on some plans.[46] The attraction of the living hall was that it had no precisely defined purpose, except for talking, sitting and slouching. It possessed all the comfortable easiness of the billiard room, smoking room and gun room, with the advantage that it was also possible to enjoy the company of the opposite sex. It was not exactly intimate, since it served as a through route for family guests and servants; but it was distinctly relaxed. Sportsmen could stand there in wet and mud-spattered clothes, rather than being banished to the other end of the house, and it was even permissible to smoke there in the presence of ladies.[47]

By 1913, when C. R. Ashbee visited Hewell Grange, built with its spectacular great hall in 1884–91, the house seemed 'a noble example of something now I suppose extinct'. As he wistfully wrote in his journal, 'it is exquisitely "lived in"—things fit somehow. I mean it is not like the living of so many of the present generation we have met e.g. Lutyens' houses, when they don't fit . . . you couldn't by any stretch of the imagination dance rag-time in the Great Hall under the shadow of the Cluny tapestries.'[48] But at that date few people shared Ashbee's neo-feudal beliefs. Gravitas had gone out of style, and so had the reopening of churches, which is perhaps why the architect Mervyn Macartney felt that 'the hall has become again the favourite room in the house'.[49] Some houses, like the Red House, Chapel Allerton, seemed to become nearly all hall.[50]

The hall at the Red House was top-lit and centrally placed, the form deriving from the kind of nineteenth-century top-lit saloon seen, for instance, at Mentmore Towers. The type of living hall that grew out of the Gothic Revival great hall, however, was off-centre, had the staircase and main ground-floor rooms giving off it, and was overlooked by the bedroom corridor. Such were the halls at Broadleys and Blackwell, respectively by Voysey and Baillie Scott. Particularly in smaller houses, living halls were regarded as socially advanced because more than one activity could take place in them. Rather than having a small, box-like dining room and an equally cramped drawing room, the idea was now to have one spacious living hall, with an alcove for eating. The role of the living hall in a large house, which had a drawing room and a dining room as well, was not so universal, but the room was equally popular. Chequers, remodelled by Reginald Blomfield, had one formed out of an internal courtyard. At Madresfield Court,[51] a house which already possessed a Victorian great hall designed by P. C. Hardwick, Lord Beauchamp created a new staircase hall out of two ground-floor rooms knocked into one (Plates 40, 178). Going up through two storeys, the room became the heart of the house, at least to judge from the evocative watercolour of the Lygon family painted in 1924 (Colour

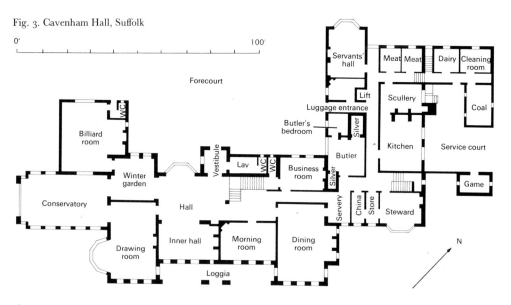

Fig. 3. Cavenham Hall, Suffolk

60

40. The staircase hall at Madresfield Court, Worcestershire

Plate xxviii). The flexibility of the living hall created an openness of plan that suited the Edwardian sense of space. Cavenham Hall (Fig. 3), in Suffolk, which was built by A. N. Prentice for H. E. M. Davies, rich from the South African gold boom, was much praised for this reason. The hall, off which was the staircase, opened into an inner hall, and the house had both a winter garden and a conservatory. Winter gardens, although sometimes placed at the side of the house, were often not detached rooms but opulent spaces that opened off other rooms or acted as through routes but would also be used for sitting, in the same way as the living hall.

The marble halls for which Edwardian grandees had such a fatal fascination sometimes functioned as living halls. Lord Wemyss, a man who 'could do most things better than other people',[52] was seventy-three when the staircase hall he added to his Scottish seat, Gosford House, was finished in 1891. He was an art lover, indeed an artist, exhibiting a statue of Venus at the Royal Academy when he was eighty-six, and the hall, designed by William Young, was astonishingly sumptuous. Nevertheless, the total, chill effect irresistibly recalls the entrance hall of Sir Ernest Cassel's London house, lined with eight hundred tons of Carrara marble imported from Italy. It was nicknamed the Giant's Lavatory,[53] and was never somewhere to dawdle.

The greatest of all Edwardian marble halls, the Indian Hall at Elveden in Suffolk,[54] was remembered by Lady Fingall as the coldest room in England. It was a dream of that most Edwardian of all Indian monuments, the Taj Mahal, planted in the cold marshes of Suffolk. But it was well used, acting more or less as a living hall. While Cassano's band played in the gallery, guests assembled there every night before dinner.[55] Lord Iveagh bought Elveden in 1894 from the estate of Prince Duleep Singh, the Indian Maharajah whom the British had ejected from the throne of the Punjab. Living on a generous pension from the civil list, the 'black prince'—as Singh was known locally—had bought Elveden in 1863, and had rebuilt it with elaborate Indian interiors. Iveagh immediately doubled the size of the house by building a new wing identical to the existing mansion externally and linked to it by a tall central block with a dome. Beneath the dome lay the Indian Hall, white and dazzling. Iveagh had visited India and brought back with him photographs of the Durbar Hall, Kerowlie, and Delvan i Khas, Delhi,[56] which were quarried for details. For further authenticity, Sir Caspar Purdon Clarke, director of the Indian Section of the South Kensington Museum, was asked to advise on the scheme, for which he shared the architect William Young's five per cent commission. Young's death, probably hastened by the volume of work involved in designing that ultimate piece of tub-thumping Baroque, the War Office in London, prevented him from seeing his plans to execution, but they were carried out by his son, Clyde, in 1900–3.

The Indian Hall rises the full height of the house and every surface is encrusted with carving. The marble alone cost Iveagh the staggering sum of £70,000, and a special railway had to be constructed from Burnham to transport it. Iveagh's Indian work contrast's severely with Singh's, which was plaster rather than stone, and—sadly evoking a warmer clime—was painted in bright colours. The Iveaghs repainted all the house white, and even painted over some of the mirrors. Duleep Singh had had the greater feeling for the spirit of India. But if, once the hall was built, the two small fireplaces, aided by underfloor central heating ducts emitting hot air beside the windows, as well as double glazing, were not enough to keep the temperature much above zero, Edward VII found

VII. Coombe Lodge, Surrey, in 1925 by Sir John Lavery, showing Lady Juliet Duff and Sir Michael Duff (private collection)

VIII–IX. Two smaller country houses: the Retreat,
Lakenheath, Suffolk, by A. N. Prentice from *Documents
d'architecture moderne*; and Broadleys, Westmorland, by
C. F. A. Voysey (RIBA drawings collection)

the house sufficiently tolerable to spend the first week of every other New Year there, alternating with Chatsworth.[57]

However, it was only after the First World War that the living hall reached, perhaps, its apotheosis, in the style which Sir Osbert Lancaster ineffably called Aldwych Farcical.[58] The informality and half-timbered cosiness suited an upper middle-class ideal. Although Rookery Nook, scene of the eponymous farce (originally a novel) by Ben Travers, was no more than a substantial house by the seaside, the description is telling:

'O eminently desirable, the modest mansion of Mrs. Mantle Ham! O for the hand of a house-agent, that we might obtain our bearings with seemly deference!'

The front door gives entrance to spacious hall, suited to additional living room and containing fine old open fireplace in Jacobean style with rich oak overmantel. Parquet flooring, valuable Turkey matting, oak-panelled walling and mullioned windowing.

The hall furniture comprises large Chesterfield, one, situated near fireplace; chairs, one set of six after Chippendale, massive hall table and other accessories. At the far end of the hall the servants' quarters and another small passage, curtained off and leading to recess for gents' hatting and a foregone conclusion for usual offices.

On the right, winding sharply, the staircase (oak).

Hiding in a cupboard under the stairs, the lovely Rhoda discovered an immense pile of back numbers of *Country Life*.[59]

41. An interior in the 'Aldwych Farcical' style, as drawn by Sir Osbert Lancaster in *Home Sweet Homes*, 1939

An Edwardian Power House

One of the grandest and most characteristic of Edwardian houses was Polesden Lacey, in Surrey.[60] Socially, Polesden Lacey was a power house. Mrs Greville, its owner, was one of the great hostesses of the age, and her guests were big fish—cabinet ministers, prime ministers, ambassadors, heads of state, several generations of the British royal family— whom she only occasionally leavened with shy young artists, writers and aesthetes.[61] But it functioned less as the centre of a landed estate than as an extension of her London house, 16 Charles Street, to which vegetables, flowers and fruit—especially the much-prized forced strawberries—from the gardens at Polesden were sent every day during the season. A bare half-hour from London and on the edge of the commuter village of Great Bookham, the thousand-acre estate, although it was farmed, was really a setting for the house—as perfect, as eighteenth-century and as beautifully preserved as the exquisite Boulle and black-lacquer cabinets that furnished the drawing room.

Like West Dean, it was not wholly an Edwardian house, because part of the previous mansion built in 1835 for Joseph Bonsor, a City bookseller and stationer, was preserved, principally the Ionic colonnade on the south front. Sir Ambrose Poynter, son of Sir Edward Poynter, P.R.A., rebuilt it in 1902–5, organising the plan round a central, grassed courtyard, rather French in feeling.[62] Externally, the house preserved the flavour of the existing building, probably because of the historical associations of the site. Richard Brinsley Sheridan had lived there, pulling an older house about until it was entirely uninhabitable and had to be rebuilt. But the roomy corridors and spacious plan betray the date of the present building. Even outside, the pergolas and porches, filled with cane seats, provided places for chance meetings, intimate conversations or lolling in the afternoon sun away from a house full of other guests—an amplitude that would have made Polesden the perfect setting for a Henry James novel.

The remodelling was done for Sir Clinton Dawkins, an Indian civil servant, whose 'first-rate brains' matched 'a *savoir faire* approaching to genius', which 'enabled him, after having exhausted the rewards of officialdom, to start on a new career in the greatest of the Franco-American banks'.[63] His marriage to Louise Johnston, which took place in 1882, had made him a social success, so his new house had every provision for smart entertaining. But he died in 1906, the year after work was complete, and Mrs Greville—or rather her father, William McEwan—bought it immediately.

Mrs Greville's presence is felt in the entrance hall (Plate 43). It was a typical living hall, screened by pillars from the broad ground-floor corridor and with the staircase giving off it. Poynter had left a framework of dark panelling, with blind rectangles of plaster waiting to be hidden by pictures or tapestries.[64] Mrs Greville did one better than that, by erecting the reredos of a demolished Wren church—St Matthew's, Friday Street—over the fireplace, where it acts as a huge, richly carved overmantel. It fitted in admirably with the existing dark woodwork. But the preceding generation would have been shocked by the irreverence. Dancing took place in front of it during balls, and above the blank panels on which the Ten Commandments were once inscribed hung a secular tapestry showing Caesar and Cleopatra.

Mrs Greville exploded into society on her marriage in 1901. Calculating the effect, she started a subscription with a press-cutting agency on her engagement, and effectively she

Larders

Floor plan labels:

Larders
Dairy
Ice
Cook's room
Kitchen court
Scullery
Butler's bedroom
Mans room
WC WC
Garden room
Butler's pantry
Still room
Back entrance
Servants' hall
Maids' stairs
House-keeper's room
Kitchen
Mens stairs
Lav
Bachelors' stairs
Lift Lift
Servery
Pergola
Gun room
Drying room
Brushing room
Store
Dining room
Smoking room
Billiard room
Courtyard
Hall
Vestibule
Cloakroom
Lav WC
Gallery
Porch
Small drawing room
Large drawing room
Library
Portico

0'   100'

42. The entrance front of Polesden Lacey, Surrey

Fig. 4. Polesden Lacey before the addition of the study next to the library

does not exist before then. She left instructions that her private papers and diaries should be burnt on her death, but she exempted the many expensively bound albums of cuttings from the court and society columns, which thus became the unofficial commemorative record of her life. Only the long obituaries of her father, an Edinburgh brewer, philanthropist, M.P. and privy councillor, give a side light on her early life, which was spent in Edinburgh, where she was born, her father having married his housekeeper, Mrs Anderson.[65] Captain the Hon. Ronald Greville, her husband, was the eldest son of Lord Greville and a long-standing friend of George Keppel. Through the Keppels, Mrs Keppel being on the closest terms with Edward VII, Mrs Greville entered the smart set. The Keppels were present over the week-ends that the King stayed with the Grevilles (either at Polesden or Reigate Priory, the nearby house which they had previously rented).[66] Mrs Greville's inscrutability and discretion, necessary for entertaining Edward VII, contributed to the 'kind of unobtrusive luxury of life and and background' which Osbert Sitwell felt he had 'never encountered elsewhere'.[67]

Ronnie Greville, a 'charming unambitious man whom she moulded affectionately into any shape she pleased',[68] is little in evidence at Polesden, because he died suddenly, aged

43. The hall at Polesden, with the reredos from Christopher Wren's St Matthew's, Friday Street, as an overmantel

forty-four, in 1908. A steeplechaser and racehorse owner, he had been steered into politics by his wife, being elected Conservative M.P. for East Bradford in 1896. 'Social duties'—and the cause of free-trading—excused his retirement in 1905. Mr McEwan, after his own wife and his daughter's husband had died, often visited Mrs Greville, and he appears in the inevitable group photographs—a thin, bearded figure giving the impression 'that his one idea was to obliterate himself'.[69] His considerable fortune (over a million pounds on his death in 1913)[70] supported the life of the house. 'It's been an easy thing for me to become rich,' as he said later in life. 'I just couldna help it: and the only pleasure it gives me is the thought that I'm able to give pleasure to others.'[71]

The house as Poynter left it was generously planned. There was a dining room, a library and two drawing rooms—the second for bridge, which needed concentration, especially when stakes were high, and so could not take place in the crowded main drawing room.[72] On the west side, the suite of gentlemen's rooms comprised a billiard room, smoking room, gun room and lavatory, and it had its own staircase leading to the bachelor bedrooms above.

The Grevilles only added a study to the end of the south front: but they entirely redecorated the house, as a result of which the drawing room became a grand climax. Reached from a dark gallery, it was a dazzling incarnation of opulence, the extravagant gilding bathed in sunlight from no fewer than five pairs of French windows. The panelling, taken from a North Italian palace and cut down to fit,[73] was lined with tall mirrors, and seemed to be dripping with gold—so much that that it took four men eighteen months and two thousand and forty-four books of twenty-four carat gold leaf to regild the room in 1961–2. The setting was rich and glittering, like the guests. Mid-Victorians would have found it dreadfully ostentatious; but a Mrs Greville would have found it difficult to storm their closed social world.

White Allom and Co. decorated the drawing room; they were probably also responsible for the Friday Street reredos, because they specialised in providing old woodwork and architectural fittings. But for the rest of the house, including the structural work, the Grevilles employed Mewès and Davis, the firm that had created, in the Ritz Hotel, Piccadilly,[74] the ultimate symbol and resort of the Edwardian rich. Charles Mewès was a Frenchman who ran an international practice, his partners in Germany, France, Spain and South America deferentially calling him 'le patron'. Arthur Davis, his English partner, was, when they joined forces, a brilliant twenty-two year old former student of the École des Beaux-Arts, who had been helping him prepare drawings for the competition for the Grand and Petit Palais, in Paris. The Ritz, which was hailed as a *tour de force*, opened in May 1906; Mewès and Davis began work at Polesden the same year. Mrs Greville was quick to see that the architects had caught the tone of her world.

Surprisingly, however, only one room at Polesden—the second drawing room, which changed its name to the tea room—was decorated in the French taste. There was no French neo-Classical staircase as at Luton Hoo. The rooms were in a sequence of contrasting styles, with a Georgian dining room to show off Mrs Greville's fine English portraits, bought from Agnew's at the top of the market.

The dining room at Polesden was important. Mrs Greville had a French chef to rival Anatole, Aunt Dahlia's chef in the Bertie Wooster stories. Some dedicated gourmets grumbled that only a handful of Edwardian hostesses served *really* good food,[75] but that was only because custom had allowed them to pitch their sights high. Consuelo Vanderbilt, from the comparatively less self-indulgent world of New York and Rhode Island, was appalled to be told by one Edwardian *bon vivant*: 'Considering that it is the only pleasure one can count on having three times a day every day of one's life, a well-ordered meal is of prime importance.'[76]

Edward VII, called Tum-Tum by his friends, was said by Escoffier to be the only Englishman truly to appreciate frogs' legs.[77] The dinner he was served at Polesden on Sunday, 6 June 1909, consisted of soup, salmon or whitebait, *boudins de volaille princesse*, saddle of lamb, quail with ortolans, salad, vegetables, sweet and savoury. Such meals were smaller in volume than those of the preceding generation, largely because, by 1890, *service à la russe*—the modern system of serving one dish after another, rather than putting a large number of contrasting dishes on the table at the same time—had become almost universal. This greatly improved the quality of eating, since delicately sauced dishes could be served straight from the kitchen and not left to congeal.[78]

A dish similar to the quail with ortolans may have inspired Austen Chamberlain to write an ode 'To a Quail', which he sent to Mrs Greville with his thank-you letter the next day:

> On the surface floating
> Of an amber sea
> In aspic coating
> Prepared express for thee,
> Like an ethereal essence
> thou breathest thy charm to me.[79]

It is terrible poetry, but has an evocative quality. And although in fact written in London, the lines could equally well have been composed at Polesden, because Mrs Greville's butlers, chauffeur and chef always moved with her when she went from Charles Street to the country.

The style of entertaining at Polesden was similar to that cultivated by Lucia, the heroine of E. F. Benson's aptly named novel *The Climber*. The week long house party she held at Brayton was to be the *ne plus ultra* of smartness:

> she planned every hour of those days, all seven of them, so that while every one of her guests would feel free to do as the spirit prompted, he would find some admirable occupation was ready, in case it recommended itself to him. Till lunch-time each day a careful blank was left by her, but she arranged that motor-cars, golf-caddies and fishing gillies were lurking like wild beasts round the corner, ready to pounce.[80]

The key-note of the week at Brayton was its simplicity, but this of course was only comparative, as it was at Polesden. The ladies in the party probably changed dresses five times a day, with a different outfit for morning, walking, afternoon, tea and dinner. This was so tiresome that experienced guests sometimes stayed in their rooms over breakfast to avoid the bother of the first change.[81] The tea-gown was the epitome of luxury, and could turn that humble meal into a feast of splendour. 'Who does not know the aspect of a magnificently furnished drawing-room in a large country house at 5·30,' asked Lady Jeune, 'with its well-shaded lamps and candles throwing a subdued light over a scene as

70

brilliant as any evening entertainment, where the brocades and silks and lace and flashing jewels make all observers rub their eyes, and wonder whether this fairy scene is not a dream?'[82] Few drawing-rooms could better have accommodated this kind of dazzling social spectacle than that at Polesden.

The Simpler Life

However, other houses expressed a fashion for simplicity in a more radical sense, shown in a growing preference for games rather than sport. The slaughter of pheasants reached a pitch of almost mechanical excellence—which some, indeed, thought rather less than sporting—in the early twentieth century. The speed and skill with which guns could be changed and reloaded, the best shots having two loaders apiece, was sometimes the chief factor in determining the size of a bag. George V, a much better shot than his father, could bring down two of Elveden's partridges in front of him, turn, and shoot another two behind, although even he was left silent at the end of the record shoot organised by Lord Burnham in 1913, in which four thousand pheasants were killed. 'Perhaps we overdid it today,' he remarked to the Prince of Wales on the train home.[83] (Shooting-party stories are legion in Edwardian memoirs, but probably the best concerns Lord Charles Beresford. Bursting into the darkened bedroom he thought to be occupied by one of his

44. The Duke and Duchess of York (George VI and Queen Elizabeth) on their honeymoon at Polesden

conquests, he leapt onto the bed with a cry of 'Cock-a-doodle-do'—only to find himself between the Bishop of Chester and his wife.[84]) But golf also gained a wide following, partly from being far cheaper and requiring less practice. 'It's an inexpensive taste, and you're lucky to find it amusing,' Lady Conybeare told her brother-in-law in *Mammon and Co*.[85] Shooting, by contrast, was probably the most difficult aspect of upper-crust life for a newcomer to master. Houses like Lutyens's Grey Walls and Blomfield's Whitehall were built as 'golf boxes'[86] near famous courses. Other houses, including Polesden Lacey, had golf courses built in the park. Edward VII was himself a devotee of the game, although he hated losing, and 'Nature', as a courtier put it, had not made his 'figure suitable for driving a long ball'.[87]

Indoor courts for real tennis, badminton and fives were also occasionally built, as at Coldicote, Whittington, Esher Place, Greyfriars and Kildonan. Squash began to come into its own as the ideal way to ease 'the unhappy lot of a sportsman prevented by frost from keeping fit in his accustomed way'.[88] Tennis could be played by both sexes and was correspondingly popular. Women were able to move more freely than the generation before, as the bustle went out in the late 1880s, and eventually the foundation skirt disappeared.[89]

By some, fresh air was held at a premium, especially after its beneficial effects had been seen in the treatment of tuberculosis.[90] Generally there was better ventilation in bedrooms, and a small but growing number of owners chose not to sleep in a bedroom at all. The ascetic Lord Leverhulme, who slept the year round under a lean-to awning on

45. The architect and writer H. A. Tipping in his open-air dining room at Mathern Palace, Monmouthshire

46. Lord Leverhulme's sleeping verandah at Thornton Manor, Cheshire, with bath

the roof of his house, Thornton Manor, sometimes woke up with snowflakes drifting across his counterpane (Plate 46). Sleeping sheds were also favoured. According to a correspondent in *Country Life* in January 1910:

> The sleeping-shed at the foot of the garden, which has become a feature of so many country houses in the last few years, represents the climax of a grand revolt against the confined and air-proof bedrooms of a former age. Curtains and blinds, four-poster beds, night-caps and warming-pans and all manner of stuffy contrivances are passing away, and we have lost that nameless terror for 'night air' which led our ancestors to believe that the quality of the air mysteriously deteriorated with the darkness.[91]

Nevertheless, even this enthusiast had to admit that the 'sleeping-shed has some disadvantages. One must reach it—unless one rejoices in a covered way—through darkness and often through rain, and while asleep one is at the mercy, more or less, of any exploring tramp or stray dog or cat.' Much more convenient, then, was a verandah on the bedroom floor, such as those at Rodmarton (Plate 209). 'If the position of the verandah was considered when the house was built,' continued the *Country Life* correspondent, 'it may be made a summer bedroom of a perfectly delightful character.' Kilteragh in Co. Dublin offered another solution. There, like Lord Leverhulme, the Irish patriot Sir Horace Plunkett 'had his own shelter on the roof, with a bed in it, where he slept, summer or winter'—but with the additional refinement of 'some mechanical device' by which 'he could turn from his bed towards the sun and against the wind'.[92]

47–8. Bathroom at Encombe, Kent, a seaside villa designed to take advantage of the fresh sea breezes in every room

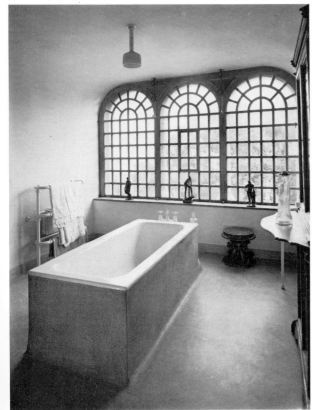 

49. A butterfly-plan or sun-trap house: Kelling Hall, Norfolk (RIBA drawings collection)

Built in 1905–7, Kilteragh was also evidence of a new desire for the sun. Unlike their Victorian predecessors, the Edwardians—or some of the more advanced—courted rather than shunned the sun's rays—indeed, a machine called a solarium or sun bath could be bought which manufactured them artificially. It was not uncommon for a mid-Victorian house, even one as progressive as William Morris's Red House, to be built facing north, but this would have been seen as a grave fault by 1900. Kilteragh, which, according to Lady Fingall, was 'designed to catch the sun in every room', was fan-shaped. 'The front of it had a blank look . . . Only the staircase windows, bathrooms and pantries looked that way, which was North. All the living and bedrooms on the other three sides, opened their windows to the sun, East, South or West, during some time of day. There was a stoep facing South, built on the model of the one Horace had seen at Cecil Rhodes's house, Groote Schuur.'[93] As the architect Arnold Mitchell wrote in 1904: 'we cannot open our British homes too generously to the sun's light and heat'.[94]

Kilteragh was one of a number of Edwardian 'sun-trap' or 'butterfly-plan' houses, designed to make the most of the sun (Plate 49). The seed of the idea was conceived by Richard Norman Shaw, when he remodelled Chesters in Northumberland, a large Classical house to which he gave a curving colonnade on one side. 'The planning of it all is a masterpiece,' wrote Lutyens, who visited it in 1901 and developed the hint the next year in the punning butterfly-plan of Papillon Hall. Sea-breezes—and, one suspects, vegetarianism, sandal-wearing and Socialism—were also important, as can be seen from the number of sun-trap houses in seaside locations. Shaw's former pupil, E. S. Prior, built

74

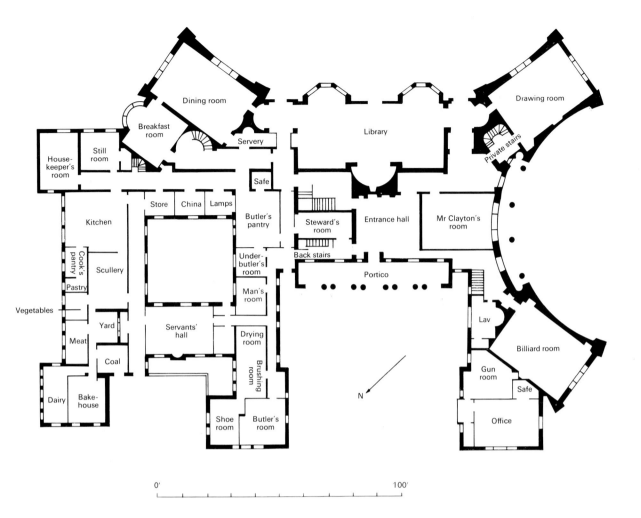

Dining room

Breakfast room

Library

Drawing room

Housekeeper's room

Still room

Private stairs

Servery

Safe

Store · China · Lamps

Butler's pantry

Steward's room

Entrance hall

Mr Clayton's room

Kitchen

Cook's pantry

Scullery

Pastry

Underbutler's room

Back stairs

Vegetables

Man's room

Portico

Meat

Yard

Servants' hall

Drying room

Lav

Coal

Billiard room

Gun room

Dairy

Bakehouse

Brushing room

Safe

Shoe room

Butler's room

Office

N

0'   100'

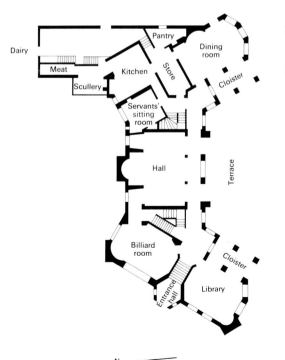

Dairy

Pantry

Dining room

Meat

Kitchen

Store

Cloister

Scullery

Servants' sitting room

Hall

Terrace

Billiard room

Cloister

Entrance hall

Library

N

Fig. 5. Chesters, Northumberland

Fig. 6. Home Place, Norfolk

75

a small, X-shaped house, with rubble walls and a thatched roof, near Exmouth in 1895–7, and later Home Place, at Holt, near Cromer (Plate 151). Indeed, the Norfolk coast was considered particularly bracing and well-suited to Arts and Crafts butterfly-plan houses: Happisburgh Manor and Kelling Hall were built there in 1900 and 1912.[95]

Butterfly-plan houses were not the only ones to make the most of the sun. Another popular plan had a corridor on the north front and the rooms in a string on the south. This was particularly satisfactory for small houses, because the comparative length of façade made a brave architectural show even when the number of rooms was not great.

Simplicity, or what was thought of as such, became something of a cult, which coincided nicely with the desire some owners had to make economies, although for others it was no more than a fashion. In a way reminiscent of Marie Antoinette's *hameau*, the rustic fantasy she contrived at Versailles, it became quite smart to live in a cottage. It had artistic overtones of the Arts and Crafts movement and the simple life, especially if the cottage was converted out of an existing building. In her country house, the fictional Lady Conybeare 'always sat in the big hall which opened straight on to the front-door, instead of in the drawing room. "Quite like hobnailed day-labourers." '[96] Evidently Arthur Martin was right to warn that 'We must not be misled by our friends' use of the word "cottage", for many cottages are so only in name.'[97]

Leopold de Rothschild turned Ascott House, an eighteenth-century farmhouse, into 'a picturesque, very original many-roomed glorified cottage', as his cousin Lady Battersea described it[98]—or, in Mary Gladstone's words, 'a palace-like cottage, the most luxurious and lovely thing I ever saw'.[99] The taste for this type of house was shown again by Lady Battersea's husband, the rich and beautiful Cyril Flower, a friend of the Pre-Raphaelites.[100] Already the owner of four country houses, he bought two inconvenient and uncomfortable villas called 'The Cottage' at Overstrand, near Cromer. The thought of sea-breezes and sea-bathing appealed to his wife, golf and tennis to him. It had no park, and some old fishermen's cottages, still inhabited, stood a little way down the lane. Lutyens converted The Cottage into a large but eccentric seaside house, which was renamed The Pleasaunce at Lord Morley's suggestion. Lady Battersea thought it a 'home-y abode'.[101] Lutyens was not proud of it, but at least The Pleasaunce was less austere than some more radical Arts and Crafts houses. Lutyens's own tastes were thought spartan by some clients, but even he came to dread going to Le Bois des Moutiers, which he built for the Theosophist Guillaume Mallet near Dieppe. 'O, I don't want to stay with the Mallets,' he wrote plaintively in 1911, 'it is so uncomfy . . .'[102]

After 1918

The collapse of the country-house building world after the First World War is vividly illustrated by the case of John Kinross, a Scottish architect with a large country-house practice in the 1890s and early 1900s, but who only kept going after 1918 by designing war memorials, some, poignantly, to sons of former clients. Masterman, who had lambasted the governing class in *The Condition of England*, acknowledged the greatness of its sacrifice—its young having perished in blood and fire, in the retreat from Mons and the first battle of Ypres—in *England After the War*.[103] The young architects A. Winter Rose and

76

50. The swimming pool at Woodfalls, a pavilion built in the grounds of Melchet Court, Hampshire

Alwyn Ball, the latter having shown the promise of great talent at Houndsell Place, died at the front. Of the architects who survived or were too old to fight, Kinross was not the only one to find that the clients had gone. Lutyens built only three country houses after 1918: he was fortunate to be absorbed in Delhi and his great public buildings, although, even so, he was not without financial worries. Robert Lorimer, who died in 1929, designed no new-built country house after the war, nor did Detmar Blow. Sir Reginald Blomfield could only remember wistfully 'that delightful country house practice which I was lucky enough to have built up before the war, and which since the war has ceased to exist'.[104]

The immediate effect of the war on such new houses as were built was the disappearance of the bachelor bedrooms. The crowds of idle, affable young men that made up the ballast of Victorian shooting parties and were usually housed in a row of smallish bedrooms in the masculine part of the house, over the billiard room, smoking room and gun room, could no longer be found—or if they could, they did not have so much time to spend in the country. The yet larger crowds of servants necessary to service big houses had also disappeared: some never returned from the front, many others never returned from the munitions factories and the town jobs that they were required to take during the war, and found more convenient than service.

There were some changes that could only indirectly be attributed to the war. It was a sign of increasing feminine influence (culminating in the vote) that the multiplicity of rooms to which a Victorian gentleman would have retreated as though to a sanctum were often no longer in evidence on post-war country-house plans. The move towards simplification visible in the Edwardian decade, with a small number of—possibly larger—communal rooms, rather than a large number of rooms highly specific in function, was accelerated. Even by 1914 smoking rooms were a thing of the past. Whereas Queen Victoria would not read a letter if she so much as suspected that the writer had smoked as he wrote it,[105] and Victorian gentlemen were intensely careful not to let the least whiff of smoke blow back into the hall of the house as they thankfully lit their cigars at the front door,[106] Edward VII smoked everywhere, and it was generally thought that his influence was decisive in ending the tobacco taboo. Old habits died hard, however, and smoking rooms were planned at Kildonan and Wallingford Court, both immediately pre-war. Billiards went out equally slowly, but it was far more likely that a new country house in the 1920s would be built with a swimming pool than a billiard room—although bathing pools, as they were generally known, were sometimes built before the war. The difference was perhaps one of design: Edwardian bathing pools tended to be picturesquely disguised as garden ponds, Andrew Carnegie's big indoor swimming pool at Skibo being an exception. Probably the only Modern Movement country house to have a billiard room was St Anne's Hill, in Surrey, and that was built for two confirmed bachelors.[107] More typical was the pool, with sliding roof (open in summer), and squash court, disguised as a chapel, built in the grounds of Stanton House, Wiltshire, in 1935.[108]

'In England this is the era of the small house,' wrote Professor Charles Reilly in 1926. 'No longer are the big country houses of the pre-war period being built.'[109] The new mood was defined by P. A. Barron in 1928: 'The wealthy woman of to-day does not desire a palace,' he wrote in *The House Desirable*; 'she prefers a service flat somewhere in W.1.; also a small country house, for preference old, but rendered comfortable by the installation of electric lighting, central heating, modern bathrooms and kitchen.'[110] Another writer,

79

51. The garden staircase at Port Lympne, Kent

52. Whiteladies House, a Modern Movement doll's house of 1935 (Bethnal Green Museum of Childhood)

Ralph Nevill, lamented the number of fine old country houses that were being shut up, sold or turned into institutions. In *English Country House Life*, published in 1925, he gave a seemingly endless list: 'Among the country houses which modern developments have affected in this way are Hamilton Palace, Trentham, Temple Newsam, Shipley, Charlton, Garswood, Worsley, Canford, Battle Abbey, Normanhurst, Ravensworth, Overstone and The Grange, which have been, or are to be, devoted to other than residential purposes.' Different fates befell different houses. 'A short time ago it was announced in the Press that the characteristic old Georgian mansion of Sudbrooke Holme, about five miles from Lincoln, was likely to be purchased by a British Film Company, who proposed to burn it to the ground in order to produce a spectacular scene on the cinematograph.'[111]

Some houses were able to carry on in the same style as before, but they came to seem curiously out of date. Polesden Lacey was one. Few hostesses of the younger generation liked to organise their guests, as Mrs Greville still did, so that each was known to be busily golfing, playing tennis, shooting or visiting the farm. A regime of comparative informality prevailed at houses such as Port Lympne (Plate 51), originally built to Herbert Baker's designs by the rich homosexual statesman and aviator Sir Philip Sassoon. To Baker's house, in the Cape Dutch style Baker had used at Groote Schuur, the South African home of Cecil Rhodes, Philip Tilden added a bachelors' wing—one of the last—around a Moorish courtyard. (Honor Channon, wife of Chips, maliciously likened it to a Spanish

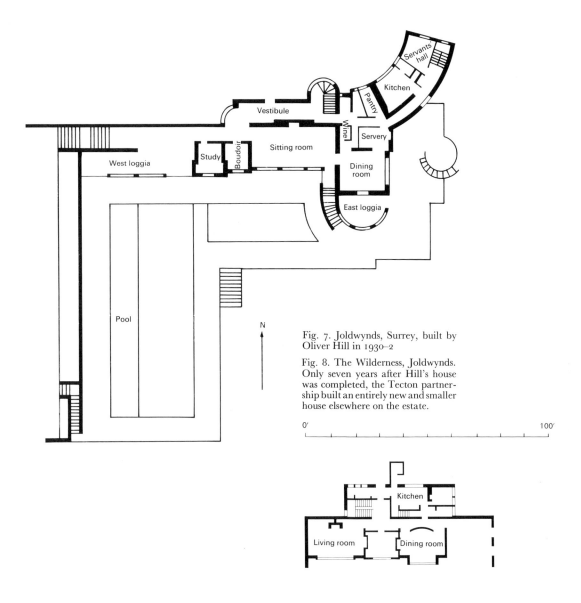

Fig. 7. Joldwynds, Surrey, built by Oliver Hill in 1930–2

Fig. 8. The Wilderness, Joldwynds. Only seven years after Hill's house was completed, the Tecton partnership built an entirely new and smaller house elsewhere on the estate.

0'   100'

brothel.) Crowds of young airmen came from the nearby flying field at Lympne to mingle with Sassoon's grand society and political friends. Partly because there was no hostess, Sassoon dispensed with formal introductions, and the atmosphere was informal—'almost American'.[112]

Hollywood was sowing weird and wonderful seeds. Some blossomed at Eltham Palace, home of the textile millionaire Stephen Courtauld, which had a silver-plated ceiling in the dining-room and a cage for Lady Courtauld's pet monkeys on the bedroom floor, directly communicating via a pole with the drawing-room beneath. At Port Lympne, the Classical garden—with its great staircase scaling the cliffside and Imperial bathing pool overlooking Romney marsh—could have been a stage set for D. W. Griffith's film epic *Intolerance*.

53. Charters, Berkshire

The cult of sun, fresh air and an informal way of life, the first signs of which had been seen in the sun-trap houses of the Edwardian decade, became more and more radical. A hot Mediterranean wind was blowing away the last suspicion of fustiness and formality. White plaster rather than brick or stone was, impractically, favoured for houses in what might be called the Hollywood Spanish style, like Encombe and Birchens Spring.[113] The Modern Movement is, strictly speaking, peripheral to a history of the country house; but when it arrived from France and Germany in the late 1920s, the new values were treated as moral principles. White walls, metal-framed windows, flat roofs and plate glass expressed what one writer called

> the habits, tastes and ideas of the people of today—the young people who are unhampered by choice possessions of old furniture or by old conventions of drawing rooms, calling hours, formal manners or privacy; a generation that in Town asks for a service flat and in the country plenty of light, a swimming pool and a house where friends can drop in in numbers any time, help themselves to drinks, and possibly come across their host or hostess somewhere or other; a generation bred in one war and living its little time of sunshine to the full before the next one.

The passage comes from the booklet accompanying a didactic, Modern Movement doll's house called Whiteladies House, designed by Moray Thomas and exhibited at the Building Centre in 1935 (Plate 52).[114] The dolls were stretched out in deck-chairs by the swimming pool, their tennis rackets in their hands. The tone is equally familiar from Evelyn Waugh's *Decline and Fall* and the architectural writings of the young Nikolaus Pevsner.

Whiteladies House, however, is the model of a small house rather than a country house. The Modern Movement did not build country houses—the very thought would have smacked of the hide-bound traditionalism it was trying to destroy. Virtually none of the houses catalogued in Jeremy Gould's *Modern Houses in Britain*[115] has more than three main rooms on the ground floor—not even High and Over, one of the largest and most prestigious. There was no need that it should, because the old notion that each function of the house had to take place in a separate room had been broken down still further. Rooms, or rather spaces, open into each other without the division of a wall or a door, and more than one activity could take place in the same room. Modern Movement houses were not built for large country-house parties, and to have just two guest bedrooms, as at St Anne's Hill, was considered perfectly adequate. Motor cars were making overnight stays superfluous; and owners—memorably characterised by Sir Osbert Lancaster in his drawing of a tweed-wearing, pipe-smoking, middle-class intellectual in *Home Sweet Homes*[116]—were as likely to choose sites in the suburbs or by the sea as in the country.

The exception would seem to be Charters (Plate 53), in Berkshire, built in 1938 for a manufacturer of electrical goods. Outside it is the very image of King's Thursday, as rebuilt by Margot Best Chestwynde in *Decline and Fall*, 'something clean and square', designed by the fictional German architect Professor Silenus who was best known for his chewing gum factory (Frederick C. Button, joint architect with George Adie, does not offer a precise parallel, although he trained with the firm that built a factory for Wrigley's—Wallis Gilbert and Partners).[117] It has a flat roof, which was intended, like the roofs of many Modern Movement houses, for use as a sun terrace, although the family preferred to sun themselves in the garden; there are staring white walls, metal-framed windows and a strict rectangularity of outline. But the walls are clad in Portland stone rather than concrete; and inside, a row of Corinthian columns supports the gallery to a room known as the great hall.

Old forms died hard; too hard perhaps. The great hall at Charters was a sign that, despite a voguish use of a new style, the tradition of building country houses in Britain was beginning to ossify, and would not stretch much further as an organic growth.

ONE SERVANT

:: USING THE ::

British Portable Vacuum Cleaner.

can clean all your Carpets, Drapery, Upholstery, and Furniture
:: without removal or disturbance to the household. ::

Can be connected with any electric-light fitting, or supplied with a petrol motor.

PRICES.

Hand Machines - 8 guineas

Electric Machines,
from 16 to 20 guineas

Please write for Illustrated Catalogue and information concerning our Deferred Payment System.

THE BRITISH VACUUM CLEANER Co., Ltd.,

15 PARSONS GREEN LANE, LONDON, S.W.
171 PICCADILLY, W.

54. Advertisement of 1909 from *Academy Architecture*

3. *The Servant Question*

*B*uilt in 1938, Charters seemed a miracle of luxury with its provision for ten indoor servants; but that number—high though it was at a time when few country houses were built with provision for more than two or three living in staff—was as nothing in comparison to the great days before the First World War. Although Sir James Miller of Manderston was not in the same league as the fifteenth Earl of Derby, who employed seven hundred and twenty-seven servants, gardeners and other staff at his death in 1893, he could still boast a small army of domestic workers which was proudly photographed at the beginning of the century (Plates 55–6). The difference illustrates the greatest of all the changes that took place in country houses between 1890 and 1920. It was called by contemporary writers The Servant Question.

Anxiety about the shortage of domestic labour was being expressed in the 1890s, and it grew throughout the next decade. Although, according to the 1901 census, domestic service employed more people than any other occupation at the beginning of the Edwardian decade, the hidden trends were disquieting. Between 1881 and 1901 the number of female indoor servants increased by one hundred thousand, to one million three hundred and thirty thousand. The rise measured just over eight per cent, which was nowhere near the twenty-five per cent increase in population. The number of young servants actually fell, despite the fact that they came from the section of the population which was expanding the fastest. 'Between the ages of 15–20, there is a decrease of 7.3 per cent while in the number of females living at those ages there is an increase of 28·1 per cent,' wrote Mabel Atkinson in 1910. 'This suggests that the difficulty of finding servants will intensify as time goes on, as is indeed borne out by observation.'[1]

To J. H. Elder Duncan, echoing the views of many people in the years before the First World War, it seemed that 'The old race of servants who laboured from six o'clock in the morning till eleven o'clock at night is now extinct; and the new order is exceedingly exacting on the question of hours and the volume of work.'[2] The problem was worse in smaller houses. After the fire that destroyed his home in 1912, Baillie Scott moved to a small Bedfordshire farmhouse, from which he wrote that his wife was so comfortable and 'so afraid of undertaking housekeeping again with all the difficulties with servants which are so great in this country now for small households that I have been obliged to put off building for ourselves yet'.[3]

The numerous editions of Mrs Beeton's *Book of Household Management* are an intriguing index of how the crisis impinged on the British imagination. The world, wrote the authors of the 1915 edition, 'has travelled of late at electric speed, and far-reaching changes of time have touched household affairs from standpoints apparently far remote.'[4] The book was four times the size of the original 1861 volume, and contained an optimistic section on colonial cookery, with recipes such as roast wallaby, kangaroo tail soup and parrot pie. Belatedly, a note on chauffeurs appeared for the first time, although it was typical that their duties turned out to be 'very similar to those of the Coachman'. It did not seem necessary to mention the fact that the First World War had already lasted a year. But in 1923, the date of the next edition, the heavens fell. Each previous edition had opened majestically with a quotation from Proverbs XXXI: 25–8, which was taken to describe 'The Mistress':

> Strength and honour are her clothing: and she shall rejoice in time to come. She openeth her mouth with wisdom; and in her tongue is the law of kindness. She looketh well to the ways of the household, and eateth not the bread of idleness. Her children arise up and call her blessed; her husband also, and he praiseth her.

This was replaced by a couplet by Hartley Coleridge:

> She was a queen of Nature's crowning,
> A smile was like an act of grace.

Mistresses had lost their God-given charter.

Worse, they were told that 'a social revolution' had been brought about by 'war and consequent heavy taxation'. 'Good servants are hard to get, harder still to keep . . . The good mistress has always been she who could not only direct but do; to-day in the majority of households, she is not only capable, when emergencies arise, but prefers in any case to do so.' It is true that one part of the 1915 edition had suggested that some mistresses were discreetly beginning to make the housekeeping budget stretch further: 'Hints to Amateur Cooks', as this section was euphemistically called, was written for ladies without the first idea of how to cook, but who were having to learn. But never before 1923 had mistresses been told that 'The continued shortage of domestic labour, and high wages, have forced housekeepers [meaning mistresses] to take a much larger part in the work of the house themselves.'[5] Never before had they had to work.

Apart from the possibility of living in a smaller house or even a town flat, there were two principal ways in which owners tried to cope with the crisis. One was to introduce some of the new technology that was making housework quicker and easier. The kitchen at Charters, for instance, had in 1938 an automatic dishwasher and waste disposal system, the first of its kind in England.[6] The other way was to make the furniture and decoration of the house less difficult to dust, polish and keep clean. 'Avoid ledges, avoid fretwork, cosy corners, and elaborate mouldings,' advised Elder Duncan;

> have solid balustrades to the stairs if necessary, and generally banish all those resting-places for dirt and dust that takes a household half its time to keep clean. Stained floors, and rugs or squares that can be easily taken outside and beaten, are far preferable to the 'all over' carpet which accumulates dirt and can never be moved without taking out all

55–6. Servants at Manderston, Berwickshire

57. Entrance hall at Eltham Palace, Kent

the furniture. Put an embargo on elaborate metal fittings that require continual and laborious cleaning. The additional comfort will always compensate for much that is lost from an artistic point of view, and truth to tell, in endeavouring to minimise the labour of the household one will escape much abominably bad art.[7]

Oak furniture was specially recommended by some writers, because it did not need polishing. As a result, the servant question was a spur to simplicity, which was the dominant characteristic of progressive country-house architecture both before and after the First World War. With equal force, it was used to justify spartan, homespun interiors by Voysey and sleek Art Deco ones by Oliver Hill.

Nevertheless, life without servants implied a social revolution too big for some to contemplate at the turn of the century; or in the uncompromising words of the fashionable magazine the *Queen*: 'As long as houses exist we must have workers.'[8] The reason for this was that innumerable things simply depended on being done by hand, and

88

there was little motive for change as long as domestic labour was cheap and plentiful. Hot water for baths had to be taken up from the basement to the bedroom floor, and for a large house party several dozen baths might have to be got ready in the hour before dinner—the same thing with the water for washing hands before and after meals.[9] Grates had to be cleared; furniture, photograph frames, plant stands and all the other objects in an over-full drawing room had to be dusted. When the family rode, let alone hunted, the scrubbing of mud-spattered clothes was long, heavy work, especially when ladies' riding habits had to be cleaned. A house steward, William Lanceley, remembered that, as a twenty-one year old footman, serving in a house where the master hunted six days a week, he would often not leave the brushing room until after midnight.[10] The numerous outfits needed for a smart Saturday-to-Monday—perhaps ten or even more—had to be packed in their swathes of tissue paper; and carrying the leather 'Saratoga' trunks, the dress baskets, the portmanteaux and the hat boxes was no mean task. Even a strapping lad of seventeen, who was six feet two inches tall, was 'advised to look for another place', because it was felt he was too weak for the work.[11] Bodices that laced up at the back could not be put on or—far worse—taken off by the wearer unaided, and one lady told the story of how, returning late after a London ball to find the servants asleep, she was reduced to calling a hansom cab—she gave the driver nail scissors and told him to cut the string.[12] 'No one will deny that servants are a necessity in every home,' wrote the author of *The Small House, its Architecture and Surrounds*.[13]

Given that there were armies of servants, however, many turn-of-the-century commentators believed that English country houses, after their long and uninterrupted evolution, functioned with almost exemplary efficiency. 'Its absolute practicality' was the 'genuinely and decisively valuable feature of the English house,' wrote Hermann Muthesius,[14] an architect sent by the German government to undertake an exhaustive, seven year study of the subject. Every element had been rigorously tested, modified and approved by long use. Having slimmed down slightly in comparison to the monsters of the 1830s and 1840s (few houses had a dairy or bake house in the 1890s), the modern servants' wing worked, as Mrs Beeton—long before Le Corbusier—described it, 'with the regularity and precision of a well adjusted machine'.[15] C. H. B. Quennell, who was then designing a large Scottish country house, Aultmore, summed up how architects thought when he compared the suite of kitchen offices in a big house to 'a modern factory, so that from the moment the food is delivered like raw material at the tradesmen's door it will pass along until it is delivered as the finished product in the dining room, and make steady progression during its journey'.[16]

Muthesius particularly admired the planning of Motcombe, in Dorset, by George and Peto (Fig. 9). One might not see why at first glance. With its lamp room, boot room, brushing room, room for riding breeches, not to mention its kitchen, housekeeper's room, steward's room, its stores and its larders, the house might look like a nightmare of over-elaboration—the sort of thing that only a railway magnate and a Grosvenor, such as the owner, Lord Stalbridge, could ever have supported. Yet it was precisely this, 'the uncommonly large number of rooms allocated to domestic purposes', that to Muthesius represented 'a high level of culture' in English country houses. Each domestic activity had its own allotted compartment to be performed in, and nothing surely could have been more logical than that.

58. Motcombe Manor, Dorset

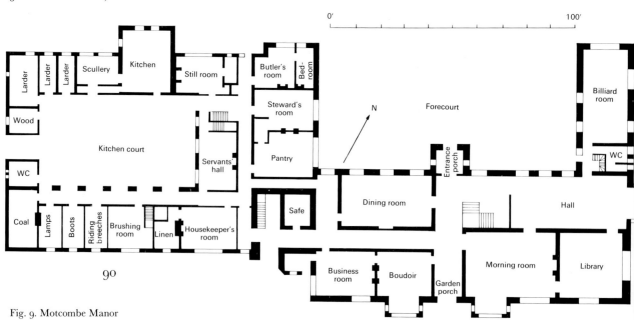

0'   100'

Larder | Larder | Larder | Scullery | Kitchen | Still room

Wood

Kitchen court

Servants' hall

WC

Coal | Lamps | Boots | Riding breeches | Brushing room | Linen | Housekeeper's room

Butler's room | Bed-room

Steward's room

Pantry

Safe

N

Forecourt

Entrance porch

Billiard room

WC

Dining room

Hall

Business room | Boudoir | Garden porch | Morning room | Library

90

Fig. 9. Motcombe Manor

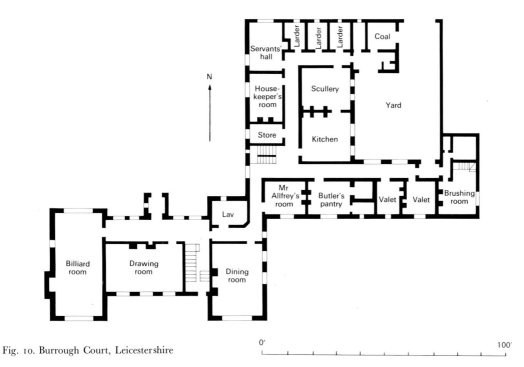

Fig. 10. Burrough Court, Leicestershire

0'   100'

There were other plans, but Muthesius thought that it was best to dispose the servants' rooms around a courtyard, as at Motcombe, so that the functions to do with food and women could be put into one range, and those to do with heavy work and men into the other. Delivering tradesmen could be directed into whichever was the appropriate wing, with the advantage that sacks of coal were not heaved past the kitchen or scullery, where food was prepared. Each side had its own staircase to the bedrooms, and needless to say there was no way through from the men's to the maids' bedrooms on any floor. The servants' hall occupied a kind of middle ground, and this—literally, symbolically and properly—was the only place where it was approved for the two sexes to meet. Muthesius felt that, ideally, the separation of functions should extend to the lines of communication with the house itself, and this was perhaps the real beauty of the Motcombe plan. Servants could reach the main rooms by a choice of two routes, one for each side of the courtyard, so that in theory the paths followed by each type of worker should never have had to cross. As the butler rushed to the dining room with the roast, he did not risk colliding with housemaids weighed down with grate-cleaning equipment. Polesden Lacey had no fewer than three routes through to the main house.

Few houses were as clearly conceived as Motcombe; even fewer, one suspects, operated with quite the impeccable efficiency Muthesius supposed. Although his view might be seen as typically Germanic, it suggests why Edwardian owners found it so difficult to reduce the size of the servants' wing, and why, when the necessity for change was forced into their consciousness, the effect was little short of traumatic. Even Burrough Court, a hunting lodge with only three main rooms and a small study, had as large a servants' wing as Motcombe, with its seven main rooms.[17] Tirley Garth, an Arts and Crafts country house

91

with a small number of family rooms, tells the same story, and the problem was exacerbated in the houses of the very grand, where a high number of personal servants were expected. Mar Lodge near Balmoral, rebuilt for the Duke of Fife, a son-in-law of Edward VII, had twenty bedrooms for family and guests, but accommodation for twenty-five menservants and forty maids.[18] Guests often arrived with their own servants, as Lady Iveagh complained after Lord and Lady Howe descended on Elveden: 'My dear, I do think it is too much when *two* people bring five servants!'[19]

Surprising though it seems, smaller country houses were regarded as more difficult to plan than the giants, because it was so hard to know where to save space. For instance, it was axiomatic that, wherever possible, the kitchen should be separated from the dining room by a long corridor with at least one right-angled bend, or else, as Arnold Mitchell wrote, 'the secrets of the menu' would 'journey about the house' inviting criticism of the architect every mealtime.[20] Even Voysey, with his liking for large, free spaces, felt bound to provide a large number of small rooms—smaller, in fact, than Motcombe's—in the servants' wings of his more substantial houses. Broadleys, with only three main rooms including the hall, had a coal room, a combined boots and knives room, a larder, a servants' room, a kitchen, a room for stores and a pantry. Moreover, no one would have felt that, money aside, the domestic arrangements at Broadleys were better than at Motcombe. Quite the reverse: saving space, Voysey cut out the corridor, so that the only way of bringing coal into the house or for a maid to reach the outside servants' W.C. was through the kitchen. But compromises had to be made.

'Why I dislike domestic service'

The Servant Question presented itself first as a problem of supply; only when it became apparent that the supply of willing labour could not be increased did owners begin to look seriously into the alternative possibilities described later in this chapter. But why could they not find servants? The root cause did not seem to be wages. Lady Jeune, like other observers, pointed out that servants were likely to be better paid than if they had taken industrial jobs; and she went on to list a depressing number of comparable trades, such as shirt-making, tie-making, parasol- and umbrella-making, matchmaking, book-binding, laundering, collar-ironing—even dock labouring and tailoring—all of which paid less than domestic service.[21] Domestic service had the further incomparable advantage that it guaranteed regular employment, whereas industrial workers were subject to short-time and lay-offs. Servants did not have to work apprenticeships: 'The servant earns from the first day she enters service, and is often carefully trained by a mistress in cooking or waiting at table, only to leave that mistress for a better situation the moment she thoroughly understands her duties.'

There were other attractions. Meals in the servants' hall were generally plentiful, and they could always be supplemented by direct access to the kitchen. 'The old Edwardian servants had enormous appetites as a result of their years of good living,' wrote the royal chef, Gabriel Tschumi, 'and rationing [in the First World War] almost broke their hearts.'[22] Lady Jeune was not alone when she wrote of servants: 'One cannot refrain from the suspicion that the quantity of meat eaten, and the strong tea and beer which they

92

consume, are, more often than over-work or under-feeding, the cause of the illnesses among them.'[23] This was extreme, although beer, constantly available and often home-brewed, was undoubtedly sometimes a cause of undoing (a footman at Woburn was sacked for drinking the contents of the bucket with which he was meant to be swabbing the oak floors).[24] It is a signal contrast to the broken health of the people at large, which was partly the result of poor diet. Some forty per cent of volunteers for the Boer War were rejected on medical grounds, despite a reduction in the minimum height to five feet, and by 1917/18 there had been no improvement: forty-one per cent of the two and a half million men examined for conscription in those years were graded C3 and unfit to fight.[25]

One may not think that servants' rooms represent a high standard of luxury. A die-hard Victorian like J. E. Panton did not believe that servants could appreciate beauty in their surroundings or live with breakable objects. 'I should like myself to give each maid a really pretty room,' pleaded the author, '. . . but alas! it is impossible. No sooner is the room put nice than something happens to destroy its beauty; and I really believe servants only feel happy if their rooms are allowed in some measure to resemble the homes of their youth, and to be merely places where they lie down to sleep as heavily as they can.'[26] Other views were prevailing, however. Philip Webb insisted on light and airy rooms for the servants at Clouds (1879), and the Wyndhams came to appreciate it, because they moved into them when the main block burnt down. 'It is a good thing our architect was a Socialist,' wrote Mrs Wyndham, 'because we find ourselves just as comfortable in the servants' quarters as we were in our own.'[27] Perhaps Arthur Martin was thinking of Clouds when he wrote that 'In large houses servants are better housed, with their separate bedrooms and luxurious bathrooms, than many of the poorer gentry in the

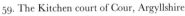

59. The Kitchen court of Cour, Argyllshire

60. Henry Moat, the Sitwells' butler at Renishaw Hall, Derbyshire, by C. R. W. Nevinson, 1918 (University Art Collection, Hull)

neighbourhood.'[28] It was a hyperbole, of course, yet to many servants their modest, plainly furnished bedrooms in the basement or attic, singly occupied or shared with only one other person, really did represent amenity of a high order. William Lanceley, who began work as a foot-boy in the local squire's mansion, was given his first holiday at the end of four years. It lasted three days. Hard conditions, one would have thought, but Lanceley found the break 'quite enough at the time'. His room and food at the hall were far better than what he experienced at home.

However, the reason large numbers of working-class girls did not go into service was as much to do with their changing, and improving, sense of social position as with pay, work or environment. The latter, of course, were important, but it was the looming social objections which made the servant question so difficult to handle. Winifred Hurlstone-Jones put what she saw as the servants' side of the argument in an article called 'Why I dislike Domestic Service', which appeared in the *Lady* in 1919.[29] She summarised the case against service under the following headings: '1. It means loss of caste. 2. It means loss of freedom of action—a girl is not on her own. 3. Long hours when they are on duty, if not actually working. 4. It is dull, the work is fairly hard, and distinctly monotonous.' Most writers—whether servants or employers—would have agreed that these disadvantages, in roughly this order, were the root cause of the problem.

94

William Lanceley knew from experience that low status prevented many young people from entering service:

Service has no attraction for the fairly educated young man or woman. It is looked down upon—they want to do something better, and often school friendships are broken through sheer snobbishness. One gets a clerkship or post as a shop assistant and another if he or she goes into service is dropped in a very short time. New friends are found and the snobbish spirit comes to the top—'I like Lettie better than any girl, but you know I cannot introduce her to my new friends as she is a servant.'[30]

Americans especially were appalled to find that the English class system was as deeply entrenched in the servants' wing as it was in the main house, a state of affairs symbolised in the ritual of the mid-day meal at houses like Longleat. The upper servants—housekeeper, house steward, head butler, cook, lady's maids, valets and the groom of the chambers—pompously trooped out at the end of the main course, in a procession headed by the second footman who carried what was left of the roast, to eat the rest of the meal by themselves.[31] Such a hierarchy was the product of the division of labour which seemed to Muthesius so efficient. As the system ossified and the lines of demarcation (on the factory principle) became more finely drawn, the formula 'That is not my place' was increasingly heard from servants not wishing to lose caste by doing something they felt was beneath them. The butler at Blenheim would not put coal on the fire, and when he offered to call the footman to perform the task, the liberal-minded Consuelo Vanderbilt, Duchess of Marlborough, was so exasperated she did it herself.[32]

New servants suffered a double dose of inferiority, being on the lowest rung of a system that, in the eyes of their outside companions, was itself 'regarded as a peculiarly menial occupation'. On the whole, employers, taking their lead from Edward VII, were beginning to be more considerate. 'My good man, I'm not a strawberry,' was the King's mild rebuke to a footman who slipped and accidentally emptied a jug of cream over him—when his mother would almost certainly have said something else.[33] Socialists, like the architect Detmar Blow, who had become sufficiently well-off through his connection with the Duke of Westminster to build his own country house, Hilles, were particularly anxious that no artificial distinction should exist between those who happened to be servants and those rich enough to employ them. Neville Lytton described the regime at Hilles in *The English Country Gentleman*:[34] 'For the better welfare of the children, there is no nursery, and, for the better welfare of the servants, there are no servants' quarters.' The whole household—family and servants—ate together in the kitchen, an arrangement which turned out to be as embarrassing for the servants as it was for the Blows and, as the awkward pauses became more and more agonising, was eventually abandoned. Other owners began to use euphemisms like 'domestic' and 'help', current in America since the 1820s at least, to avoid giving a discouraging impression of superiority. However, it was not so much the attitude of their employers that rankled, as the snobbishness of other members of the servants' own class. The American domestic economist Lucy Salmon was shocked to find that, in England, domestic servants were the targets for 'the satire and ridicule of the press'.[35]

'The lack of personal freedom,' wrote an observer, '. . . may seem a mere sentimental objection not to be weighed in the balance for a moment by sensible persons as against the

61-2. Mrs Greville's maids and butlers at Polesden Lacey, Surrey

solid advantages of domestic work.'[36] But values were changing; besides which, not everybody at sixteen or seventeen—the age at which the decision to go into service was taken—was so prudent. It meant a young girl leaving her family and friends, perhaps leaving the neighbourhood, to be shut up for most of the week with only the other servants for company. Mabel Atkinson had 'very little doubt that one of the greatest objections to domestic service is that it removes the young woman from her own class just at the marriageable age'.[37] Large country houses had their own life 'below stairs', and social activities were encouraged by employers who feared the allure of the town. But when the Household Club was established by Lord and Lady Aberdeen at Haddo Hall in 1889, few people can have been surprised to find that the annually elected committee was made up of the heads of department—butler, housekeeper, head gardener, head coachman, head forester, head gamekeeper, estate clerk of works, farm manager, head laundry maid and poultry manager.[38] It was hardly an escape from the usual routine. Meeting the opposite sex was not easy, but if a servant did reach the stage of deciding to marry, he or she (or both, if the bride and groom were each in service) would have to find a new place unless the employer could give them a cottage. It took a very staunch supporter of the system to miss the irony in the bachelor house steward William Lanceley's comment: 'The only thing that brings anxiety is [the desire for] marriage.'

The very long hours were in themselves an impediment to social life which was increasingly resented. A housemaid at Nether Swell Manor, built by Sir John Scott in 1903-13 and inherited by his two sisters, was generally on duty from four a.m. until the Misses Scott's dinner, a fifteen hour day.[39] It could be longer if the Misses Scott went up to London, because the housemaids would wait up until they returned. The work was tedious rather than physically hard; or as Lady Jeune put it, citing the benefits of a servant's life, 'ordinarily the routine is so monotonous as to be mechanical, and, therefore, not arduous'.[40] However, this could not be said of scullery maids, young girls who might have to wash up until one a.m. and then get up early the next morning to prepare breakfast. The law had it that servants were at their masters' disposal twenty-four hours a day. Of course, they were given time off—an evening a week and every other Sunday—but elsewhere the hours were shorter and, above all, they were better defined. Shop and factory girls had more time of their own and they could make use of it as they wished. Maids, on the other hand, were forever watched over by maternalistic employers. Lady Iveagh's twenty or thirty housemaids were kept 'somewhat as novices in a convent, not

96

being allowed to go out alone, or to visit the neighbouring cottages'.[41] Mistresses felt they were *in locus parenti*, whatever the age of the maid.

But standards were wavering. The *Book of Household Management* found it necessary to insert a stiffening paragraph in its 1915 edition, to emphasise the burden of care:

> A lady should never allow herself to forget the important duty of watching over the moral and physical welfare of those beneath her roof. Without seeming unduly inquisitive, she can always learn something of their acquaintances and holiday occupation, and should, when necessary, warn them against the dangers and evils of bad company. An hour should be fixed, usually 10 or 9 pm, after which no servants should be allowed to stay out. To permit breaches of this rule, without having good and explicit reasons furnished, is very far from being a kindness to the servant concerned. The moral responsibility for evil that may result rests largely on the employer who permits late hours. Especial care is needed with young girls. They should be given opportunities for welcoming respectable friends of their employer's house, and not be forced by absence of such provision for their comfort to spend their spare time out of doors, often in driving rain, possibly in bad company.[42]

Victorian employers would not have needed reminding.

63. Scullery maid at Thurston Hall, Berwickshire

Then there was the work. Many writers, William Lanceley included, did not think that servants worked hard. A butler, for instance, led 'a life of leisure, ease and excessive comfort, seldom having to exert himself even to his capacities,' wrote Arthur Ponsonby.[43] And this was true of the upper servants. The lion's share of the work fell on the juniors, such as the scullery maids. 'Poor little devils, washing up and scrubbing away at the dozens of pots, pans, saucepans, and plates, up to their elbows in suds and grease, their hands red raw with the soda which was the only form of detergent in those days,' said the great butler, Nancy Astor's 'Lord' Lee of Cliveden. 'I've seen them crying with exhaustion and pain, the degradation, too, I shouldn't wonder. Well, let's hope they got their reward in heaven.'[44] Earthly ambitions might be satisfied when one of them rose to become housekeeper or cook, but that looked a long way off to a girl of sixteen.

Remedies to increase the supply of servants were suggested and, in some cases, put into practice. Domestic economy schools such as the one Lady Mary Clive attended after the war were established.[45] A pioneering university course called 'Home Science and Economics' was started in 1911. A few years earlier the idea that domestic service might, on revised terms, answer the needs of distressed gentlewomen gave rise to an experiment in Cheltenham called the Guild of the Dames of the Household. As a contemporary newspaper reported: 'Where the Association of Trained Charwomen has in a small way shown that one path of solution at the lower end of the scale is by way of daily service, with

64. The scullery at Castle Drogo, Devon

the greater independence it gives, this guild affords another solution at the other end of the scale, by encouraging women of gentle birth to enter the "profession", thus removing the stigma which has so absurdly stuck to service.'[46] Significantly, Dames did not fit well into large staffs, because they were too refined to put up with the living conditions of ordinary servants.

None of these proposed solutions effectively tackled the essence of the problem nor did anything to improve its most critical symptom, the shortage of maids. There was simply no need for girls to be given formal education to learn housework—the housekeeper could teach them. 'Improvement is much more likely to result from alterations in the condition of domestic service,' wrote Mabel Atkinson, and mistresses would not yield ground on the terms of employment until there was no other choice.

That time came all too quickly with the outbreak of war. A *Punch* cartoon of 1915 shows a lady asking a cottager if her very recalcitrant-looking young son, who has just left his last job, could work for her as a gardener. 'Well, Mum,' replies the self-satisfied mother, 'there's bin 'alf a dozen after 'im this morning. But I shall be very 'appy to put you on the waiting list.' This was a reversal of roles, and applied to all branches of service. Enlarged experience made former servants reluctant to accept the old, pre-war conditions. Working in munitions factories, wrote Randal Phillips in *The Servantless House* (1920), 'girls who formerly accepted the shackles of what was little better than domestic drudgery came into a new liberty. They got good wages for what they did and they got far more time of their own than they ever had before in domestic service.' William Lanceley believed that 'hundreds' were 'spoilt for future service' by the taste of good pay for short hours.

To some, change dawned quickly. Servants' attics were provided at Langoed Castle, built on the eve of the war, but they were never plastered. Sir Mark Sykes ignored the signs and added a large servants' wing, Victorian in scale, to Sledmere in 1915; but it was doomed from the start and had to be demolished in 1944. E. F. Benson's account of the 'parable house', Hakluyt, in *As We Are*, published in 1932, accurately described the way things were no longer the same. First its owner, Lord Buryan, had a disagreeable experience with a Socialist in the Temperance village club that he had given the village in earlier days. Then the congregation at church began to drop off. But most telling of all was the demise of another old custom, the New Year's servants' ball. In former years it had always begun with the old dance 'Sir Roger de Coverley',

> the butler leading off with my Lady and my Lord with the housekeeper. But this year, the butler, very deferential and diffident, put it to Lady Buryan that he and his lordship's valet and the ruptured footman were the only men in the house and that the women (the difficulty about getting servants at all in the country had begun to be acute) were not quite of the sort to which her ladyship was accustomed. He had talked it over with the housekeeper and, if her ladyship would excuse him, they both thought it would not quite be such an evening as they had always enjoyed so much in previous years. So perhaps . . . And she thought so too, and there was no servants' ball.

But there were other means by which a house could be kept going than brute manpower, and fortunately many of the new labour-saving devices that were marshalled for use had been developed before the war.

Labour-Saving Technology

Ernestine Mills, in a book dedicated to her 'kind and helpful maids', envisaged the day when the upper classes would herd together in 'barracks with communal kitchens and public restaurants' to make the most of the few servants that remained.[47] A less radical alternative, she said, was to use cheap foreign labour; but it was above all the labour-saving inventions—some of them foreign, some of them British—that enabled country-house life to survive after the end of the First World War.

The first signs of this technology were in evidence in the most up-to-date houses at the very beginning of the twentieth century. Manderston, in Berwickshire, rebuilt in 1901–5, showed several advances on Motcombe, notably in the provision of electric light—in fact available from 1897, when the power house by the home farm was constructed. The first house in the country to have filament lamps was Cragside, home of the hydraulics engineer Sir William Armstrong, in about 1880; the system at Hatfield was slightly later, although there Lord Salisbury and his family threw cushions at the sockets when they sparked and the gardener was actually killed by it, giving point to Hilaire Belloc's mock-heroic lines on 'The Benefits of Electric Light':

> Behold the Electrician where he stands:
> Soot, oil, and verdigris are on his hands;
> Large spots of grease defile his dirty clothes,
> The while his conversation drips with oathes.
> Shall such a being perish in his youth?
> Alas! it is indeed the fatal truth.
> In this dull brain, beneath that hair unkempt,
> Familiarity has bred contempt.
> We warn him of the gesture all too late:
> Oh, Heartless Jove! Oh, Adamantine Fate!
>   Some random touch—a hand's imprudent slip—
> The Terminals—a flash—a sound like "Zip!"
> A smell of burning fills the started Air—
> The Electrician is no longer there!

The engines in the power house, with their gleaming brass and finely adjusted motion, were driven either by steam, as at Paddockhurst (Plates 67–8), or by gas; this of course meant that gas also had to be produced on site. Water-powered turbines were sometimes used in hilly districts. At Ardkinglas (Plates 65–6), the home of Sir Andrew Noble, who succeeded Armstrong as chairman of Armstrong Whitworth and Co., Lorimer's turbine house was a fortress-like structure designed to harmonise with the forest setting; and the carefully landscaped dam, which provided a twenty-two foot fall, included a salmon ladder. Inside, the instrument panel was faced with marble.[48] Turbines were also used at Cour, the romantic house (Plate 59) which Oliver Hill built in Argyllshire immediately after the First World War.

Lamp bulbs were such a novelty that, even in Lorimer's elaborate brass electroliers for Ardkinglas, they were not always covered with shades. Even so, they offered new freedom to the designer, because they could point in any direction (unlike gas) and they could be at

65. The turbine house at Ardkinglas, Argyllshire

66. In the dynamo room at Ardkinglas. The instrument panels were faced with marble.

67–8. Two steam generators, both in use at Paddockhurst, Sussex, and attached to the central switching gear shown on left below

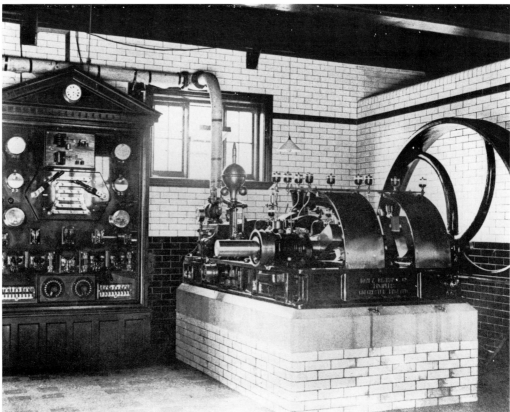

any height (unlike oil lamps, which needed to be within easy reach to be taken down, cleaned and filled). But electric lighting met with some resistance, especially from ladies who—perhaps having suffered under arc lighting, which preceded the filament lamp—feared that 'no one who was not made up as for the stage could possibly show herself in the glare of such cruel search lights without alienating the affections of every man who loved her'.[49] After 1900 most new country houses had electricity, which was universally recognised as the best although not the cheapest method of lighting, but there were also other possibilities. The discovery that thoia mixed with a small percentage of ceria gave off a brilliant light in a gas flame had been made by Welsbach in 1883 and led to the incandescent gas mantle, which prolonged the life of gas as a serious rival to electricity. Acetylene was also used, although principally in smaller country houses and, because of the ease of installation, in old ones which needed converting. All were an alternative to oil and did away with the lamp man. However, as regards saving labour, electricity was particularly praised as being less hot than the other forms of lighting; it consequently did not attract dirt rings to the same extent and ultimately saved work in cleaning.

Apart from electricity, the two most obvious advances Manderston showed were the telephone and the ice-room. A large switchboard was housed in two cupboards in the basement corridor, and handsets were installed in each room. The system did not communicate with the outside world. Few country houses had outside telephone lines before 1914, and even if they did, other people did not.[50] But internal telephones saved housework. Rather than ring for the maid who then had to make a special journey to find out what was needed, return and make another with the article required, members of the

69. Telephone switchboard beside the owner's bed at Sennowe Park, Norfolk

70. The laundry at Carberry Tower, Midlothian

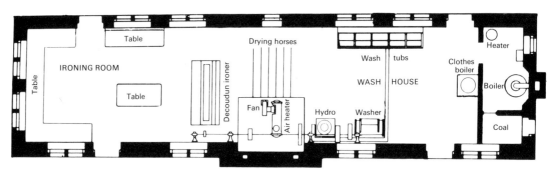

Fig. 11. The laundry at Dundas Castle

71. The ironing room at Carberry Tower, with an ironing machine in the foreground

family could telephone requests and instructions to whomever's duty it was to fulfil them, cutting out a great deal of unnecessary leg work. That, at least, was the theory, although one suspects that telephones—like other aspects of early technology—could also be sophisticated toys for the owner. The switchboard at Sennowe was not in the servants' quarters but on one of the walls of the owner's bedroom, so that he could operate it from bed (Plate 69).

The Manderston ice-room was opposite the fish larder, and its significance is shown by Lucy Salmon's comment that the 'little use of ice' was 'one of the ways in which domestic service is much harder [in Europe] than it is in America'.[51] Throughout the nineteenth century, ice was taken from frozen ponds in the winter, packed in straw and stored in ice-houses, which were built partially under ground or beneath heavy shade. It is unlikely, however, than Manderston had much more than a glorified ice-chest, which was all that was meant by the term 'refrigerator' in the 1890s and early 1900s. But huge 'store cooling' and ice-making machines like the Zero were in production and being recommended for country houses by 1912. The one at Sennowe was connected by a tile-lined underground pipe filled with brine to a cold room beneath the clock tower. Cold-storage plants were recommended by *Country Life* in 1920 because of difficulties in food supply following the war; but as yet they had been installed by a comparatively small number of owners despite the 'frequently ample, even excessive', quantities of game, fish, beef, mutton and dairy and garden produce on hand at most country houses.[52]

Because it was originally an eighteenth-century house, Manderston's kitchen, servants' hall, housekeeper's room and other service arrangements were below the main house, in which it was uncharacteristically out of date: basements were held to be a great disincentive to servants. The principal walls being lined with white tiles, it had—perhaps deliberately—a permanent chill, which was good for the game, fish, pastry and meat in the row of larders, but bad for the footmen and butler who slept at this level. However, there was also a small service court, which was sunnier and, because it contained both the laundry and the motor house, freer (laundry maids were less strictly supervised than the maids in the house, and at least one butler 'had little time for chauffeurs', who were townies, probably flirtatious and did not fit into the below-stairs hierarchy).[53] The laundry itself was below ground and dirty clothes were sent down by a shute.

The specifications for the new laundry at Sledmere dated January 1913 show the state reached by laundry technology on the eve of the First World War.[54] There was a washing machine, mangle or 'wringer' and box mangle, powered by a single, four-horsepower motor; the drive was transmitted to the machines by means of shafting, pulleys and leather belts, as in a factory. The cylindrical drum of the washing machine, which held the clothes, was made out of a double thickness of wood, pine on the outside, maple within. Summerscale's 'Patent Automatic Reversing Motion and Locking Gear' ensured that the drum changed directions after a few revolutions. The mangle was above the washing machine, while the other equipment to be supplied comprised three pitch-pine wash-troughs, a rinsing and blueing trough (with an improved 'Neptune' hand-operated wringer) and the box mangle. The latter, built on a French-polished mahogany frame, pushed a heavy weight over washing laid on a bed to squeeze out the water. There was a complete drying closet, in the form of a brick-built chamber with a central stove to heat the air; 'drying horses'—rails laden with clothes—were pushed in or pulled out on runners (see Colour Plate XI).

In 1913, the year of the Sledmere laundry, *Country Life* described a similar building—run 'on factory lines'—at Carberry Tower, the seat of Lord Elphinstone.[55] Here the machinery, as at Sledmere, was driven by shafting from a central electric motor, although houses without electricity would have found that steam provided 'quite as satisfactory a drive'. In addition to the other equipment, Carberry had an early spin-drier, called a 'hydro-extractor'.

Yet, although the power laundry in large country houses had become an established fact, according to *Country Life*, the new laundry at Dungavel Lodge, Lanarkshire, a seat of the Duke of Hamilton and Brandon, was still powered by hand,[56] though it was contemporary with that at Carberry. The boiler used seven hundredweight of coal a day to feed steam to the washing machine, the copper boiling tank, the steam-heated coils in the drying chamber and the hot water generator (the latter, otherwise known as a 'calorifier', could supply three hundred gallons of hot water an hour up to a temperature of 180 degrees Fahrenheit). Processing eighteen hundred pieces of laundry a week, it employed a staff of seven, including the engineer, who had the unenviable task of operating the hydro-extractor, which was turned by hand at a rate of six hundred revolutions per minute. Washing machines with their own motors were made after the First World War, but problems with insulation made some types less than totally safe until the 1930s.

Ironing in the days before the electric iron could be a tedious and frustrating occupation:

> Either the iron was too hot which caused a brown mark called a burn, or else it was too cold which caused a brown mark called iron mould; and well meant efforts to remove either by dipping them in blue-water merely turned the material pea-green. And then if I didn't iron in all the wrinkles, I found, after toiling laboriously round yards of skirt, that the sleeves had meanwhile been crumpling themselves up and gone back to start or that the bodice had become suddenly damp again owing, apparently, to spontaneous condensation. If, however, I did glide home with a decent bit of ironing it merely revealed how completely I had failed to wash out any of the original dirt. It was a heart-breaking, back-breaking business, particularly as the floor was concrete and we ran to and fro to the stove in an atmosphere of steam and short tempers, carrying our heavy red-hot implements, bumping into each other as we all frantically tried to exchange bad irons for good, spitting hopefully and knocking each other's *chef d'oeuvres* of laundress' art off the line onto the floor.[57]

The electric iron brought incalculable benefits. Most Victorian irons were solid and had to be heated in tiers on a stove, although some were hollow and had a door at the back through which a slug of hot metal could be dropped. Neither sort stayed hot for very long, and the temperature was not constant; also, the irons were in danger of picking up smuts from the fire. Experiments were made with irons heated by gas, petrol and paraffin, and the 1923 *Book of Household Management* enthusiastically recommended ironing machines, in which the articles to be ironed were fed between a roller and a heated bar, as in a mangle. Electric irons were made in the 1890s but they were heavy (one weighed 14 lbs). Handier versions were produced after the First World War.

The sewing machine was another labour-saving invention, although one that was not used so regularly. Sewing machines were available from the mid-nineteenth century. Nearly all the upholstery at Minterne Magna was sewn by Lady Digby, helped only by Mrs Sims, the odd man's wife: 'I got through a most wonderful lot of needlework,' she wrote in her diary, 'quite miles and miles on the machine.'[58] The housemaids at Nether Swell Manor, who spent their afternoon quietly mending the footmen's gloves and sewing nightdresses for the Misses Scott, found sewing machines equally useful: the Misses Scott were both very large and each nightdress took six yards of crepe de chine.[59]

Manderston did not have a vacuum cleaner. Probably the first British house to contain one was Minterne Magna, built in 1903–7. Minterne also had electric luggage and service lifts to spare the footmen. The vacuum cleaner was a centralised system. A large pump in the basement was connected by a series of tubes to the major rooms in the house (see Plate 72); there were outlets in the skirting boards—covered by brass flaps—into which housemaids could plug hoses and nozzles. In some houses, there were only outlets in the hall, which meant that rugs and carpets had to be carried out for cleaning. The idea of this system was patented in 1903, the year work on Minterne began.

The basic idea of the vacuum cleaner had been patented by an Englishman, H. Cecil Booth, in 1901. Booth, an engineer who also designed wheels for fairgrounds such as the Vienna Prater, founded the British Vacuum Cleaner Company. Its first machines, large pumps mounted on carts, stopped outside the house to be cleaned and hoses were fed in through the windows. Obviously the range was limited, and smaller movable machines

72. The centralised vacuum cleaner at Sennowe Park, Norfolk

73. Radiator cover at Balmanno Castle, Perthshire

were introduced within a few years. The Ohio harness-maker W. W. Hoover began to manufacture a range in 1908. Early movable vacuum cleaners were expensive and distrusted by servants; even so they were bought by some very large houses, where one would have thought the labour problem was not acute. Dunrobin, in Scotland, still contains two pre-1914 models, a Pulvo, powered by electricity, and a Baby Daisy, which did not have a motor. It was worked by hand, like a bellows in reverse. Hand-operated or foot-operated machines were cheaper, but many required two people to work them. A drawback to machines driven by electric motors was the absence of power-points in many houses, which meant that they had to be plugged into light sockets. Remarkably, most large, new country houses were still built with centralised vacuum cleaners right down to the Second World War; examples are Eltham Palace (1936) and Charters (1938).

By 1890 nearly all new country houses had central heating of some kind, with the radiators—concertinaed pipes looking like giant intestines—discreetly hidden behind carved or wickerwork panels, usually under bench seats in the window embrasures (Plate 73). The question was no longer whether they were provided but how effectively they worked. At best, they took the chill off a room, the screens diminishing still further the modest amount of heat given off by the radiators. In no pre–First World War house was the architect rash enough to rely on central heating alone. All rooms had open fires, which had to be stoked, cleaned and emptied of ash. Central heating only really began to

75. Bedroom at Eltham Palace, Kent, with electric fire

74. The boiler room at Charters, Berkshire

76. (right) A shower at
Ardkinglas, Argyllshire

77. Shower at Sennowe Park,
Norfolk

save labour when it cut out the need for auxiliary fires, doing away with the need to carry coal. That was not until the 1930s, by which date coal grates had been replaced by electric and gas fires in new houses (Plate 75).

As late as the 1920s it could be regarded as positively unhealthy to have central heating in bedrooms. Lord Grimthorpe thought so and W. H. Brierley, then remodelling Easthorpe Hall, agreed.[60] Brierley had second thoughts when he realised 'What a cold house it is' and advised his client that, when he was away 'in winter or early spring, or when the visitors' rooms are empty, heat would be invaluable to keep them aired without the expense and labour caused by fires'. Lord Grimthorpe—steeled by Eton and Oxford—demurred: 'I think on the whole that I would sooner not have radiators in the bedrooms, as they are rather stuffy things.' Brierley, who was certainly not one to be brow-beaten by clients, was for once of like mind: 'If you are prepared for the extra expense and labour of fires in cold weather, there is no doubt they are the healthiest and best.'

Bathrooms were common if not plentiful. Most owners had bathrooms *en suite* with their bedrooms, but few enjoyed the opulence of Sir James Miller's at Manderston, with its silver-plated tub enshrined beneath a marble, groined vault. The other bedrooms generally had about one bathroom between three. This did not mean they were used. Despite the fact that there were three bathrooms at Nether Swell Manor, the Misses Scott insisted on having hot water carried up in jugs well into the 1920s. Lord Ernest Hamilton, looking back to his mid-Victorian youth, shuddered to remember the 'large iron tanks encased in mahogany, evidently designed to do duty as baths and—judging from their size—designed to accommodate several people at once'. Switching on the hot tap produced a succession of sepulchral rumblings 'succeeded by the appearance of a small geyser of rust-coloured water', which stopped after a couple of minutes and was in any case stone cold.[61]

Lord Digby—progressive when it came to the vacuum cleaner—refused to have any bathroom on the main bedroom corridor at Minterne, although Leonard Stokes prudently laid pipes in case they would be wanted. Even in the 1920s, Lady Fry could dismiss bathrooms as 'only for servants';[62] her reasoning was presumably like Oscar Wilde's in scorning the plumbed-in wash-stands at the Savoy: he said that if he needed hot water, he liked to ring for it.

Typically, Muthesius had a more advanced view of technology. He believed that a modern bathroom was 'like a piece of scientific apparatus, in which technique of a high intellectual order rules, and if any "art" were dragged in it would merely have a disturbing effect'.[63] By 1912 Elder Duncan could write that 'educated people look upon their baths as an enjoyable pleasure, and not, like many of our forefathers, as a necessary but troublesome item of cleanliness to be undertaken with fear and trembling and extraordinary preparations and precautions'.[64] Things had undoubtedly improved. Heated towel-rails, for instance, were an Edwardian innovation. And, as comfort increased, so more attention was paid to bathroom design, which—for all Muthesius's strictures—was already showing hints of caprice. Lutyens made drawings of one with a sunken bath in a shell alcove for Lady Wimborne in 1905.[65]

But the great change came after the war, when adequate supplies of hot water from central tanks began to gush into more streamlined bathtubs. The result was commonly known as the 'stew bath', and the 1920s girl was prepared to wallow in one without her

78. The kitchen at Dunham Massey, Cheshire, in about 1910

79. The kitchen at Birchens Spring, Buckinghamshire, in 1938

x. The kitchen at Manderston, Berwickshire, of 1905

xi. The drying room at Hill of Tarvit, Fife

XII. (right) Edward James's bathroom at Monkton, Sussex.

XIII. (below) A bathroom at Castle Drogo, Devon

XIV. (facing page) Mrs Parkinson's bathroom at Charters, Berkshire

mother's fear for her complexion. Arthur Oswald waxed lyrical: 'The glossy porcelain-enamelled bath made in one piece or having an enclosure of marble or tile positively invites you to step (not climb) into it. Instead of a lukewarm trickle from the tap marked "Hot", a carefully tempered mixture of hot and cold wells up with a dance of bubbles from below.'[66] The bathroom became the most characteristic Art Deco contribution to the country house. The hard, water-resistant surfaces of chromium-plating, glass, marble and enamel were supremely appropriate, and hundreds of old houses needed modernisation—thirty bathrooms were installed at St Donat's Castle alone. High points were reached in Mrs Parkinson's bathroom at Charters (Colour Plate xiv) and Edward James's at Monkton, in which the sun and moon—in the form of electric lights—shine through the onyx walls and the circular shaving mirror is in the guise of a map of the earth (Colour Plate xii).

The real change to the kitchen, which was the heart of the servants' wing, came after the First World War, when progressive writers began to talk about abolishing the scullery—although most large country houses had a scullery until 1939. The progress in other aspects of design was chartered in the breathless captions to a picture feature in the *Lady* in 1930. 'Still the old range!' read one of the first. 'Flues to clean, grates to blacklead, ashes to sift, walls to be distempered every year.' Then came: 'A step in the right direction! Washable walls so far up and a gas stove in its recess. Sink with cold water, but minus the hot. Dirty linoleum in lieu of a draining board. Think of the germs!' At last: 'Excelsior!' the modern age had arrived, with tiled walls, rubber floor, electric refrigerator, and a servery into the dining room.[67] From the mid-1920s, heat-storage ranges like the Aga, designed by the blind Swedish physicist Gustav Dalen, a Nobel prize winner, began to replace the old type, in which the temperature was not constant (although the latter retained the advantage that they could be stoked up to a greater heat quickly when required). Stoves run on gas and electricity were also introduced.

The kitchen offered the greatest scope for labour-saving devices. By 1923 electric grills, waffle irons, toasters, coffee percolators, and hot plates were available. Electric food mixers were being made by 1918, and by 1930 ones from the United States were capable of 'mincing meat, beating eggs, grinding coffee and about a dozen other kitchen operations'.[68] Electric kettles became practicable: pre-war models had the element strapped underneath, so they took a long time to boil. The 'Bullpit', which appeared in 1921, was the first kettle to have its element in the water. Very soon Ernestine Mills applauded the fact that 'thanks to modern devices even the most foolish old lady is now more independent of her maids, and instead of going without an extra cup of tea for fear of raising a storm, would probably be provided with the means of getting it for herself'.[69]

117

4. *The History Men*

*T*he most obvious difference between the architects of the social and the romantic country house was their attitude to historical precedent. Andrew Prentice, the author of *Renaissance Architecture from Spain* (1894), once met C. F. A. Voysey at the Arts Club, and was rash enough to ask in the course of conversation if he had 'ever designed anything after the manner of the Spanish Renaissance?' 'Mr Prentice,' replied Voysey, 'I have only one book in my office, and it is Bradshaw's Railway Guide, which, I am sorry to say, I have to use much oftener than I like.'[1] It was not that Voysey shunned precedent altogether, but he liked to derive his style from cottages and manor houses to which no architect's name could be attached, rather than the masterpieces of the history of architecture. But there were country-house architects who took the contrary view. They felt that it was right to make use of stylistic convention. They were less wayward than they would have been in the 1870s and 1880s, and probably more timid than in the 1850s and 1860s. The most striking thing about them is that they generally did not take sides.

The Battle of the Styles, wrote Reginald Blomfield in 1897, had become 'about as much out of date as the controversies of the schoolmen'.[2] A few old campaigners, like the church architect G. F. Bodley, true to the colours until his death in 1907, soldiered on under the flag of the Gothic Revival until the turn of the century; but two decades of light-hearted skirmishing by the motley troops of the Queen Anne Revival had blustered most architects out of their prejudices. To A. W. N. Pugin, style had been nothing less than a *causus belli*, now, if you cared about historical precedent at all (and Arts and Crafts architects probably did not), it was once again a question of taste. Blomfield, who had gone to public school and Oxford before he began work in his uncle's architectural office, could view the matter with more academic detachment than architects of the mid-nineteenth century, the majority of whom had begun working life early, without the benefits of a Classical education. He was heavy-handed when it came to designing a cornice, but he was a sensitive and fair-minded scholar. Others shared his interest in history, and architectural publishing went through something of a golden age.

The giant who still dominated country-house architecture in the early 1890s was Richard Norman Shaw, but even his last houses show no clear sense of direction. They are in a bewildering succession of styles, some inventive, some not. Bryanston and Chesters were in English Baroque, the one bringing elements of what was to be neo-Georgian to the

80. Baroque doorcase and window surround on the garden front of Barnett Hill, Surrey

81. Cupboard doors at Falkland Palace, Fife, carved with portraits of the children of the third Marquess of Bute

country house, the other sowing the seeds of the butterfly-plan. Haggerston Castle, which Shaw remodelled, was in a bleak Classical style, with echoing interiors and a strange, stripped Gothic water-tower, now the only part to survive. Then in 1894 the Old English style of the 1870s made a late and final reappearance with The Hallams, in Surrey. By style alone it would be difficult to guess that one architect designed all four within a five year period.

Shaw was an eclectic in the two senses of the word: he both used different styles in different buildings, and combined motifs from different historical periods or cultures within the same building. Even Bryanston, which looks as though it is soundly based in one historical time and style, contains an essence of Mme de Pompadour's chateau at Menars, a sprinkling of Vaux-le-Vicomte, a solid helping of Coleshill, and garnishings of Stoke Edith and Cobham Hall. Many of the younger generation, including a strong contingent of Shaw's own pupils, who were entering practice in the years that Bryanston was being built had an equal aversion to stylistic pedantry, although they also disliked ostentation and thought Shaw himself was too flashy. In the 1890s the sensitive country-house architect Ernest Newton, still imbued with the spirit of the Gothic Revival and Pugin's dictum that a building's plan should be expressed on the exterior, used the

82. The architect: John Kinross

83. The patron: Sir James Miller of Manderston, Berwickshire

Georgian style with flexibility, without regard for the most basic rule of true Georgian architecture, symmetry; and he was equally prepared to combine the Tudor idiom with the 'rational' use of sash-windows.

After 1900 even architects like Newton and his more dazzling contemporary, Luytens, were won over to a more strict use of style. However, on the conservative wing of the profession, many architects had been working in a variety of styles all along. Often they were not part of a coherent movement and are therefore little known. They looked carefully at the new books on architecture that were being produced, but otherwise followed their own course. Their work expressed the convictions of men and women who wanted to establish their position in the continuum of history.

The most scrupulous in his use of historical precedent was the Scotsman John Kinross. He had a highly successful private career but was not greatly influential or widely known outside Scotland, because he never needed to seek publicity and, although he exhibited drawings at the Royal Scottish Academy, his work was not published. Kinross's career reflects the growing awareness of the history of architecture caused by restoration work, and his major country-house commission, Manderston, in Berwickshire, clearly suggests the kind of considerations that weighed with clients in the choice of a style.

Keeping up with the Curzons

Kinross had the kind of practice that many architects dreamed of, working in particular for two discriminating, private clients of very great wealth. He first met the third Marquess of Bute in 1885, when he was thirty years old. He had been born in Stirling, the son of a coachbuilder, and had served his apprenticeship first with John Hutchinson of Glasgow, then with the Edinburgh firm of Wardrop and Reid, which specialised in Scottish Baronial country houses. Bute, who had been William Burges's patron twenty years earlier, was a scholar, traveller, linguist and, as the son of the builder of Cardiff docks, one of the richest men in Britain. He had seen Kinross's *Details from Italian Buildings Chiefly Renaissance* published in a limited edition of three hundred in 1882. Kinross, aged twenty-five, had borrowed £250 from his mother—repaid with five per cent interest in due course—to spend two years in Italy, an experience which encouraged his 'inherent aristocracy of taste'.[3] The architect spoke fluent Italian, read Italian newspapers throughout his life, frequently visited the Continent, and, unlike most of his contemporaries, had a genuinely cosmopolitan outlook: Rodin was among the foreign artists and architects who visited his house in Mortonhall Road, Edinburgh.[4]

Bute was an ardent convert to Catholicism and was committed to restoring the ruined

84. The stables at Manderston

religious houses as well as the other buildings on his one hundred and seventeen thousand acres of estates. Over the next fifteen years Kinross restored for him a priory at St Andrews, a friary at Elgin, a palace (Falkland Palace) and began work on restoring an abbey (Pluscardine). Each was done with meticulous scholarship. Kinross would go off and stay in religious houses in Britain and on the Continent to understand how each Order worked in practice. Although Kinross did not belong to the SPAB inner circle, his work shows that he shared its principles. Rather than replace the rotten timbers in the ceiling of the royal chapel at Falkland Palace, for instance, he hung them from steel girders concealed overhead—just the kind of 'repair' (as opposed to, in his sense, 'restoration') that Morris advocated. But Kinross did not idealise the craftsman. His view was that 'To design an article is one thing, to make it another, and the ability to make it does not confer the power to design it; nor does the power to design it give the ability to make it.'[5] This was the down-to-earth attitude of the practising architect, which, ironically, is perhaps why the craftsmanship in his country houses is superb. Ashlar is cut razor sharp and jointed with mathematical precision, the thin bands of moulding are carved with exceptional crispness, and gates, doors, doorhandles and bell-pulls are invariably of the very best materials. Restoration work, which involved the intimate study of the fabric of old buildings, heightened his awareness of texture, as it did some of the SPAB architects; but it also refined his perception of style.

Bute died unexpectedly in 1900, and Kinross found he had lost his most sympathetic and valuable client. It was an anxious moment, but the suspense only lasted a year. On 27 May 1901 Sir James Miller returned from the Boer War along the flower-decked route from Berwick station to his country house, Manderston: a golden *M* in a frame of tulips hung from an evergreen arch over the drive from the south lodge, and from there his carriage, the horses unyoked, was dragged by a team of tenantry headed by the Duns Volunteer Band. The house which came into view as Miller's vehicle lurched up the beech-lined drive was thought to be far from satisfactory, and the next month Kinross was employed to remodel it.[6]

Architect and client were already well known to each other. Miller was undoubtedly smart in both tastes and appearance, although he never quite made the smart set. The son of Sir William Miller, first baronet, who had made a pile out of trading in hemp and herrings with the Baltic, he had been an officer in the Hussars (he failed the 'examination' for the Blues, which probably meant he was not up to the mark socially) and was a racehorse owner of note. His horse Rock Sand won the Triple Crown in 1903. In the mid-1890s Kinross erected the nearby house of Thurston, in a neo-Baroque style, for Miller's sister. In 1894 Miller commemorated his ambitious marriage to Eveline, the fourth daughter of Lord Scarsdale and sister of the future Lord Curzon, Viceroy of India, by employing Kinross to design a clapboarded boathouse with candystick chimneys. It gave Miller the taste for building. Within a year, Kinross was at work designing a neo-Classical stable block of staggering extravagance. The stalls for the horses had teak sides and solid brass posts, and the horses' names (all of which, like Milton, Margot and Matchless, began with *M* for Miller and Manderston), framed in brass, were mounted on marble tablets (Plate 84). The harness room, with its rosewood doors and glass-fronted cases for whips and reins, was a kind of gentlemen's club for the stableboys.

Soon afterwards, Kinross rebuilt the home farm and the nearby village of Buxley in a

Scottish Baronial style (Plate 85). The contrast to the stables shows his versatility. The cloistered courtyard of the home farm, with its four-centred arches, is Spanish Gothic in feeling—evidently Kinross had read Prentice's book. Milk was carried through an arch of Berwickshire alabaster to the model dairy, made out of marble and alabaster from seven different countries. The roof boss, which literally weighed half a ton, showed the dairymaid milking a cow (Plate 86). On first attempt, the cow faced the wrong way, but, horrified by this agricultural solecism, Miller had it taken down and recarved. The tea room over the dairy, which was modelled on a room in Holyrood Palace and used to round out an afternoon's tour of the farm, was built entirely of Spanish oak, which was joined without nails (Plate 87).

So by 1901 Miller had complete faith in his architect. When Kinross asked him how much the remodelling of the main house ought to cost, he replied nonchalantly: 'It doesn't really matter.'[7] It says a great deal for Kinross's instinctive sense of restraint that Manderston was not made into a monster. Instead, he rescued the house from the strange hybrid state in which he found it. Originally a modest Classical house probably designed by Alexander Gilkie in the late 1780s, it had been enlarged by Miller's father. He gave the house a French Renaissance style mansard roof and added a Doric *porte-cochère* to the giant Ionic portico. Architecturally, the result was disastrous. Besides which, by 1901, even the enlarged house was too small. Kinross's work involved enlarging the main body of the house, adding a wing, a service court and a basement, and rebuilding the attic storey. The

85. The home farm at Manderston

86. Roof boss from the dairy at Manderston

87. The tea room above the dairy at Manderston

whole entrance front was demolished and the roof was removed. The entrance façade was rebuilt in a position in front of the old one, so that the house was made deeper (Plate 88). This made only one additional room, but the other rooms were enlarged. A new wing full of gentlemen's rooms—bachelor bedrooms, gun room and office—was added to the west. Only the garden front of the eighteenth-century building survived, and that was refaced (Plate 6).

Opulent Classicism for country houses survived longer in Scotland than in England, possibly because of the nationalist associations of Robert Adam. In 1897 E. J. May, better known for his small, sensitive Arts and Crafts houses in the Home Counties, remodelled and greatly enlarged Jardine Hall, Dumfriesshire, adding sumptuous marble interiors. The client was a man very similar to Miller, the adventurer, big game hunter and racehorse owner David Jardine. In 1913 C. H. B. Quennell, again more familiar in Hampstead than the Highlands, built the large Classical house Aultmore, near Elgin, for H. Millet, owner of a Moscow department store.[8] But by contrast Manderston, although Classical, was strikingly austere. Kinross worked in the style of the eighteenth-century house, but added the stamp of his own personality in, for instance, the tablet rather than pediment over the giant entrance portico.

Kinross built country houses in Scottish Baronial and Tudor as well as Classical styles, but the choice of Classicism for Manderston was not his alone. The Millers had particular reasons for wanting to live in a neo-Classical house. Lady Miller had been brought up at Kedleston, in Derbyshire, where Sir James proposed to her. Before his marriage, *Vanity Fair* had written that: 'Being a good fellow, one of the most wealthy Commoners in the country, and a bachelor, he is a very eligible young man.'[9] But in point of antecedents he fell a long way behind the fourth Viscount Scarsdale with his Norman ancestry. Since Oxford days, Miller's brother-in-law had been characterised in the tag:

> My name is George Nathaniel Curzon,
> I am a most superior person.
> My cheek is pink, my hair is sleek,
> I dine at Blenheim once a week.

Lady Miller wanted a house that would recall her childhood home; Sir James wanted to keep up with his relations-in-law.

Inside Manderston, several details were unashamedly poached from Kedleston. The hall fireplace and overmantel and the circular pattern of inlaid marble in the floor of the hall (Plate 89) are based on those in the Marble Hall at Kedleston. Two torchères actually came from a set in that room. The ballroom ceiling is based on the dining-room ceiling at Kedleston. Wall sconces with Wedgwood plaques from the Kedleston Saloon inspired those in the Portico bedroom. Miller went so far as to start a collection of bluejohn vases to rival the bluejohn at Kedleston. Happily, Curzon was not a man to be abashed by homage, and proof that he found the house, with its many little acts of deference to his personal taste and possessions, agreeable, if not gratifying, is shown by his choice of Manderston as the house in which to spend several months recuperating from a motor accident after his return from India. The stay is commemorated by the Old English well he gave his sister as an act of thanks; she placed it, incongruously, in the Japanese Garden.

126

88. The entrance front of Manderston

Whatever the motives behind it, Manderston shows the social country house at its best, and also, which is not quite the same thing, its most luxurious. But in 1906, only a year after the house was finished, Miller caught a chill on the train to Scotland, insisted on hunting the next day, developed pneumonia, and died. The house was inherited by his brother and still exists as a family home. But Kinross had no more clients who said the cost did not matter.

The English Renaissance

Architects like Kinross, working in different styles in different buildings, believed that the merits of the available styles were essentially relative. This attitude was encouraged by architectural publishing.[10] A modest landmark was the appearance in 1896 of what was to become a Bible of style to several generations of architectural students, Banister Fletcher's *A History of Architecture*. Fletcher's famous 'comparative method' was in no way innovative, but emphasised the impartiality with which his eye passed over the whole history of styles, from Egypt onwards. Architects were encouraged not to have *parti pris* about style.

The sheer volume of architectural books published between 1890 and 1910 was prodigious. Buildings, being immobile, were an ideal subject for early photography, and this gave publishers the opportunity to open up a new market.

The development of high quality, half-tone block-making coincided with—and perhaps fuelled—the new concern for the texture of materials. A mid-nineteenth-century architect like Salvin, who designed several monumental Elizabethan piles, including Harlaxton and Thoresby Hall, had no shortage of published source material, notably Nash's *Mansions of England in the Olden Time*, which came out in four folio volumes between 1839 and 1849, and Shaw's *Details of Elizabethan Architecture*, published in 1834 and republished in 1898. But engravings, though they could be accurate, as in Shaw's line illustrations, or romantic, as in Nash's views, peopled with Elizabethan figures, could not give the same sense of brickwork and stone as a full page photograph in one of the turn-of-the-century folio volumes, their long exposures having been set on an apparently endless succession of dreamily motionless afternoons.

The principal subject for new architectural books was the English Renaissance. J. A. Gotch's *Architecture of the Renaissance in England*, illustrated by the distinguished photographer Charles Latham, was published in 1891–4. Gotch was principally concerned with Elizabethan and Jacobean rather than Caroline or Georgian architecture. However, interest in Wren had been growing since A. H. Mackmurdo published *Wren's City Churches* in 1883. Blomfield's *History of Renaissance Architecture in England, 1500–1800*, illustrated with prints and drawings, appeared in 1897. It was shortly followed by *Later Renaissance Architecture in England* in 1898–1901, by the architects John Belcher and Mervyn Macartney and originally issued as a series of plates with the minimum of text. It did not seek to illustrate the history of the English Renaissance so much as 'its adaptability to every purpose, large or small, monumental or domestic'. It was one of the few books known to have been in Lutyens's architectural library. Macartney later become sole editor of the *Architectural Review*, another magazine founded, like *Country Life*, to take advantage of new techniques for printing photographs. In 1906 the *Architectural Review* began publishing a series called 'The Practical Exemplar of Architecture', which every month carried eight or nine pages of details—gatepiers, chimneystacks, doorways—mostly from eighteenth-century buildings, providing a handbook for correct neo-Georgian.

The English Renaissance provided a kind of half-way house between Gothic and the more rigorous forms of Classicism. By 1900 it had become overwhelmingly popular with country-house architects (those, that is, who were interested in historical precedent), but it could come Early or Late (Plates 90–1). The chief protagonist of the Early Renaissance was Ernest George, who, when Norman Shaw stopped building country houses in the mid-1890s, became the leading country-house architect in Britain, until he in turn was toppled by Lutyens. George is an important figure. He was by no means a progressive: his clients—like Willie James—were new men who nevertheless had solidly old-fashioned tastes and wanted to live in big houses surrounded by plenty of land and all the feudal trappings. He found no shortage of such people until about 1910, when he was building his last house, Putteridge Bury. By then he was seventy-one. Conservative though he was, from his office, as from Shaw's, came a stream of talented young architects, including Baker, Dawber and Lutyens. Lutyens in later years remembered disparagingly

129

89. The hall at Manderston

90. Early English Renaissance: North Bovey Manor, Devon   91. Later English Renaissance: Ditton Place, Sussex

a distinguished architect who took each year, a three weeks' holiday abroad and returned with overflowing sketch books. When called on for a project he would look through these and choose some picturesque turret or gable from Holland, France, or Spain and round it weave his new design. Location mattered little, and no provincial formation influenced him, for at that time *terracotta* was the last word in building. All honour to Philip Webb and Norman Shaw (in his later period) for their gallant attempt to bring England back to craftsmanship and tradition.[11]

Poor George: Lutyens's entertaining, contemptuous portrait has understandably stuck, but it was far from fair as regards the mainstay of George's practice, his country houses. It is true that he was a charming watercolourist, and liked to travel on the Continent and produced a series of books of lithographs to pay for his holidays. With his different partners, he was also a follower of fashion, designing Rousdon, with Thomas Vaughan, in Old English, and Buchan Hill, with Harold Peto, in Queen Anne. These houses were full of Flemish, German and even Japanese motifs. But by 1890 George had settled down into the faithful Early English Renaissance style from which he never subsequently departed in his big country houses.

By coincidence, the commission for the first country house to exhibit this style came in the year Lutyens joined George and Peto, 1887. It was for Batsford Park (Plate 222), near Moreton-in-Marsh, later the childhood home of the Mitford sisters. Guy Dawber, who was to become president of the Royal Institute of British Architects and founder of the

130

Council for the Preservation of Rural England, but then in his late twenties, was the clerk of works, which may explain the sensitive texture of the lovely grey Cotswold stone. The style of the house, which was large but not enormously so, was based less on the very grand sixteenth-century houses soon to be published by Gotch than on their more modest contemporaries—Chastleton rather than Longleat. The garden front, with its banks of mullioned windows, is a simplified version of Montacute, down to the garden pavilions. However, it has triangular rather than curly gables, a form more fitted to a house the size of Batsford, but still an unexpected piece of architectural restraint.

At first sight, Batsford looks disarmingly like a genuine Elizabethan manor house. It set the tone for Motcombe, Eynsham Hall (Plate 92) and Putteridge Bury. Eynsham was a slightly scaled down version of Burton Constable, the Jacobean house outside Hull. Only Crathorne Hall, in Yorkshire, the handsome stone house built in 1906–9, broke the mould, and only then because George was using the style of the locality, in which Renaissance motifs, surviving unexpectedly long, were combined with Palladian fronts.

Other architects building Early Renaissance country houses were Aston Webb, who designed Hildon, in Hampshire, and Yeaton Peverey, in Shropshire, and the elusive W. H. Romaine Walker, a society architect and decorator, who designed luxurious Elizabethan pastiches at Rhinefield and Danesfield. Lutyens toyed with the style in the entrance façade of Little Thakeham, although it is not the elevations so much as the great hall—bleak, baffling and Baroque—that makes the house memorable.

The Later Renaissance did not properly arrive until the late 1890s and brought with it neo-Georgian. Intimations that it was coming can be seen in the 1870s, with W. E. Nesfield's Kinmel Park, Webb's Smeaton Manor and Wilfrid Scawen Blunt's Crabbet Park. With Bryanston (Plate 223), the style was almost there; but Bryanston was premature. Elements of the Later Renaissance were taken up around 1890 but used asymmetrically. Symmetrical designs began to make their appearance at the Royal Academy in 1898.

The Later Renaissance itself fell into two parts. For big country houses, the sturdy, full-blooded style of the mid-seventeenth century was preferred. Blomfield took the lead, remodelling Heathfield Park, Sussex, from 1898 (work did not finish until 1910), and about the same year designing for Hudson Kearley, politician and founder of the International Stores, a smaller country house, Whittington, in Buckinghamshire, later rebuilt in the style of Groombridge Place. He developed this manner in a number of substantial Edwardian commissions, of which the most splendid was Moundsmere (Plates 102, 238), with its flavour of Wren's work at Hampton Court Palace. He was still using it in Wretham Hall in 1912. Earlier, his cousin A. C. Blomfield's rebuilding of Stansted Park after a fire in 1900 was a textbook essay in the style of Wren (Plate 93).[12] But for smaller country houses something lighter was looked for. Macartney's Frithwood of 1900 is one of the first houses that can be called neo-Georgian, derived from the discreet eighteenth rather than seventeenth-century precedents. He used it again in Kennet Orley, the small house he designed for himself in 1910. The most sophisticated expression of neo-Georgian before the First World War was Houndsell Place (Plate 94), designed by the twenty-eight year old Alwyn Ball in 1912. Elegance replaced sturdiness as the ideal of the inter-war years, and is expressed at its best in Rex Whistler's painting of the remodelled south front to Godmersham Park (Colour Plate XVIII).

92. Neo-Jacobean: Eynsham Hall, Oxfordshire

93. Neo-Wren: Stansted Park, Sussex, rebuilt after a fire

94. Neo-Georgian: Houndsell Place, Sussex

By comparison to Blomfield, Lutyens—for all his inventiveness—was for once not especially quick to discover the Wrenaissance. The east front of Crooksbury, which was designed in 1898 for an old family friend (and fervent admirer of Lady Emily), Arthur Chapman, had all the elements, but the Baroque doorcase was placed boldly off-centre. The first signs of a stricter interpretation of the seventeenth century came in the St John's Institute, in Tufton Street, Westminster, a modest enough building when it was designed in 1899, and even more modest when it was built. Two years later, in 1901–2, he experimented with Georgian in a mysterious house he hoped to build in Berkshire, Rush Court. From the outside, this house would not have been a success: it was immensely long (over twenty bays), only two storeys tall, and was to have had an unbroken parapet on the south elevation. The glory of the building would have been the domed, double-storey hall, for which sketches survive. Monkton, the next essay in Georgian, was a very hesitant design. When Lutyens's Wrenaissance did appear, it was with the splendour and confidence of a trumpet voluntary; but that was not until the Country Life building of 1904. Nevertheless, once it had been achieved, Lutyens brought to the Later English Renaissance style a lightness, a panache and an exquisite sense of proportion, such as it never had under the heavier hand of Blomfield. Despite his erudition, or perhaps because of it, Blomfield designed too massively. The simple forms of the seventeenth and eighteenth centuries allowed Lutyens's sense of geometry full rein; the plasticity of Middlefield foreshadows the Mannerism of Heathcote or the French Classicism of Gledstone.

95. Gledstone Hall, Yorkshire, showing Lutyens turning to French Classicism after the First World War

Heathcote, on the outskirts of Ilkley, was one of Lutyens's jokes. This, his most architecturally complex house, and the only one in which he used the Classical orders in the grand manner, was not a country house at all, but a substantial suburban villa. In fact, the Baroque was rarely used for country houses. To most architects, it was a style of the town—especially public buildings like the War Office (1898–1906) and the Old Bailey (1900–6). The Baroque elements of Chesters and Bryanston had largely been forgotten by 1900, with two exceptions: W. D. Caröe's South Lytchett Manor (Plate 241), in Dorset, finished the year Heathcote was begun, 1904 (Sir Nikolaus Pevsner commented that the entrance front, with its giant gable combined with a niche, 'has to be seen to be believed'), and Sennowe Park, in Norfolk, begun in about 1905.

Sennowe Park

Ebullient is the adjective unavoidably brought to mind by Sennowe Park (Plate 96), which shows the Edwardian country-house tradition at its most vigorous.[13] However, although its flamboyance seems more Central European than English, the house is a good case study for the English Renaissance, because it shows the wide range of sources that architects quarried. It is one of a large number of houses in East Anglia of about the same date—Elveden, Culford Hall, Pickenham Hall, Wretham Hall, the Arts and Crafts houses on the coast—but undoubtedly the one that best expresses the supposed optimism of the age.

The self-confident tone of the house owes something to the owner, T. A. Cook, and something to its no less self-confident architect, Skipper of Norwich. The Thomas Cook who built Sennowe (incorporating but completely transforming an earlier house) was a very different character from his grandfather and namesake, the travel agent. The elder Cook, born in 1808, began life as a Baptist evangelist.[14] Having at one time been apprenticed to a drunken woodturner, he was a natural convert to the Temperance Movement, gathering momentum after the Beerhouse Act of 1830. It was entirely through the Temperance connection that the travel firm came into being. The epoch-making first excursion took place in 1841, when Cook engaged a special train to take five hundred and seventy people from Leicester to Loughborough to attend a Temperance meeting. Forty-four years later, the British Government was turning to T. A. Cook's father, John Mason Cook, to conduct the military expedition it sent—in the event disastrously late—to relieve General Gordon at Khartoum. By the end of the century, when T. A. Cook sold out to buy Sennowe and its good sporting estate, the firm had developed highly profitable banking interests through investing the large sums left with it, interest free, for travellers' cheques.

T. A. Cook was a *bon viveur*. Like Andrew Carnegie, his hobby was to drive four-in-hand. An evocative oil painting by A. de Faxthorn shows him bowling down the carriage drive in front of the newly built Sennowe, with his wife beside him and his only son and two footmen behind (Colour Plate xvII). It is said that, breaking the bye-laws, he once drove five-in-hand through Hyde Park. When stopped by a policeman and told that five horses were not allowed, he returned the next day with the permitted four—and a mule in place of the fifth. He is also remembered for his appearances in Fakenham, where he

96. The entrance front of Sennowe Park, Norfolk

would draw a large bag of pennies from the bank, heat the coins on a shovel in the fire of The Crown, and shoot them across the market place for small boys to try to pick up. A giant electric spotlight was erected at the top of the water-tower at Sennowe for duck shooting on the new seven or eight acre lake. This practice had to be stopped by the coastguard, who feared that mariners would mistake the tower for a lighthouse.

Cook went to the local architect, George Skipper, born in East Dereham.[15] As Sir John Betjeman described him, Skipper 'is to Norwich rather what Gaudi was to Barcelona'. The son of a builder, his earliest wish was to be a painter, but his father persuaded him to go into architecture, and he entered the London office of J. T. Lee in 1873. After six years he began his own practice in East Dereham, and the next year transferred to Norwich. After working in Somerset for W. S. Clark of Clarks Shoes, he won the competition for the town hall at Cromer. He rarely worked outside his home ground again. He built the three largest hotels in Cromer, the Grand, the Metropol and the Hôtel de Paris. Then came the Royal Arcade in Norwich with its Art Nouveau tiling (described by a contemporary as 'a fragment of the Arabian Nights dropped into the heart of the old city').[16] His masterpiece was the Norwich Union Life Assurance Office in Surrey Street, the competition for which

135

98. The winter garden at Sennowe

he won in 1901. Although his design had been entered under the title 'Utility', he persuaded his clients to buy a quantity of extremely fine marble that had originally been intended for Westminster Cathedral. Consequently the walls and floors are laid with marble, and a colonnade of veined monoliths surrounds the circular central office, at an extra cost of £5,000. This was the spirit of sumptuousness with which he set about Sennowe.

Skipper was an individualist, with a special feeling for rich, plastic, slightly hectic effects. For the opulent curved bay on the entrance front he may have looked as far as Vienna : the figures and carved panels above the cornice would have been too extravagant for English precedents. Nevertheless, Skipper also shared Blomfield's enthusiasm for Wren. His sketchbook for May to September 1905, about the time he received the commission for Sennowe, shows that he visited St Paul's Cathedral and the Wren Library at Trinity College, Cambridge.[17] The notes that he made were not used in the house, although St Paul's may have suggested the figures on the skyline, unusual in English Baroque houses except the grandest, like Blenheim and Castle Howard. The windows in the attic of the semi-octagonal turrets show another debt to Wren : they were derived from the oeil-de-boeufs at Hampton Court, although made oval not round. Red brick was the favourite material of the English Renaissance : Skipper refaced the original house, which had been built of white brick, with red tiles.

Inside, the English Renaissance is still more in evidence. The staircase (Plate 99), with its three flights surmounted by an oval cupola, was based on the famous one at

137

97. H. C. Fehr's statue of 'Evening' at the end of the south colonnade at Sennowe

100. The fireplace in the saloon at Sennowe

Ashburnham House, Westminster, then thought to have been by Inigo Jones. Belcher and Macartney, who published photographs and measured drawings of the Ashburnham House staircase, commented that its 'planning and design may be considered one of the greatest achievements of English architecture'.

While the Ashburnham House staircase had balusters, the staircase at Sennowe has richly carved panels. These, although similar to ones at Cassiobury, were probably derived from a staircase in a house in Guildford High Street, again illustrated by Belcher and Macartney, with both a drawing and a photograph. At Sennowe, each panel is different. A third source was the staircase at Dunster Castle, on which the newels were modelled. It cannot have been a coincidence that Arnold Mitchell incorporated another staircase modelled on that at Ashburnham House at Barnett Hill, built for Frank Cook, T. A. Cook's brother, about 1906.

The library was Early Renaissance rather than Later, with a coved ceiling and door set at an angle, almost certainly based on the Whispering Door at Broughton Castle, illustrated by Gotch. The saloon, which is fifty feet long, has a little bit of everything. The gigantic fireplace, for instance, is in the form of a Baroque altar, has a trophy of dead game birds in the style of Grinling Gibbons, and a garland that is neo-Classical French. Unlike Blomfield or Newton, Skipper was too irrepressible to confine himself to any one style for long.

139

99. The staircase at Sennowe

There was even a bit of Art Nouveau. T. A. Cook, having approved the plans, left for a two-year world cruise while the house was being remodelled. When he returned, his one criticism was: 'But where is my ball room?' To remedy the omission, the winter garden was made large enough to accommodate dancing (Plate 98). Credence is lent to the story by a watercolour perspective showing Skipper's first thoughts for the remodelling, at which stage it was intended to retain the old conservatory with its pitched roof. Inside, there is a centrepiece formed of six green monolithic stone columns around a pool, with a lithe Art Nouveau bronze figure of a girl as a fountain.

The stone carving at Sennowe, both on the house and on the Italianate terraces, was so extravagant that a team of Italian masons was specially brought over. An old photograph (Plate 101) shows them in their masons' shop, in the full glory of their moustaches, berets and smocks. Descendants of some of these craftsmen still live in the neighbourhood of Ryburgh, the village at the gates of the park.[18] More than anything it is the stonework—urns and beasts, garlands and figures—which sets the tone of the house.

But even Skipper calmed down, eventually. His practice, which continued after the First World War, later included a commission for a large country house, Framingham Hall, in Norfolk, built in 1930. It was not as big as Sennowe, although still substantial; and it could not have been more suave, polite or neo-Georgian. Skipper, most Edwardian of architects, was also a survivor, and that may have been evidence of his vigour.

101. Italian stonemasons at Sennowe

But to many architects Sennowe would not have seemed quite the thing. There was a suggestion of foreignness about the house, and it drew attention to itself at a time when most new houses were trying to merge into the background. The English Renaissance was valued precisely because it was English. The greater the architect, the more English his work was thought to have been. Thus, according to Blomfield, 'Wren was not only the greatest but the most English of all English architects. He went to see Bernini in France, and talked with Mansard and Perrault, yet their influence on him was merely superficial. It spoilt his ornament, but left his essential faculty untouched.'[19] Was it for his greatness or his Englishness that he was valued?

British architects were confirmed in their complacency from abroad. Not only did they hear themselves being called independent, home-loving and uniquely fortunate in their domestic arrangements by the German Hermann Muthesius, but numerous country houses were being built by British architects overseas. R. S. Wornum, having worked for the Queen Regent of Spain, became the favoured architect of the Iberian aristocracy. Baillie Scott, who won the international Dulce Domum competition run by a Darmstadt magazine for an advanced country house (Colour Plate XXXI), had commissions from Switzerland, Rumania and Russia. Arnold Mitchell built a royal villa and golf pavilion for the King of the Belgians outside Ostend.[20] The best contemporary architecture of Germany, in the plain style of Peter Behrens, was known as *Mackintoshismus*. Even at the height of anti-English feeling shortly before 1914, the Crown Prince of Germany could commission an 'English house', albeit from a German architect, Paul Schultze-Naumburg, which was triumphantly published by the *Builder* in 1916.

The ideas that Blomfield and his friends had about England had as much to do with public school notions of gentlemanliness as they did with architecture. Blomfield would rather have given the impression of being a squire than an architect. He shot, hunted, played cricket, and was glad to leave another prominent resident of Rye, Henry James, in the tea-tent with his back to the game.[21] Despite his scholarship, he was not averse to being thought a bit of a philistine. His view of architecture was strongly coloured by his social ideal. 'The English tradition,' wrote Blomfield in *The Formal Garden in England*, 'has always been on the side of refinement and reserve.' In an essay actually called 'The English Tradition', he defined its three great qualities as 'steadfastness of purpose, reserve in design, and thorough workmanship'.[22] Ebullience was thought distinctly bad form, although English Baroque was admitted on sufferance: 'Even Vanbrugh's architecture, huge, enormous, unwieldy, if it was not English, was certainly nothing else.'[23]

The England Blomfield loved was the England of Elgar, the England of Housman, the 'England, my England' of W. E. Henley, the England of *Country Life*. It was the England Lady Flora Burne, in John Buchan's *A Lodge in the Wilderness*, recalled in her wistful vision of an Africa peopled with younger sons, who would found a new aristocracy: 'What a delightful society it would be: I can picture country houses—simple places, not palaces like Musuru—and pretty gardens, and packs of hounds, and—oh, all that makes England nice.'[24] These were also the values of Blomfield's clients, as expressed at Moundsmere.

Blomfield's Englishness at times comes close to self-parody, but it was not confined to himself, or even to architects with his background and beliefs. 'Simple, well off house-

102. The entrance hall at Moundsmere Manor, Hampshire

Fig. 12. Moundsmere Manor

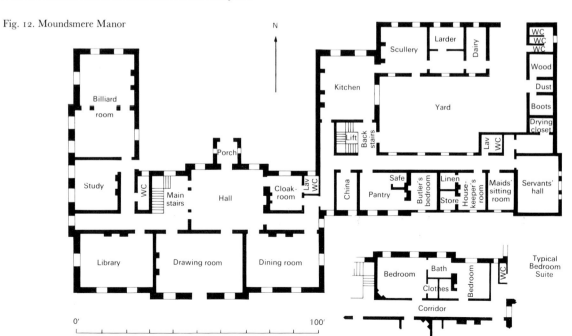

N

0'   100'

keeping, with tea in the garden,' wrote the Socialist W. R. Lethaby in 1916; 'Boy-scouting, and tennis in flannels. These four seem to me our best form of modern civilization, and must serve as examples of the sort of spirit in which town improvement must be undertaken.'[25] The vision of England he and the SPAB sought to preserve was one of 'old towns, tilled fields, little rivers, farms, churches, and cottages'.[26]

A house like Bryanston, let alone Sennowe, seemed altogether too boisterous. 'It is probable that time will greatly improve the exterior which at present seems to need much toning down,' was the conclusion reached by the members of the Architectural Association who visited it in 1899. 'Under the blazing sunlight, the red and white of the walls made one blink . . .'[27] All extremes, whether of elaboration or bareness, were to be shunned in case they 'might seem affected posing and advertising,' according to Webb. 'I never begin to be satisfied,' ran another of his dicta, 'until my work looks commonplace.'[28] By 1900 most country houses were quieter than those of the mid-nineteenth century. Towers were out of favour (Sennowe and Tylney Hall were exceptions).[29] The change had been expressed by J. J. Stevenson in *House Architecture* (1880), where he stated the belief that, however 'conspicuous and commanding the building', the 'low level lines of the English Tudor house are in better taste, and more in harmony with English scenery', than a Gothic house, full of vertical accents. And by 1911, when Ernest Willmott published *English House Design*, repose and restfulness had become the dominant aesthetic values.

There developed a school of architects, mostly designing small country houses, who made a virtue of reticence. Guy Dawber was impeccably and sometimes enchantingly modest. In its details, proportions and materials, his small house, Burdocks (Plate 103), in Gloucestershire, is almost indistinguishable from the West Country manor houses on which it was based. Ernest Newton was almost equally unassuming. As his son, W. G. Newton, wrote: 'growing out of more commonplace origins, [Newton's work] is less exciting and dramatic very often than is the work of Shaw or Lutyens. You will less often say on seeing one, "This is a Newton house"; but perhaps more often, "This is the house for this position."'[30] Lawrence Weaver had a word for it. Writing about Ardenrun Place (Plate 104)—in the English Renaissance style—in *Country Life* in 1911, he told a rather literary joke about a lady wearing a poke-bonnet in eighteenth-century London. Two blades pursued her, overtook her, peered round the bonnet and, in profound disappointment, gave vent to the groan: 'Extraordinaryornary, by Gum!' Kinder and more suggestive was W. G. Newton's phrase which he used of Fouracres: 'that nothing which is everything'. It is the undemonstrative excellence of their craftsmanship and materials that raises Newton's houses above the 'extraordinaryornary'.

Ardenrun shows the degree to which Newton came to accept stylistic conventions after 1900; he also worked in Elizabethan and, at Oldcastle, a lyrical Tudor.[31] But the most radical Edwardian architects sought to escape from the influence of tradition altogether. As Mackintosh said as he handed over The Hill House, newly completed, to W. W. Blackie in 1904: 'Here is a house, It is not an Italian Villa, an English Mansion House, a Swiss Chalet, or a Scots Castle. It is a dwelling house.'[32] But Mackintosh never had the opportunity to build a country house.

Voysey drew on tradition, but it was an even simpler tradition than that of the manor houses which Dawber and Newton admired. His low roofs, rough-cast walls, hipped gables and leaded lights were ultimately derived from the cottages of the Home Counties. They had been revived by Norman Shaw and Nesfield in their Old English style of the 1860s, but they were now put together with a fairytale freshness, described impishly by H. S. Goodhart-Rendel as 'Only-little-me-ishness'.[33] It owed something to the ground plans, which were severely geometric (preferably rectangular), and much to the colours: bright red tiles or green slates for the roof, bright green for the guttering, shutters, and if there was one, which was likely, the barrel that served as a waterbut. The effect was charming, inexpensive, but not really suitable for larger houses.

Whether Voysey would have felt it appropriate to use historical motifs had he ever designed a large country house is an unanswerable question. It is possible he was not quite as inflexible as he appeared. When commissioned to build a house for T. S. Cotterell, general manager of the Bath and Portland Stone Firms, he designed an appealing, stone-built bungalow in the castle style. With its buttresses, crenellations and oriel windows, Lodge Style (Plate 232) suited the client. Not only did Cotterell want a house to show off the quality of his stone, but he was a keen Dickensian and, in 1909, the year Lodge Style was designed, took a leading role in promoting the Bath Historical Pageant, to celebrate the one thousandth anniversary of the city.[34] And Lodge Style was not a unique deviation from Voysey's better known style. Five years earlier he had proposed building a house for Lady Henry Somerset in a similar style; and, had it been finished to his designs, which included even a chapel, it would have been his largest country house.

103. Burdocks, Gloucestershire

104. Ardenrun Place, Surrey, drawn by F. L. Griggs (RIBA drawings collection)

Minterne Magna

The best example of a large country house designed by a stylistic radical is Minterne Magna (Plate 106),[35] in Dorset. Again, it shows the tendency for houses to become quieter and more horizontal, being long and comparatively low, with a stumpy tower which only pushes a short way above the roof ridge. The architect was Leonard Stokes, an uncompromising, irascible man, best known for the scandal he caused by sitting for his portrait as president of the Royal Institute of British Architects in a fawn-coloured dressing gown. In one of his few recorded comments on his profession, he said that architects 'ought to try to develop individuality in our modern architecture'.[36] That was his aim at Minterne.

If, in the crisis of stylistic faith, one may imagine John Kinross preserving a conservative piety, Stokes was an architectural Theosophist, practising what has been called 'Free Style'. Theosophists prided themselves on their openness to all types of religious thinking, however foreign or strange. Stokes had the same attitude towards style, choosing architectural motifs by eye rather than because they consistently conformed to a period or style.

For all that, Minterne, which replaced an eighteenth-century house, also embodies another attitude to the past, a deep affection for what was known and what had gone. This was the contribution of the owner, the tenth Baron Digby, one of the few aristocrats to build a new country house in the twentieth century. So Minterne is, like Manderston, an unusually interesting study in how an architect and a client responded to history.

It is not clear why Lord Digby chose Stokes, who might seem an unusually progressive figure for a backwoods peer to have found. Before Minterne, his experience of country-house work had been limited. In 1893 he had designed a rambling, rather perverse house called Innisfall, on Loch Allen, Co. Leitrim, and later Shooter's Hill, Pangbourne, Berkshire, for D. H. Evans of the Oxford Street store. Stokes was principally an ecclesiastical architect, although after his marriage in 1898 to Edith Gaine, daughter of William Gaine, general manager of the National Telephone Company, he received a large number of commissions for telephone exchanges—twenty in the decade before Gaine's death in 1908.

Perhaps that helps explain the radical toughness at Minterne. To an historian, the entrance front, built of narrow courses of hammer-dressed Ham Hill stone ashlar, is a slightly unnerving experience. It is a strong-looking house from the outside, but the L-shaped entrance front seems to yearn for the past   or for a past. Because as you come closer you realize that it does not hint at one historical period but many. It is a composite past, eerie, veiled and obscure. Each element of the composition suggests a different historical period. The porch is eighteenth-century, the tracery in the big window is Perpendicular, the vestigial machicolation along the parapet suggests the age of castles, the chimneys recall Hawksmoor. It is as though an actor had gone to the property shop and picked out parts of a costume at random, and gone on the stage in doublet and hose, a frogged coat and top hat. The difference was that Minterne does not flaunt its contradictions, because the age of ostentation was past.

Inside, the atmosphere is less rugged. It is light and spacious, some of the rooms always having been painted white, and there are characteristically Edwardian vistas down the

146

105. The hall at Minterne Magna, Dorset

106. Entrance front of Minterne

broad, arched corridors that run along two axes of the house. Nevertheless, the Free Style principles are just the same as outside. The form of the main hall (Plate 105), with its minstrels' gallery, ultimately derives from Gothic great halls, and the two tall windows have Perpendicular tracery and stone mullions (seen from the entrance court). Yet the stuccowork of the room, the joined pairs of the Corinthian columns and the elegant barrel vault are in the spirit of Hawksmoor, and so are the heavier ceilings to the drawing room and the Tapestry Room (now called the dining room). While Kinross used different styles in different buildings, Stokes used different styles—or parts of styles—in the same house.

How did it come to be built? Lord Digby had been perfectly satisfied with the house he had inherited in 1889, although his young wife, whom he married in 1893, was rather less so. She was then twenty-two, he forty-seven. Family tradition has it that, newly married, she persuaded him to build a new house; he acquiesced, but insisted it should be done out of income, not capital. So they waited nine years before undertaking the work.

But the real reason for rebuilding was probably far less romantic. The old house developed a series of worrying smells. Lady Digby's diary for 22 February 1902 sounds the first ominous note. 'Eddy and I,' she wrote, 'had to turn out of our bedroom as a horrible smell turned up in the middle of last night which we think must be a dead rat in the wall,

148

XVIII. Mr and Mrs Robert Tritton having tea in the garden at Godmersham Park, Kent, by Rex Whistler (private collection)

XVII. (previous pages) T. A. Cook driving his family four-in-hand past the newly built Sennowe, by A. de Faxthorn (private collection)

but at present we cannot trace it.' On the 26th she found the Tapestry Room was smelling strongly of gas—'they fear something wrong with the drains'. Nine days later, a hitherto unknown barrel drain was discovered, giving rise to further alarm. 'Eddy is much troubled as to what ought to be done. He feels the house is not worth spending a big sum on, and he feels that it must be a big business, what with drains, dry-rot and rats in the house.'

Lord Digby asked Stokes to prepare a survey. At this stage they still hoped that it would not be necessary to rebuild completely, but Stokes's verdict on Minterne's condition was not favourable. Rebuilding could not be avoided. By May the next year Minterne's contents were gradually being put into store, the best pieces going to the Digby's town house in Belgrave Square. A special excursion was made 'to see Leonard Stokes about the plans—also to bustle him up a bit'. The housekeeper and the head housemaid stayed in the increasingly empty house until August, when the builders took over. A cottage, formerly the stud groom's, was furnished for the Digbys to use when they visited the site.

Lord Digby was a typical conservative, loving home-life, rarely going to London and dividing his time between field sports and public duty in the locality. He was happy with the existing house and insisted that, if it had to be rebuilt, the new Minterne contain something of the spirit of the old. For the sake of economy, the old foundations were re-used, so that the plan changed very little in outline (the only departure being the billiard room at the end of the garden front, set at an angle). A new Tapestry Room was built to replace the old one. It displayed the set of Flemish tapestries given to a former owner, General Charles Churchill, brother of the first Duke of Marlborough, by the States of Holland in reward for his governorship of Brussels. In April 1907 the tapestries were put in 'exactly as they were in the old house, the room being practically a duplicate', including the bow window.

One wonders what Stokes thought of this cosy attitude towards the past. He was notorious for his bad temper and irritability but on this occasion he must have been tactful. It is considerably to his credit that on 24 February 1908 Lady Digby entered in her diary: 'to-day Eddy attended Petty Sessions and hunted after. He has been keeping very well and is I think really pleased to be settled home again, with all the worries of building done and finished with, and to his satisfaction. He says that if he had to do it over again, there is very little, if anything that he would do different.' Between them, Stokes and Lord Digby had created a very elegant house, rooted in the past but of its own age, gaunt from the outside but deliciously comfortable once you are in. It is a triumph of contradictions, and as such one of the best and most typical essays in Edwardian country-house style.

5. *The Tudor Taste*

The country houses described in the preceding chapter were built by architects who all believed to some extent in a conventional concept of style. They made conscious reference to a tradition of grand country houses in which they hoped their own buildings would naturally take a place. Although some edged closer and closer to producing what might seem, from a distance, virtual replicas of buildings of past times, none of their houses could—when you get nearer—really be mistaken for the work of any other age than the late nineteenth and early twentieth century. They used a vocabulary that was redolent of the past, but the grammar and idiom were modern. However, many, more romantic architects did not have any devotion to style in that sense. Arts and Crafts architects believed that methods of construction were more important, socially and morally, than end results; and anyway they had a natural preference for labourers' cottages over aristocrats' mansions. Their ideals and some of the country houses which best expressed them will be described in chapter seven. This chapter and the next will describe an equally romantic approach to the country house, which probably appealed more to owners than to their architects. It was nothing less than to reproduce the exact appearance of an old—preferably half-timbered—building, so that it genuinely did look like the real thing, down to the last wobbly beam and lichen-covered tile. Not only were new country houses constructed out of old building materials, which had already become gnarled with age; but whole buildings were transported entire and tacked on to new ones to ensure that verisimilitude was absolute.

The taste was immensely popular in the 1920s, when the old buildings of the English countryside seemed more than ever to recall an idyllic pre-Industrial age, incapable of producing the recent horrors of mechanised destruction which had scarred the imagination of the civilized world. In England, the Edwardian decade had been haunted by nostalgia—for the vanishing crafts of the countryside, for the folk songs and country dances which Cecil Sharp and Vaughan Williams were recording before they faded for ever, and for the once-sturdy, self-sufficient peasant culture, the last signs of which were about to die in the face of wage labour and encroaching villadom.[1] This feeling became all the more poignant when it seemed that continuity would be broken for ever. 'When I return from the observing post at dark, after changing from wet muddy things, I get some tea,' wrote a twenty-year-old officer from the front; 'then out comes my pipe, and the latest *Country Life* from England, and I sit down in front of my dug out and read about old

155

107. Detail of the entrance front of Bailiffscourt, Sussex, incorporating a two-light medieval window from Somerset

houses.'[2] The writer never returned to the countryside he loved, but Gordon Russell, the furniture designer, was more fortunate, and lived to remember 'the nostalgic longing for the sight of the first dry-stone wall' experienced in the first days of leave.[3]

In 1915 the *Studio* devoted a special number to romantic engravings of old English mansions. On that occasion Alfred Yockney wrote: 'We look on the distant past as we do on a beautiful sunset, conscious only of warm, glowing reflections.' This was the spirit of what might be called the Tudor Taste. Sometimes the style—if style it can be called—was used deliberately to evoke an image of a world removed from war. The most striking example is Wyke Manor, in Worcestershire, which was originally an unassuming Georgian farmhouse, rebuilt on the site of an earlier half-timbered building. In 1923 it was virtually rebuilt as a memorial to the owner's son, Alban Hudson, who had been killed at the Battle of Messines in 1917.[4] To begin with, it was intended to be the centre of a scheme that would have included two long rows of almshouses for disabled servicemen—establishing a community for the wounded that would have recalled, through the buildings, an Elizabethan charitable foundation—but only the work to the house was carried out as planned. The almshouses were built, but to a different design and elsewhere in the village.

Wyke Manor (Plate 108) was transformed from a brick box to a very convincing imitation of a sixteenth-century yeoman's hall. The only portions of the Georgian structure to survive were parts of the two rooms in the centre of the entrance front, and even these are not obvious from the outside. The new plan was meant to follow as closely as possible the outlines of the original house; but the architect, Cecil G. Hare, who continued G. F. Bodley's old practice (Bodley would have turned in his grave), was probably wilfully irregular. None of the walls makes a right-angle with another, and the planning is self-consciously inconvenient, with a deliberately cramped staircase, an absence of corridors on the north side of the courtyard, and living rooms at opposite ends of the house. An oratory was constructed in the north-east corner of the house to contain Lieutenant Hudson's tomb, and it was a condition of inheritance in his father's will that commemorative services be regularly held.

Another war-time connection is the work of Major Kenneth Hutchinson Smith, a Canadian who served with the Royal Engineers, married an English girl after the war, and built fifty or so houses for businessmen in the Wolverhampton area.[5] The first job he undertook, gained as a direct result of his experience with the Engineers, was to move the half-timbered Elizabethan mansion Bradley Hall from Kingswinford near Dudley to the side of the Avon at Stratford, where it became known as Bradley Lodge. A number of old timbers were somehow left over when Bradley Hall was rebuilt; Smith acquired them in the early 1930s to build Tudor Close on a nearby site. Other old materials became available from Lymore Hall, in Montgomeryshire, demolished after Lord Powys's offer to give the house to the nation had been refused for lack of endowment (the staircase was bought by William Randolph Hearst for St Donat's Castle, but never installed).

Smith's amateur approach was typical of the Tudor taste, and so was the size of his buildings, which are too small to be called country houses. Nevertheless, although the Tudor taste seems a characteristically post-First World War phenomenon, the first signs were in evidence some time before 1914. And like most themes in country-house architecture of the first quarter of the twentieth century, the idea can be traced back to

Lutyens—however loath he might have been to admit paternity. An early indication of the way things were going was the British Pavilion Lutyens designed for the Paris Exhibition of 1900. It had been decided (again the idea was not the architect's) that this should be a faithful reproduction of Kingston House, an elaborate early seventeenth-century building at Bradford-on-Avon. However, even earlier than that, the architect Robert Lorimer's description of Munstead Wood, the small country house Lutyens built for Gertrude Jekyll, suggests the real roots of the Tudor taste in the Arts and Crafts movement and the veneration of the very stones of an old structure inspired by the Society for the Protection of Ancient Buildings:

It looks so reasonable, so kindly, so perfectly beautiful, that you feel that people might have been making love and living and dying there, and dear little children running about—I was going to say 1,000 years—anyway 600. They've used old tiles which of course helps but ... it has been built by the old people of the old materials in the old 'unhurrying way' but at the same time 'sweet to all modern uses'.[6]

108. Wyke Manor, Worcestershire

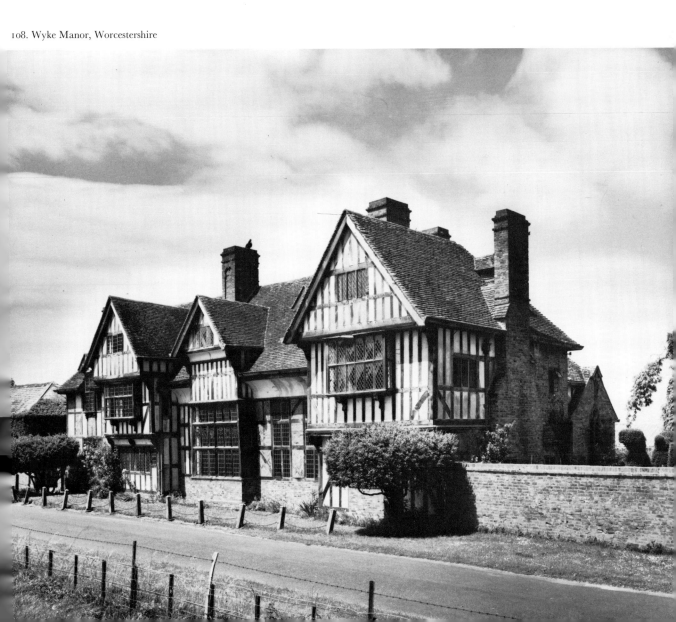

It was not so great a step to the Tudor taste, although not one that in this case either client or architect would have wished to have taken.

But Lutyens did take it, if unwillingly. He first added to the seventeenth-century manor house of Ashby St Ledgers in 1904. The Hon. Ivor Guest, the eldest son of Lord Wimborne, had bought it the year after his marriage to Alice Grosvenor in 1902. Further alterations, financed by a steel fortune, a directorship in Barclay's Bank and eventually the income from the eighty-three thousand acre Wimborne estate, were planned and sometimes executed over the next thirty-five years. There were reasons for the work. Lord Wimborne abandoned the family home of Canford Magna on inheriting his father's title in 1914. There was 'a terrible squash', wrote Lutyens, when the Prince of Wales visited in 1921, which made the Wimbornes 'add lavishly in spite of taxes and hard times'.[7] But the principal reason was the joy of it, which was no doubt what led client and architect to talk enthusiastically about building a model town as part of the original scheme in 1904. The plan was to 'bring in the Grand Junction Canal in a lovely way with horses on the tow path, rubbed green by the brass work of their harnesses'.[8] Inevitably at that date, the new buildings were to shelter a community of craftsmen. 'The trades we shall encourage and develop are: Tapestry, wrot iron, Barge building, boots, tapestries, linen, fabrics, clocks, etc etc. Great fun!'

109. The Tudor house at Ashby St Ledgers, Northamptonshire

Nothing came of the idea, but Guest must have had even greater fun bodily moving an old half-timber Tudor house (as it was called on the plans) from between Carr Street and Cox Lane in Ipswich to his Northamptonshire home, where he persuaded Lutyens to tack it on to the east front (Plate 109). It was just such small-scale, timber-framed buildings— modest but full of character and charm—that seemed most likely to disappear from Britain's towns and countryside. The first building acquired in 1896 by the newly formed National Trust was of exactly this type—the Clergy House, at Alfriston, in Sussex. 'The essentially national type of fifteenth and sixteenth century domestic architecture which is [Britain's] precious heritage,' wrote Arthur Stratton in the preface to Garner and Stratton's *The Domestic Architecture of England during the Tudor Period*, published in 1908, the year the Tudor house was moved, 'has hitherto received no adequate recognition, and in too many instances no effort has been made to stop the work of destruction, which has already robbed the country of many of its finest works of craftsmanship in materials of widely different natures.'[9] But for once the fun was lost on Lutyens. He was probably referring to the Tudor house when he wrote: 'we have arranged a scheme, but not got my way with the big simple lines I wanted, and have had to put in a good deal of fuss fuss to please I. Guest'.[10] Despite his efforts to discourage the project, each timber was numbered and lettered and the building was transported from Suffolk by an Oxford Street firm.[11]

Lutyens's doubts were proved right. The ideas of comfort held by a sixteenth-century Ipswich merchant were not up to those of a twentieth-century politician, banker and aristocrat. Draughts were no longer acceptable. Shortly before Lord Wimborne's death, Lutyens wrote to advise him 'in all humility' to face the lower storey of the Tudor house in stone; 'you could then get symmetrical windows wind proof etc.', Charles II panelling could be installed, and the fireplace could be moved to the centre of the room and the garden door to the side, so that they would be in a better relation to one another.[12] The Tudor house (which was then used as a 'common room') could then have been entered via a screens passage in the manner of a traditional hall—except that Lutyens envisaged a cocktail cabinet opposite the garden door. Lord Wimborne did not take up the suggestions; he probably did not wish to alter so radically the character of the building.

The Tudor taste appealed to the collecting as much as the architectural instinct. Detmar Blow's Little Ridge, Wiltshire, a successor to William Beckford's eighteenth-century folly, Fonthill House, was built to provide a setting for the owner's art treasures in 1904. The entrance front incorporated parts of the manor house of Berwick St Leonard, which was itself regarded as a choice and collectable *objet trouvé*.

However, for Lutyens, the sequel to Ashby St Ledgers came a few years later. Although he had tried to shoot down the idea of moving the Tudor house, he did something very similar when enlarging Great Dixter, Nathaniel Lloyd's small but delightful country house in Sussex (Plate 110). Lloyd was himself a connoisseur of old buildings, and architect and client had happened on a yeoman's hall at Benenden when touring the countryside together in search of correct period details to use in work on the fifteenth-century house. The Benenden hall was about to be demolished, so Lloyd bought it; and the whole structure was re-erected on the south side of Great Dixter, forming the principal bedroom.

A postscript to Great Dixter was Lutyens's creation of picturesque, sixteenth-century street scenes, mostly half-timbered, for the Shakespeare's England exhibition at Earl's

110. The Benenden Hall at Great Dixter, Sussex

Court in 1912. Although the scale was smaller than life size (this had not been the case with the Kingston House of 1900), it was uniform. Many—but not all—the buildings were copies of existing ones, reproduced in a spirit that was partly scholarly, partly self-indulgent.

The Tudor taste seems so much to have suited the mood of the times—a mood which was less and less confident after 1909[13]—that it appeared in a number of simultaneous manifestations between which there was almost certainly no thread of connection. The moving of old buildings extended the principle of moving old fireplaces and panelling and installing them in new buildings, which had not been uncommon in the 1890s, for instance in Rosehaugh (Plate 219), the Scottish house William Flockhart designed for Douglas Fletcher, millionaire chairman of the Highland Railway. About 1908 two other architects were at work in a very similar vein to the Tudor house at Ashby St Ledgers: one was Baillie Scott, who would have been known to Lutyens and who published his own designs in 1909;[14] the other was George Crawley, a quasi-amateur, probably unknown to both Lutyens and Baillie Scott and who had no designs in the conventional sense to publish.

At Burton Court, in Dorset, designed by Baillie Scott, it was once again the client, E. W. Barlett, a solicitor educated at Sherborne School, who determined the style of the house, having already salvaged windows, fireplaces, oak partitions and beams from the Court Farmhouse, Batcombe, before the architect arrived on the scene.[15] These fragments—and others from Yetminster, Stock Marston, Tintinhull and Sherborne—were incorporated into a small courtyard house that looks as though it has been mellowing above the Dorset soil for centuries. Baille Scott claimed he had no intention to deceive, but nevertheless quoted the ultimate unconscious compliment paid by an old farmer who said: 'I've come along this road all my life, but never noticed that old house on the hill before.'[16]

Crowhurst Place

George Crawley[17] was very different from either Lutyens or Baillie Scott, the hard working professionals. He was educated at both Eton and Harrow, and then at Trinity College, Cambridge, where he 'took little or no interest in the serious side of University life'. An aesthetic awakening came through the things he began to collect at this time, and he finally came to find that he could make money simply by having an eye. Not immediately, however. He first had thoughts of a business career, and various ventures were tried, though none with success. Circumstances were sometimes a little tight, especially when collecting precipitated the crises during which the 'budget of bills used often to burst its elastic bands'. Eventually he achieved a directorship in the Silicate Paint Company, which eased the immediate strain.

Crawley was essentially an amateur. It is true that his architectural commissions provided an income that must at times have been considerable, but he had no formal training and none of the naked ambition necessary to pursue and capture large numbers of clients. The thought of Lorimer's hard sell[18] would have appalled him. All Crawley's work came from contacts made as he eddied around the wealthy, middle-class world to which he belonged. The fleet of liners that he decorated after 1912 for Canadian Pacific Ocean Services was the result of his friendship with the company's European manager, Maitland Kersey. It was only through knowing his first client, Henry Phipps, socially (they were neighbours in Hertfordshire) that he fell into the business of architecture and decoration at all. Phipps was the millionaire partner of Andrew Carnegie. After dinner one night, Crawley talked with such enthusiasm about Phipps's plans for decorating his new house in New York that, a few months later, Phipps asked him to undertake it. This led to other work done for Phipps and his son, Jay: decorating a house in Westbury, New York, a tenement in Allegheny City and skyscrapers in Pittsburg. Money seemed limitless, and when Crawley insisted on using English stone carvers, they were brought over specially, despite the fact that they had to spend six months idle before they could join a union and so become entitled to work. But, as an amateur, cost was a secondary consideration with Crawley. 'Any niggardly bargaining with artists used to stir him to intense irritation,' wrote his friend Cuthbert Headlam in a memoir, 'for to him money had little value for its own sake, whilst a beautiful picture or other work of art meant everything in the world.'[36]

The only country house that Crawley designed from new was Thornhaugh Hall, near Peterborough, for his brother-in-law, Stanley Brotherhood. It is in an unexciting Jacobean style. Crawley's ability to handle the true quality of architecture, form, was necessarily limited. He was at his best when given a theme, in the shape of a suggestive pre-existing structure: this would inspire him, and he would weave around the core of an old building lyrical, fanciful and impossibly romantic variations 'like a rhapsody on Igtham Mote'.[19] His masterpiece was Crowhurst Place, near Lingfield, in Surrey, a fifteenth-century house which Crawley acquired for himself in about 1907.[20] It was a place to recover after two years' of working 'at fever heat' (his wife's phrase) in New York.

Peaceful it must have been. Pre-alteration photographs and drawings show Crowhurst as a tumbledown farmhouse reached only by a wooden bridge across the willow-fringed moat, with ducks paddling up to the foundations. Mrs Crawley was distinctly unimpressed: she knew what she would be letting herself in for if she consented to live in the house while restoration went on around her, and she was right. Headlam's memoir contains a harrowing account of the first Christmas at Crowhurst. One of the two guests who managed to get to the feast huddled by the fireplace as snow gusted in through the cracks. Externally the house was not even particularly attractive, beyond the moss-covered roofs and tile-hanging. There was no half-timbering, none of the quaint bits of character that proliferated later. The real splendour of the house was a short but magnificently timbered hall of 1423;[21] and Crawley worked to bring the rest of the house up to that standard. He was forced to go slowly, as income permitted—hence the discomfort. Nevertheless, he developed ideas about farming and was intensely proud of his home. 'There was nothing which George liked more than to pick up a congenial friend in London and to take him down to Crowhurst in a taxi,' wrote Headlam. But he had only just finished restoring the house when his wife, suffering in health, found she could stand it no longer, and he was forced to part with Crowhurst in 1910.

Happily, an ideal new owner came forward in the form of Consuelo, Duchess of Marlborough.[22] Crowhurst was a refuge to her also—this time from Blenheim during the period of her divorce. Nothing could have been a greater contrast to Vanbrugh's Baroque palace, which she hated, and this was perhaps why she chose it. She felt that Crowhurst 'had the charm of an old engraving', and it was convenient for London. But it did not have enough space for the servants, so she retained Crawley to add a wing on the north-east side. The wing was not entirely new, because it kept the ground floor of the north-east corner, which was made into the kitchen, intact, and the foundations of a demolished range were re-used. But the end product was a storey taller, jettied out over a wall faced in a picturesque medley of stone, half-timber and diamond-patterned brick. Out of the deep stone roof rise chimneys of elaborate but traditional design—much more interesting than the ones they replaced. It does not look new; Crawley took pains that it should not. The first-floor windows, for instance, are all of different sizes and do not sit above the bressummer but dig into it, as though they were later additions. At the other end of the house Crawley added new sitting and garden rooms in half-timbered style. Between the two new extensions, he added on the north-west front a new half-timbered gable and a porch (both based on the Guildhall at Lavenham, illustrated in Garner and Stratton's book) and an elegant semi-circular bay window to the hall (Plate 112). The bay window is the only thing to give the date away.

111. The new wing at Crowhurst Place, Surrey, built by George Crawley in 1912. Only the foundations are old.

112. The garden front at Crowhurst. The porch and window bay were added by Crawley.

Such melodious results were achieved against odds. 'It was only natural,' states Headlam ingenuously, 'in view of his total lack of technical training, that George was less efficient on the practical as opposed to the creative side of his work as an architect.' His obituary in the *Architects' Journal*[23] described how his vision was realised. It compared his method of working to Balzac's endless correction of proofs: 'Crawley, having unfolded his ideas to a conventionally-trained architectural draughtsman, would correct the drawings until, finally, they took the shape of the building he had conceived.' Laborious, possibly haphazard, yet the infinite care Crawley took, working as an artist rather than an architect, created a piece of pastoral fantasy akin to Marie Antoinette's *hameau* in the grounds of Versailles. Indeed, Consuelo Vanderbilt still talked of the farmyard, although the moat was now stocked with swans rather than ducks.

Crowhurst was (and still is) enchanting—at least Consuelo Vanderbilt thought so, and her eulogies are a tribute to Crawley, even if she does not once mention his name. 'The simple charm of Crowhurst,' she wrote, 'the fact that one lived in a garden, the roses and honeysuckle climbing into one's windows, the flowers at one's feet as one opened the door, awakened in everyone a gentleness sometimes wholly unexpected.' During the First World War it was a retreat. Consuelo used to sit on the lawn waiting for news from the front, and she experienced a mother's anxiety every time the butler came out waving a telegram. Margot Asquith came down, and so did her husband, the prime minister. Lord Hugh Cecil and Lytton Strachey played tennis like 'figures in an Italian primitive come to life'. It was idyllic. Yet sometimes the comparison with the *hameau* at Versailles seems rather too close for comfort. One night during dinner, Asquith, as was only natural under the circumstances, slated the Kaiser, and it was agreed the latter ought to be hanged. After Asquith had left the room, another guest, the Grand Duke Dmitri, turned to his neighbour and said: 'De quel droit ces gens-là se permettent-ils de nous critiquer?—What right have such people to criticise us? Consuelo Vanderbilt was appalled; revolution was not to be the way England would change. But change there would be, and nobody imagined that things would be the same after the war.

Tudor in the Twenties

Like many another, George Crawley's practice was hard hit by the war.[24] But the early 1920s did give him one chance to lyricise in the Tudor vein. This was the restoration of Old Surrey Hall,[25] a fifteenth-century hall that had, like Crowhurst, fallen into decay during use as a farmhouse. Old Surrey Hall (Plate 113) had been built by a branch of the Gainsford family that lived at Crowhurst, which was only some half dozen miles to the south-east. It was probably the example of what had been done at the latter house that made the Hon. Mrs George Napier[26] go to Crawley for hers. First, the internal divisions that had disfigured the hall had to be removed to open it up again to the roof. But this cut down on the already limited accommodation, so from either end of the hall Crawley brought forth new wings in half-timber and stone to contain bedrooms on one side and a kitchen, pantry and servants' hall on the other.

Seeing Old Surrey Hall today, one might have thought he did more; but it was Walter Godfrey who closed the mouth of the U-court in 1937 (Crawley had died eleven years earlier) and added a further range to the south (Plate 114). Godfrey's work is slightly less

13. Crawley's additions at Old Surrey Hall. The fifteenth-century hall is out of sight between the two projecting wings

14. Old Surrey Hall, with Walter Godfrey's wing of 1937

plausible than Crawley's: the first-floor corridor that links the north and south wings is a shade too self-consciously picturesque, although there were sound reasons for it—the hall having been restored to one storey, servants had to go through it on the way from their wing to the bedrooms; the alternative route via a dark subterranean passage had presumably become unacceptable by the late 1930s. Godfrey also introduced some Classical details. But the spirit is the same, and shows that the Tudor taste continued in full spate well after the architectural establishment had become dominated by the Modern Movement.

Strangely, in view of what was finally done, Godfrey's client, Colonel Ian Anderson,[27] had originally employed a modernist architect. Joseph Emberton, the architect of Simpson's store, in Piccadilly,[28] was a personal friend, but pressure of work prevented him from making more than internal alterations; and, as H. Dalton Clifford, who had worked in Emberton's office, wrote in *Country Life*, 'it is perhaps just as well that none of his work appears on the outside'.[29] The switch of architects suggests that to Anderson, a stockbroker, although certainly not to all Tudor taste clients, the style was not part of a larger view of life. Out of the garage that Crawley had enterprisingly created from a medieval barn by the approach to the house would emerge Anderson's Rolls-Royce, with the ultimate *nouveau riche* gimmick of gilded lion-head masks on the ends of the exhaust pipes.[30]

But this was 1937. Chronologically, it is necessary to return to Crawley's time at Crowhurst, and the burst of—again apparently unrelated—Tudor taste building before, during and after the First World War. Maurice Webb created Ellens, at Rudgwick, in Sussex, for Frederick Warburg in 1914.[31] An old farmhouse was engulfed in new, old-looking accretions. Webb ransacked the countryside to find sufficient old Horsham stone slates, which were carefully removed so as not to damage the moss, and timbers from derelict farmhouses and barns. The workmen were forbidden to use plumblines or levels in case they inadvertently built a straight line. As an interpretation of Elizabethan architecture it could not have been a greater contrast to Yeaton Peverey House, Shropshire, built by Maurice Webb's father, Sir Aston, in 1890.[32]

Again in Sussex, but on a slightly larger scale than Ellens, a traditional-looking manor house was evolved out of an unsatisfactory Regency building at Nymans (Plate 117), which Lieutenant-Colonel Leonard Messel, father of the decorator Oliver Messel, inherited in 1915. The Messels had an attachment to the house, which had been Leonard Messel's boyhood home, but required a building that would set off Mrs Messel's oak furniture. Consequently, Norman Evill built a 'Tudor' front and Walter Tapper a mock fourteenth-century great hall. Christopher Hussey entered into the spirit of the thing and wrote a spoof topographical history for *Country Life*.[33]

In the years after the First World War, architects of an erudite turn of mind found they had time to devote to these witty, piecemeal undertakings. Philip Tilden launched into the restoration of Long Crendon Manor, in Oxfordshire, as a kind of therapy for his client, Mrs Hohler. He had been introduced to her by Vita Sackville-West, whom he had met at the house of another client, Sir Louis Mallet. The Hohlers had bought Long Crendon when Arthur Hohler returned wounded from the front, but he died soon after. Under Tilden's hands, Long Crendon grew 'from a mere farm of four or five bedrooms and a couple or so of sitting rooms, into a house of five sitting rooms, each of them large and

115. Detail from the front doorway at Ellens, Sussex

116. Panel depicting the Arts of Building over the Great Marlborough Street entrance of Liberty's, London

individual, with nearly twenty bedrooms'.[34] The primitive planning arrangements were retained by providing independent staircases to the bedrooms to save the anachronism of corridors. Although Tilden was a professional architect, he worked with a small team of builders from the local firm, and had no clerk of works. During the restoration he and his wife and Mrs Hohler actually lived in the old house, until it became too draughty and they moved into a nearby thatched cottage. Some of the work of stripping stucco from the Tudor beams they did themselves, 'when we felt energic enough,' Tilden remembered. Bouts of activity were interspersed with jaunts by bicycle and pony and 'jingle' (a kind of trap) to explore the local building traditions, with Tilden doing stunts on his bicycle to keep their minds off worse things.

By the mid-1920s, the examples of small half-timbered houses being moved or smaller country houses being built in faithful Tudor styles out of old materials had become too numerous to catalogue.[35] The Prince of Wales even used one as his 'summer residence' in 1926.[36]

The same year Sir John de Fonblaque Pennefather, first baronet, a Lancashire cotton broker and M.P., employed B.C. Deacon to remodel Eastwell Park, in Kent, a very long and ungainly building that, having been leased to the first Duke of Edinburgh, Edward

117. Nymans, Sussex

xix. Dovecote at Nymans

VII's younger brother, had been one of the smart country houses of the Edwardian age. The central block (Colour Plate xx) was turned into a replica of Sir John's former home in Hertfordshire, Markyate Cell, while a lyrical Tudor range was built to create an enclosed courtyard on the entrance front (Plate 9). Sir John quickly found he could not live in the house and sold it to Viscount Dunsford almost as soon as work was finished in 1927.

A few years earlier two London buildings of 1924 had confirmed that the style had arrived. At the Wembley Exhibition, on a site near the British Government Pavilion, the Federated Home-Grown Timber Merchants' Association erected an Old English house, faithfully imitating a half-timbered building 'assumed to have been constructed in 1480'.[37] But the real weather vane of taste was Liberty's store. When it came to rebuilding their Great Marlborough Street shop, the directors decided on a large but intimate Tudor taste building, which, as Ivor Stewart-Liberty himself wrote, 'would express their own ideals, give room for expansion at a reasonable cost, and enable them to show their goods in rooms of a height and kind in which people are in the habit of living, and where dress and decoration can be seen in their proper proportion and judged on their true merits.'[38] By this date, in contrast to Blomfield's views on the English Renaissance, it seemed that 'The Tudor period is the most genuinely English period of domestic architecture.' The timbers came from old two-decker men-of-war, H.M.S. *Hindustan* and H.M.S. *Impregnable*. At the insistence of the ground landlords of Regent Street, the Office of Woods, Forest and Land Revenues, the Regent Street frontage was built in a grand Classical style; yet this only served to bring forth another quaint device—a three-storeyed bridge to connect the Regent Street and Great Marlborough Street blocks.

The response of the building papers reflects the attitude of the architectural profession to the Tudor taste. The *Building News* was patronising, where it could be, but fair: 'not the layman only,' wrote the correspondent, 'but the critically-minded architect, has to admit, reluctantly as it were, its charm'.[39] The same writer felt it necessary to absolve the architects, the late E. T. Hall and E. Stanley Hall, from the responsibility of having chosen the style: left to themselves, it was 'by no means improbable' that they 'might have wished to have designed in a style more commonly accepted as being suitable to the twentieth century'. Messrs Liberty had to shoulder the blame. But they had wanted a building that would be popular, and popular it was. When it was finished the owners were sent a petition signed by all the workmen employed asking if they might bring their wives and children to see the completed job. How much stronger must its appeal have been to the Liberty's customers, venturing up, perhaps, from the half-timbered commuter and seaside colonies of Oxted, Angmering and Thorpeness.

Built in London, there was never any chance that Liberty's would be as quaint or cranky as the more extreme Tudor taste country houses. Consequently it looks surprisingly like the half-timbered buildings of Victorian Chester or the country houses of Grayson and Ould. It is worth remembering that these buildings were still admired. In 1929 Sir Ernest Royden, a ship-owner, demolished his late father-in-law's house in Frankby, Cheshire, called Hill Bark, and transported his own—Bidston Court, Birkenhead, built by A. E. Ould for the soap manufacturer R. W. Hudson in 1892—to the site: Birkenhead had become too suburban. 'The removal and rebuilding should result in preserving in delightful surroundings an excellent piece of modern architecture,' commented the *Builder*.[40]

171

xx. Eastwell Park, Kent

In that same year, 1929, the style even acquired its own literature in the form of *The House Desirable* by P. A. Barron.[41] This document is peculiarly of its age. The author saw the countryside entirely with the motorist's eye, and if the impression received was slightly blurred as a result—well, that would be all to the benefit of the Tudor taste. 'Why cannot such homes be built to-day?' Barron expects his readers to ask on seeing his illustrations. In fact, nearly all the buildings had been built since the First World War, and the author showed how they could be obtained. This was not necessarily to be done by employing a professional architect. Barron applauds the artist and plain builder—a sentiment George Crawley would have approved—and offers advice on how to persuade professional bricklayers, likely to take an awkward pride in the regularity of their work, to lay old bricks 'all wibbly wobbly', as a craftsman might have expressed it. He suggests ruses to win round the district surveyor to the use of time-worn timbers and walls out of plumb; and there are the inevitable jokes about new houses being visited by tourists admiring their (as they think) quaint old workmanship.

Some of Barron's illustrations show old buildings that have been extended or adapted in the Tudor taste; others are converted barns; and a whole chapter is devoted to 'new houses which are designed and built in such fashion that it is difficult to distinguish them from truly old buildings'. He finds an extraordinary number of examples: Tudor Close, Rottingdean, a close of small houses erected by developers 'who realised that the old-world charm of Rottingdean was of commercial value'; Normandy Hall at Worthing, which L. J. and I. Williams of Oxted (specialists in this type of work) built as a copy of Stragglethorp Old Hall, in Lincolnshire; and several houses by Blunden Shadbolt, L.R.I.B.A., of which the most fanciful is Smuggler's Way (Plates 118–20), in Hampshire, of 1925—so crooked and full of so many 'old world' motifs that it strays across the border from pastoral idyll to *opera buffa* or Aldwych Farce (it was in fact so inconvenient that the owners sold it in 1932 and built another house, more modern in style, close by).[42] Even so, despite the fact that the author by his own estimation motored many thousands of miles collecting material, he failed to discover Crowhurst, Old Surrey Hall, Long Crendon, Wyke Manor or any of the works of Major Smith. There is no doubt about the Tudor taste's popularity, but the different practitioners often do not seem to have known about each other's works. Nothing could be in more absolute contrast to the Modern Movement and Amyas Connell, building the first concrete house—High and Over—in 1928. The one was doctrinaire, liked by intellectuals (the client at High and Over was a professor of Classics at London University), but low in mass appeal; the other was essentially a spontaneous movement, had no core or theory, and was akin, however remotely, to the semi-detached houses about to line by-passes and arterial roads throughout the country.

Barron saw no dichotomy between motoring and the Tudor taste: he thought it would particularly suit the 'wealthy woman of to-day' who would prefer a week-end cottage to a country house. Few of his examples, including the larger ones like Ellens and Smuggler's Way, have more than a few acres attached. There is no suggestion that the fantasy should have gone beyond the architecture. But that was not the attitude of the wealthy woman of the day, the society hostess Lady Moyne, who was the driving force behind the most extreme—and most successful—of all Tudor taste country houses, Bailiffscourt (Plate 121).

172

118–20. Instant antiquity: before, during and after construction of Smuggler's Way, Dorset, 1925

Bailiffscourt

The architect of the new house was Amyas Phillips, and it was his only architectural commission.[43] He had not been trained as an architect, having left Christ Church, Oxford, early to work in his father's antiques business at Hitchin, in Hertfordshire. It is his father's name, F. W. Phillips, which apears on the plans. The connection with the Moynes began when they called one day to look at furniture. Phillips began to advise them on antiques, and from this it was a relatively small step to decorating their town house at No. 10 Grosvenor Place. Phillips decorated Grosvenor Place in a Strawberry Hill Gothick style, with a lift that looked like 'a tiny medieval closet'.

> The downstairs rooms were lined—panelled is not the word—with rough, blackened wood. The fires were encouraged to smoke and smoulder, because the effect Lady Evelyn wished to create was that of a house so 'early' that chimneys had not been invented. The furniture, besides refectory tables black with age—or with simulated age—one did not always quite believe in the Grosvenor Place furniture—consisted of dozens of Spanish chairs, of various sizes but similar designs, a strip of dark, hard leather for the back, another for the seat, with many a rusty nail to catch a stocking here and there in the crumbling wooden frame. The lamps were made of bent pieces of iron holding sham yellow candles with yellow bulbs of about five watts shaded in thick old parchment—tallow, not wax, was the note.[44]

Success for Phillips at Grosvenor Place led in turn to Bailiffscourt. There the maids wore long medieval gowns, which could sometimes catch out unsuspecting guests. The young Duke of Bedford (then Marquess of Tavistock) spent some time in desultory conversation with one of them before realising that she was not a fellow guest.[45]

Living the part as Lady Moyne did was not wholly new. In 1920 E. F. Benson published a novel, *Queen Lucia*, about the arrival of an Indian guru in Riseholme, an artistic village near Stratford-on-Avon. The heroine was Mrs Lucas, the wife of a successful barrister, who lived in The Hurst, a house made out of three cottages knocked together, with a new wing—'if anything a shade more blatantly Elizabethan than the stem on to which it was grafted'—at the back. The bedrooms were named after Shakespeare plays like *Hamlet* and *Othello*, and it was the new wing that contained

> the famous smoking-parlour, with rushes on the floor, a dresser ranged with pewter tankards, and leaded lattice-windows of glass so antique that it was practically impossible to see out of them . . . Here, though in the rest of the house she had, for the sake of convenience, allowed the installation of electric light, there was no such concession made, and sconces on the walls held dim iron lamps, so that only those of the most acute vision were able to read. Even to them reading was difficult, for the book-stand on the table contained nothing but a few crabbed black-letter volumes dating from not later than the early seventeenth century, and you had to be in a fanatically Elizabethan frame of mind to be at ease there. But Mrs. Lucas often spent rare leisure moments there, playing on the virginal that stood in the window, or kippering herself in the smoke of the wood-fire as with streaming eyes she deciphered an Elzevir Horace, rather late for inclusion under the rule, but an undoubted bargain.[46]

121. Bailiffscourt, Sussex, built in 1931

122. The courtyard of Bailiffscourt

123. Doorway to the courtyard at Bailiffscourt

There was a good deal of Mrs Lucas in Lady Moyne, although the latter had married a Guinness not a barrister and her guests were likely to be Dukes and cabinet ministers rather than the artistic, retired professionals of Riseholme. Lord Moyne (then Walter Guinness)[47] bought Bailiffscourt and an estate of seven hundred and fifty acres in 1927. Although the house that was built is a country house in the traditional sense of a nobleman's seat and a family home, and has a farm attached, the reason for choosing the site was to be near the sea. Lord Moyne was a keen yachtsman, and even before the house was built Lady Moyne, her children and their friends used to stay in a construction known as 'the huts'—a long, weatherboarded bungalow in a field next to the beach.[48] And there was also a social reason, because Bailiffscourt was convenient for Goodwood.

The name derives from the twelfth-century house from which lay-brothers and a bailiff-monk administered the Sussex estates of the Abbey of Seez.[49] All that remained from this period was the so-called Norman chapel (the twelfth-century building was in fact demolished and rebuilt in the thirteenth century, re-using some of the original stones).[50] The farmhouse was an early Georgian building, chiefly remarkable for having

176

124. Chevron-moulded doorway to the guest house, Bailiffscourt, reconstructed from fragments found in the walls of the demolished farmhouse

125. Room at Bailiffscourt with pseudo-medieval furniture

126. Wardrobe at Bailiffscourt made from pieces of old oak

been the home of 'Colonel' Barker, a notorious local woman who dressed as a man and married a local girl (the subject was *not* discussed in the presence of Lady Moyne). When the building was demolished, the walls were found to contain fragments of the Benedictine structure.

Phillips described himself as an 'antiquarian' rather than an antique dealer, and the distinction is both just and suggestive. He was capable of erudition, as when he wrote a ten-page dissertation on the architectural history of the Norman chapel at Bailiffscourt. He produced several beautiful books, including *Old English Chintzes*, privately printed, which must have been one of the first publications to take a serious interest in the history of fabrics.[51] But there was another side to his mind, and he was happy to abandon scholarly principles to design pseudo-medieval two-pronged forks and pewter plates for Lady Moyne (the plates were hammered out by the chauffeur in his spare time). And guests were right to suspect the authenticity of the furniture. The main rooms at Bailiffscourt were furnished with splendid tapestries and antiques of the richest kind, but strange hybrids lurked in the bedrooms and corridors (Plate 126). These were made in Phillips's Hitchin workshops from sections of old carving that once belonged to quite different types of object. Chests, tables and cupboards were made in this way:[52] they evince an extraordinary reversion in taste to the mid-nineteenth-century fashion for cobbling together disparate bits of 'olde oake' that was started at Charlecote. Chips Channon hit the right note when he said that 'every guest room is decorated to resemble the cell of a rather "pansy" monk'.[53]

Architecturally, Bailiffscourt is a blend of fantasy and scholarship. The plan, without a hall or screens passage, is unlike that of any existing medieval house. But it is genuinely medieval in spirit. The principal rooms are not connected by corridors, but communicate directly into each other. As at Long Crendon, the bedrooms are reached by individual staircases giving off the courtyard—guests would have had to go outside to get to them. Most of the details Phillips designed were based on medieval examples, such as the Fish House at Mere, Wiltshire, or the St Mary's Guild building at Lincoln. He also restored. Old stones found in the walls of the demolished farmhouse were carefully reassembled into their original form as doorways and windows. These, like the twelfth-century doorcase that forms the entrance to the detached guest house (Plate 124), were used again in the new Bailiffscourt, and Phillips's restoration of the Norman chapel is an exemplum of care and restraint.

Other details in the new building came from elsewhere. Some were taken from Somerset, perhaps to be in sympathy with the tawny Somerset stone out of which Bailiffscourt is built. The entrance archway was once part of Holditch Priory; the fifteenth-century oak door to the entrance hall originally belonged to South Wanborough church and was discovered in the stables of a nearby farmhouse; and a two-light oak window on the entrance front of the house was rescued from a derelict building near Muchelney Abbey. But Hertfordshire, where Phillips lived, was another source: the fireplace in the dining room and the oak screen in the bedroom above it both came from buildings in Hitchin that were being destroyed by the local authority.

A number of whole buildings were transported bodily and set down in the rough grass around the house. A fifteenth-century gatehouse (Plate 127), otherwise doomed to be pulled down and sold for building materials, was brought from Loxwood, in Sussex. Adjoining it is a seventeenth-century half-timbered house from Old Basing, in Hampshire. What is now a sandstone and thatch electricity sub-station came from Bignor, in Sussex. The only new outbuilding is the garage, a thatched, stone-walled building, with tiny medieval windows and a buttress—very much a 'garage desirable'.

The buildings were cossetted during removal. Phillips developed a special technique to ensure the minimum disturbance. 'Each brick panel in the timber framework was first strengthened with cement on its reverse, or invisible, side so that these panels could be removed intact, complete even to the old mortar joints.'[54] As many of the buildings would otherwise have been destroyed, this was an effective way of preserving them. Indeed, the Moynes had been partly motivated by preservationist feelings when they bought the Bailiffscourt site, which was due to be covered in small houses by a speculative developer. Altogether it is an indication of Phillips's antiquarian rather than sentimental or purely picturesque approach that the outbuildings are grouped randomly and do not 'compose'. The effect is more like an open-air museum—or a genuinely medieval settlement—than Nash's Blaise Hamlet.

For all that, there was a strong element of caprice. A block built separately to the north was linked to the main house by an underground passage. Plans call this the 'guest house', although the Duke of Bedford remembers that Bailiffscourt was really two houses: 'Lord

127. The gatehouse at Bailiffscourt, constructed from a fifteenth-century building from Loxwood, Sussex, and a seventeenth-century one from Old Basing, Hampshire

and Lady Moyne lived very much their own separate lives . . . Lady Moyne lived on one side of the tunnel and he and the children lived on the other.'[55] Perhaps this is why the guest house was extended in 1933, in a style which was consciously more picturesque than the rest and intended, it seems, to suggest a ruin.

In *Queen Lucia*, The Hurst was approached through a Shakespeare garden, in which only the flowers distributed by Ophelia were planted. It was consequently a Spring garden, bare in July and August, although there was celebration when the first violet or daffodil appeared above the soil. Lady Moyne went further, and allowed no cultivated flowers at all at Bailiffscourt.

Her passion was for wild flowers, but the soil was so bad that cow parsley, grasses and

180

bullrushes were grown in bowls, and even dandelions and other weeds were raised under wires to protect them. On the train down from Victoria and Arundel Lady Moyne would scatter weeds and wild seeds from the windows. 'Walter doesn't quite approve,' she told Diana Mitford (soon to be married to the Moynes' eldest son, Bryan); her husband was then Minister of Agriculture.[56]

Sir Philip Sassoon used to say that the wild flowers were as expensive as orchids. It is perhaps a token of her conviction that Lady Moyne spent so much on them. Even so, their much prized simplicity was in stark contrast to the coveys of Duchesses and fashionable Goodwood guests who used to stay in the house. Lady Moyne did not herself wear medieval gowns but dressed at Paquin and this paradox is expressed in the grounds. The approach to planting trees was the same as to erecting buildings. Dozens of big trees, some twenty-five years old, were dug up from the Downs and transported with their roots encased. Cranes were used to erect them, and they were kept upright by steel hawzers. Amazingly, most survived this treatment, although their roots never took.

This practice would have been unforgivable according to eighteenth-century picturesque theory, by which landowners were expected to plant not for themselves but for ensuing generations. However, such confidence in the future was no longer possible, and the symbolism of the trees was proved right. Bailiffscourt had a tragically short life as a family home. Lady Moyne died in 1939, six years after the house was finished; Lord Moyne was assassinated by the Stern gang while serving as British Minister in Cairo in 1944. The family did not go back to the house after they had vacated it during the Second World War. After thirty or forty years Lady Moyne's transplanted trees blew over one by one as the hawzers rusted through.

Low-built, almost lost in the summer haze rising from the surrounding cornfields, the house possessed, as Chips Channon wrote, 'a stillness that reminds one of the Emilian plains near Ravenna'. There was nothing frenzied. Nevertheless, if the houses of the Modern Movement were built for occupants living their 'little time of sunshine' between two wars, Bailiffscourt and other Tudor taste country houses are equally the product of a generation that was too impatient to allow time to take its course. Even age had to be instant.

6. *Castles of Comfort*

'*I* do wish he didn't want a Castle, but just a delicious loveable house with plenty of good large rooms in it,' wrote Lutyens when Julius Drewe offered him what should—at £50,000—have been the commission of a lifetime to build Castle Drogo.[1] In the south, the building of castles—popular with the chivalrous Victorians—had come to seem too obvious a way of expressing a sense of romance. The quaintness and discomfort and historical associations of an old castle, such as Lutyens restored on Lindisfarne and Lambay, were far more suggestive to the twentieth-century imagination. Millionaires like William Waldorf Astor and William Randolph Hearst thought so too, and wanted to buy the real thing rather than build their own, even if comfort and a good number of bathrooms were also priorities. The restoration of Hever and St Donat's Castles show many of the stylistic attitudes of the Tudor taste, and the assumptions underlying them, writ large.

The scene was rather different in Scotland, however, where a tradition of fortified architecture was the native building style. The great five-volume source book on Scottish Baronial, Ross and MacGibbon's *The Castellated and Domestic Architecture of Scotland*, was not published until 1887–92. The style was not only expected of a vast and unoriginal pile like Sydney Mitchell's Sauchieburn (Plate 129), described as 'one of the biggest houses in the country' when it was built in 1890,[2] but became the vernacular for Arts and Crafts architects. To Lorimer, pepperpot turrets and bastions were the equivalent of Lutyens's half-timbering, tile-hanging and hipped roofs. Individually, the elements that went to make up Sauchieburn were of the same race as those in Lorimer's Ardkinglas (Colour Plate XXI)—the difference lay in the lyricism of Lorimer's composition, in the drama of his planning, which made maximum capital out of the traditional disposition of rooms on several floors, and in the quality of the materials. Having been intimately bound up heart, mind and soul with Ardkinglas for two years (a staggeringly short period of building, but the client was over seventy when work began), Lorimer had a lump in his throat as if 'saying goodbye to a child' when he made his final tour of inspection.[3]

Lorimer, who had himself been brought up at Kellie Castle, also restored several castles, including Lympne, Dunderave and Balmanno. The latter, which he did for the Glasgow ship-owner W. S. Miller, was said to have been the only commission in which he would have liked to have lived himself. Although in silhouette the house remained largely the same except for the roof and a new service wing, he restored the interior, rearranged it,

·183

128. The parapets at Castle Drogo, Devon

129. Sauchieburn Castle, Stirlingshire

130. Ardkinglas, Argyllshire

furnished it and laid out the gardens. But, as at Lindisfarne, an element of discomfort was an inescapable part of the romance, and it was not one that the owner's wife much appreciated. She could not be tempted away from her flat in Pollockshields where she liked to live in surroundings of distinctly unromantic cosiness 'with red petticoats round all the lights'.[4]

But there were also other Sauchieburns. When George Bullough, created a baronet in 1910, pulled down the house he inherited on the island of Rhum in 1891, he is supposed to have declared that he wanted a house as long as his yacht.[5] The yacht in question, the *Rhouma*, was big enough to be turned into a hospital ship during the Boer War and had taken Bullough on a two-year cruise to celebrate his twenty-first birthday. For an architect he went to the big municipal firm of Leeming and Leeming in London, who were well known for their outstandingly ugly addition of 1884 to the Admiralty in Whitehall. Kinloch Castle (Plate 131) on Rhum was long and low, roughly square in plan, and built of red sandstone brought over from the Isle of Arran. It had a lavish organ in the corridor, a kind of proto-Wurlitzer costing £2,000 and fitted with drums, trumpets and bells. It was not a very convincing castle.

In emulation of Balmoral, a piper played round Kinloch Castle every morning. The same routine was followed at Skibo, which was like Kinloch but bigger. Andrew Carnegie bought the estate in 1898. A contemporary estimate had it that from 1900 to 1903 he spent £100,000 altering and extending the nineteenth-century building already on site. That is not impossible, because he sold the United States Steel Corporation in 1901 for £100 million. Virtually all trace of the original house was lost in the remodelling.

131. Kinloch Castle on the Isle of Rhum

132. Skibo Castle, Sutherland, rebuilt by Andrew Carnegie

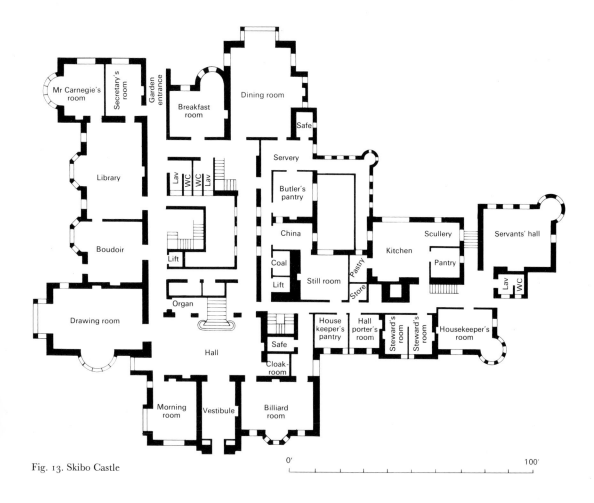

Mr Carnegie's room

Secretary's room

Garden entrance

Breakfast room

Dining room

Safe

Servery

Library

Lav WC WC Lav

Butler's pantry

China

Scullery

Servants' hall

Kitchen

Boudoir

Lift

Coal

Pastry

Pantry

Lav WC

Lift

Still room

Store

Organ

Drawing room

Hall

House keeper's pantry

Hall porter's room

Steward's room

Steward's room

Housekeeper's room

Safe

Cloak-room

Morning room

Vestibule

Billiard room

Fig. 13. Skibo Castle

0'   100'

At first sight, Skibo seems a kind of parody of the social country house. Although Carnegie's own tastes were comparatively simple, the castle was so big that he had to build another house, Altnager Lodge, a couple of miles away for him and his wife to go to as a retreat: Skibo itself was used for entertaining Carnegie's powerful Liberal friends, like Lloyd George and Lord Morley, Gladstone's biographer. Two hundred tons of steel from Carnegie's Pittsburg steelworks were used in the alterations. When the house was finished, it was, almost inevitably, visited by Edward VII for luncheon—an occasion which, like the screaming checks and plaid of Carnegie's coaching attire, was evidence both of the owner's desire to be part of the top level of Edwardian society and of his almost wilful failure to sound the right note. Carnegie received the king in the library and read a poem composed for his birthday by Joaquin Miller, 'the poet of the Sierras'. The opening lines included the invocation 'Hail, fat Edward!' which Carnegie jocosely underlined by saying, 'That's you, Sir.'[6] It went down like a stone. Carnegie was too much of a democrat to be part of the smart set, and Skibo had not—for all its vast bulk—been conceived principally for social reasons. Having been brought up in a Perthshire weaver's cottage, he returned to the Highlands out of sentiment. 'I will lift up mine eyes unto the hills' was carved on the balustrade of a terrace constructed on the south side of the house to take advantage of the view across the Dornoch Firth to the hills of Ross. Originally Skibo was to have been simply a home for himself and his family; he seems not to have envisaged how it would turn out.[7]

The architects were Ross and Macbeth of Inverness. The senior partner, Dr Alexander Ross, was an old-fashioned Victorian who had done very well out of the Highland boom of the 1850s and 1860s, building houses and shooting lodges as well as schools and—his *magnum opus*—Inverness Cathedral.[8] As a composition, Skibo is not a thing of great subtlety, although the pinkish granite is well cut and the decoration—beasts over the window and thistles on the skyline—is restrained. Inside, the house is planned around the hall, panelled in dark fumed oak and hung with trophies of stags and moose. A broad staircase of Sicilian marble sweeps down next to the organ, and over the landing is a big stained-glass window by Gerald Moira telling the story of the house and Carnegie's own fairy-tale of capitalist endeavour.[9] It was typical of Carnegie's didactic interest in history. The inner lights show owners of the previous house on the site—the thirteenth-century Bishop Gilbert of Dornoch, the Viking Chief, Sigurd—and the Marquess of Montrose, imprisoned at Skibo in 1650. The outer lights depict, on the left-hand side, the humble croft in which Carnegie was born and the sailing ship which first took his impoverished family to America when he was a child. On the right-hand side is the liner on which, years later, he made his return—shown steaming out of New York harbour with the Statue of Liberty in the background—and, below, Skibo Castle itself, pink, glittering and the symbol of self-made triumph.

It used to be said that the hen house at Skibo was better than any dwelling house at Dornoch, because the hen house had electric light. The big power house constructed towards the loch had a long underground chimney to prevent smoke blowing back onto the house higher up. But the real luxury at Skibo was the swimming pool (Plate 133)—a big stone building, with capitals of lizards and leaves. It was roofed in glass and iron like a conservatory, but the pool itself was made out of marble. The seawater for swimming was heated. The main space was big enough to act as a ballroom when the pool was covered over with a dance floor. 'Huge electric arc lamps and chandeliers glittered overhead,' remembered one visitor. 'Tubs of evergreens were spaced along the walls, and festoons of coloured paper chains and bunting hung overhead ... Mrs Logan's dance band from Inverness played in the balcony, varied by bagpipe music for Scotch Reels, Eightsome Reels, Highland Scottische and so forth, played so harmoniously by the Castle piper.'[10]

The contrast with Skibo makes Castle Drogo seem all the more remarkable (Colour Plate XXIII). It was built for Julius Drewe, who had made a fortune from the Home and Colonial Stores by the time he was thirty and retired shortly after. The site was chosen largely because of Drewe's romantic self-identification with Drewsteignton, the parish in which Castle Drogo is situated, which means 'Dru-his-town-on-the-Teign'. The castle pretence was carried through with romantic dedication. Drogo is a real castle, built in a position that was truly defensive and—on a promontory nine hundred feet above sea level overlooking Dartmoor—equally inconvenient. The look of the castle was carefully considered, and wooden mock-ups were erected to judge the effect of parts before building began. But the way of building was traditional. Every stone of the granite walls was laid by one of two masons, Devon-men called Cleeve and Dewdney. At one point Drewe

188

133. The swimming pool at Skibo, roofed in glass and lined in marble

insisted—although it was not ultimately possible—that every wall had to be six feet thick, like a real castle. And the long period of building, which lasted two decades, and the halts and changes of strategy made the comparison with medieval practice complete. Lutyens, dreaming of feudal England on a liner en route to South Africa, originally planned the castle to be three times its final size. It was partly Drewe's insistence on thick walls that caused the reduction in scale.

The architect pulled off a characteristically brilliant trick when he married a wing of three floors (for family and servants) with one of two (for state rooms), with a staircase between them (Colour Plate XXII). But the virtuosity of it does not make the house, with its granite staircases and corridors, livable. Nevertheless, it was initially conceived as a family home. Touchingly the site was chosen on a family picnic with Lutyens in tow, Mrs Drewe pulling up a mangold in a field to mark the spot where the drive was to begin. Unfortunately there was little time for Castle Drogo to function as it was intended, because Drewe died the year after it was completed.

Architects found that there were no more castles to build on that scale. 'It has been said that an Englishman's home is his castle,' mused Baillie Scott in 1933. 'This seems to be an overstatement. It is much more likely to be a jerry-built suburban residence, or perhaps a duplicated compartment in some vast honeycomb of flats. The castle as a model for a modern country house seems to have been strangely overlooked.'[11] The romantic impulse that led clients to castles had gone into restoring or adapting old ones rather than building from new.

Millionaires' Tudor

The first article to appear in the *Pall Mall Magazine* for 1907 was entitled 'Hever Restored'. The author frothily described how the elegant late fourteenth-century fortress, 'the daintiest of castles, a castle in miniature, a castle-ette, of the femine gender', was rescued from 'the possession of humble farmers whose ducks and geese swam in the old moat, whose kitchens were the once proud Hall, whose bacons and hams hung seasoning from the ancient beams, whose spades and shovels and hoes were piled in the ancient guard house, whose corn and potatoes lay stacked in the chambers that were haunted by so many memories'. It was signed coyly 'A Visitor', but anyone who read the publication regularly would have been familiar with those rhetorical, piled up phrases, and others could have made a simple deduction about the authorship: the *Pall Mall Magazine* was owned by William Waldorf Astor, the very man who had bought Hever in 1903.[12]

Astor wrote copiously. It has been said that he started the *Pall Mall Magazine* because the editor of the *Pall Mall Gazette*, which Astor had bought in 1893, tactfully refused his pieces on the grounds that they were too literary for a newspaper. He was a passionate romantic, writing terrible novels with titles such as *Sforza* and *Valentino* and dialogue full of Renaissance idioms like: 'By the keys of St Peter, you send me upon a thorny quest.'

To T. H. S. Escott, Astor generally satisfied 'the ideal of an Anglo Saxon gentleman'[13]—an unexpected judgement from so acerbic a critic, and one that leaves us still farther from penetrating the complexities of Astor's character. Although once a diplomat, he could be monstrously tactless—not only did he become a naturalised British subject but he incensed his fellow countrymen with his widely reported comment on leaving the United States in 1893: 'America is not a fit place for a gentleman to live.'[14]

The story of the Astor fortune is an American legend.[15] The family originated in the village of Waldorf, near Heidelberg. At about the time of the American War of Independence John Jacob Astor, the fifth son of a butcher, left to become an instrument maker in London, and then set out for the New World, taking with him five pounds in cash and some musical instruments with which he intended to open a business. An extraordinary meeting diverted his course. The brig that he crossed on, the *North Carolina*, became ice-bound in the Chesapeake Bay with a number of other ships; passengers walked from one to another over the ice, and it was in this way that Astor met a young fellow German who traded in furs. He became intrigued by the lucrative business and soon entered the fur trade himself. He was able to make a profit in London of one thousand per cent on skins that the Iroquois on the Candian border were happy to part with for cooking pans and pocket knives.

A portrait of John Jacob Astor hangs in the library at Hever (Plate 135), copied from one painted in 1794. By then he was reputed to be worth over $50,000. Profits were even more extravagant after 1800, when the Napoleonic Wars forced him to look for new markets and he began trading with China. The surplus was invested in land. It was an obvious enough decision perhaps—but what land! Astor bought farms on the edge of the expanding port of New York. He began with a half share in the seventy acre Eden estate, which cost him $70,000: it ran from what is now Broadway to the Hudson River, just north of 42nd Street. Newspapers at the time of his death calculated Astor's fortune at $20 million, which made him the richest man in America by far.

William Waldorf Astor, John Jacob's great-grandson, was not cast in the family mould. Although he remembered that his father had never taken a holiday beyond the week-end for seventeen years, he himself hated business. He once described his joyless childhood in a letter: 'I was myself brought up severely and kept upon a pitiful allowance [from coming of age until he was twenty-five he received the comparatively meagre figure of $1,800 a year] . . . The hellfire sermons of my childhood the like of which no congregation out of Scotland would listen to today frightened me silly and I knew those red hot things were being made ready for *me*.'[16] Spiritually, Astor was waiting to rebel against the Calvinist ethic. When, at the age of eighteen, he was introduced by his German tutor to Greek philosophy, the experience was one that he later compared to the conversion of St Paul. Professor Hinkel 'talked eloquently of the Greek ideal. To him the human body, brought to Grecian perfection, was the most splendid thing in the world.'[17] Like a character in a Henry James novel, Astor became devoted to beauty, although it was Italy rather than Greece that claimed his heart in the end.

Although introspective by nature, Astor nevertheless sought to establish an appropriate place in the world. In 1880 he was elected to the New York State Legislature and while

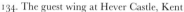

134. The guest wing at Hever Castle, Kent

135. Portrait of John Jacob Astor hanging in the library at Hever

136. (far right) The Long Gallery at Hever, with F. L. Pearson's ceiling

there introduced a number of bills, of which the most significant was one that required poisons to be sold in clearly labelled, dark-blue glass bottles with roughened sides. But he was not elected to Congress or re-elected to the State Legislature. However, his talents were recognised in the best possible way, because he was appointed American minister in Rome. There he took a suite in the Rospigliosi Palace and 'had so little to do' that he could devote himself to 'Archaeology, pictures, Renaissance history, and excursions in the thrill and glory of the Campagna'.[18] His official receptions were magnificent, but even these won little favour at home, since he was condemned for placing 'the mission to Italy beyond the occupation of anyone without private means'. In Rome he began forming the collection of Italian sculpture that Pickfords transported to Hever in 1905.

Astor bought Cliveden from the Duke of Westminster in 1893. It was redecorated and later became one of the great political centres of the country under the regime of his

192

forthright, teetotal daughter-in-law, Nancy Astor, the first woman to take her seat as an M.P. But Astor did not find English society easy to broach. His most famous and revealing gaffe was made at a concert at his town house in Carlton House Terrace. Captain Sir Berkley Milne, R.N., went in Lady Oxford's party, although he had not been personally invited. When Astor saw him, he asked him to leave and, despite a written apology, inserted a paragraph in the *Pall Mall Gazette* the next day stating that Sir Berkley had been there uninvited. Society was outraged, and the Prince of Wales promptly asked the unfortunate captain to his box at the theatre the next night—an unequivocal judgement from the highest authority.

That he built an addition containing twenty-five guest bedrooms at Hever shows that he continued to entertain. 'But how can I give up these parties of pleasant friends?' he replied when asked why he did not go to his villa at Sorrento during an attack of gout. Yet he was also intensely suspicious. After his London parties he did not sleep at Carlton House Terrace; instead, he went to the Astor Estate Office on the Embankment, where he had a small bedroom with a very large François Premier bed. 'There at least I am safe,' he mysteriously told Lady Warwick, whom he showed round the building. In one of the upstairs rooms he pointed to a lever by the side of his chair. 'If I were to press that,' he said, 'every door in the house would close, and you could not possibly get out without my permission.' Then he smiled as he added, 'you have nothing to be uneasy about, as you know, but I must take precautions.' They went into a room lined with steel, which Astor used as a strongroom. He produced a bag full of sovereigns:

> 'I keep ten thousand pounds in cash in this room,' he said. 'You never know when you may want money or when cheques may be difficult to cash. A man who succeeds as I have done has many enemies, and if he is wise he avoids all risks' . . . To think of this big man, with his prominent eyes, broad forehead, and the appearance of rugged strength, as one who was going about in fear of his life, seemed absolutely absurd, yet he meant every word he said.[19]

Security was equally important in the country, and it presented a vivid motive for buying a castle. At Cliveden he built tall walls around the park and stopped the public using the lake for boating. When he did the same thing at Hever, it gave rise to the joke that his real middle name was Walled-Off. 'It is necessary,' he said, 'to live securely.' Patrols of smart young policemen who might have been taken for house guests could be seen regularly combing the grounds. The drawbridge was restored and pulled up at night.

Astor's architect for restoring and adding to Hever was Frank Pearson, who had already worked on the Astor Estate Office begun eleven years earlier. In name, the Estate Office had been designed by his father, J. L. Pearson, but the elder Pearson was seventy-five years old and reluctant to take on the commission. Consequently, Frank designed much of the rich carving—showing Italian Renaissance as well as Gothic influences—that encrusts friezes, spandrels and pilaster strips. J. L. Pearson died in 1897, and the greater part of Frank's career was spent in completing his work, notably the cathedrals at Truro and Brisbane. Hever was his largest independent commission.[20]

Having bought the castle, Astor, according to his article in the *Pall Mall Magazine*, 'wished to live in comfort in his medieval stronghold, having no desire to call up from the past the phantoms of the Plague, the Black Death, or the Sweating Sickness, and other deadly dwellers in the castle of the Middle Ages. Again, he naturally wished to entertain his friends, but to house them in his Castle would necessitate the most radical changes in the very chambers he was bent on preserving intact.' The outside of the castle was left almost untouched, except for necessary repairs to the stonework. By building the guest rooms in a separate wing, the interior of the castle proper was given over, on the ground floor, to reception rooms, with only a few bedrooms on the upper floors. Unfortunately, the courtyard had suffered in a restoration campaign undertaken only a few years earlier. One Captain Sebright had demolished the genuine Tudor stables together with an old barn that stood two hundred yards from the house. He seems also to have replaced the gables of the inner courtyard with a parapet. This was altered again when the courtyard was virtually reconstructed around the surviving Tudor timbers, Pearson adding gables with elaborately carved bargeboards and dormers.

137. Open-work panel in the hall at Hever

Visitors were greeted by two figures in armour opposite the entrance door on the north side of the courtyard. No more than a corridor, the first room they entered was nevertheless 'furnished with cabinets, coffers, settles, noble chairs, and many a precious specimen of the artificer's skill and taste', preparing them for riches to come. Passing under a wooden four-centred arch, a few steps took them to one of the richest rooms in the castle, the inner hall: 'a lovely chamber, with a great fireplace of Verona marble, and panelled from floor to ceiling with the choicest examples of Italian walnut'. A staircase runs up behind a panelled screen to a gallery, the front of which is composed of elaborately carved open-work panels (Plate 137).

On the walls of the inner hall is a collection of sixteenth-century portraits, commemorating the moment when Hever, home of Anne Boleyn, entered national history and was visited several times by Henry VIII. Anne Boleyn appears in a portrait by Holbein, and there is another Holbein of Anne of Cleves, who lived at Hever from 1540 to 1557. To Astor, history was a source of endless romance—the piquant detail, the curious fact were themes for his imagination to play on. Besides pictures, he bought objects like the layette worked, according to tradition, by the future Elizabeth I for the expected child of Mary Tudor and Philip II of Spain. Even the richly carved screen of columns dividing the inner hall from the passage had a story. According to the article in the *Pall Mall Magazine*, the columns were made from a tree cut down in Caserta in 1747, later turned into a winepress. 'Fire and tempest, the lightning's blast it escaped: wars and revolutions left it untouched'; finally it was bought by the timber merchant who sold it to Astor. 'Nor, indeed, does its history end here, for a piece of an ancient rapier was found embedded in its heart, a romantic circumstance which our imaginations may interpret as they will.'

At times the opulent craftsmanship of the ground-floor rooms may be too rich for some tastes—for instance, in the elaborate minstrels' gallery to the dining room, largely carved by Nathaniel Hitch in 1906—although it was exactly this intricacy of workmanship that most appealed to Astor.

> Wherever the eye turned it fell upon some object which illustrated the devoted care which has been bestowed on the most minute details of the Hall. No plane has been allowed to touch the panels of wall or ceiling, but only the adze, as you may see by glancing at their surface; whilst the long table, the buffet, the tapestry, the coffers, the chairs, the armour, the heraldic emblazonments in the lofty windows, are eloquent of the period when Hever was in its glory

—although they had all been installed in 1903–6. In the drawing room, the oak panelling is inlaid with bog oak, lance-wood and holly. The Grinling Gibbons–style carving in the library—on the chimneypiece, the frieze and the bevelled edges of the panelling—is the work of W. S. Frith, chief craftsman at Hever. Although the design of the bookcases was taken from Magdalene College, Cambridge, the wood is a naturally scented one, sabicu, from South America, and the ceiling was based on a room at Hampton Court. The billiard room is in the form of a miniature Tudor hall.

The guest rooms were built in what was intended to look like a small Tudor village on the other side of the moat, with a bridge connecting it to the castle (Plate 134). To keep up the fiction, different parts of this irregular wing (roughly in the shape of a square courtyard with a spur or two to the north) have names like Cobham Corner, Medley Cottage, the Smuggler's Room and Orchard Cottage. The idea of the arrangement was simple: 'I cannot imagine a more natural way of providing guest-rooms,' wrote Astor. 'It is impossible to add to a castle; a village street in the medieval style would savour of the stage; and yet if the rites of hospitality were to be exercised at Hever, some considerable extension was, of course, necessary.' Like the Tudor taste houses which it predated, the Tudor village at Hever was intended to look old, in keeping with the castle. Masons and timber merchants in Kent still talk of how the Home Counties were scoured for old tiles. Once again, Astor himself described the expected response: 'For a moment I could not believe that they had been built a few short months ago, they seemed so old and crooked, and possessed such individuality as though they had grown up one by one in various ages, as those old villages did which we sometimes see on our travels, sheltering themselves under the walls of the overlord.' The kitchen court (Plate 138), with its stone walls apparently patched with brick, its low arches supporting half-timbered upper floors, half seriously pretends that it has been built in several stages, much in the spirit of Devey's Betteshanger nearby. Pearson designed the Home Farm in the same style in 1908.

196

138. The kitchen court at Hever

Once, when baited by the American press, Astor had his estate office release the false news of his death, so that he could read glowing tributes on every front page in New York. Restoring Hever gave Astor a chance to play another little game with the newspapers, by allowing absolutely no public admittance. He knew perfectly well that 'since the estate passed into the hands of the present owner many fantastic stories have found their way into print'; and it evidently amused him to think that no one beyond those directly engaged on the project knew what lay behind the forest of scaffolding poles that had sprung up round the castle. A small army was engaged on the work. In December 1904, seven hundred and forty-eight workmen were employed on the castle, village and garden, each receiving a Christmas present of two pounds of beef, a slice of cake, and threepence worth of tobacco, at a cost of two shillings a head. That was before work had begun on excavating the lake, which in itself employed eight hundred navvies. One man's job was carrying forty-five gallons of beer to How Green every day for them to drink. During the restoration the work force was put up in a temporary village of huts to the north of the river Eden, and Astor had a small cottage built near the castle for his own use: a stone tablet carved with the words 'Hic Habitat' was laid to mark the exact site. Security was characteristically tight, with eight detectives employed to work in shifts round the clock. Workmen were issued with passes, and it was forbidden to take photographs.

Astor was right to expect criticism. The SPAB would have been outraged, and Philip Tilden, who restored Allington Castle, probably expressed a popular view when he wrote: 'Hever Castle might indeed have been another Bodiam, infinitely alluring as it sat as I first saw it in the 'nineties, with its grey skirts sweeping the waters of the moat, set

197

around with the blue swords of the wild flag; but instead it has now become a miniature Metropolitan Museum of New York.'[21] It seems difficult to believe that the Edwardian inhabitants were not polished daily and stowed away in satin-lined leather cases at night. But Astor had his argument for the work. 'Only an anchorite,' wrote 'A Visitor',

> would dream of living in a medieval castle without taking some such measure. It is all very well for a Scott or a Dumas to hide from us by their vivid pens the ugliness of the rugged masonry, to stifle the rank odour rising from the rush-strewn floor, to quell the winds that rush in through loopholes and howl down cavernous chimneys, nay, even to disguise the revels in the banqueting-hall, but the magic spell soon loses its power, and we regard the old times and ancient manners with qualified regret, much as we pretend to look askance at modern luxuries and conveniences. A moat cannot defend us from a clammy dampness, coating even the inner walls and floor with a mysterious growth where lurks a host of ills which prey on man. So modern wit steps in, and Hever Castle now rests upon a lower floor of asphalte.

Unlike Lindisfarne, Lytton Strachey would not have found it uncomfortable.

139. Telegram from William Randolph Hearst to Alice Head, his London factotum

WESTERN UNION

WESTERN UNION TELEGRAPH COMPANY.

ANGLO-AMERICAN TELEGRAPH Co. LD.

No.

CABLEGRAM. Via Western Union.

RECEIVED AT 22, GREAT WINCHESTER STREET, LONDON, E.C. 2.

1925 AUG 13 AM 5 00

DEFERRED CABLEGRAM

MCY3PZ 1588

SANSIMEONCALIF 42

LCO HEAD

NASHS MAGAZINE

LONDON

WANT BUY CASTLE IN ENGLAND PLEASE FIND WHICH ONES AVAILABLE STDONATS

PERHAPS SATISFACTORY AT PROPER PRICE BUT PRICE QUOTED SEEMS VERY HIGH SEE

IF YOU CAN GET RIGHT PRICE ON STDONATS OR ANY OTHER EQUALLY GOOD

HEARST

No inquiry respecting this Message can be attended to without the production of this paper.

'Want buy castle in England'

The Tudor Taste had been the offspring, albeit heartily disowned, of the SPAB, with its intense regard for old craftsmanship. At St Donat's Castle, bought by the American newspaper tycoon William Randolph Hearst in 1925, the monster-child turned on its parent. Hearst had begun to look for an English castle in August that year. 'WANT BUY CASTLE IN ENGLAND' read the telegram he sent to Miss Alice Head, managing director of his English subsidiary, the National Magazine Company.[22] Astor—the man of letters, the romantic, the lover of history—would have been horrified to think that what he did at Hever could have foreshadowed, even inspired, the barbarisms Hearst was to commit at St Donat's, but so it was: the example of one millionaire was followed by another. When Hearst considered acquiring Leeds Castle, in Kent, Miss Head wrote to her chief that, given investment, it could 'be made quite as attractive as J. J. Astor [sic] has made Hever Castle'.

But Leeds did not fit the bill. 'MADE THOROUGH INSPECTION LEEDS CASTLE LAST SATURDAY,' ran the wire. 'QUITE UNIQUE AS ANTIQUITY BUT NEEDS EXPENDITURE LARGE SUM TO MAKE IT HABITABLE NOT A BATH IN PLACE ONLY LIGHTING OIL LAMPS SERVANTS QUARTERS DOWN DUNGEONS AND IN STEEP BATTLEMENTED TOWERS STOP PART COULD BE MADE FIT TO LIVE IN BY SPENDING ABOUT FOUR THOUSAND.' When Leeds was sold the next year, the purchaser—the Hon. Lady Baillie—if not American, was at least half American, and she employed the fashionable decorator Stephan Boudin to create interiors not unlike those at St Donat's; Boudin imported a French Gothic staircase and a seventeenth-century room from Thorpe Hall. Before that, however, Leeds could not compete: 'PERIOD PLACE IN EXCELLENT REPAIR WITH CENTRAL HEATING MODERN SANITATION,' wired Miss Head after visiting South Wales to see St Donat's (Plate 140). 'DONT WANT MISS IT.'[23] It became Hearst's—or strictly the National Magazine Company's—in October.

As yet Hearst had seen it only in photographs. He did not visit his new possession until three years later, when he reached England at the end of a Continental tour in the company of Marion Davies and other Hollywood friends. 'Let's go down to St Donat's and look it over,' he said when the entourage reached London.[24] He arrived late one afternoon having been driven down by Miss Head, another Hearst executive, and Sir Charles Allom, his architect and decorator. He was entranced by what he saw, and explored the castle until ten p.m. The next morning he left again for New York. But the brief visit was enough to enable him to write a few weeks later a twenty-five page letter about the restoration proposals.

Sir Charles Allom had recently redecorated Buckingham Palace.[25] It was probably this that persuaded Hearst to employ him, although he was also closely associated with the notorious art dealer and impresario Joseph Duveen, from whom Hearst bought paintings. Allom, who had founded the firm of White Allom and Co. (of London and Montreal), had a personality as large as those of his millionaire clients. His entry in Who's Who mentioned that both his grandfathers, Thomas Allom and Thomas Carrick, were painters; but sporting enthusiasms were given as much prominence as artistic accomplishments. Fellowship of the Royal Society of Arts unexpectedly rubs shoulders with president of the Boat Racing Association, member of the Shorthorn Society of Great Britain and chairman of the Board of Control of the World's Sculling Championship. He

owned his own racing yacht, *White Heather*, belonged to four yacht clubs, four golf clubs and two general sporting clubs—but not to the Athenaeum.

'This is our home,' says Orson Welles in *Citizen Kane*. The irony in the line, spoken to his dejected mistress, comes from the fact that 'home' was Xanadu, a megalomaniac dream castle of gargantuan proportions. Kane, modelled on Hearst, at that moment is seen standing at the foot of a sweeping marble staircase seemingly made for a colossus; the woman he addresses cowers beneath a French Gothic fireplace that is itself as big as a house. Xanadu was a parody of Hearst's twin-towered castle in California, San Simeon (called, with false modesty, 'the ranch'). This was the final resting place for many of the crate-loads of antique furniture that he had shipped over from Europe. St Donat's never became a Xanadu, or even a San Simeon; but nowhere else does the romance with old materials for their own sake reach such a pitch of naked obsession. Romance, in fact, gave way to rape.

Hearst's twenty-five page letter to Miss Head has been lost. However, one of the topics broached must have been the acquisition of parts of old, preferably Gothic buildings, because White Allom and other firms began supplying old chimneypieces the same year (Plates 142–3). This was nothing new to Hearst. As early as 1891 he had seen a well-head that he liked in Verona; he bought it, shipped the five tons of stones back to San Francisco and re-erected it there, before transporting it eventually to Mexico, where it gave the

141. The courtyard at St Donat's

140. Medieval gatehouse at St Donat's Castle, Glamorgan

142. Fireplace in the Lady Anne tower at St Donat's, with a cut-down hood resting on jambs from a different medieval source

143. View into the banqueting hall at St Donat's through the fifteenth-century Gothic screen imported from Devon

name to his Hacienda de Pozo de la Verona. During the 1920s he kept up an energetic correspondence with the loyal Miss Head. The subject was usually art or furniture sales but a communication such as the following, dated 8 February 1924, was not uncommon: 'ARE THERE ANY IMPORTANT CEILINGS TO BE HAD IN ENGLAND ALSO STAIRCASES OF TUDOR OR JACOBEAN PERIOD WOULD LIKE ALSO ONE TRUSSED CEILING OF GUILD HALL TYPE HEARST'. The pieces he bought were shipped to San Simeon or fitted into the Clarendon apartment block in New York (when the owner had refused permission for Hearst to remodel the space he rented by removing two floors, his solution was simply to buy the whole building). Not all the purchases could be found a home, however. Many went to one of Hearst's two warehouses in the Bronx. When, with new management trying to save the Hearst Corporation from financial disaster, these disgorged their treasures in 1937, one was found to hold ten thousand seven hundred crates containing the stones of a Spanish monastery.[26] On the set of a Colonial scene in one of Marion Davies's films, Hearst thought the fireplace looked inauthentic. 'I bought a real one some years ago. Find it and we'll use it,' he said. It was located, with difficulty.[27]

According to a National Magazine Company inventory of 1945 (entitled 'Mr W. R. Hearst's Property Insured as "Built In"'), Hearst had eighteen or so old chimneypieces or fireplaces moved to St Donat's. Most came from Acton Surgey Ltd or White Allom. They included a stone fireplace from Cadbury House, Yatton, as well as several fifteenth-century chimneypieces, Gothic screens and minstrels' galleries, doorways and whole rooms. Not all fitted, so some had to be cut down, or else—in the case of a fireplace—the hood and frieze were supported on jambs from a different piece. The new banqueting hall created in the west range of the castle is reached through a fifteenth-century stone screen taken from a Devon church. In 1930 the elaborately carved and gilded ceiling was

202

xxi. Ardkinglas, Argyllshire

XXIII. The entrance front of Castle Drogo

XXII. The main stairs at Castle Drogo, Devon

144. Medievalising wrought-iron light fitting at St Donat's, with the Virgin and Child in the centre

removed from St Botolph's, the famous parish church of Boston, in Lincolnshire, known as Boston Stump (it had been found above the early nineteenth-century vault and sold, surreptitiously it seems, for just over £2,000 to pay for Sir Charles Nicholson's restoration of the church.[28] The fireplace, with its tall hood (truncated by the comparatively low ceiling) and armorial shield of fleurs-de-lys, came from a chateau in Beauvais.

But Hearst's greatest quarry was Bradenstoke Priory, in Wiltshire. In 1929 the medieval tithe barn was taken down stone by stone amid great secrecy; the workmen did not even know who was employing them. The western range of the cloister, including the prior's lodging and the refectory, soon followed. All that was left above ground were two fourteenth-century undercrofts and a tower. The magnificent early fourteenth-century double collar-beam roof of the refectory was fitted into a specially devised hall, which functioned as an 'assembly room', on the south side of the castle (Plate 145). Part of the outer curtain wall was demolished to accommodate it, and the windows from the prior's lodging were built into the walls. Questions were asked in Parliament as to whether an American millionaire could be allowed to jumble the national heritage in this way.[29]

The SPAB was outraged. It went to the unprecedented lengths of putting up posters in underground stations showing before and after photographs (Plate 146). 'Protect your

207

XXIV. Hever Castle, Kent, showing the guest wing beyond the moat

PROTECT YOUR ANCIENT BUILDINGS

BRADENSTOKE, WILTS.,
BEFORE AND DURING
DEMOLITION

THE SOCIETY FOR THE PROTECTION OF ANCIENT BUILDINGS
HAS WORKED FOR OVER FIFTY YEARS TO SAVE THEM
AND NEEDS YOUR HELP.
WRITE TO 20, BUCKINGHAM STREET, ADELPHI, W.C.2

146. Poster issued by the Society for the Protection of Ancient Buildings, 1929

ancient buildings,' ran the slogan. 'Bradenstoke, Wilts, before and during demolition for the sake of old materials.' It was found to be actionable, so the words 'for the sake of old materials' had to be masked out with pieces of white paper and paste. Letters appeared in *The Times*. 'It is more than an ordinary act of vandalism; it is an attack on the soul-life of our people,' wrote Lewis R. Farnell.[30] A. R. Powys, secretary of the SPAB, used a patient, schoolmasterly tone in appealing to Hearst's better feelings. 'England at present suffers much from the removal of old buildings and fittings from places where they were originally set,' he explained; 'but it must be said that this damage to our heritage is more the result of our own people than that of the citizens of the United States of America. My society asks Mr Hearst to set Englishmen a good example in this instance, to shame them, perhaps, into better behaviour.'[31]

Hearst was inured to worse things than this; Theodore Roosevelt called him 'an unspeakable blackguard' who combined 'all the worst faults of the conscienceless, corrupt and dissolute monied man',[32] and some people used stronger epithets. Miss Head was handling the SPAB correspondence. 'Mr Hearst and I are well aware of your views,' she

209

145. The roof of the refectory at Bradenstoke Priory, Wiltshire, built into St Donat's

wrote primly, '. . . You must please allow us to hold our own opinions.' Allom tried to
pour oil on the waters by stating publicly that, since it would cost too much to restore the
Bradenstoke barn where it was, it would be erected as part of St Donat's, replacing a
modern wing 'which is incongruous and hurtful to the artistic sense'.[33] At least it would
not be lost for ever, he said; but it was. The barn was not incorporated. Only the doors and
windows of the prior's lodgings and the roof of the guest house were used. The barn simply
disappeared, and today nobody knows what became of it.

There were two other barns at St Donat's. They were used as smaller versions of the
Bronx warehouses and stored bits of old buildings for which no immediate use could be
found. They still held a number of pieces in 1945, including thirty-three cases containing
a tracery window from St Albans Cathedral, 'returned from Los Angeles'.[34]

The photographic inventory of the furniture at St Donat's fills twelve fat volumes. As at
Hever, some pieces were bought for their historical associations rather than intrinsic
quality as *objets d'art*: a plaque on Hearst's bed, for instance, recorded that Charles I had
slept in it in 1645. Often his acquisitions came from the houses of living aristocrats. Most
significant of these were the Craven bed from Combe Abbey and an English State bed

147. (far left) The armoury at
St Donat's

148. Marion Davies's bedroom
at St Donat's

from Lord Vernon's collection, although both had been bought from dealers. A Queen
Anne State bed was purchased at Sotheby's. Altogether, the castle possessed a remarkable
collection of beds: Elizabethan beds, Jacobean beds, Hepplewhite and Chippendale
beds—some shipped to America and then shipped back to St Donat's. Typically, the
'small XVth Cent. Oak Gothic Bed' bought from Acton Surgey in July 1930 appeared in
a later inventory as 'bed made up from old wood', a true Tudor taste piece. Luckily the
exterior of the castle was left comparatively unchanged, except for the bay thrust out for
the dining room, the demolition of part of the curtain wall and an extra storey given to the
Lady Anne Tower. From the latter there is a superb panorama seawards over the falling
terraces of the Edwardian garden laid out by a previous owner. Above the ancient rose
garden Hearst built an Italian summer house, with a telephone to call his editors. It is said
that the telephonist at Llantwit Major fainted when she was first asked to call California.
At the bottom of the terraces was perhaps, in a Welsh climate, Hearst's greatest folly: the
swimming pool, one hundred and fifty feet by fifty and filled with salt water, although
happily there was provision for heating.

Hearst never used St Donat's as a family home. His wife did not even know he had bought it. (When she was told it was Norman, she is said to have replied: 'Norman who?')[35] Altogether, Hearst's visits, which he made with Marion Davies, add up to a bare four months. The castle served as an expensive Hollywood-style backdrop, with crateloads of medieval stage props waiting to be wheeled out from the wings.

St Donat's is an aberration in the history of taste. It was an oddity, which in the end even Hearst could not afford and nobody else wanted. As Hearst lost his grip on his empire, he was banned from St Donat's in case it later incurred death duties. The National Magazine Company, in whose name St Donat's and much of the contents had been purchased, looked dolefully at a supremely unremunerative asset. As the report to the parent Hearst Corporation ran at the time: 'The National Magazine Company Ltd has an investment in the Castle and in the lands surrounding it of approximately £281,500. If the place were put up for sale it is most unlikely that £100,000 could be realised.' The company consulted the best solicitor they could find, Major Milner, the deputy speaker at the House of Commons. Sadly he

> ventured his opinion that he knew of only one man who might be able to use the premises to good advantage. That man is a Mr Butlin, a Canadian, who has a chain of holiday camps throughout the British Isles, and who has amassed a tremendous fortune from these operations . . . The consensus is that we have at St Donat's a white elephant of the rarest species, and that Mr Hearst should be prevailed upon to authorise the disposal of the premises without delay in view of the fact that in no circumstances will he be able to occupy them short of three years.

In the event St Donat's did not become a holiday camp or even a home for William Butlin. The place just would not sell, and it was not until 1960 that the National Magazine Company was able to take the castle off its books, having sold it to the United World College of the Atlantic.

The Ideal Restored

If Hever, Skibo and St Donat's look fantastic, and perhaps even absurd, it is because their owners were trying to do with castles something that was wholly against their character. Castles were never built for comfort, and even Hever, originally constructed at the time when the castle was yielding ground to the country house and fortifications were becoming something of a chivalrous pretence, offered only a relative degree of luxury to its late fourteenth-century owners, the Boleyns—it had always been low-lying and damp. But not everyone wanted transatlantic standards in bathrooms and central heating, or even—like Edward Hudson, making the best of chilly stone walls and smoking fires—the average level of convenience found in Edwardian country houses.

Apart from Lorimer and Lutyens there were other architects at work restoring and converting castles with sensitivity, and their numbers grew. Philip Tilden restored Allington Castle for the scholar, traveller, mountaineer and politician Sir Martin (later Lord) Conway, taking over the work from W. D. Caröe and proceeding by gradual stages until 1929.[36] At Herstmonceux, the fifteenth-century brick castle in East Sussex, restoration was begun by the Conservative M.P. Colonel Claude Lowther in 1911.[37] It

149. Herstmonceux Castle, Sussex

was only finished after Lowther's death in 1929 by Sir Paul Latham, a millionaire Labour politician whose aim was partly to give work to unemployed men during the Depression. His architect was Walter Godfrey, more familiar to contemporaries from his regular scholarly articles in the *Architectural Review* and other papers.

Allington and Herstmonceux (Plate 149) were restored as houses, but it was a logical progression from the scholarly attitude of their owners to restore castles just as pieces of history, without the compromise of adapting them, however sensitively, to modern needs. This was what Lord Curzon, politician and former Viceroy of India, did with Bodiam and Tattershall. Bodiam was his first love, although in 1911 it was still owned by Lord Ashcombe, who would not part with it but offered Curzon first refusal if and when he did. Curzon found a 'magnificent substitute' in Tattershall Castle, in Lincolnshire, the brick tower built by Henry VI's Lord Treasurer, Ralph Cromwell, in 1434–45. This, as he wrote in his book *Bodiam Castle*, 'I was able to reserve for the nation from a fate that was not merely imminent, but had already been partly consummated.'[38] Sixteenth-century

213

150. Barbican to the castle Gordon Selfridge proposed to build at Hengistbury Head, Hampshire

fireplaces had already been taken out for shipment to America; Curzon bought them back and returned them to Tattershall in triumph—he was photographed sitting on top of them as they were carried by cart in the last stages of their journey. William Weir of the SPAB was architect of the restoration. In 1914 he was ready to order five museum cases from Ernest Gimson, whom he also commissioned to build bridges across the moat. 'I am very pleased too that Lord Curzon and yourself think we have done some good carpentry and joinery,' wrote Gimson when the job was completed. 'The men who did the work are now taking in hand the most delicate and expensive inlaid and veneered cabinet making and I shall find that they will do it all the better for their six months bridge building.'[39] Such was the virtue of labour.

Finally Curzon had the opportunity to buy Bodiam on Lord Ashcombe's death in 1917. Symmetrical, towered, lapped round by a lake or moat, it was 'the most romantic and, notwithstanding its rather austere appearance, the most fairy of English Castles,' felt Curzon. It had been built at about the same time as Hever, in 1385. Again Weir was the architect for the restoration. 'A certain amount of conjectural work' was needed to reinstate a missing portion, but Weir did 'not consider there would be any great difficulty in the undertaking that could not be overcome with care'.[40]

214

To begin with, Curzon had thoughts of 'restoring, in the sense of rebuilding, a portion of the interior of the Castle, and making it again practicable for residence,' and plans were drawn up to that effect. But he decided not to: 'on reflection I felt that a new gem does not usually do honour to an old setting; I realised that while saving something I should sacrifice more; I remembered what Viollet-le-Duc had done with Pierrefonds and in a lesser degree with Carcassonne; and I desisted from what would have been an interesting architectural experiment, but might easily have degenerated into an archaeological crime.'

Restoring Bodiam finished in 1919, but the First World War had not completely killed the chivalric dream as expressed in stone—or at least on the drawing board. Gordon Selfridge, American millionaire owner of the Oxford Street store, confidently bought a dramatic parcel of headland opposite the Isle of Wight called Hengistbury Head, on which he intended to build the biggest castle in the world.[41] Sir Martin Conway of Allington organised a lunch at the Ritz at which he could meet Philip Tilden. Plans were made, and a dazzling series of perspectives drawn (Plate 150). Selfridge had a passion for Gothic architecture, although he wanted the overall plan of his palace to be Classical, with 'mighty vistas, balance, and the co-ordination of parts'. For some time, beginning in early 1919, Tilden indulged his imagination in dreams of Piranesian grandeur and Watteau-like romance. The only way that he could get down the result on paper was to make the scale one in sixty-four.

The basic scheme included four miles of rampart punctuated with towers, a 'small castle' (itself the size of a substantial house) perched above the sea and a 'large castle' on the higher ground. As well as the usual living rooms, the latter was to contain a Gothic hall, a three hundred foot tower, a theatre, a winter garden, a covered lake, long corridors and galleries for pictures, tapestries and craft-objects, and 'at least two hundred and fifty suites of rooms for guests'. It would have taken so long to build that another house would have been necessary for use during the period of construction, hence the small castle.

Tilden took it very seriously. Every month he would go and see Selfridge in Oxford Street or at Highcliffe Castle, his country house, where there was usually a gathering of other millionaires like Sir Thomas Lipton, Sir Ernest Cassel and James Beck of America. Everyone was enthusiastic and encouraging, and in the process Selfridge and his friends gained an enhanced intellectual reputation as connoisseurs and (at least potential) patrons of architecture. Nothing was actually built beyond a plaster model of the small castle. 'Never mind,' wrote Tilden bravely, 'the whole ideal was a great and grand one, for Heaven knows, no man in these days would ever consider building a palace. It was all a sign of the times, a sign of hope that fear had been strangled, that culture was to be fostered, that men and women were to be happier.'

But in the end it was Curzon and the National Trust (to which his restored castles were eventually given) that won the day, and men and women find happiness in visiting Bodiam rather than living in a fantasy palazzo.

7. The Country House as Cottage

'Our house-building now has its chance,' wrote E. S. Prior in 1901.[1] The architect of Home Place, Holt (Plate 151), probably the most eccentric of all Arts and Crafts buildings, Prior was referring to house-building at a romantic but doctrinaire extreme: no copying from past styles; the money saved 'by the rejection of counterfeit ornament' to be used to buy solid stone, thin rough bricks, hand-made tiles, English oak carpentry; the cost—because he blandly admitted it would be more expensive than conventional architecture—not to be counted, since it was morally better to have *good* building rather than *cheap* construction; the materials and labour to come from the locality. His hope was that a 'rational and purposelike' manner of building should 'come back in place of the fret and fume of archaeological designing; so that our own habits and ways of living might have a chance of asserting themselves'. The London-based architect, with his numerous assistants and hectic schedule of visits to all parts of the country, was despised. 'To be quite candid,' declared another Arts and Crafts hard-liner, Robert Weir Schultz, 'I am not hopeful that a good general type of modern building will be seen until all we architects are abolished, swept away root and branch.'[2] Salvation lay in the crafts.

Life in the country was idealised by Arts and Crafts architects—it was more natural than urban living, it was in direct contact with the disappearing rural traditions, and there were still parts of England that were virtually untouched by the Industrial Revolution. Country Houses were the ideal Arts and Crafts building type, because their owners were often rich enough to afford expensive handmade products, and country areas were still generally free from the district surveyor (who would have forbidden the use of thatch, for example, in the towns or the suburbs).[3] Rather than rehearse the growth of Arts and Crafts principles among the young men in the offices of Norman Shaw and Ernest George, the ideal of the medieval craftsman shared by Ruskin and Morris, the foundation of the Art Workers' Guild, the Arts and Crafts Exhibition Society (the title of which was the first use of the term 'arts and crafts'), and the Society for the Protection of Ancient Buildings, all of which has been told at length elsewhere,[4] this chapter will taste the fruit of the theory as it was expressed in four of the most radical Arts and Crafts country houses: Melsetter, Rodmarton, Hilles and Madresfield Court.

Melsetter, where W. R. Lethaby enlarged and remodelled an existing house, shows

151. The garden front of Home Place, Norfolk

how an Arts and Crafts architect (London-based, as it happens) responded to the spirit of the place, and also put into practice the rational ideas of architecture evolved through the study of old buildings under Philip Webb's guidance. Rodmarton was the ideal of an Arts and Crafts country house carried out on a basis of hand-work and sound building, and became the centre of a craft revival in the community. Hilles, built by the architect Detmar Blow for himself and his family, represents the Arts and Crafts social ideal; and in the chapel at Madresfield the perfect union of the arts and the crafts was achieved. Although, ironically, the latter was associated with the family tragedy that formed the background to Evelyn Waugh's *Brideshead Revisited*, it is arguably the most thorough expression of Arts and Crafts theory in Britain, and perhaps too its most lovely. The four commissions—Melsetter, Rodmarton, Hilles and Madresfield—were executed for, respectively, an industrialist, a banker, a professional man and an aristocrat.

The Romantic Country House : Rationalism

To May Morris, William Morris's daughter, Melsetter 'seemed like the embodiment of some of those fairy palaces of which my father wrote with great charm and dignity. But, for all its fitness and dignity, it was a place full of homeliness and the spirit of welcome, a very lovable place'.[5] The house, which was in former times a stronghold of the wild and powerful Moodie lairds, stands at the north end of Longhope Bay, one of the most southerly points in the Orkneys. Even today the island of Hoy is wild and remote; but it is also a place of wild flowers, because of the comparatively mild climate, and Melsetter is surrounded by drifts of bluebells and daffodils in the Spring. Both May Morris and Lethaby responded to the two aspects. A fairy palace was no longer, like Skibo, a thing of bristling turrets and waving pennants; the task Arts and Crafts architects were setting themselves was to combine intimacy with the size expected of a substantial country house.

From Melsetter Hill (Plate 152), there is nothing to suggest that, in its present form, the house was built for an industrialist from Birmingham; and that is exactly what Lethaby would have hoped. It stands at the end of a string of outbuildings—most of them earlier than Lethaby's time—from which it is not very different in either scale or materials. There is a courtyard, which possesses a sense of enclosure but does not seek big effects; and if the garden front seems more rugged, showing that the character of the Moodie stronghold partly survived, it does not try to hide the fact that it was built in additions.

By the end of the nineteenth century the railway and the suburbs and the motor car made it increasingly difficult for romantics to find complete isolation in the countryside; so if they were rich enough they bought islands. Lindisfarne, Lambay and Rhum were all the scene of major country-house work, and so was Lewis, where Lord Leverhulme spent his retirement in a disastrous attempt to revitalise the crofting community (starting Mac Fisheries for the purpose) and remodelling Lews Castle. The railway reached Thurso in 1876, and with that even the northernmost tip of the mainland of Scotland was relatively accessible. Lethaby's client, Thomas Middlemore, looked beyond the mainland in 1898 and bought not merely one island but several—the Melsetter estate comprised Hoy, Walls, Fara and Rysa.

152. Melsetter House from Melsetter Hill, on the island of Hoy in the Orkneys

Middlemore at first sight seems an unlikely romantic. He came from a Baptist and Liberal family that had banking and manufacturing interests in Birmingham. On graduating from London University, he managed the Birmingham Wagon Company for seventeen years before selling out and buying Melsetter. But he was also on the fringe at least of an artistic Liberal circle—the Birmingham equivalent of the one the Prestwiches of Tirley Garth had enjoyed in Manchester. Middlemore's brother, Sir John Middlemore, M.P., gave an impressive series of Pre-Raphaelite paintings—including Burne-Jones's Pygmalion series and Holman Hunt's *Finding of the Saviour in the Temple*—to the Birmingham Art Gallery, and almost certainly knew C. E. Mathews, chairman of the Parliamentary Committee of the National Education League, a close friend of Joseph Chamberlain and a keen supporter of Birmingham's progressive art movement—Lethaby had worked for Mathews at The Hurst, Sutton Coldfield, in 1893.[6] Moreover, Middlemore's wife, Theodosia, was a craftswoman and friend of May Morris, also an embroideress, so she may well have come into contact with Morris himself. She exhibited textiles at the Arts and Crafts Exhibition Society and ordered embroidery pattern books

219

153. The garden front of Melsetter

154. The courtyard at Melsetter

from Morris and Co.[7] Crafts were practised at Melsetter. One outbuilding was converted into a spinning room and another into a museum.

After Ruskin and Morris, Lethaby was the great thinker of the Arts and Crafts movement. Although his response to the 'brown-bread and dewy morning ideal of beauty' rather than the 'late champagne supper ideal'[8] was at bottom emotional, he believed, like Prior, that his theories of sound building—derived from an idealisation of the medieval craftsman—had their basis in reason. The classic statement of his values was made in an assessment of the importance of the Society for the Protection of Ancient Buildings as a teaching body: 'Dealing as it did with the common facts of traditional building in scores and hundreds of examples, it became under the technical guidance of Philip Webb, the architect, a real school of practical *building*—architecture with all the whims which we usually call "design" left out.' And again: 'this Society, engaged in intense study of antiquity, became a school of rational builders and modern building'.[9] The lessons Lethaby derived from old buildings were at the opposite remove from Lutyens's response to their texture and quality of materials, expressed at Munstead Wood—let alone the way the architects of the Tudor taste reacted. It was the approach of the head rather than the heart.

Lethaby himself (again like Prior) built little—just six buildings. He retired from active practice after the practical problems of trying to realise his ideal of the architect indirectly supervising construction at Brockhampton church nearly led to a nervous breakdown in 1902. However, 'rational' remained the key word in his theory—so much so that, influenced by the mid-nineteenth-century French architect and theorist Viollet-le-Duc, he increasingly saw the architect as an engineer rather than a craftsman. Eventually, his part in founding the Design and Industries Association, with its implied acceptance of machine production, fragmented the never willingly cohesive ranks of the Arts and Crafts movement in 1915, and prevented them from ever regrouping after the First World War.

Lethaby had been chief clerk in Norman Shaw's office. He was born in Barnstaple in 1857, but Shaw saw some of his drawings in the *Building News*, invited him to London, and eventually set him up on his own with a 'starter commission' generously passed on from his own busy office. It was for a large house for Lord Manners ('Hoppy' as Margot Asquith knew him)[10] in the New Forest called Avon Tyrrell (Plate 220). But Lethaby's real master was Webb, who 'by the austerity of his life and the signified reticence of his design' seemed 'the ideal of what an architect ought to be'.[11] They were both Socialists. They first met at a meeting of the Labour Emancipation League in Hoxton and later lived near each other in Gray's Inn. At Melsetter, the joined gables on the east front—a motif ultimately derived from sixteenth and seventeenth-century manor houses—is a gesture of homage, Webb having used similar gables on most of his principal houses.

Lethaby's enlargement of Melsetter does not quite follow the letter of the SPAB manifesto, since Morris had insisted that, when an old building became inconvenient for use, another completely separate structure should be erected. But this rule, soon seen as both hopelessly impractical and unnecessary, was abandoned, and in all other respects Lethaby behaved impeccably according to SPAB principles. He kept nearly all the structure that already existed and even incorporated a row of old outbuildings on the north side of the entrance courtyard into the main house. Like the old house, the new work was harled, with dressing of local red sandstone.

There was no attempt to make the house self-consciously picturesque—that would have been anathema to Lethaby's ideas of rational building. The windows were regularly spaced, but that was only because, following Gothic Revival precepts, they reflect the disposition of the rooms they give light to. On the east elevation, to take one example, the bedroom and the drawing room on the corner have fewer windows than the other rooms on this front because they are also lit from the south. But it is inside that Lethaby the rational theorist shows his flash of real brilliance. This is in the fireplace in the entrance hall (Plate 155). There is no mantelshelf, only five corbels beneath a row of seven coats of arms in low relief; the corbels were intended to hold candles (although early photographs show they were also used for pots), which threw a dramatic light onto the shields.

Avon Tyrrell had been roundly condemned by Lorimer in a letter to his Australian friend Dods: it was not

> the masterly affair I expected from the one who 'lets his tongue rage like fire amongst the noblest names'. What does the man preach? That modest work fails because it's all done in the office and isn't worked out on the spot as in the old days afore time! Well if you'd been with me (I wish to God you had been) we'd have agreed a dozen things that failed in this very particular . . . The proportions of a lot of it was poor and the staircase I simply would not have owned.[12]

But it is said that when Lethaby first arrived at Melsetter he immediately tore up the plans he had drawn in his office in London, and the story is probably true. At Melsetter he succeeded where at Avon Tyrrell he had failed, and his veneration of local traditions and reverence for the building already on site are all the more remarkable since the house as he found it was comparatively modest. However, he worked carefully and slowly, researching the local building traditions for details such as the crowstepped gable on the south elevation, similar to those seen in Tankerness House, Kirkwall, and the other larger houses of the Orkney mainland. This, as he would have said, was architecture without the caprice of design.

Melsetter also displays another side of Lethaby's rationalism—rationalism that was in this case laced with a good deal of mumbo-jumbo—in the cluster of small symbols on the south gable of the east front: a star, a moon and two tiny heart-shaped windows (Plate 156). Lethaby believed that his contemporaries should evolve their own language of symbolism, free from what he regarded as the obsolete and meaningless vocabulary of the styles. Further, he believed that symbolism was the very stuff of architecture. The theme of *Architecture, Mysticism and Myth*, which he published in 1891, was that the architecture of the Assyrians, Egyptians, Greeks and other early civilisations was in origin essentially symbolic rather than utilitarian. As he put it later: 'All over Europe the early morning of architecture was spent in the worship of great stones.'[13] The star, moon and heart-shaped windows at Melsetter represent the only time he put these ideas into practice outside a church or a chapel; but—alas for poor Lethaby—not only are they modest in scope, it is far from clear what they mean.

Like much of the Arts and Crafts movement, the symbols at Melsetter are top-heavy with theory. But the house does possess the 'magic quality' Lethaby believed was the desideratum of architecture. Something of it is suggested in a sketch map of the garden which May Morris sent to a friend.[14] It shows a walled garden to the south, a kitchen

155. The hall fireplace at Melsetter

156. Symbols on the south gable of the east front at Melsetter

garden to the north-east, and an 'old garden laid out with daisy bordered beds' to the east. A row of clipped yews alternated with miniature pieces of ordnance to form one border of the 'great lawn where seagulls and ravens often sit'; the tea room, with its romantic view, had a fireplace for cooler evenings; and beside the great lawn was a grass nut walk—all of which was a foil to the wild moorland and bleak turnip fields that otherwise surrounded the house on all sides.

Perhaps because the wild, romantic setting touched a vein of poetry in his imagination that was not active elsewhere, Lethaby felt that Melsetter was the most successful work of his small oeuvre. The courtyard to the south in particular has exactly that sense of the ordinary raised to something more that all Arts and Crafts architects sought. If the internal planning is awkward, that may be put down to the sacramental need to preserve the old house; and perhaps it was Lethaby's misfortune that, for his best building, the local tradition dictated harling, with its hard surface, so that the house does not always seem as warm and home-like as May Morris recalled. It was for the latter qualities that Arts and Crafts architects went to the Cotswolds.

224

The Cotswolds—unpretentious, comparatively remote, still unfashionable and full of lovely old grey buildings—were becoming prime Arts and Crafts country.[15] Guy Dawber, who moved there as clerk of works at Batsford and established a practice at Moreton-in-Marsh, the village outside the gates, had been sketching around and about since the 1880s, and sometimes had published the results in the *Builder*. Broadway had already acquired something of an arty—if not yet arty-crafty—reputation: Sargent went there, so did Henry James, and a farmhouse in the village was praised by Morris for exactly the qualities Gimson and the Barnsleys were to admire. ''Tis no ideal house I am thinking of,' Morris admonished a lecture audience, 'no rare marvel of art, of which but few can be vouchsafed to the best times and countries; no palace either, not even a manor house, but a yeoman's steading at the grandest, or even his shepherd's cottage . . . 'tis in fact beautiful, a work of art and a piece of nature, no less . . .'[16]

Perhaps influenced by this feeling for the modest, humble and unspectacular, the Hon. Claud Biddulph, a City banker, would refer to his country house, Rodmarton Manor, as his 'cottage in the country'.[17] The use of the word was of course intended as a humorous piece of false modesty, but it was not so absurd as it might sound. By any standards Rodmarton is a large country house, with a long entrance front snaking lazily round what looks like an enchanted green in front of the house. The manor itself dates back to the Conquest, although the ancient manor house had been demolished by the time Biddulph's father, Michael (later Lord Biddulph), gave him the estate in 1894. Nevertheless, for all its size the house does have a calculated modesty that could at a stretch be called cottage-like; it is only one room and a corridor deep, with a big main living room.

The house itself was designed by one man, Ernest Barnsley, whose only other major architectural works were Sapperton village hall, built with Norman Jewson in 1912, and Bledsilowe Lodge, near Cirencester, rebuilt in 1921 using stone from a demolished mansion on the outskirts of Birmingham. But the conception, execution and furnishing of Rodmarton belong to a small community of architect-craftsmen founded by Barnsley and his brother, Sidney, and Ernest Gimson, all of whom left London to live and work in Gloucestershire in 1893. Jewson, inspired by their example to make a similar move fifteen years later, gave an account of the principles by which he and the three older architect-craftsmen were motivated:

> The professional side of architecture had never appealed to me. I was aware that it was generally considered to be impossible to become a successful architect without living in a town, spending much of one's time making social contacts while most of the actual work was done by one's office staff, but for me it was architecture I was interested in, not making a large income as an architect. My own buildings I wanted to have the basic qualities of the best old houses of their locality, built in the local traditional way in the local materials, but not copying the details which properly belonged to the period in which they were built.[18]

Private means were desirable—in fact essential—for this kind of life, which involved renouncing worldly success. The irony of Gimson and the Barnsleys' adventure was that

157. The curving entrance front of Rodmarton Manor, Gloucestershire

the private incomes which made it possible ultimately derived from the kind of industrial business which, as utopians, they so much disliked: Josiah Gimson, father of Ernest, had been an ironfounder and machinist in Leicester, while the Barnsleys' father was a director of the big building firm John Barnsley and Sons, which constructed Birmingham Town Hall and did well out of the expansion of the Birmingham suburbs in the late nineteenth century.

The failure in 1892 of Kenton and Co.—a furniture firm founded by Lethaby, Blomfield, Gimson, Sidney Barnsley and Mervyn Macartney—had precipitated the move to Gloucestershire the next year. First, Gimson and Sidney Barnsley settled at Ewen near Cirencester, then they persuaded Ernest Barnsley to join them. Ernest was married, unlike the others, but not doing well as an architect in Birmingham, where he had tried to establish his practice. In 1894 all three transferred to Pinbury Park (Plate 158), on Lord Bathurst's estate, said to be haunted by the ghost of a nun-housekeeper who used to roll Double Gloucester cheeses down the avenue. They stayed there until 1902, when the Bathursts took it back to use as a summer home and 'more particularly', as Sidney Barnsley rather sardonically wrote to Philip Webb, 'for their children to live and learn country ways—if possible?'[19] The craftsmen were all given sites for their own cottages to be built in Sapperton at Lord Bathurst's expense, and the ancient manor house of Daneway, half a mile away across the fields, was made available to them for workshops and for displaying furniture. The finer pieces of furniture made for Rodmarton came from Daneway. Earlier, in 1902, Sidney Barnsley described the arrangements there: 'My brother and Gimson have already started workshops at Daneway having 4 or 5 cabinet makers and boys so far, with the hopes of chairmakers and modellers in the near future. I

226

am remaining an outsider from this movement—still going on making furniture by myself and handing over to them any orders I cannot undertake, and orders seem to come in too quickly now as we are getting more known.' Two years later he reported that he was 'still occupied principally in making good solid oak furniture with occasional pieces of a more delicate kind as a rest and change'. Considerable physical labour as well as skill was involved in making the larger pieces: 'by night time I have felt fairly tired out'.[20]

The greatest influence on the furniture from Daneway was that of the traditional country crafts which could be still seen in Gloucestershire villages at the turn of the century, but which were on the point of extinction. The chamfer motif—originally used on carts and hayrakes to make them lighter—was elaborated and used decoratively (Plate 160). Stretchers for tables were inspired by the shape of old-fashioned hay rakes. The 'wishbone' table was a development of this theme, with an extra strut from the stretcher to the table top (Plate 161). The craftsmen also developed a series of complicated joints of which the most interesting were the cogged dovetail (a row of dovetails at a corner which looks like the teeth of a cog) and the three-dimensional dovetail. The latter was used for joining the planks of tabletops, and was dovetailed in plan and also in section. Although it might have been true of Oxford Street imitations, Gordon Russell was quite wrong to say that three-dimensional dovetails were liable to be washed off when the tables were scrubbed.[21] As with all Arts and Crafts furniture designers, the Sapperton craftsmen

158. Ernest Gimson's cottage, Pinbury, with (left to right) Sidney Barnsley, Ernest Gimson and Ernest Barnsley, and families

160. Chest from Rodmarton carved with chamfer motif, and detail (seen under construction in Plate 159)

159. (previous pages) The Pinbury workshop

161. Wishbone table from Rodmarton

believed in Pugin's axiom that 'all ornament should consist of enrichment of the essential construction'—although in practice this sometimes meant an appearance of massiveness going beyond the strict dictates of function. 'These could be omitted and the table be quite firm and rigid,' reads a note on the wishbones in one of Barnsley's table designs.[22]

Sidney Barnsley executed his designs himself, but Gimson employed professional cabinetmakers (his own production of furniture was largely limited to rush-seated chairs). However, for the plain oak furniture intended for cottage use, these craftsmen were literally too skilled. The care with which they finished their work not only refined away the slight roughness of surface that Gimson liked, but made it too expensive for village people to afford. It was a paradox of Arts and Crafts furniture design that there was little demand for what were thought of as cottage-style products: Gimson and Barnsley, like Morris, found themselves 'ministering to the swinish luxury of the rich'.

Rodmarton itself started life as rather more of a cottage than it became. Biddulph originally intended to build a small house, on which he would spend £5,000 a year for a number of years. Work began at the east end in 1909 with the kitchen court, and that is far more cottagey than the rest. Barnsley used all the motifs that could be culled from the Cotswold vernacular: hipped roofs, eaves of different heights, two lanterns like Saracen's helmets, quaint chimneystacks (Plates 162–5), walls and flags and tiles of Cotswold stone. It was a romantic interpretation of the vernacular—so many pieces of individuality would have been far too expensive for a labourer—but it was vernacular nevertheless. When the house was finished in 1926, work having been slowed down because of the war, it ended with another burst of romanticism in the chapel and garden loggias. But the building in between, with its big gables (giving it, as the *Builder* unkindly remarked, the 'unfortunate skyline effect of an upturned and magnified saw'),[23] seems to have been more massive than the initial conception. The jovial Ernest Barnsley was a persuasive advocate of the Arts and Crafts life.

From the start Rodmarton was conceived with a social object, which was expressed in the lines from Goldsmith's *Deserted Village* inscribed on the side of the porch:

> Ill fares the land, to hastening ill a prey,
> Where wealth accumulates, and men decay;
> Princes and lords may flourish, or may fade,
> A breath can make them, as breath has made;
> But a bold peasantry, their country's pride,
> When once destroy'd can never be supplied.
> A time there was, ere England's griefs began,
> When every rood of ground maintain'd its man;
> For him light labour spread her wholesome store,
> Just gave what life requir'd, but gave no more;
> His best companions, innocence and health;
> And his best riches, ignorance of wealth.

It was 'Mrs. Biddulph—austerely elegant, her benevolence intermittently masked by her caustic wit—who, presiding over house and village like the abbess of some great medieval religious house, was the animating and directing force.'[24] She was strong-willed and unconventional. She had been to horticultural college, and it was there that she had met her future head gardener, whose name, with that of the foreman, but not, typically of the Arts and Crafts movement, that of the architect or owner, was put up over the door to the garden in a tablet which reads:

> A. Wright Faber Tignarius
> W. Scrubey Hortorium Cultor

'I've seen no modern work to equal it,' wrote Ashbee after a visit in October 1914,

> nothing I know of Lutyens or Baker comes up to it. And when I ask why I find the answer in the system, the method rather than the man. It is a house built on the basis not of contract but of confidence and Barnsley has been allowed a free hand to put all his personal knowledge and technique into the work. The Eng. Arts and Crafts Movement at its best is here—so are the vanishing traditions of the Cotswolds.[25]

The stones and slates for building were quarried near the house, brought to the site in farm carts, and shaped and laid by local masons. Timber for the oak floors and rafters was felled and seasoned on the estate. The tree trunks were even sawn by hand, using a two-man saw in a sawpit, although the method had long been made obsolete by machine-driven circular saws.[26] In fact everything was done by hand, and as much as possible by estate workers—even the inkwells were made by the local blacksmith; and Barnsley, if a

232

162–5. Cotswold stone chimneys at Rodmarton

166. (above) Rodmarton library in use as village workshop

167. (right) Rocking-horse made by Rodmarton estate workers

168. (middle) Light sconce from Rodmarton, probably to a Gimson design

169. (far right) Lead downpipe at Rodmarton embossed with an owl

newcomer, at least lived locally, and pedalled over to inspect progress with a book open on the handlebars of his bicycle. With Home Place, Rodmarton was one of the very few Arts and Crafts country houses which—true to principle—were actually constructed without a contractor.

Inside, a broad passage runs the length of the north front. Behind it is the hall (now library), which could be used as a theatre for village performances. Like a medieval hall, it is entered by a door at one end, and opposite this door another gives into the garden, hinting at the arrangement of a medieval screens passage. At the west end is the dining room, coming forward in one arm of the garden front's U. The whole of the east wing separates it from the kitchen so that—with a suggestion of self-conscious primitivism— every meal had to be carried past Mr and Mrs Biddulph's rooms. The library, which balances the dining room at the west end, was originally used as a work room for the villagers (Plate 166). The rural atmosphere of the house is indicated by the names of the bedrooms upstairs: Jackamants, Lordsdown, Stonehill . . .

Although Sidney Barnsley designed much of the furniture in the house, he set up a workshop so that the estate workers could have a part in making it. As at Daneway, each man saw his job through from the beginning to end, thus avoiding the evils of the division of labour. The most impressive piece made in the workshop is the dining-room dresser, the design for which is dated 21 June 1924.[27] Like most Barnsley designs, it relies for its effect on the contrasting geometrical planes of the wood. In addition, the estate workers also made beds, tables, chests chairs (some covered in tapestry designed by Alfred Powell, an architect who lived in the village); and other local crafts were encouraged. The Rodmarton Women's Guild made a series of appliqué work hangings to the design of Hilda Sexton, on local themes such as Hunting (1921), the Village Green (1922, Colour Plate xxv), Farmyard at Irongate (1923) and Archery. The rugs in the entrance hall, which are white with a brown chevron repeat, were also made in the village.

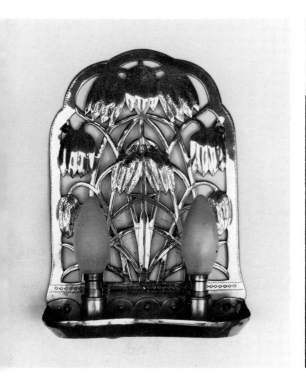

Most of the ironwork was made—often to Gimson designs—by Gimson's old blacksmith, Alfred Bucknell of Tunley. Gimson 'discovered' him, installed him in a shop at Sapperton, and set him to work copying medieval latches and making casements for his own cottage. Later, he was given more delicate work, including handles for furniture, and he took on apprentices, so as many as four or five smiths were sometimes at work. The Rodmarton window casements were all made by hand. Jewson made the decorative leadwork on gutters and downpipes outside the house (Plate 169), which have brackets embossed with owls, cocks, rabbits and other local creatures, the craft having been revived following Lethaby's *Leadwork Old and Ornamental*, published in 1893. Unfortunately, Gimson had died in 1919 before Rodmarton was ready to receive decoration; but his work can be seen in numerous other Arts and Crafts houses, and Jewson executed friezes in the Gimson style at Rodmarton village hall.

The Romantic Country House: Domestic Ideals

Rodmarton was a triumph of craftwork revived and applied. Even so the Sapperton enterprise did not fulfil the broader social vision the architects had set out with. In the early years it seemed that Gimson and the Barnsleys had hoped that their endeavour would be the first step in establishing a larger community of craftsmen. In 1901 Sidney Barnsley wrote to Webb: 'At present we have a small workshop in Cirencester with two or three men making furniture we cannot undertake—the idea being to get hold of a few capable and trustworthy craftsmen and eventually have workshops in the country where we should all join together and form a nucleus to which in time others would attach themselves.'[28] Nothing came of this immediately, although Gimson continued to lay plans for a craft village and, according to Jewson, 'got as far as to buy the land and make sure of a water supply for it about two miles from Sapperton. Then the 1914–18 War prevented any further progress and he died so soon after that the whole project came to nothing.'

C. R. Ashbee (the 'artist and furniture freakist' whom Lutyens found 'most to me distasteful')[29] thought ruefully of the more modest but more permanent enterprise at Daneway when his own Guild of Handicraft—a band of whose craftsmen, their wives and children, totalling one hundred and fifty souls, had left Whitechapel to settle in the village of Chipping Camden in 1902—went into liquidation in 1907. But conversely Sidney Barnsley and the others felt that, with its wider social aims, the Guild of Handicraft had partly achieved what they themselves set out to do.[30] The Sapperton enterprise was more permanent, but it was unable to halt the changes taking place in the countryside. In part, the craftsmen themselves misunderstood the problems of rural England. Although Gimson smiled when cab-drivers, seeing him in his hobnailed boots on a rare expedition to London, called out, 'Hullo, guv'nor, how are the crops?', he was not a countryman by birth. The same quotation from *The Deserted Village* that was put up at Rodmarton was used on the frontispiece to George Sturt's study of rural life, *Change in the Village*, published in 1912. Sturt lived all his life in Farnham, in Surrey, where he observed at first hand the poverty and demoralisation of the local villagers whose traditional way of life was vanishing. But he understood his neighbours and did not think

236

170. The staircase at Besford Court, Worcestershire

171. The staircase at Besford Court

they would 'be sympathetic at all to those self-conscious revivals of peasant arts which are now being recommended to the poor by a certain type of philanthropist'.[31] The old peasant culture had been sturdy but there had been misery and ignorance in it too, and the people who really knew it did not want it back.

Rigidly true to their principles, the Sapperton craftsmen also had a conviction about what was good for other people. Gimson had a way of making both friends and potential customers feel guilty, as Arthur Benson, Master of Magdalene, found. 'I have had to part company with Gimson,' he wrote to William Rothenstein, who had recommended him, 'he wouldn't design me what I wanted, only what he thought it right of me to want'.[32] That attitude was perfectly justified in the case of an architect-craftsman who refused to compromise his standards, but it became a serious flaw when applied to his social perceptions. However much they might laugh at the vicar, they would not truly become part of the village they lived in without going to church. Never, never would they do that.

Through the determination of the three principal participants the Sapperton community successfully lived out the ideals of practising crafts and living in the countryside to the end. On a personal level it was haunted by the suggestion of failure and

238

xxv. The Village Green, 1922, one of a series of appliqué work hangings made by the Rodmarton Women's Guild for Rodmarton Manor

xxvi. The entrance corridor at Rodmarton Manor, Gloucestershire

XXVIII. Lord and Lady Beauchamp and their family in the staircase hall at Madresfield in 1924, by W. B. Ranken (private collection)
XXVII (left). The chapel at Madresfield Court, Worcestershire, looking west
XXIX. The chapel at Madresfield, looking east

ARDENRVN PLACE · SVRREY
· THE ENTRANCE PORCH ·

172. Portrait of Detmar Blow
by Augustus John, 1913
(private collection)

even tragedy that befell so many Arts and Crafts undertakings. In the early 1900s, at about the time of the move from Pinbury, the two Ernests—Barnsley and Gimson—quarrelled badly. At this distance it is not possible to be certain of the cause, although a disagreement between the wives may have been at the root of it, and there is no doubt that Mrs Ernest Barnsley, who was markedly less enthusiastic for the rural life than the others, spoke her mind. The result was that, although they both continued to live within a stone's throw of each other in the tiny village of Sapperton, the Gimson and the Ernest Barnsley households broke off all communication.[33] Good relations were never restored, which perhaps was the greatest failure of the Sapperton community.

From the point of view of a single country house, the worst Arts and Crafts tragedy was at Besford Court (Plates 170–1): work on the big new courtyard there finished abruptly when the architect, Randall Wells, eloped with Lady Noble, the wife of the owner.[34] The couple married and started a craft workshop called the St Veronica's Guild, but Wells received only one more major commission—for St Wilfrid's church, Halton, built in the late 1930s—and his wife eventually went mad.

Architects—especially Arts and Crafts architects with feudal beliefs—occupied an uneasy position at the beginning of the century. The feudal question could be seen from two vantage points, the labourer's or the lord of the manor's. Neither was readily accessible to the professional man, who found himself somewhere in between. Gimson and

243

xxx. Ernest Newton's Ardenrun Place, Surrey, in a watercolour perspective by Alick G. Horsnell, 1910 (RIBA drawings collection)

173. The garden front of Wilsford Manor, Wiltshire, with chequerwork on the main block and thatch on the servants' wing

the Barnsleys were some of the few who took the flinty road of craftsmanship and gave up thoughts of worldly success. The other way required a large and successful practice—just the kind of practice, in fact, that was most difficult to reconcile with locality, hand-work, personal care and the other Arts and Crafts values. The architect who tried hardest to make the reconciliation was Detmar Blow (Plate 172), who, by his success and failure, was almost a metaphor for the whole Arts and Crafts movement.

After Munstead Wood, Lutyens was never quite as serious about the Arts and Crafts movement as some contemporaries would have liked: his houses have a streak of individuality which, although it makes them architecture, ran counter to the cult of the anonymous craftsman. But Blow, who was his friend as well as his successful rival, was more dedicated to the cause. His houses are solid and substantial and intentionally lacking in meretricious brilliance; their quality lies in the use of the best materials worked in the best possible way. Blow was an innocent. A lovable, fastidious personality and a joy in simple things permeate his own house, Hilles, in Gloucestershire.[35] Thrust up on a bastion because of sloping ground, the house looks as though it grew out of the soil. Begun in 1914, it was built on a site chosen for its spectacular views of rolling countryside and woods, but the house was not orientated to take advantage of the view. In Elizabethan fashion, it turns its shoulder to the panorama, only casting a backward glance, so to speak, through a comparatively small number of not very large windows. On the ground floor, only a bay at the end of the Long Room looks out on this side. Hilles was built in stages; but even allowing for this, it does not seek to make a triumphant, unified impression. The broad window bay which goes up above the thatched eaves of the roof is disproportionately big, fitted to need rather than to conventional notions of architecture. The rooms—with their Mortlake tapestries, their panelling, their seventeenth-century

244

174. The garden front of Hilles, Gloucestershire

furniture—are not without a sense of grandeur; but equally the stone flags of the hall, the elm floorboards and ceilings throughout the house, the plainness and solidity of the architecture, and the simplified mouldings to the windows and fireplaces suggest a relish for the natural qualities of materials unadorned (Plates 175–6). The way the life of the house was organised, socially and domestically, completed the aesthetic whole.

Blow imbibed his inspiration from John Ruskin, the fount of all Arts and Crafts theory. The great sage, then in his declining years and suffering from intermittent bouts of madness, happened upon Blow, aged twenty-one, sketching in Abbeville Cathedral. They crossed France together and went to Italy, the young architect reading nightly from the works of Gibbon. 'Detmar is good as gold,' wrote Ruskin in a letter of 1888.[36] To his diary of the same year he committed the poignant, scattered images of happiness in the Alps before his last onset of madness (Morez, Jura, 2 September): 'Detmar sketched a Jura cottage, and I painted it for him yesterday at St. Laurent . . .' Then in a letter (Merligen, 11 November): 'The gentians I sent you a day or two ago were gathered by Detmar—higher than I can climb now . . .' From Ruskin came Detmar's passionate love of fine craftsmanship and also his socialism, which shaded over into the romantic toryism expressed at Hilles. He gave up his conventional architect's training and apprenticed himself, under Ruskin's influence, to a builder at Newcastle-upon-Tyne. This gave him the experience to become Ernest Gimson's foreman and builder at Stoneywell Cottage; and it was Gimson who gave Blow the idea for the butterfly-plan of his first big house on his own, Happisburgh Manor—one of the group of radical Arts and Crafts seaside houses in Norfolk, which included Prior's Home Place at Holt.

After this unworldly start, Blow's career took off swiftly. The young idealist was taken under the wing of Philip Webb, who introduced him to Percy Wyndham and his family at Clouds. Through Wyndham's son, George, Blow became inducted into the blue-blooded, intellectual world of the Souls. As the self-styled wits of their generation, it might have been expected that they should have gone to Lutyens, who was witty both in his conversation and in his buildings. But—although Hudson and Riddell eddied on the outer circles of the vortex—the only true Soul Lutyens hooked was the cricketer, barrister and M.P. Alfred Lyttleton, who was Gladstone's nephew, although he also built for his brother-in-law, H. J. Tennant, brother of Margot Asquith. In politics most of the Souls were Conservatives; perhaps this led them to prefer Blow's architecture, with its unquestioning reverence for tradition. Whatever the case, it was Blow—a familiar figure at Clouds under George Wyndham's regime—who became their favoured architect. He built Mill Hill in Yorkshire for Hugh Fairfax-Cholmeley, Wilsford Manor (Plate 173) in Wiltshire for Lady Glenconner (the sister of George Wyndham and sister-in-law of Margot Asquith), and the north-east wing of Stanway for Lady Glenconner's sister, Lady Elcho, who had a long-standing relationship with Arthur Balfour.

He added a chapel at Hewell Grange, in Worcestershire, and reciprocated by buying furniture from Gay Plymouth's workshop there for Hilles. The Souls were high-minded about Empire, and Blow designed the Government Buildings in Rhodesia. By the early years of the new century, prestige with the Souls had led to country houses for clients who were not Souls at all. They included North Bovey Manor for Lord Hambleden, grandson of the newsagent W. H. Smith, and Little Ridge, in Wiltshire, for Hugh Morrison, art collector and heir to a haberdashery fortune.

246

175. The Long Room at Hilles

176. Staircase at Hilles

In 1910 Blow married Winifred, the second daughter of the Hon. Hamilton Tollemache. The obvious comparison is with Lutyens's marriage to Lady Emily Lytton, and equally the Tollemache connection was not made to advance Blow's career—he was forty-three, had established his practice, and had already done most of his best creative work. But Blow's own ancestry—he was the son of a shellac, tea and coffee merchant in Mincing Lane—was artistic rather than aristocratic; an ancestor was Dr John Blow, Purcell's tutor, and his mother was taught the piano by Clara Schumann. There can be no doubt about the romantic nature of the circumstances under which they met: Blow was making a sketching trip through Suffolk in a gipsy caravan, and had ended up in the grounds of Helmingham Hall, where Winifred was raised. Detmar's less successful brother Sydney, an actor and playwright, was to view the marriage as evidence of the social ambition which he described with fraternal lack of delicacy, and even perhaps some jealousy: 'Detmar always had rigid ideas for raising the family up! Up! UP!'[37]

Hilles was begun in 1914 but, interrupted by Blow's service as an ambulanceman during the First World War, still had not been completely finished at his death in 1939. It was a house Webb would have approved of: 'The rooms are large and full of light,' wrote Detmar's friend the Hon. Neville Lytton.[38] 'The hall is paved with stone, which does not fear the muddiest boots. The long drawing-room has a floor of raw elm, which also cannot be injured by large boots with nails in the soles . . . There is little furniture—one or two beautiful chests and chests of drawers; three or four tapestries and three or four pictures; a splendidly solid dining-table, a few good chairs; an old organ, and one beautiful frieze carved by the owner.' The Long Room served as a living hall, and a wide staircase, without banisters or any other ornament, gave off it. All the bedrooms faced south.

Blow ran his little kingdom on 'sovietic' lines. Contrary to usual practice, Mrs Blow did everything herself for the children. She breast-fed and washed them, and the nurse who was also employed was 'merely an understudy'. The children were not beaten when they were naughty, but corrected by means of persuasion, example and kindness—although even Lytton had to admit that the drawback to this system was 'a period of monstrous anarchy between the years of five and ten'. There was no nursery to keep the children out of the way of the rest of the family; and there were no proper servants' quarters. For a time, family and servants ate together in the kitchen, at separate tables but sharing the same food and some of the same conversation, but this proved so embarrassing to both parties that the experiment had to be abandoned.

Since the Blows were agnostics, daily prayers were abolished; folk culture, however, had a kind of sanctity in Arts and Crafts households, so each morning the children sang a hymn or a folksong in the hall before starting work. The two maids and the odd man as

177. The kitchen at Hilles

often as not joined in too. Generally there was country dancing after tea, with the servants helping to make up the sets. But Blow, with a Church of England living in his gift, did not neglect the established church: he supported the parson because he was part of the traditional fabric of the countryside. His attitude to the farm, which could be seen from the front door of the house (Plate 1), was equally romantic. 'Having had a terrible struggle to acquire his own small fortune', he was 'determined that those who live by the land and on the land should have no other enemies but fickle nature and still more fickle politics'. Consequently he only charged his farmer a peppercorn rent.

'A terrible struggle': Blow had only been able to achieve his domestic ideal at a cost. In 1906 he was so busy with country-house work, having just taken on North Bovey Manor that he was forced to look for a partner. He found one in the Frenchman Fernand Billery, whom he had met through the sculptor John Tweed, a pupil of Rodin. For someone of Blow's radical ideals, it was an almost inexplicable choice. Commercially, as other architects were quick to point out, there were clear arguments in its favour. The Ritz Hotel, Piccadilly, had just opened its doors, and Beaux-Arts Classicism was at the height of its vogue as the smart style in London. It may have been that Blow thought the French manner more appropriate for the metropolis: the Arts and Crafts movement failed to find a style for the town. Its architecture as well as its ideals was essentially rural. Blow and Billery saw no irony in announcing their intention to build Wallingford Court in a style 'typical of an Englishman's country residence, quite free from foreign influence'.[39] But some people saw a contradiction. 'We are informed by an assertive though small clique, whose aims are not entirely disinterested,' said John Kinross, 'that nothing good can be done except by the Craftsman . . . Mr. Detmar Blow implores us in Gilbert's words "to be Early English ere it be too late", turns craftsman, builds his own house walls as is self-evident, but with an eye to the main chance keeps a partner who can do work in the best French style.'[40] At least some of the money to build came from the suave London town houses.

Worse was to come. For years Blow had known 'Bendor', the playboy second Duke of Westminster, whose mother, Lady Sibell Grosvenor, married George Wyndham in 1887. Bendor was heir to the vastly lucrative Grosvenor Estate, which not only owned large swathes of Cheshire but most of Mayfair in London. Before the war, Blow worked for Westminster as a private architect. Among other things, he built a French hunting lodge, Mimizan, in the Landes, and would travel there with the Duke, stopping off to look at buildings on the way. Eventually he came to take a hand in the Duke's business affairs. At the very time Hilles was rising, 1917, Lutyens wrote: 'he is doing no work except for a house for himself and living with Westminster, running his house, a sort of bailiff and maître d'hôtel, as far as I can make out.'[41]

It was a bizarre relationship but continued after the war when Westminster persuaded Blow to become his agent. Although Wallingford was proposed in 1913, it was never carried out. The year 1914 was an ominous date for Hilles to begin. The Westminster connection was perhaps Blow's answer to changing circumstances, but only an innocent could have failed to foresee the consequences. Westminster had the charm of an aristocrat and a millionaire, but he was self-indulgent, and could be both changeable and cruel. When he married for the third time in 1930, his new wife, Loelia Ponsonby, objected to the swarm of sycophants she saw as forming his entourage, and particularly took exception to Blow. The end came on board the Duke's yacht *Flying Cloud*, which in earlier days Blow had designed to resemble an eighteenth-century country house.[42] As well as the Westminster menage, Blow had ended up running the Grosvenor estate property in London; his reward seems to have come in the form of the occasional gesture of largesse from the Duke. Now an accusation was made against him—it may have been over the assigning of leases, it may have been, as some thought, about something as trivial as the new car Blow had bought for the chauffeur at Eaton. But the result was that Blow, in his late sixties, was ignominiously dismissed; and whenever he tried to see his former friend and employer to heal the wound, Westminster would not have him admitted. Blow suffered a nervous collapse and retired to Hilles for the six remaining years of his life. He continued to do some modest work locally and to care for old buildings, but he never recovered.

Poor Blow. Every Arts and Crafts venture—from Morris and Co. to the Guild of Handicraft and even the Sapperton craftsmen—foundered on the rock-like facts of the economic system in late nineteenth and early twentieth-century Britain. By nature an innocent, Blow never lost the Arts and Crafts ideals expressed in his private life at Hilles. To acquire and preserve the fortune necessary to realise them, however, involved compromise. A worldly man would have seen the dichotomy, but it was Blow's strength and his weakness that he kept his innocence intact to the end.

The Romantic Country House: Solidarity of All the Arts

The dreadful Bendor was the ogre of the Arts and Crafts movement. He was directly responsible for another tragedy, which became the background to Evelyn Waugh's *Brideshead Revisited*. William Lygon, the seventh Earl Beauchamp, known as 'Boom' to his family and whose seat was Madresfield Court, had married Westminster's sister, Lettice. Waugh came to know four of the children of the marriage, meeting Lord Elmley and his younger brother Hugh at Oxford, then becoming a particular friend of their sisters, Lady Mary and Lady Dorothy Lygon. Lady Dorothy remembered a conversation in which Waugh talked about the novel: 'It's all about a family whose father lives abroad, as it might be Boom—but it's not Boom—and a younger son: people will say he's like Hughie, but you'll see he's not really Hughie—and there's a house as it might be Mad, but it isn't really Mad.'[43] Physically, Brideshead was modelled on Castle Howard rather than Madresfield, but from Madresfield Waugh borrowed the chapel, decorated as a wedding gift from Lady Beauchamp to her husband, and perhaps the most complete realisation of Arts and Crafts theory in Britain. When Charles Ryder entered the chapel at Brideshead, his response was simply, 'Golly'. But as one of the Guild of Handicraft wrote to Ashbee, 'Well I expect you must expect anything from a man, that has his private chapel decorated like a barber's pole and an ice cream barrow.'[44]

Lord Beauchamp's record of public service was outstanding. He was Governor of New South Wales in 1899–1902, Lord President of the Council twice, First Commissioner of Works in 1910–14, Lord Warden of the Cinque Ports in 1913–14, Chancellor of the University of London in 1929 and Liberal Leader in the House of Lords. Ashbee, however, although he commented on the 'splendour and pomp' that surrounded his life,

250

178. Crystal balusters in the staircase hall at Madresfield Court, Worcestershire

also observed that Lord Beauchamp had unusual sensitivity and a 'touch more human tenderness'. That, he commented, 'comes I should say from the homogenic side of him, for that side is there without doubt though I have not gone near enough to discuss it'.[45] To Ashbee and his circle, 'homogenic' was a private word for homosexual (preferred since both halves of the word derived from the same language, Greek). With some prescience he continued:

> His lordship knows doubtless what a mighty solvent it is, and caste is caste. But I chuckle to myself when I look into the eyes of a man whom I know to feel as I do, and think how if I chose to put forth the power of the word I could make all the splendour and pomp pass away like smoke, and leave only the bare soul of the man, naked as the Italian Quattrocentist might have drawn it in its progress to heaven or hell.

Lord Beauchamp was not only a patron but—in dramatic contrast to his hunting neighbours—something of an artist and craftsman in his own right. In the small library at Madresfield is a set of chairs upholstered in materials that he embroidered, and he also sculpted a small statuette in the same room, which tackles the difficult pose of a naked young golfer in full swing.

Madresfield, a Tudor house extended in the late sixteenth century and largely rebuilt by P. C. Hardwick in 1863–88, is entered by a low, dark porch.[46] This does not give into an entrance hall but what is really a broad passage, running around two sides of the inner courtyard and panelled in dark oak. This in turn leads into an equally dark ante-room, hung with tapestries. But the staircase hall, remodelled at the turn of the century, is a contrast of light and spaciousness, rising up through two storeys and lit by three glass domes. It was made from a number of smaller rooms knocked together, so its proportions seem slightly strange. But then that is very much part of the character of the room. The stair and the gallery, together running round three sides of the room, have balusters of solid crystal (Plate 178), and the original Art Nouveau light fittings were each made of two octagonal bands of opaque glass at right-angles to each other. The motto carved in the cornice clearly suggests the self-consciously artistic mood of the seventh Earl's work in the house, which is not without a ray of poetry: 'Shadows fly: life like a dome of many coloured glass stains the white radiance of eternity until death tramples it to fragments. The one remains, the many change and pass: Heaven's light forever shines.'

It seems likely that the alterations to the staircase hall were carried out by Ashbee and members of the Guild of Handicraft, founded in 1888, who were also responsible for work in the library.[47] Ashbee first visited the house on 6 January 1902, a couple of months before the Guild moved to Gloucestershire. He returned again in March and December, when he was apparently advising on who should paint Lady Beauchamp's portrait. Presumably the decoration of the library (Plate 179) was mooted in this year. The work was delayed but it was underway by 1905, because on 3 March Will Hart, one of the carvers in the Guild of Handicraft, wrote to Ashbee: 'Lord Beauchamp came down to the Court today, he seemed very pleased with the deepening results of the "Tree of Life" end, he is making an addition of another motto in Greek, which I should term swank, having already one in Latin on the end.' But in the end only the Latin motto—the leaves of the tree are the salvation of the people—was carved, scrolling through the upper branches of the Tree of Life that runs up through a miniature Jerusalem on the end of the bookstacks.

On another end, a human-headed serpent slithers down the Tree of Knowledge while Eve tempts Adam with the forbidden fruit (Plate 180).

A door carved with the Crucifixion leads to the chapel. After the pleasant gravity of the library, where the only suggestion of colour comes from the rich bindings of the books, the chapel is radiant with flowers. Its poetry is that of an idyllic family life, and all the more poignant since in the end that life was denied Lord Beauchamp. The chapel had been built by Hardwick in 1867. When it was finally decorated (Colour Plates XXVII, XXIX), it perfectly expressed the ideal embodied by the Arts and Crafts organisation the Art Workers' Guild—as Selwyn Image, a master of the Guild, put it—of 'the Unity, the Independence, the Solidarity of all the Arts'.[48]

H. A. Payne painted the murals in tempera. On the east wall Lady Beauchamp is shown in her bridal gown, kneeling in the attitude of a donor; her husband kneels in his robes of state on the other side of the altar. Although work began soon after the wedding in 1902 it took so long to finish the frescoes that the additional figures of the Lygon children were worked into the design at the west end. Lord Elmley, the future eighth Earl Beauchamp, kneels with a broad-brimmed straw hat on his back, and next to him is an angel playing the harp. Lady Sibell and Lady Lettice sit on a carpet of flowers above this

179. The library at Madresfield

group, studying a book. The youngest brother, Richard, stands alone on the other side of the arch, while on the opposite wall Lady Mary and Lady Dorothy, the youngest sisters, play at the skirts of an angel in red, who is said to have been their nanny. Because they were added at intervals over a period of years, all the children look about the same age.

The joyous, delicate colours were intentionally flower-like. An unsigned and undated book on the chapel, presumably written by Payne (who certainly designed the woodcuts) and published in about 1907, opens with the verse from the Song of Solomon: 'A Garden enclosed is my sister—my spouse'. This links the theme of the garden to the nuptial celebrations, although the chapel also seems the perfect expression of the Edwardians' desire to open their rooms out to the fresh air and sunlight, and to unite the garden with the house. The book describes the mood of the chapel in characteristically Arts and Crafts language:

> Through the open window steals the scent of blue-spiked lavender and jessamine with stars of white; the litany of gentle doves rises Heavenward to the music of the humming bees. The world without is glad with a thousand colours and a thousand songs, for every flower turns its face in praise to God, and every throat of things created has a song of Glory to His Name. And the walls within have caught the glory of the world outside: overhead is green, colour of charity and peace; honeysuckle clings to the rafters, doves circle about them.

180. Bookstacks at Madresfield

181. A door from the library at Madresfield

The figures above the dado, the armour-clad St Michael and the Virgin and Child on the opposite wall, stand on a narrow verge radiant with old English flowers: crown-imperial, fritillary, primrose, snow-drops, violets. 'Here twines convolvulus, and here the saffron scarcely blooms, love-in-the-mist, pale eye of faith looking dimly from a cloud of green, the pomp of sweet carnation, the purity of meek lilies, the crimson secret of the rose.' A trellis with climbing roses is skilfully used to define the space on which the figures stand.

Painted above the altar on the east wall, Christ is enthroned in the Tree of Life. 'Angels kneel before Him offering as incense the prayers of all mankind.' The reredos shows Christ in a chasuble offering the invitation to communion. 'Behind Him is spread the table of the Marriage-feast, attendant angels hold the wedding garments, "the garments of praise", to be put on in place of the spirit of heaviness by all who would come to the Marriage-feast.' Jerusalem can be seen through windows at the back, perhaps a reference to the new Jerusalem of this world, inhabited by craftworkers and sparkling with their creations, to which some Arts and Crafts thinkers looked forward. Certainly the figures in the flanking panels of the triptych, the Reaper and the Vine Dresser, rather tenuously combine Biblical allusion with the principles of William Morris.

Apart from the murals, much of the decorative scheme was executed by members of a band of craftsmen known as the Birmingham Group, most of whom were teachers at the Birmingham Municipal School of Art, which was particularly associated with the revival of tempera painting. The link may have been provided by Robert Hilton, who made the chalice, since Hilton was a Chester metalworker who had already done work for the Grosvenor family, and had studied briefly at the Municipal School of Art in Birmingham.[49] The altar frontal was worked by the two daughters of the local vicar.

If in *Brideshead Revisited* the reason for Lord Marchmain's absence abroad is mysterious, that for Lord Beauchamp's self-imposed exile, taken up in 1931 to avoid a scandal of Oscar Wilde–like dimensions, was all too palpable. It was nothing less than that his brother-in-law, Westminster, having discovered what Ashbee called his 'homogenic side', ruthlessly set about to destroy him.[50] First he told George V, who had made him a Knight of the Garter, then Lady Beauchamp. The age and society in which she lived were such that she did not understand what the term 'homosexual' meant. At the Duke's insistence, a warrant for Lord Beauchamp's arrest was issued after he had left the country. He was not allowed to return to England for his wife's funeral in July 1936, and the Home Secretary only relented for that of his son Hughie, who died from a fractured skull after a fall in Germany in August the same year. In 1937 he returned to Madresfield, where he intermittently stayed for long periods.

The flowers in the chapel had not faded, and the children still looked angelic. But the freshness and promise and air of hymeneal celebration in this most lovely of all Arts and Crafts rooms had been blighted. The Arts and Crafts movement was a romance for an innocence that it was impossible to recover, and the chapel at Madresfield was its most poignant symbol.

8. *The Road to Good Taste*

At first sight, it might seem that the most palpable differences between the social and the romantic country house lay inside. The way in which owners lived was probably more clearly revealed in the way they furnished their rooms—whether with gilt sofas and palm stands in the *Style Louis Seize* or with austere oak dressers and benches—than in the external style of their buildings. Façades might be for dignity or display or idealism, but not only were chairs for sitting in, which made them subject to considerations of comfort, but their choice and arrangement was likely to be the one aspect of the commission that was securely in the owner's rather than his architect's grasp. There were undoubtedly some dramatic contrasts—between Standen and Manderston, for example, or between both and Wickham Hall (Plate 183). But there also existed an increasing area of common ground between the extremes, especially in the use of antiques and the general dislike of clutter. Both the social and the romantic country house were in their way important as contributing to the shared ideal of Good Taste which was especially associated with neo-Georgian interiors before the First World War, and which—with their tactful mixture of objects and furniture (mostly old), their reticence, their light colours and their freedom from overcrowding—has survived as the ruling principle of innumerable interiors down to the present day.

There were two principal reasons for architects wanting to furnish more simply, the first of which was the servant problem. 'Most rooms are woefully overcrowded,' lamented Walter Shaw Sparrow. '. . . In these days of continuous effort to diminish the burden of service, every piece of not strictly necessary furniture means so much more labour for the housemaid, so much more area for the accumulation of dust and dirt, and so much more opportunity for accident and damage.'[1] It was desirable both that there should be fewer pieces of furniture, and that each piece should be free from unnecessary ornament: one of the 'striking characteristics' of the best articles of furniture was 'the ease with which they can be dusted and kept clean'. Elder Duncan was of the same mind. 'A multitude of small tables, chairs, palm-stands, and other articles, so disposed as to leave but narrow lanes through which one must thread one's way gingerly and warily, is a common defect.' He was appalled at 'the enormous amount of labour entailed day in day out in dusting and cleaning'.[2]

However, the second impetus towards simplicity was aesthetic, and came in the

257

182. *Style Louis Seize* at Culford Hall, Suffolk

183. The billiard room at Wickham Hall, Kent

184. The Abbot's Parlour at Forthampton Court, Gloucestershire

example of Philip Webb. Although Webb worked closely with Morris and Co., his own taste in decoration was austere. A house like Stanmore Hall, decorated by Morris and Co. in 1890, reflects the legacy of Morris's own preference for ornament and plenty of it. Every inch of the main rooms was covered in colour and pattern, whether painted, woven or dyed. Very different, however, is Webb's contemporary Standen, with its largely white-painted panelling and period furniture, where Morris and Co. fabrics and wallpaper were used, but only sparingly.[3]

A few years earlier, Webb had enlarged and 'repaired' Forthampton Court (Plate 184) for John Reginald Yorke, father of the novelist Henry Greene.[4] Webb, who took infinite pains about every aspect of his work, went with the Yorkes to Morris and Co.'s show room in London to choose some hangings and a carpet for the drawing room. This room was made out of the upper part of the medieval hall, at that time divided into two storeys and known as the Abbot's Parlour. Webb made his views felt. 'Practically,' he wrote in a letter dated 18 November 1890, 'with the fine roof, the wall hangings, and the carpet, the room would be quite furnished, anything else added would be for convenience of use only; any other furniture could not be too scanty and should be, I am sure, simple in the extreme.'[5] Mr Yorke, however, a friend of Balfour and Lord Randolph Churchill, was not to be dictated to, and four days later Webb wrote again, evidently in reply to a bristly letter from Forthampton: 'I had no wish to limit the moveable furniture for the Abbot's Hall to two cricket stools and a toasting fork—but, I thought to stimulate your enthusiasm for the noble room by showing how it made itself without the assistance of the modern furnisher who, in these days of the art dilettante, chokes up space as if it were a thing offensive, and to be got rid of as much as possible.' As usual, the client seems to have been won round, for a year later Webb could congratulate Mrs Yorke on having kept the house 'simple and quiet when fitting it for use'. Morris fabrics were here more in evidence than at Standen; and it is difficult to believe that the room was really all that simple and quiet from the late nineteenth-century photograph showing it with Christmas decorations hung from the roof timbers. Nevertheless, the intention was there; and the room was in fact considerably less cluttered than most contemporary drawing rooms.

Webb was not the only architect to encourage simplicity. 'It is disconcerting, you will admit,' wrote Norman Shaw, 'when you find that your host and hostess are less noticeable than their wall-papers and furnitures.'[6] With their admiration for cottage interiors and simple, country furniture, Shaw's pupils and their brethren at the Art Workers' Guild reacted still more vehemently against over-furnishing. One even suspects Voysey of a Puritanical distaste for comfort in his very sparing use of upholstery. Others certainly fell victim to mortifications of the flesh: 'There are certain moods when one feels a kind of pleasure from any slight physical inconvenience, and this may, if desired, take the form of sitting on a hard seat, especially when one feels it may be ended at will, by the aid of handy cushions.'[7] Lutyens's personal tastes were almost as spartan, so it is no wonder that he was aghast when he saw the oak hall at West Dean (Plate 17). On his last site visit to Monkton in 1904, the week before the Jameses' annual Goodwood house party, he spent the couple of hours he had to wait before his train came helping Mrs James rearrange it. Assisted by three of the servants, he took out the polar bear, a sedan chair, two screens and various other pieces of furniture; and he found it still over-full.[8]

If an owner wanted advice on how to furnish his new home, or even to have the whole

thing done for him, there were a number of possibilities. He could ask the architect. Lutyens, although he designed a limited amount of furniture, in particular for Delhi, was in fact not as interested in furniture or decoration as some contemporaries. He did design a number of plain oak pieces for his Arts and Crafts houses, such as the dining-room sideboard at Deanery Garden, with a faceted front and shelves that were piled high with pewter; but most of his Arts and Crafts rooms were furnished with antiques. But Voysey, Ambrose Heal Jnr and above all Sidney Barnsley were making unstained oak almost the inevitable material for Arts and Crafts furniture in the 1890s and early 1900s. Of oak too were the roof timbers, floorboards, wall braces and panelling of the architect-designed rooms that it was used in. Nevertheless, there were some who felt that cottage-style furniture was inappropriate to a big house. Contrary to reputation, the lead was given by Morris and Co. From the first they had made bobbin-turned chairs based on seventeenth-century originals, and by 1890 their stylistic range was much wider. According to Muthesius, Philip Webb, who designed much of the furniture, 'was extremely catholic in his choice of means: he used Gothic and Renaissance forms, such materials as oak and mahogany, his treatments always included polished and natural wood, inlay and painted ornament. He always aimed for simplicity. But Morris furniture does not shun echoes of historical art; and it always retains a certain degree of refinement.'[9] Webb largely furnished Standen with Chippendale and Sheraton revival pieces made by Morris and Co. The 1912 Morris and Co. catalogue advertised that the company specialised 'more particularly in two classes of furniture,' the first of which was 'cabinet work of the highest standard as regards design, workmanship, seasoned woods, figured veneers, and inlaying ... equal to the best productions of Chippendale and Sheraton'. Recently they had obtained some Classical designs from Mervyn Macartney, consulting architect to St Paul's Cathedral and an acknowledged authority on English furniture of the best periods. The second type was its joiner-made or 'cottage' furniture, 'solidly made in oak, stained ash, or painted pine' and specially recommended for bedrooms. By this date Macartney's designs were clearly the ones for the country-house market.

186. Doorhandle from Ardkinglas, Argyllshire

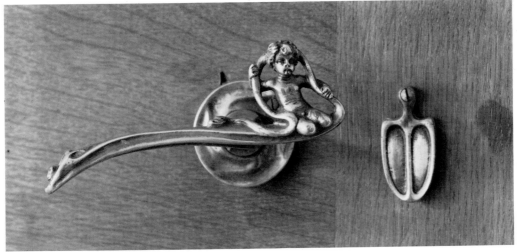

185. The eastern half of the sitting room at Lambay Castle, Co. Dublin

187–8. Lorimer furniture designs and floor plan for the drawing room at Balmanno Castle, Perthshire, and the room as actually furnished

Of all Arts and Crafts architects who designed furniture in a variety of styles, Robert Lorimer—sometimes called the Lutyens of Scotland[10]—probably achieved most. Much of his furniture was made by the Edinburgh firm of Whytock and Reid, although he also liked to think of himself as 'coaching up' other craftsmen, notably the village joiner William Wheeler. 'The only real way to approach design was through a knowledge and appreciation of the material in which your design was to be carried out'; this, he told the Edinburgh Architectural Association, was to him the essence of William Morris's teaching.[11] Lorimer was a member—somewhat grudgingly—of the Art Workers' Guild ('Suppose I ought to be proud to be associated with C. R. Ashbee, Voysey, etc. Anyway I accepted, as it only cost 10/- a year,' he wrote to his friend Dods); and there was a true Arts and Crafts massiveness about the lintel over the drawing-room fireplace at Ardkinglas, which weighed no less than five tons. Not surprisingly, his first furniture designs were Baronial, the North-of-the-Border first cousin to Gothic.

But Lorimer's tastes widened rapidly. He was influenced by visits to museums in Holland, and liked French furniture too, especially if it was inlaid. The extent of his ecleticism can be seen in the pieces he designed for Balmanno, although it seems they were not made (Plates 187–8). The exact position every piece was to occupy was carefully marked on ground plans of the rooms. At Balmanno, Lorimer was combining the role of architect and decorator much as his countryman Robert Adam had done. Like Adam, he could provide designs for firedogs and plasterwork ceilings, and also tapestries and embroideries.

Because he did not work with lathe and chisel himself, he possibly fell some way short of the Arts and Crafts ideal. (He did leave a considerable amount to the intelligence of his craftsman, since he only gave them the briefest scraps of drawings to work from, but it is not possible to say whether that was by accident or design.) The elegance of his designs was appropriate to the handsome rooms for which they were made, and where Sidney Barnsley's massive oak furniture—which Muthesius found 'primitive to excess'—would have been out of place.

Although even the *Lady* (hardly an avant-garde publication) recognised the influence of the Arts and Crafts Exhibition Society on the standard of contemporary production, Arts and Crafts furniture could—because of the means of production—only be possessed by the few. That may be one reason why it never became generally popular, except in the debased—and cheaper—form known as the Quaint Style sold by the London shops. But it could be seen in far more country houses than the new art or *art noveau* furniture, which was so fashionable on the Continent. Although work by Mackintosh, the Glasgow School and Baillie Scott was constantly illustrated in the *Studio*, hardly any country-house owners were tempted to build or decorate in the style. The three largest Art Nouveau houses— Baillie Scott's Blackwell, Mackintosh's The Hill House and George Walton's Wernfawr—were none of them country houses in the sense used in this book.

French Art Nouveau seemed glaringly out of place in Britain. Architects wrote to *The Times* in disgust when George Donaldson donated a high quality collection of contemporary French furniture to the Victoria and Albert Museum. 'Hitherto our British solidity and self-sufficiency have saved us as a nation from foreign contagion,' trumpeted the *Magazine of Art*.[12] But even that journal had to admit that 'certain signs of its presence indicate that here and there some unfortunate has been infected with the hideous disease'.

263

189. Design for an Art
Nouveau billiard room by
George Walton from
*Documents d'architecture
moderne*

It would have pleased the writer to know that the misguided sufferers had little chance to practise the new art on a large scale in British country houses. Strangely, though, the response of certain Continental aristocrats was the reverse of that shown by the British upper classes. Ashbee and Baillie Scott were received with unaccustomed enthusiasm when they visited Darmstadt, home of the artists' colony established by the Grand Duke of Hesse, to decorate rooms in the ducal palace. Baillie Scott arrived by train with a small bag in his hand. He was met at the station by two of the Duke's coaches, one for the luggage, complete with footmen in livery. It was very different from England.

Baillie Scott received other commissions in Central Europe and Russia, the most attractive of which was for the Duke of Hesse's twenty-three year old sister-in-law, Crown Princess Maria of Rumania. For her he designed Art Noveau interiors for Le Nid, a delicious rustic fantasy in the form of a log cabin on stilts—built out of tree trunks in the depths of a pine wood on the family's summer estates and borne aloft by eight living trees. The principal room (a space for praying, sleeping and living) was called 'The Salon of the Sun and the Sunflower', and suns appeared on tiles, seats, windows, ceiling, fireplace, friezes, rugs and tapestries—but it all blew down after the First World War.[13]

Further international recognition came in 1901, when Baillie Scott was awarded the highest prize in a competition for a House for an Art Lover organised by the Darmstadt magazine *Zeitschrift für Innendekoration*. Mackintosh's entry was disqualified since he did not submit the correct number of perspectives; but it pleased the judges—who included Olbrich and Hoffmann—so much that they awarded it a purchase prize all the same (Colour Plates XXXI–XXXII). Both show a sense of colour—dramatically monochrome in the Mackintosh rooms, seductively pretty in Baillie Scott's—very different from most contemporary British country houses, however much their owners were moving away from the sombre purples and greens of the previous decade. Unfortunately neither was built.[14]

Dulce Domum and Der Vogel (as the competition entries were called) were designed for total decorative effect. In this they were unlike many Arts and Crafts rooms, including Lorimer's, which tended to be the sum of their individually crafted items. However, a sense of overall style was becoming increasingly felt in social country houses, where the fashionable decorator—perhaps because owners were tending to buy old houses rather than build new ones—was becoming a more and more vivid presence.

The idea of getting a firm to take care of all the internal appointments of a house was not new. It dated back to the eighteenth century, when not only architects like the Adam brothers but cabinetmakers like Messrs Gillow were ready, at a price, to do everything. Holland and Son, founded in 1815, even supplied the coffin-plates beneath which their clients were buried.[15] By the time the Aesthetic Movement had got under way, other large and equally wide-ranging firms, like Collinson and Locke, Jackson and Graham and Liberty's, had come into existence. Soon Mrs Haweis was warning unsuspecting young home owners against possible displays of temperament or overbearing demeanour: 'He may guide you,' she wrote of the decorator, 'but he must not subjugate you . . . Such stipulations as professional decorators are apt to make—that having undertaken to decorate your room, they are to do it in their own way, and not be "hampered by your prejudices" is, I think, a principle *a priori* false, though I can well understand the professional views and reasons.'[16]

By 1890—somewhat before either the *entente cordiale* or the Ritz Hotel, Piccadilly, with which is it associated—the smartest decorating style was French eighteenth century, whether Louis XV, Louis XVI or something between the two. 'Of course,' commented the *Lady* in 1897, 'the Parisian styles have not got it all their own way, for "Chippendale", "Tudor", "François Premier", "Empire", and "Flemish Renaissance" are all in evidence, but still nothing is so popular as the Louis Quinze and Louis Seize.'[17] Readers had already been recommended to go to the exhibition of French furniture at Harrods, and a Louis XVI drawing room by Messrs Waring and Co. was illustrated. Of the two French styles, Louis XV was in slight decline. Having been overexposed in numerous restaurants, hotels and theatres, it had begun 'to be considered rather common by many people'.[18] On the other hand, the *Lady* felt that 'few decorative styles have ever been devised which possess the fascination of the Louis Seize'.[19] At the middle and bottom end of the market, what went by the name of Louis XVI did not always bear much resemblance to the austere, delicate, straight-legged originals, but on the whole it was considerably more correct than it would have been thirty years earlier. The best furniture was stylistically very accurate. Magnificent collections of French furniture had been formed in the mid-nineteenth century by Lord Pembroke, by the Marquess of Hertford and Sir Richard Wallace, by members of the Rothschild family, and by the Duke of Hamilton. The last mentioned collection, when it was sold in one of the most sensational art sales of the century in 1882, undoubtedly helped to stimulate public interest in French taste; and some commentators unhesitatingly dated its popularity in England to the mid-1880s.[20] It could still be said that 'rooms fitted up in the French style' were becoming 'increasingly popular' in 1907.[21]

Expensive, glamorous, comfortable, cosmopolitan, it was essentially a style for the town. Numerous French decorators—or decorators with French sounding names—were at work in late nineteenth-century Mayfair,[22] but comparatively few ventured into the country. Walter Burns, brother-in-law of J. Pierpont Morgan, was typical in his response. He employed the Parisian decorator Bouwens van der Boijen to create the opulently theatrical interiors, Louis XVI and Rococo, in his town house in Brook Street, where—as so often—old French *boiseries* were reused; but it was Ernest George at his most Elizabethan who enlarged and remodelled Burns's country house, North Mimms Park.[23] To use a French style in a country house implied an attitude to life in the country; it was only done by the smartest of the smart, and largely by those who were already, or aspired to be, members of the Prince of Wales's set. The Duke of Marlborough and Lord d'Abernon both employed Achille Duchêne, one to redecorate the west wing of Blenheim, the other to build Esher Place. The Willie Jameses called in Charles Mellier and Co.

Mellier was typical of many firms doing French work. Despite the name, they do not seem to have been French; certainly there was no office in Paris. The company apparently got under way in the mid-1860s, since the name first appears in the trade directories in 1872. They were not only decorators, in the sense that they could make and install wall hangings, curtains, drapes, ceilings, mouldings and door surrounds, but they also employed craftsmen to make furniture, usually French in style and always done to a very high standard. Pieces have been recorded at Hornby Castle, Sledmere, Lowther Castle and Minley Manor.[24] In 1904 Mellier and Co. represented Great Britain at the St Louis Exhibition, for which they made a replica of the Kensington Orangery. By 1907 they were doing so well that they could occupy a building in Albermarle Street pretentiously named Mellier House.

When George and Peto had finished their work at West Dean, the drawing room and library, the two rooms at the south-west corner of the house, were joined by double doors, and the drawing room had a fan-vaulted ceiling. Mellier and Co. threw over this arrangement, which had survived from the Regency house, in favour of a more characteristically Edwardian space. They opened the two rooms into each other, marking the division by a pair of Corinthian columns; and pushed out a bay on the west side of the room. The result was one room, more spacious, more convenient for large house parties, and more conducive to that flow between guests and activities that a hostess like Mrs James sought to achieve. In style, it was more or less Louis XVI. Certainly it was more accurate than a 'French' room would have been in the mid-nineteenth century,

190. Mewès and Davis's staircase hall at Luton Hoo, Hertfordshire

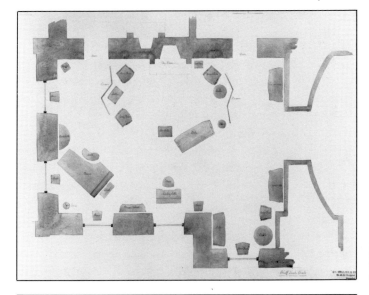

192. Mellier and Co.'s floor plan of the Manderston drawing room showing the intended arrangement of furniture

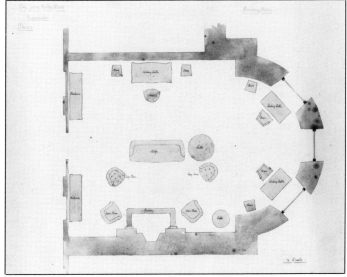

193. Floor plan of the smoking room at Manderston

although—unable to resist extra gilt ornament on the columns—Mellier and Co. made it both richer and more frivolous than the real thing.

Mellier and Co.'s biggest country-house job was Manderston. Inside the house the architect, John Kinross, allowed himself only one un-British touch (the staircase which had a silvered balustrade and was modelled on the Petit Trianon at Versailles) but the Millers were just the kind of people to want the *style Louis Seize*—even when their ceilings were 'Adam'. They had already employed Mellier to decorate their London house, 34 Grosvenor Square.

The easy opulence of the Mellier style is suggested by the local newspaper's report of the first ball which the Millers gave in the newly remodelled house, held on 7 November

269

191. Looking through the ballroom doors to the drawing room at Manderston, Berwickshire

1905.[25] An additional retiring room and supper room had been erected to the south, on the terrace which, presumably, had not yet been planted. The walls of the retiring room were hung with green satin, and with fifteenth and sixteenth-century Gobelins and Flemish tapestries. These, the antique Persian carpet and the 'Louis XV' furniture—seen under the soft electric light coming from a fifteenth-century candelabrum—gave, it was thought, 'a vivid idea . . . of old time luxury'. Beyond the retiring room, the supper room was decorated in primrose and white, which were Sir James's racing colours. They set the tone of the temporary decorations throughout the house. Arriving guests, their wraps having been ushered away to the groin-vaulted cloakroom beside the vestibule, were greeted by a display of lilies and white and yellow chrysanthemums in the hall, arranged between the inevitable potted plants. The drawing room, ballroom and boudoir were furnished with complete suites of reproduction Louis XV and XVI. The pelmets, gathered drapes, *boiseries* and mirrors were equally French; the walls were hung with silk and the curtains in the ballroom were woven with silver and gold thread.

Although the design of individual pieces of furniture was often historically accurate, the arrangement was likely to be purely Edwardian. Floor plans like those at Balmanno survive for Manderston (Plates 192–3). They show that the very formal, neo-Classical furniture was disposed in a wholly informal way. The chairs were placed in pairs or groups to encourage conversation among their occupants—what Henry James would have called 'admirable corners'. The only vestige of symmetry was in the drawing room, where pairs of chairs and commodes faced each other at the north and south ends of the room. This informality was itself highly studied, since Mellier's plans were precisely drawn to a half-inch scale; but their real interest is that they show that the rooms, even if provided with the odd palm stand, were comfortable but not too overcrowded. Even the French decorator was an influence for simplicity.

Not all Manderston was Louis XVI, however: the dining room was solidly furnished with Chippendale, and the library returned to Adam. (The library was originally intended to be a writing room, with the billiard room next door and no ballroom. Then the ballroom took the place of the billiard room, so the billiard table was moved into the writing room, which was renamed the library. The *Journal of Decorative Art* commented that libraries were often used as second drawing rooms—perhaps a reflection of the priorities of the age.) The ideal was to contrive a sequence of rooms in contrasting styles within the same house. H. P. Shapland discussed a number of ideas in *Style Schemes in Antique Furnishing*, published in 1909, which illustrated how a number of different rooms might be handled in different styles. Most of the schemes were eighteenth-century, whether Chippendale, Sheraton, Hepplewhite or Adam, except for the hall and billiard room (Jacobean), where a more masculine note was appropriate.

Most eighteenth-century and early nineteenth-century English furniture styles had been revived in the course of the nineteenth century. As early as the 1830s there was sufficient interest in Chippendale and his contemporaries for their designs to be republished for use by practising cabinet makers.[26] By the early 1860s the clock had moved forward to the age of the Adam Brothers, Hepplewhite and Sheraton. The furniture firm of Wright and Mansfield showed some neo-Adam pieces in the International Exhibition of 1862, and five years later one of its cabinets in the Adam style was bought by the South Kensington Museum as an example of contemporary design.

194. Georgian dining room at Thornton Manor, Cheshire

195. French drawing room at Thornton Manor

Soon the Regency and Empire styles were being taken up by the avant-garde, led—surprisingly—by the Pre-Raphaelite Dante Gabriel Rossetti.

In 1890 the *Furniture Gazette* observed that: 'It would considerably astonish the Brothers Adam . . . to find that the chimney-pieces, overdoors, and glass frames designed for them in 1790, are still in stock and still the latest fashion . . . Off and on during the past thirty years, the "Adams" style has never been quite "dead".'[27] In the next decade Muthesius found—to his deep disappointment—that 'imitation eighteenth-century furniture accounts for by far the largest part of present-day demand . . . Large factories, each employing hundreds of workers, devote all their effort to the production of this furniture, furniture shops are full of new copies of Sheraton and Chippendale, for these are the pieces that the English public most desires.'[28]

Some people reacted against what they saw as incipient chaos; but others recognised that there was a fitness in using certain styles for certain rooms. H. J. Jennings, author of *Our Homes and How to Beautify Them* (1902), considered that:

> For the dining room, you may have it Italian Renaissance, François Premier, Elizabethan, Jacobean, eighteenth-century English, or modern English Renaissance. French styles may be put on one side for an English dining room; so may the Gothique Anglais . . . For the drawing room there are available the whole range of the French styles, from Louis XIV to Empire, also the English Chippendale to Adam period, and, if these give not scope enough, the English Renaissance as practised by the English School. A breakfast or morning room . . . is essentially of the national character.[29]

In fact, this was a rationalisation of the way in which numerous country houses throughout the country were already furnished. Crome in *Crome Yellow*, published shortly after the war and modelled on Lady Ottoline Morrell's Garsington, would have been typical, were it not for the whiff of modernity in some of the pictures.

> There was the long gallery, with its rows of respectable and (though, of course, one couldn't publicly admit it) rather boring Italian primitives, its Chinese sculptures, its unobstrusive, dateless furniture. There was the panelled drawing room, where the huge chintz-covered arm-chairs stood, oases of comfort among the austere flesh-mortifying antiques. There was the morning-room, with its pale lemon walls, its painted Venetian chairs and rococo tables, its mirrors, its modern pictures. There was the library, cool, spacious, and dark, book-lined from floor to ceiling, rich in portentous folios. There was the dining-room, solidly, portwinily English, with its great mahogany table, its eighteenth-century chairs and sideboard, its eighteenth-century pictures—family portraits, meticulous animal paintings . . . Among the accumulations of ten generations the living had left but few traces.[30]

Clearly this was the effect Mrs Greville hoped to create at Polesden, with its seventeenth-century dark, panelled hall, its gallery lined with Old Masters (and some Italian primitives), its opulent drawing room, delicate boudoir and eighteenth-century dining room—the latter hung with portraits by Reynolds and Lawrence, even though the sitters had no connection with her own family.

This approach survived surprisingly long. When White Allom remodelled Stanford Hall in Leicestershire in 1928, they gave it a medieval hall; but this opened into a

196. Pewter and oak at Mathern Palace, Monmouthshire
197. Bedroom at Frensham Hill, Surrey

Classical stair hall, furnished with Chinese Chippendale sofas, and other rooms included a Louis XVI drawing room, a Charles II library, a Georgian mahogany dining room, an Adam morning room and—supremely appropriate—an Art Deco theatre. Waring and Gillow supplied a *moderne* style sitting room for the ground floor, complete with niches and indirect lighting. Upstairs the bedrooms were named after the styles in which they were decorated—Adams, Charles II, Spanish, Italian, Louis XVI, of which the last was the master suite.[31]

With the rise of the decorator, and perhaps associated with his expertise, antiques became more and more prized. The position of furniture in the Gothic Revival had been comparatively simple. Since very few genuine Gothic pieces survived at all, and those that did were generally unsuitable for Victorian purposes, furniture in the Gothic style had to be manufactured from new designs. But the status of old furniture changed when more recent historical styles were revived. A Louis XVI chair or a Sheraton bureau was still a serviceable object, and the authentic period look was desired. However, a choice still had to be made. Owners who did not care for antiques could have very convincing imitations made, either from old designs or from existing pieces of furniture.

One of the several elusive firms to make high quality reproductions was Edwards and Roberts, founded in the mid-nineteenth century.[32] 'Old oak though it still fetches a good price is not as much in demand as it was,' reads an account of the firm written in 1898; 'and the "rage" during the last twelve years has been for the furniture of "Chippendale", "Sheraton", "Hepplewhite" and "Adams".' Edwards and Roberts also made French styles and 'a representative of the firm told us . . . that high class furniture imitations of old furniture were very costly'.[33] The last point was certainly true. Sir James Miller paid the firm of Hodgekins the staggering price of £2,400 for a *Régence* style cupboard at Manderston. The Edwardian attitude to reproductions was that they had an advantage over the real thing, since they were still in perfect condition.

The parents of the art historian Lesley Lewis were typical of their generation in their ideas about furnishing. The chairs in their Edwardian dining-room were of a shieldback Hepplewhite design,

> copied from one pair of genuine old ones which had pieces of stamp paper stuck on their undersides to remind us to spare them undue wear and tear. The reproductions were so good as to be virtually indistinguishable . . . If [the owners] liked an old design, whether of furniture or silver, they had it copied to make up a set by the excellent craftsmen working at the time, and without any intention to deceive. No old design was tolerated for merely historical reasons. If it were uncomfortable or too large or too fragile it failed to earn a place: thus the antiques and the reproductions, or frankly modern oak, walnut and mahogany; the eighteenth-, nineteenth- or twentieth-century silver, Sheffield or Electro plate, jogged along in harmony engendered by long use and wear.[34]

Nevertheless, the dividing line between a copy, albeit in modern materials, and an object that was intended to deceive was necessarily narrow. The best Victorian and Edwardian craftsmanship was extremely fine, and only recently have furniture historians become aware of the prevalence of style revivals before the First World War. When the South Kensington Museum acquired its first example of supposedly eighteenth-century

xxxi. Dulce Domum, M. H. Baillie Scott's entry in the House for an Art Lover competition, Darmstadt, 1901

xxxii. Music Room from Der Vogel, C. R. Mackintosh's entry in the same competition

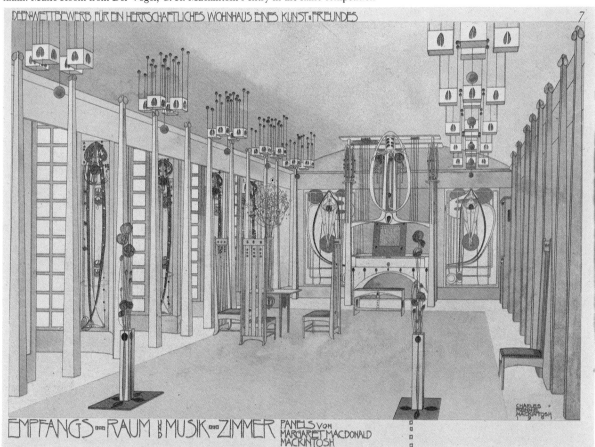

furniture—a satinwood dressing table—for no less than £200 in 1870, it almost certainly bought a fake. The piece was probably made between about 1862 and 1865. Muthesius was appalled at the number of furniture fakers that he encountered in London.

'This is the age of old furniture,' wrote Elder Duncan in *The House Beautiful and Useful*.[35] Inventories show that, for instance, the Jameses' shooting box, Monkton, Sussex, was almost completely furnished with antiques, reproductions or pseudo-antiques.[36] The sitting hall contained a pair of cabinets 'of Chippendale design', a Jacobean chest, a Sheraton secretaire, a Sheraton card table, a Jacobean side table, a Chippendale table, a pair of Chippendale chairs, a 'Hepplewhite pattern' elbow chair, a Japanese screen and a William and Mary clock, as well as several overstuffed chairs. This was not untypical of even Lutyens's more Arts and Crafts houses: Deanery Garden was furnished in a similar, if choicer, style. The interest lies in the mixture of objects, styles and woods, the colour and variety of which were set off by the white painted walls. Thinned out, this kind of eclecticism became an ingredient of post-war good taste; in the Edwardian decade it was used to create rich effects, as at Coombe Lodge (Colour Plate VII).

However, there was a limit to the combinations that could be made, and in any case the hybrid approach was thought only to be appropriate for the drawing-room or other sitting rooms, such as that at Monkton, where a suggestion of informality was desirable. And even there Elder Duncan thought that the practice was fraught with danger. 'Old furniture possesses a glamour from its mellowness and surface that new articles do not possess, but I question whether even this mixing of old furniture of all periods, styles and contours is quite satisfactory.'[37] Muthesius commented seriously that the 'deliberate informality' of the average drawing room 'all too often degenerates into confusion'.[38] One-period schemes were safer, they were easier for decorators to handle, and they appealed to an age that was indecisive about style.

Naturally, the way in which a room was furnished expressed its use, and every eventuality had to be anticipated. The entrance hall was particularly tricky because of its ambiguous role. According to Elder Duncan, 'A large roomy hall should have several chairs and a table', while 'a bureau for writing hasty notes, messages, or replies to telegrams is also useful'.[39] Furnished as a small sitting room, 'it forms a very useful waiting-room for strangers and others whom it is not necessary or desirable to admit to the sitting-rooms, but whom it is equally undesirable, or unhospitable, to keep waiting outside the door'. And if there was no music room, then the entrance hall was the only place left to put the organ, as at Sennowe, Skibo and Manderston. However, living halls required a different treatment. 'Halls of this sort always house a grand piano for music-making and sometimes a billiard table.'[40]

The House Beautiful and Useful[41] contains a check-list of principal articles of furniture in the sitting rooms of large houses. The dining room was likely to have a broad mahogany dining table and chairs to match, although circular tables became fashionable after 1900. There might even have been several small tables, since 'the splitting up of the diners into groups of three or four at separate tables' was sometimes preferred. For a time this was the practice at Knole. An innovation in both the dining room and the breakfast room was the dinner wagon, a movable extension of the sideboard.

Although the author was passionately opposed to overcrowding, he expected the drawing room to contain items from each of the following ten groupings: chairs of various

277

XXXIII. Bedroom corridor at Monkton, Sussex, as transformed for Edward James in the 1930s by Kit Nicholson and Hugh Casson with the help of Salvador Dali

kinds; flower and palm stands; settees; small revolving bookcase (occasionally); screens; stools for lounge chairs; china or curio cabinets; curio tables; card table; occasional or pier tables. They could be mahogany, stainwood, stained sycamore, inlaid or gilt; French and English styles of the late eighteenth century were preferred. Muthesius commented on the English liking for very low armchairs, which were 'conducive to intimate chats'.

On the whole, decorators were not often asked to design bedrooms, which could be completely furnished by the large London shops; but Muthesius gives them his fullest attention. Bedroom planning shows the meticulous detail in which Edwardian architects considered their clients' welfare, especially as regards their health. Ideally, bedrooms faced south-east, so that they were bright when the owner woke up and sunny by day— but not too much so, because the afternoon sun would have made them too warm. The bed invariably stood with its head to the wall and both sides free. It was an acknowledged rule—although one frequently broken—that the bed should not face the window, or the occupant would be disagreeably dazzled on opening his eyes; but this was not easy to achieve, since the other walls were usually taken up by the fireplace and the door to the dressing room. Draughts had to be avoided at all costs, so that 'a line drawn from the door to the fireplace must not touch the bed'. But the room had to be sufficiently ventilated: Voysey often incorporated small leaded panes which could be opened without opening the whole window. It was most important that the door opened with its back to the bed 'to avoid embarrassing situations': maids bringing early morning cups of tea would probably be entering the room before the master or mistress got up. Of course, to satisfy all these requirements was almost impossible, but Muthesius published a plan which showed it could be done.

Surprisingly, Muthesius was luke warm about the most progressive item of English bedroom furniture, the build-in cupboard, which had become popular after R. W. Edis's books of the 1880s.[42] The only way of airing the cupboards was by taking out all the contents, which was seldom done: 'To sleep in the midst of these crammed cupboards is like sleeping in a warehouse.' More acceptable were the clothes closets that were, in effect, separate rooms. Moundsmere Manor had a particularly up-to-date bedroom floor, which was praised by Lawrence Weaver.[43] The bedrooms were arranged in pairs, with a bathroom and two cupboards between each one (Fig. 12)—although it was still necessary to go outside the suite to reach the lavatory. At all times hygiene was at a premium. Wicker baskets might be used to hold dirty clothes, but Elder Duncan reacted with horror at the thought that they might contain dirty underwear; the latter 'should be at once removed from bedrooms, and kept in some convenient basket or cupboard, ready for the laundry'.

Between the Wars

The arrival of Diaghilev's Ballets Russes in 1911 caused a sensation, and almost at once there arose a cult for the bright, clashing colours of Leon Bakst's sets. In the country, this was realised with most gusto at Port Lympne (Plate 198). Sir Philip Sassoon had a voracious appetite for aesthetic stimuli. Consequently, the main rooms in the house have no more than what Arthur Oswald called 'a personal relation to each other'.[44] Although

198. The dining room at Port Lympne, Kent

the octagonal library was panelled in sycamore, the dining room was decorated in the
barbaric taste associated with the Ballets Russes, with lapis lazuli walls, an opalescent
ceiling, a grey carpet and gilt chairs containing jade cushions. Above the cornice ran a
chocolate and white-coloured frieze painted by Glyn Philpot representing an African
procession. The drawing room, in which Lloyd George conferred with Marshal Foch
prior to the Treaty of Versailles, was conceived as a painted salon, the walls covered with
an allegory of France attacked by Germany and eventually triumphing. Painted by
M. Sert, from Paris, the theme is loosely treated, with France portrayed as a shrinking
maiden attacked by eagles. Her allies are shown symbolically, with a pair of gloriously
exotic, trumpeting elephants over the chimneypiece, rather in the style of Andrea Pozzo's
frescoes in Il Gesù, Rome. This was the style that Sir Osbert Lancaster called Curzon
Street Baroque. A whiff of it can be felt at Coombe Lodge, home of the Marchioness of
Ripon, where Nijinsky himself danced.

It is significant of the growing vogue for Good Taste that by the late 1920s, Sassoon had
swung round completely to an appreciation of English reserve. This was personified at

279

Trent Park (Plate 199), in Hertfordshire, an unexceptional Victorian house which he had Philip Tilden remodel, and which he increasingly preferred to Port Lympne. As described by Christopher Hussey, the interiors were a timeless, tactful pot-pourri of lithographs, old books, antiques and odds and ends: Sassoon's imagination and quick perception had been at work 'catching that indefinable and elusive quality, the spirit of a country house . . . an essence of cool, flowery, chintzy, elegant, unobtrusive rooms that rises in the mind when we are thinking of country houses'.[45]

The appearance of a British drawing room with any pretensions to chic in the mid-1920s—the very time when Britain was making its notoriously poor showing at the 1925 Exposition des Arts Décoratifs in Paris—has been admirably described by Loelia Ponsonby, who married the second Duke of Westminster in 1930:

[It was] painted a heavy green picked out in gold and there was sure to be a Knole sofa piled with small brocade cushions, much fringed and be-tasselled. Tall gold venetian lamps and lampshades stuck with real-prints torn from books or made of parchment sheets of old music, and real old prints were plastered on to cigarette boxes, wastepaper baskets, bridge-boxes and every other flat surface. The picture over the mantel piece would probably be of the lady of the house dressed in veiling and painted by de Lazlo, and on an easel on a table there might be a tinted drawing of her daughter by Olive Snell. At one moment a fashionable eccentricity was to have the room divided, for no apparent cause, by wrought iron gates.[46]

The taste for the more opulent styles of antique furniture—Spanish and Portuguese as well as Italian, and preferably gilded—could be seen at Anglesey Abbey (where the guests had their shoelaces ironed before breakfast)[47] or at Encombe.

Things began to look up in the late 1920s, when fashionable magazines started to carry articles on what had recently been coined 'interior decoration', as opposed to just 'decoration' or 'furnishing'. The sophisticated, aggressively modern styles emanating from France made perfect journalistic copy. Then strong colours went out under the influence of Syrie Maugham, Somerset Maugham's wife who ran a decorating business, and it became 'literally impossible to buy bright coloured material of any sort'.[48] By this date, the architectural aspect of modern rooms had been considerably simplified: the dado rail (which had usually run between three and four feet above the ground, the area beneath it being decorated in a different way from the wall above) had disappeared, cornices and other mouldings had become less elaborate or gone altogether, and wallpaper was frowned upon. Advice was given as to how the modern wife might tackle those 'rooms still retaining the fearsome features of the Victorian age.'

Modern taste demands that all this must be swept away. Plain wall surfaces are needed, to be finished preferably with paint. The fireplace is generally quite impossible and is replaced by a simple surround and interior, often without a shelf. It may be necessary to modify the cornice and to remove the ceiling rose. The doors may be inoffensive when suitably painted, but it is often more successful to face them with a flush plywood surface and add an architrave of modern type.[49]

Soon, in *A Handful of Dust*, Evelyn Waugh was to describe Mrs Beaver at work in much the same spirit on the boudoir at Hetton Abbey.

281

199. Trent Park, Hertfordshire

'But, my angel, the *shape*'s all wrong,' said Daisy, 'and that chimney-piece—what is it made of, pink granite, and all the plaster work and the dado. *Everything*'s horrible. It's so *dark*.'

'I know exactly what Brenda wants,' said Mrs Beaver more moderately. 'As Veronica says, the structure does rather limit one . . . you know I think the only thing to do would be to disregard it altogether, and find some treatment so definite that it *carried* the room, if you see what I mean . . . supposing we covered the walls with white chromium plating and had natural sheepskin carpet . . . I wonder if that would be running you in for more than you meant to spend?'[50]

As M. Dane commented in 1930, 'the salient feature of interior decoration today is a complete reconstruction of the whole'.[11]

A growing mystique surrounded the art as decorators became known as individuals rather than firms. Instead of going to Mellier and Co., Lenygon and Morant or Trollope's, you were now more likely to try Sybil Colefax, Syrie Maugham, Marcel Boulanger or Basil Ionides. Before the First World War a big firm would send down its representative, who ate in the servants' hall; now decorators (perhaps emulating Sir Charles Allom, a friend of Queen Mary) arrived in person, probably for the week-end, and possibly—like the self-promoting Mrs Beaver—even before you had thought of having anything done.

Unlike the architects of the MARS (Modern Architects Research) Group, for instance, who had a moral commitment to Modernism to the exclusion of everything else, decorators were by nature less single-minded. 'A few short years have vastly altered the public attitude towards furniture and modern design. It has now taken its own place in the long succession of styles.'[52] Modernism was (rightly, as it transpired) seen as a style like any other, and decorators and some architects treated it as such. Oliver Hill, *Country Life*'s favourite architect in the 1930s, could design or decorate more or less in any style the client might favour, and the result would be equally suave. M. Dane wrote that decorators would sweep away the banalities of an existing interior to 'create (within the same four walls) a pine-panelled Georgian parlour or a modern setting suited to the latest examples of chromium-plated steel chairs or plate-glass dressing tables'.[53] To them, one was much the same as the other.

The French *moderne* or 'modernistic' style (Plate 200), with its dazzling use of glass, was praised for its flexibility: 'Silver leaf on the walls or on coved ceiling, softly gleaming on the curves of pillars or pilasters, is as fittingly allied with the walnut of William and Mary as the tubular chromium plating and crystal of the most modern school of furnishing.'[54] No one loved antiques as much as the English, and there were a large number to go round. However common it was in bedrooms, only the most advanced houses—like High and Over and St Anne's Hill—had built-in furniture in the reception rooms; and even High and Over had a rather traditional looking table and set of chairs in the dining room.

There were even more extreme contrasts at Charters, a house which also illustrates one way in which country houses, with their larger rooms and broader wall surfaces, offered greater possibilities to the decorator than small town houses or flats: this was in mural painting. As the 1930s wore on, the severe, white style of the late 1920s gave way to something altogether more confused. Colour crept back into wallpapers, carpets and rugs, the latter influenced by the designs of Marion Dorn. An International Exhibition of

282

Surrealism held at the New Burlington Galleries encouraged a taste for the more complicated phases of art, notably the Baroque. This was championed by Sacheverell Sitwell, whose brother Osbert was one of the first collectors of Victoriana. Henry Tonks, professor of painting at the Slade School in the late 1920s, had already encouraged his pupils in the direction of mural painting, having suggested large wall decoration as an exercise. He arranged for Rex Whistler and Mary Adshead to paint the walls of a boys' club in Shadwell, which was run by Etonians. The success of this scheme led to two public commissions: Rex Whistler painted the tea room at the Tate Gallery, and Mary Adshead the new Bank underground station. Rex Whistler's witty, virtuoso *trompe-l'œil* style—the quintessense of English good taste—went down particularly well in the country, where he decorated rooms at Mottisfont Abbey and Plas Newydd. Sassoon, who had already employed Sert and Philpot, commissioned Whistler to paint the delightful tent room at Port Lympne. The murals Martin Battersby painted on the east and west walls of the Great Hall of Charters were framed by *trompe-l'œil* drapes.

But Charters, designed in 1938, brought modern and traditional taste into conflict (Plates 201–2). The client, Frank Parkinson, was chairman of Crompton Parkinson Ltd

200. The dining room at Eltham Palace, Kent, with silver-leaf ceiling

201. Perspective drawing of Charters, Berkshire, by H. G. Hammond, 1938 (De Beers Industrial Diamonds Pty)

of Chelmsford, which manufactured electrical goods. He was a convinced modernist, although also by second interest a farmer—and so, unusually, desired his severely white and rectangular house to have a home farm. Charters is much larger than most Modern Movement houses, and it is clad in Portland stone rather than concrete; yet there is no mistaking the debt to the Bauhaus and to Le Corbusier—if perhaps also to Wallis Gilbert, the Art Deco factory architects with whom Button trained—from the outside. Provision was made for a modern scheme of decoration, with concealed lighting throughout the house, usually above the cornice, and an imaginative use of a new form of glass in the window wall over the entrance (it was made of glass bricks, which were hollow and vacuum sealed; they were supposed to give both light and privacy).

Apart from the bathrooms (Colour Plate xiv), that was where the progressive style stopped. Mrs Parkinson felt that her husband 'kept her in a gilded cage', and she was determined that the cage would not be Modern Movement. To the despair of Adie and Button, the architects, she declared that she liked antiques and would furnish the house with them. Consequently, the gallery to what is revealingly called the Great Hall is supported by Corinthian columns; and all the main rooms are furnished either with genuine eighteenth-century pieces or with high quality reproductions. The concealed lighting was supplemented with chandeliers; the dining room with its Chinese Chippendale chairs and reproduction table was decorated with chinoiserie wallpaper. The house was the perfect example of Good Taste triumphant.

284

202. The great hall at Charters

9. *Postscript:*
The Edwardian Garden

One of the themes of this book has been the contrast between the social and the romantic country house. Visually, the difference principally lay in the quality and texture of the materials used in building and in the varying emphasis placed on methods of construction rather than style. A conflict of a similar kind was being waged outside the house, in the garden, which was seen as being of increasing importance to the house itself. Architects were laying claim to the garden as the frame which married the architecture to the landscape. Architectural publications encouraged architects to submit garden designs with their house plans. Gardeners, on the other hand, promoted the wild garden and natural effects at the expense of architectural design. This conflict, however, was resolved. The harmony between formal planning and informal planting in a Lutyens–Jekyll or Harold Peto garden represents an ideal synthesis, in which the country-house garden was possibly more successful than the country house. The garden cannot come within the scope of a book principally about new country houses, because many of the best gardens were created for houses that were old; but it is appropriate to leave the subject with an image of this achieved ideal lingering on the retina.

In many ways the conflict was more perceived than real. It arose because of two books championing formal gardens, J. D. Sedding's *Garden Craft Old and New* and Reginald Blomfield's *The Formal Garden in England*, published within months of each other in 1891 and 1892. Both developed the concept of the 'old-fashioned' garden of the Aesthetic Movement, which had been particularly associated with Rossetti and his admiration for old topiary.[1] The old-fashioned garden had been given the imprimatur of William Morris's approval. Morris believed that a garden, whether it was large or small, 'should look both orderly and rich. It should be well fenced from the outside world. It should by no means imitate either the wilfulness or wildness of Nature, but should look like a thing never to be seen except near a house. It should, in fact, look like part of the house.'[2] The formal gardens Morris admired were seventeenth-century and English, with clipped hedges, topiary, pleached avenues and espaliers, but not elaborate Italianate terraces or vivid displays of tender plants. Sedding followed their example: 'The old fashioned country house,' he wrote, 'has almost invariably, a garden that curtseys to the house, with its formal lines, its terraces, and beds of geometrical patterns.'[3] But Blomfield was more

287

204. T. H. Mawson's design for the garden at Broadleys, Westmorland, from his *The Art and Craft of Garden Making*, 4th ed., 1912

205. A secluded garden from Walter Godfrey's *Gardens in the Making*, 1914

aggressive in his emphasis on the architectural character of formal gardens. 'The question at issue is a very simple one,' he stated on the first page of his book. 'Is the garden to be considered in relation to the house, and as an integral part of a design which depends for its success on the combined effect of house and garden; or is the house to be ignored in dealing with the garden?' Gardeners were trounced for venturing outside the greenhouse: 'it is evident that to plan out a garden the knowledge necessary is that of design, not of the best method of growing a giant gooseberry'.[4]

For years the old-fashioned garden had existed on equitable terms with what is often considered the dominant strand in late nineteenth-century gardening, represented by William Robinson. The first signs of the old-fashioned garden can be perceived in about 1870, at just the time that Robinson was publishing his widely influential books *Alpine Flowers for English Gardens* and *The Wild Garden*. Robinson belonged to the 'gardenesque' school associated earlier in the century with Loudon. He had been born in Ireland in 1838, began work in the grounds of the big house at Ballykilcannon, and rose to take charge of the greenhouses by the age of twenty-one. He left and made his way to London, where he found a job in the Royal Botanic Society's garden in Regent's Park. The superintendent there was Robert Marnock, who had introduced both herbaceous plants in borders and a small collection of English wild flowers. Robinson taught himself French, went to the 1867 Great Exhibition in Paris as the *Times* gardening correspondent, and two years later made his first walking tour in the Alps. At about this time he met Ruskin, whose prose style influenced the rhetoric of his books.

288

Both the old-fashioned garden and Robinson's ideas were in some measure a reaction against the showy Italianate parterres that had been unrolled like carpets in front of many great Victorian country houses by Paxton and William Andrews Nesfield. Brightly coloured half-hardy plants like begonias were tended in greenhouses throughout the winter, then brought out in bloom and put in flower beds that were shaped like crescents, stars and circles. At its best, it could achieve a blaze—or several blazes—of colour with absolute predictability virtually overnight. A huge staff of gardeners was required, but that was not yet the problem it would become after 1900. Bedding out, as the practice was known, was Robinson's *bête noire*. The aim of his books—and the popular journals, *The Garden* and *Gardening*, which he started—was to show how it was possible to naturalise plants from the Alps and elsewhere, so that they could remain in the ground all the year round. They could be planted in 'fields, woods and copses, outer parts of the pleasure grounds, and in neglected parts in almost every kind of garden'.[5] The ruined garden described in *Elizabeth and her German Garden* by the Countess von Arnim (née Mary Annette Beauchamp) shows the Robinsonian garden at its most extreme, with dandelions sprouting in the lawns, meadows filled with weed, hepaticas, white anemones, violets and celandines growing in sheets beneath the trees, and clumps of lilacs—'masses and masses of them'—near the house. 'My days,' wrote Elizabeth, 'seem to melt away in a dream of pink and purple peace.'[6]

When Sedding and Blomfield produced their books in the early 1890s, the Irish in Robinson scented a fight. In their plea for alleys and arbours he saw his old enemy of bedding out raising its head again, and he struck out. His refutation appeared in the form of a short book called *Garden Design and Architects' Gardens*, published in 1892. The tone was vituperative. 'Mr. Blomfield writes nonsense, and then attributes it to me,' he wrote on page thirteen; 'a passage full of nonsense!' he exclaimed ten pages later; 'the very name of the book is a mistake' (page twenty-five); 'here is a poor sneer at true art' (page thirty-seven). There was much more in the same vein. Blomfield hit back in the preface to the second edition of his book, which, with his Oxford education, he was rather proud of as an elegant piece of destructive criticism. But the dispute did not end there; it smouldered on until the First World War, with Walter Godfrey restating Blomfield's position in *Gardens in the Making* of 1914.

It took the comfortable figure of Lutyens's 'Aunt Bumps', Gertrude Jekyll, to sit in judgement over the two factions, which she did in the *Edinburgh Review*.[7] An article of 1896 weighed up both sides of the controversy and concluded 'Both are right, and both are wrong.' The supporters of the formal garden were 'undoubtedly right in upholding the simple dignity and sweetness and quiet beauty of the old formal garden,' but they were undoubedly wrong in ignoring the horticultural advances made over the last twenty-five years. William Robinson, by then a personal friend and mentor of over twenty years' standing, was praised for his practical knowledge and pioneering use of Alpine plants; but it was implied, if not stated, that a pergola occasionally would have been appreciated. This was the key to the gardens she herself designed with Lutyens. 'It is much to be desired,' she wrote in another context, 'that the formal and the free ways shall both be used.'[8] As H. A. Tipping wrote of Hestercombe: 'The old school of formalists aimed at banishing Nature, just as the late landscapists sought to banish formalism. Our best schools of to-day . . . rightly insist upon combining the two.'[9]

206. The water garden at Batsford Park, Gloucestershire

The synthesis can be seen, for instance, at Le Bois des Moutiers, where the path leading up axially to the house is flanked by waving herbaceous borders; or at Hestercombe (Plate 203), where the rock plants cling to the walls of the Classical design, which were carried out in rough-hewn local stone. Towards the end of her life, Gertrude Jekyll came to deplore the habit of planting fumitory, chiranthus and campanulas in the cracks between the stones of a terrace or a flight of steps, although her own example had done much to encourage it. Even T. H. Mawson, who revelled in Baroque vistas and elaborate geometrical designs, wished his stonework 'to take on an appearance of age as quickly as possible'. It reached lengths comparable to the Tudor taste, but not always so appreciated. His carefully contrived plans misfired at Rushton Hall, where the client, the

207. The flower garden at Gravetye Manor, Kent, from William Robinson, *Gravetye Manor*, 1911

American millionaire J. J. van Allen, called in a quantity surveyor and refused to pay for what he mistakenly took to be bad workmanship when he saw Mawson's rough stonework, with its deliberate crevices, and the corners knocked off the flags for the path.[10]

As the nineteenth century turned into the twentieth, labour shortages made it impossible for most people to contemplate a return to bedding out. This was elevated to become an aesthetic principle. Apart from the affectation, Gertrude Jekyll disapproved of the long row of falling terraces at Hewell Grange because 'the mind of the spectator is disturbed by a consideration of the amount of summer labour that the good keeping of the grass steps and slopes must entail'.[11]

The irony of the Blomfield–Robinson controversy was that the two sides were really much closer than they would admit. Robinson had formulated his theories of the wild garden for outlying areas and woods, where the ordinary principles of gardening did not apply. He was prepared to admit that 'Formality is often essential in the plan of a flower garden near a house', although '*never* as regards the arrangements of its flowers or shrubs'. When Blomfield built himself a house at Rye, he did so on the side of a cliff, where it was impossible to make a formal garden; when Robinson bought 'a new residence', as Lawrence Weaver observed to the conference on Garden Planning in 1928, 'the only practical solution of his problem was a formal garden and he proceeded to lay out a very beautiful one'.[12] Similarly, it might have been expected that Robinson, with his feeling for

208. A. Brazier, woodman at Gravetye, from Robinson, *Gravetye Manor*

209. Garden compartments at Rodmarton Manor, Gloucestershire

wild nature, should have advocated the use of English plants. Instead, he held the contrary view: 'The true use and first reason of a garden is to keep and grow for us plants *not* in our woods and mostly from other countries than our own!' It was Blomfield, English to the last, who championed English garden plants called by English names, in the tradition of William Morris and the old-fashioned garden, even if not all of them were strictly speaking indigenous:

Gillyflowers and columbines, sweet-williams, sweet-johns, hollyhocks and marigolds, ladies' slipper, London pride, bergamot and dittany, peace everlasting, batchelors' buttons, flower of Bristol, love in a mist, and apple of love—these are a few old names to contrast with the horrors of a nursery gardeners' catalogue, and these, too, are the sort of flowers for the garden.

When he published *The Formal Garden*, Blomfield was still in the Arts and Crafts phase of his career, and it is characteristic that the perfect realisation of his precepts was not in

292

XXXIV. Plumpton Place, Sussex, where Lutyens also created the setting of garden and three lakes for Edward Hudson

xxxv. The boathouse at Sennowe Park, Norfolk (private collection)

xxxvi. The Pergola at Trent Park, Hertfordshire, by Sir Winston Churchill (Chartwell, Kent)

XXXVII. The Pillar Garden, Hidcote Manor, Gloucestershire

a garden but on the walls of the chapel at Madresfield. 'Roses climb about the trellis that encloses our garden, the crown-imperial droops its head to hide a tear of shame, the painted fritillary is humble too, primroses, orphans of the flowery prime.'[13]

The real importance of Blomfield's book was its influence on the compartmental garden. The special quality that both Sedding and Blomfield admired in formal gardens was their seclusion. Blomfield liked the way they possessed a sense of 'quiet and retirement' and were 'sheltered from the outside world by a yew hedge or a tapestry of roses and jasmine against the garden wall'. By means of paths, hedges and walls, he wished the broad expanse of the garden to be divided up into separate, enclosed areas, each one of which was a private world. The best pre–First World War example was at Rodmarton Manor (Plate 209), designed by Ernest Barnsley. In the 1930s the idea was developed by Vita Sackville-West and Harold Nicolson at Sissinghurst. 'The garden is seen as a continuation of the rooms of the house,' wrote Hermann Muthesius in 1904–5, 'almost a series of separate out-door rooms, each of which is self-contained and performs a separate function, thus the garden extends the house into the midst of nature.'[14] Just as sunshine and fresh air were penetrating inside the house, so the house itself was reaching out to embrace the garden.

The great advantage of the compartmental garden was that it provided a way to cope with the immense range of Edwardian gardening styles. Because each compartment was secluded from the rest, it offered an opportunity for a different treatment, without threatening the unity of the whole. Garden designers, open to geographical as well as historical influences, were often even more eclectic than architects. There was a comparable literature on garden history, with books like Alicia Amherst's *A History of Gardening in England* and Rose Standish Nichols's *English Pleasure Gardens*. The eclectic approach at its most far-reaching can be seen at Friar Park.

Built for the solicitor and baronet Sir Frank Crisp, Friar Park, in Oxfordshire, is by far the most eccentric house of its age.[15] Living up to the name, Crisp filled it with punning jokes about friars: you switch on the electric light by pushing a friar's nose, and friars hold lamps and dreadful mottoes throughout the house. They also appear in the garden, but this was organised on a different principle. Crisp wrote a guidebook warning I.Vs (ignorant visitors), as he called them, not to think that the Japanese and Topiary Gardens were designed 'as indubitably pleasing objects in themselves'; rather, they were 'designed, as it were, as specimens in a museum to illustrate the taste of the period or a Nation, leaving the observer to come to whatever decision he pleases for or against the particular idea, an opportunity having been given him of forming an opinion from an actual object lesson'.[16]

Among other 'special gardens' at Friar Park were the Water Caves, Iris Garden, Herbaceous Gardens, Garden of Sweet Smells and Savours, eight Medieval Gardens (based on miniatures and other fifteenth-century paintings), the Elizabethan Herb Garden, the Rose Garden, the Topiary or Dial Garden (laid out on the plan of the labyrinth at Versailles, with sundials instead of fountains, each of which had a sentimental motto) and a Rhododendron Glen. However, Crisp was cautious enough to include a paragraph of 'Anathemas, where to be pronounced': 'If any I.V. (male or female) feels compelled to anathematize the owner, it would be obliging if it could be arranged to be done outside the grounds, or, if this is not possible, at least that it should not take place in the presence of any of the gardeners.'

As Crisp's explanation indicated, geographical influences were prominent. The cult of Japan, hallmark of the Aesthetic movement of the 1880s, did not reach the garden until the publication of J. Conder's *Landscape Gardening in Japan* in 1893. Manderston had a Japanese garden, complete with miniature pagoda, and so did The Pleasaunce. Crisp's included flowering cherries, almond trees, plum trees, wistaria, camellias, maples and dwarf pines, and a loquat or Japanese medlar. The Japanese garden at Fanhams Hall, which had been remodelled by W. Wood Bethell in 1901, was laid out by an expert from Japan, Professor Suzuki. Two Japanese gardeners came over every summer and stayed in a house familiarly known as Jap Cottage. There was a genuine Japanese tea house by the lake, called House of the Pure Heart—although this was not the only foreign note, since an Austrian house had been brought over after it had been exhibited at the Paris Exhibition of 1900. Lord Redesdale published *The Bamboo Garden* after cultivating his own at Batsford Park.[17]

The glory of Friar Park, however, was Alpine rather than Oriental. Robinson's *Alpine Flowers for English Gardens* and Ruskin's *Proserpina* created a vogue for the pretty flowers of the mountainside, and nearly every big Edwardian garden had a rock garden to reproduce their natural habitat. Crisp's rock garden, which covered four acres, culminated in a scale model 'of very faithful appearance' of the Matterhorn (Plate 211), which he had sent his head gardener to Switzerland to study. Twenty thousand tons of millstone grit went into the construction. There were miniature Alpine torrents, a little chalet and even tiny model chamois (visible through a telescope Crisp provided) made of tin. Despite his eccentricity, Crisp was a serious plantsman, and the rock garden contained some four thousand species. Clouds of saxifrage and other plants covered what would have been the foothills, and the famous alpinist Henri Correvon could not resist 'a shout of admiration at the richness and variety of the floral carpet'. On one visit he counted more than four hundred species in flower.

Other visitors were less enthusiastic.[18] Of these, the most vociferous was Reginald Farrer—a life-long traveller, a notable plant collector, something of an adventurer, a failed novelist and failed politician, whose book, *The English Rock Garden*, published after he had met his death plant-hunting in Burma, was a monumental work of scholarship and horticultural lore. It is difficult not to sympathise with his criticisms.

Hidden away in the Matterhorn were a Skeleton Cave, an Illusion Cave (in which an optical illusion showed 'the upper part of a Friar who had instantaneously passed from life to death, after the manner of an American "electrocution"') and a Gnome Cave ('so called from the representations it contains of Gnomes of all sizes and conditions'). The burden of Farrer's attack was that Crisp's garden was unnatural, a point that was self-evident to all except Crisp. Nevertheless, it was distinctly unfortunate that Farrer chose to deliver his barbs in the preface to a book by someone else, *My Garden in Spring* by E. A. Bowles. Crisp, in a towering huff, issued a pamphlet entitled *Mr. E. A. Bowles and His Garden*, with the sub-title *A New Parable of the Pharisee and the Publican*. And it was distributed by Miss Ellen Wilmott, a great gardener who unaccountably had a grudge against the inoffensive Bowles, at the gates of the Chelsea Flower Show in 1904. Beside the Alpine fantasy at Friar Park and the furore it aroused, Lord Devonport's rock garden at Whittington, with its boulders imported from Derbyshire at a shilling a ton, looks comparatively modest.[19]

210. (above) Friars at Friar Park, from Sir Frank Crisp's guidebook

211. (right) The rock garden with the model of the Matterhorn at Friar Park, Oxfordshire

212. View of the man-of-war garden at Sedgwick Park, Sussex, from the masthead

Themes other than geographical and historical ones were pursued. Gertrude Jekyll planted single colour borders, in which, for instance, grey-leaved plants like gypsophila, echinops, pink hollyhock, heliotrope and silver thistle were grouped together. A grey garden was planted at Clinthurst Hill in 1893. Although, as she put it, 'careful eye-cultivation' was necessary for this type of garden work, she believed the principle could be extended and wished to experiment at Munstead Wood:

> Arrangements of this kind are sometimes attempted, for occasionally I hear of a garden for blue plants, or a white garden, but I think such ideas are but rarely worked out with the best aims. I have in mind a whole series of gardens of restricted colouring, though I have not, alas, either room or means enough to work them out for myself, and have to be satisfied with an all-too-short length of double border for a grey scheme. But, besides my small grey garden I badly want others, and especially a gold garden, a blue garden, and a green garden; though the number of these desires might easily be multiplied.[20]

This passage was probably the seed of many other single-colour gardens, like the famous white garden at Sissinghurst. By 1912 Percy Noble had a blue garden at Park Place, which was illustrated by Alice Martineau in *The Herbaceous Garden*. In addition to single-colour gardens, Martineau advocated Iris gardens, Michaelmas daisy gardens and Paeony gardens, and she wrote that she had even heard of a Ghost garden, although unfortunately she does not give details.[21]

Sometimes literary ideas provided inspiration. The garden laid out in the 1890s by the lovely, scatter-brained Countess of Warwick at Easton included, as well as a rock garden and lily garden, a rosery, a Border of Sentiment and a Garden of Friendship (the latter containing gifts of plants made by friends, each of which was commemorated on a heart-shaped label). Her greatest triumph, however, was the Shakespeare Border. Here she 'grouped the flowers and herbs that the immortal bard loved so well', a quaint selection that—apart from roses, primroses, violets and marigolds—included leeks, garlic, flax, cabbages, hemp, mustard and carrots. The appropriate quotations from the plays with their references were inscribed on the wings of pottery butterflies.[22] In Sussex, the garden at Sedgwick Park (frontispiece) was hardly less fanciful. It was laid out to evoke a man-of-war, with topiary portholes, bulwarks, quarterdeck, masthead and fortifications.[23]

The cult of Italy, which gave rise to the Italian garden, was an American rather than English phenomenon. In the United States, Italian gardens complemented the opulent Italian Renaissance style of decoration, which never really took root in England, except in isolated examples like the dining room at West Dean. It was an American, Edith Wharton, who published *Italian Villas and their Gardens* in 1904, although other books on the same subject quickly followed: Charles Latham's *The Gardens of Italy* (1905), H. Inigo Trigg's *The Art of Garden Design in Italy* (1906) and Sir George Sitwell's essay *On the Making of Gardens* (1909). The Italian garden, wrote Edith Wharton, was meant to be 'lived in'; the grounds were planned with broad paths leading from one division to another; there was 'shade easily accessible from the house, as well as a sunny sheltered walk for the winter'; it offered 'effective transitions from the dark wooded alleys to open flowery spaces or to the level sward of the bowling green'. The house should be surrounded by terraces and formal gardens, and clipped ilex or laurel walks should lead off into the landscape. As interpreted by William Waldorf Astor (himself an American) and Harold Peto, Sir Ernest George's former partner, the Italian garden became another example of synthesis between Classical and informal values, and perhaps showed at its most evocative the Edwardian romance with the past.

The pleasure grounds at Hever Castle were begun the year *Italian Villas and their Gardens* appeared, 1904. Work on the great Italian garden began the following year, and continued until the Nymphs fountain carved by W. S. Frith was put in place in 1908. It was conceived to incorporate the collection of Classical statuary which Astor had acquired during his period as American minister in Rome in the 1880s.

The Italian garden was one of a number of different gardens at Hever. The others included a maze and an Anne Boleyn garden, which contained a set of topiary chessmen in golden yew, modelled on ones from the reign of Henry VIII which Astor had discovered in the British Museum. The plan of the Italian garden was probably drawn by Frank Pearson, who certainly designed its architectural features. In length, the Italian garden measures some two hundred yards, and comprises two lawns divided by a sunken garden which originally contained a Roman bath. At the further end from the Castle, the lake opens out in a broad sheet of water covering thirty-five acres (Plate 214). It was one of those ridiculously extravagant Edwardian undertakings. The excavations took eight hundred men, using six steam diggers and seven miles of railway line, two years to complete. The effect is imperial, but irresistibly reminiscent of Lake Michigan as well as Lake Maggiore.

But the genius of the scheme lies in the northern border, the so-called Pompeian wall, where Astor, Pearson and the local gardening firm of Cheals of Crawley created a dazzling homage to Ancient Rome (Plate 215). Astor's collection of statuary—gods, goddesses, sarcophagi, porphyry columns, well-heads—was massed down the length of the border, creating a seemingly endless vista of civilisation yielding to Nature. The composition was arranged entirely for visual effect, without any of the archaeological considerations that might have affected the display of what was, in effect, an open air museum. Flowering trees, climbing plants and shrubs were planted among the marbles, so that it looks as though at any moment the luxuriant vegetation will take over. Loggias and buttresses, steps and fountains divide the Pompeian wall into sections, to provide variation to the eye and a sense of surprise as you walk down it. Even if there may be a lingering doubt as to the propriety of creating an Italian garden beside a sixteenth-century castle, the result is a feast for the imagination, a fantasy in stone and shrub as dizzying, of its kind, as Piranesi's engraving of the Appian Way.[24]

Harold Peto bought Iford Manor in 1899. When he left Ernest George in the early 1890s, he developed an extensive garden practice, working much in the south of France. His largest garden undertaking was begun in 1910, when Annan Bryce, M.P., asked him to transform the thirty-seven acre island of Garinish off the west coast of Ireland. The whole island was given over to garden, although—perhaps because the First World War intervened—it never had a country house, only a small cottage and a martello tower. It shows his skill and even daring as a plantsman, since, because of the island's mild climate, he extensively used exotic species, including some from Australia and New Zealand. But that was not his idea at Iford. His concept of the Italian garden was even more austere than Edith Wharton's:

213. Digging the lake at Sennowe Park, Norfolk

214. The lake at Hever Castle, Kent, covering thirty-five acres and dug by eight hundred men over a period of two years

215. The Pompeian wall at Hever

The entirely subordinate place in the scheme that flowers occupy gives a breadth and quietude to the whole which is sympathetic, the picture being painted with hedges, canals and water tanks, broad walks with seats and statues and tall cypresses . . . It is difficult to understand what pleasure anyone can derive from the ordinary herbaceous border that one sees without the slightest attempt at form, and the taller plants tied in a shapeless truss to a stake, and the most discordant colours huddled together.[25]

Like Hever, the garden at Iford was partly conceived for the display of statuary. As an architect, Peto had always been interested in buying such antique, Gothic or Renaissance fragments as he came across them in his travels, and he had a discriminating collection. It included, for instance, a pair of fourteenth-century lions made of red Verona marble, which he had come across in Venice. The antique dealer from whom he bought them had at

304

216. The staircase at Iford Manor, Wiltshire

one time been an architect and concerned in the so-called 'restoration' of the Casa d'Oro, against which Ruskin inveighed in *The Stones of Venice*. 'The palace had been bought by Taglioni the dancer,' Peto recalled in the 1920s, 'and I found that my two lions had been stowed away all these years since Ruskin had seen the destruction.'[26]

To display his treasures Peto at first built a Spanish style loggia, which he called a *casita*. Unlike Astor, he felt that it was better to group the greater number of his objects together, rather than scatter them throughout the garden. For this purpose he built a free-standing cloister, constructed of old stone and weathered tiles, with new dressings from a nearby quarry. Inside the cloister, the antiquities were arranged more or less chronologically, although with no intention of creating a museum-like atmosphere. One of the corner columns was an ancient one, bought in Naples and made of Brescia Africano. It delighted Peto's historical imagination to think that this marble had not been quarried since Roman times and that even the great Brescia Africano pilasters in St Peter's were made from Roman columns plundered from the Baths of Diocletian. In the picturesque tradition, the objects in the cloister were placed where they would most please the eye. Wistaria and a pink-flowering rose twined round the arcading.

Iford was not the last Italian garden. The great Italian garden at Port Lympne, with its terraces and breathtaking views over Romney Marsh, was created at the end of the First World War, but it was dedicated to different gods. As Sir Philip Sassoon circled in his

217. Rex Whistler's *trompe l'œil* map of the gardens at Port Lympne, Kent

218. (far right) Harold Peto in his garden at Iford

aeroplane overhead, he knew that statues of Pericles and Constantine stood at the top of the magnificent staircase that scales the cliff. The mood was imperial rather than introspective. Iford—with its mood of reverie, its tinge of nostalgia, its suggestion of a man too sensitive to tear away the enveloping tendrils from his beautiful possessions—was the symbol of a different age. With his clipped beard and his fastidious eye, Peto was first and last an Edwardian. Towards the top of the stairway which crosses the great terrace is a tall column surmounted by an old Roman capital. On it Peto placed a figure of the infant Zeus and inscribed the column with the legend:

To
King Edward VII
The Peace Maker
Harold A. Peto
Dedicated this Column
in the midst of
The Great War
1916

At Iford, an ideal was realised, but the age for which it had been created had already passed away.

Catalogue

IN the following catalogue I have tried to list all the houses mentioned in this book and also the most conspicuous country houses, in terms of size and architectural importance, which have not been discussed. The difficulty in compiling it has been drawing the line between country houses proper and smaller country houses or houses in the country; just to list houses on estates would rule out much of the best domestic architecture of the age. It is a remarkable fact that Lutyens, most often thought of as a country-house architect, built no houses on estates during the 1890s, but to omit reference to Orchards, for instance, as well as to all the work of Voysey, Mackintosh, Baillie Scott or George Walton, would obviously paint a disappointing picture of architectural activity in the period. Consequently, the catalogue includes a selection of the best smaller country houses, although as far as possible I have tried to state when houses were not built on estates. The references at the end of the entries refer to periodicals only. However, the following books can be consulted on individual architects or aspects of the period. For Lutyens, *The Life of Sir Edwin Lutyens* by Christopher Hussey (1950) and the catalogue of the exhibition 'Lutyens' at the Hayward Gallery, London, in 1981–2; for Ernest Newton, *The Work of Ernest Newton, R.A.* by W. G. Newton (1925); for R. Weir Schultz, 'Robert Weir Schultz (1860–1951): An Arts and Crafts Architect, by David Ottewill in *Architectural History*, 22, 1979, 88–115; for Robert Lorimer, *Lorimer and the Edinburgh Crafts Designers* by Peter Savage (Edinburgh, 1980); for Richard Norman Shaw, *Richard Norman Shaw* by Andrew Saint (New Haven and London, 1976); for Baillie Scott, *M. H. Baillie Scott and the Arts and Crafts Movement* by James D. Kornwolf (Baltimore, 1972); for broader aspects, *Das Englische Haus* by Herman Muthesius (Berlin, 1904–5), republished in translation as *The English House* (edited by Dennis Sharp, 1979), *The Gentleman's Country House and Its Plan, 1835–1914,* by Jill Franklin (1981), and *Dream Houses* by Roderick Gradidge (1980); for specific houses, *The Buildings of England* series edited by Sir Nikolaus Pevsner.

ABBREVIATIONS

A	*Architect*	*AR*	*Architectural Review*	*BN*	*Building News*
AA	*Academy Architecture*	*B*	*Builder*	*CL*	*Country Life*
	(ed. Alexander Koch)	*BA*	*British Architect*	*S*	*Studio*
ABJ	*Architect and Builder's Journal*	*BJAR*	*Builders' Journal and*	i	illustration
AJ	*Architects' Journal*		*Architectural Review*	p	plan

219. Rosehaugh House, Ross and Cromarty

ABBESS GRANGE, Hampshire

By Banister Fletcher for George Miles Bailey. 1901.
The house already on site was pulled down in favour of the
new one, which, as the *Building News* wrote, is in 'a
quiet, mullioned type of design'.
BN 18 Oct 1901, 519, i, p; *BN* 20 Dec 1901, 835, i.

ABBEY HOUSE, Lancashire

By Edwin Lutyens for Messrs Vickers Ltd, shipbuilding
and armaments firm. 1913.
It was perhaps an indication of the impact of the 1909
Budget that Lutyens's last house before the First World
War was commissioned not by an individual but by a
company, although there were also quarters for the
firm's managing director, Sir James McKechnie. The
house, built in a style similar to Castle Drogo but of red
sandstone rather than granite, was principally for
entertaining the potentates visiting the Barrow-in-
Furness shipyard. Consequently, the plan looks surprisingly old-fashioned.
CL 2 Apr 1921, 398, i, p.

ANGLESEY ABBEY, Cambridgeshire

Re-creation by various architects, including A. E.
Richardson, for Urban Huttleston Broughton, first Lord
Fairhaven. 1926–38.
Little survives of the thirteenth-century conventual buildings beyond the calefactorium, which Fairhaven used
as a dining room. The interior was otherwise completely remodelled, and a new library and picture
gallery were built. The house, now owned by the
National Trust, contains a rich, millionaire's collection
of works of art, tapestries and furniture, with a series of
Etty nudes in the corridor to Fairhaven's private
bedroom wing. According to James Lees-Milne, Fairhaven was invariably served first at meals, before his
guests, 'in the feudal manner which only the son of an
oil magnate would adopt'.
CL 27 Dec 1930, 832, i, p.

ARDENRUN PLACE, Surrey (Col. Pl. xxx, Pl. 104)

By Ernest Newton for Woolf Barnato, a racing motorist.
1906–9.
A perfect if not especially original essay in the Later
English Renaissance style beloved of Blomfield, with
hipped roofs, dormers, Portland stone dressings, deep
red Wrotham bricks, and cupola that was connected to
the bachelor quarters. Newton said that it cost him
'some hard thinking'; perhaps it shows. The materials
inside were unusually rich, partly because a French
decorator was employed. The house was burnt in 1933.
AA 1909 (2), 71–3, i, p; *B* 12 May 1906, 526, i, p; *B* 3 Feb
1911, 135, 142, i, p; *BN* 28 Jan 1910, 132, i, p; *BN* 4 Feb
1910, i; *CL* 21 Jan 1911, 90, i, p.

ARDKINGLAS, Argyllshire (Col. Pl. xxi, Pls. 65–6, 76, 130, 186)

By R. S. Lorimer for Sir Andrew Noble, chairman of
Armstrong Whitworth and Co. 1906.

Lorimer's Baronial masterpiece, planned round a courtyard and built out of the local, greenish, glittering
granite. The main rooms are on the *piano nobile* and
have fine plasterwork.
AR 27, 1910, 95, i; *CL* 27 May 1911, 746, i, p.

ARDMULCHAN, Co. Meath

By Sydney Mitchell and Wilson of Edinburgh for Mrs
F. G. Fletcher. 1904.
Large house in a mixture of Elizabethan and Baronial
styles.

ASHBY ST LEDGERS, Northamptonshire (Pl. 109)

By Edwin Lutyens for the Hon. Ivor Guest (later Lord
Wimborne). 1903–38.
A Jacobean manor house enlarged several times over in
four building campaigns. See pp. 158–9.
CL 27 Jul, 3, 10 and 17 Aug 1951, 274, 348, 420, 496.

ASHLEY CHASE, Dorset

By E. Guy Dawber for Sir David Milne-Watson, Scottish
governor of the Gas, Light and Coke Co. 1926.
A small, traditional-looking house on a sun-trap plan.
Dawber continued to build houses of about this size in
more or less his pre-war style into the late 1920s. It was
essentially a shooting lodge.
B 11 Jan 1929, 50, 78–80, 106, i.

ASHTON WOLD, Northamptonshire

By Huckvale for the Hon. Charles de Rothschild, son of
Nathan Meyer, first Baron Rothschild. 1903.
Lord Rothschild built this large house as a wedding
present for his son; it is said that it was ready by the time
he and his wife returned from their six month honeymoon. Charles de Rothschild rebuilt the village of
Ashton using local materials, and built an electricity
plant in the mill. He was a significant naturalist, nature
conservationist and student of fleas, discovering the rat
flea *Xenopyslla cheopis* Rothschild. The house was reduced in size by removing the top storey by the Hon.
Claud Philimore in about 1970.

AULTMORE, Inverness-shire

By C. H. B. Quennell for H. Millet, the owner of a
Moscow department store. 1912–14.
An imposing Palladian revival mansion house, with
projecting wings and a cupola. The walls were harled
and had freestone dressings. Quennell's brief included
making a reservoir on a mountainside three miles away
to provide water. A centralised vacuum cleaner was
installed.
AA 1913 (2), 34–5; *AR* 51, 1922, 154–5, i.

AVON TYRRELL, Hampshire (Pl. 220)

By W. R. Lethaby for Lord Manners, friend of Margot
Asquith and Master of the Quorn Hunt. 1891.
Lethaby's first commission, passed on from Norman
Shaw. Mannered red brick entrance front, with stone
peacocks on the skyline; disappointingly flat garden

220. Avon Tyrrell, Hampshire   221. Batsford Park, Gloucestershire

elevation, using elements of cottage architecture on a very large scale. Inside an impressively 'rationalist' fireplace constructed out of chequers of grey and black Derbyshire marble; plasterwork by Gimson. Now Guide training centre.
CL 11 Jun 1910, 846, i, p.

BAILIFFSCOURT, Sussex (Pls. 107, 121–7)

By Amyas Phillips for the Hon. Walter Guinness (later Lord Moyne). 1931–3.
See pp. 174–81. Now an hotel.
CL 19 Jun 1980, 1394, i.

BALMANNO CASTLE, Perthshire (Pls. 73, 187–8)

A sixteenth-century tower house restored by Lorimer for W. S. Miller, a Glaswegian in shipping. 1916.
See pp. 183, 263.
CL 21 and 28 Mar 1931, 344, 394.

BARNETT HILL, Surrey (Pl. 80)

By Arnold Mitchell for Frank Cook, grandson of Thomas Cook the travel agent. 1906.
A large and handsome house in the Later Renaissance style, set in twenty-six acres. There is a deep entrance courtyard formed by the billiard room on one side and staircase towers in the angles, similar to those used at Crathorne Hall by George and Yeates (Mitchell had trained in Ernest George's office). Barrel-vaulted corridor on entrance front and staircase modelled on Ashburnham House. Mitchell later built the Thomas Cook head office in Berkeley Street, W1. The Bromsgrove Guild provided lead garden statues. Now Red Cross training centre.
B 29 Mar 1912, 164, 268–9, i; *BN* 15 Mar 1912, 379, i, p.

BARNSDALE HILL, Rutland

By E. J. May for Captain the Hon. Charles Fitzwilliam, son of Earl Fitzwilliam. 1890.
A medium sized house in hunting country. Elizabethan in style. Hot air central heating. Now flats.
B 7 Jun 1890, 417, i, p.

BATSFORD PARK, Gloucestershire (Pls. 206, 221)

By Ernest George and Peto for A. B. Freeman-Mitford (later Lord Redesdale). 1887–93.
Of importance as the first example of George using style with the strictness and sensitivity that he did throughout the next two decades. E. Guy Dawber was clerk of works.
A 1 Jun 1888, i, p; *A* 29 Apr 1893, i; *BN* 4 Jan 1889, i; *CL* 1903, 18, i.

BEECHAMWELL HALL, Norfolk

By Wimperis and Best for Mrs Fielden, widow of Joshua Fielden, cotton manufacturer. 1904–6.
The previous house on the site had been burnt in 1902.
AA 1906(1), 49; *B* 10 Nov 1906, 544, i.

BESFORD COURT, Worcestershire (Pls. 170–1)

By Randall Wells for Sir George Noble. 1912.
A large new stone wing built round a cloister was added to the west of the original half-timber Tudor house, which remains. Work was never finished because the architect ran away with the owner's wife, but what exists (now used as a school) contains the extraordinary, wave-like staircase, curving and dividing as it descends, shown in Plates 170–1.

BIDSTON COURT, Cheshire

Built by Grayson and Ould for Robert Hudson, soap manufacturer. 1891–2.
Luxurious, half-timbered house modelled on Little Moreton Hall, it was taken down, moved and reassembled as Hill Bark, Frankby, by Rees and Holt in 1929–31. Now a mental institution.
A 22 Nov 1895, 332, i; *A* 10 Apr 1896, 236, i; *BA* 1894, 308.

BIRCHENS SPRING, Buckinghamshire (Pl. 222)

By John Campbell for C. Rissik. 1938.
Spanish style house in the shape of a cross, with pitched roofs but loggias and sleeping balconies for summer use, embodying the 'open-air ideal'. The walls of the dining room painted with mural by A. W. M. Rissik, drawing master at Uppingham School and a relative of the owner.
CL 20 and 27 Jan 1938, 114, 140, i, p.

222. Birchens Spring, Buckinghamshire

223. Bryanston, Dorset

BLACKWELL, Westmorland

By M. H. Baillie Scott for Sir Edward Holt, C.B.E., J.P., twice Lord Mayor of Manchester, a brewer and paper manufacturer. 1898–9.

The brilliance of this house, Baillie Scott's largest, lies in the spatial and stylistic contrast between the lofty, half-timbered living hall and the comparatively low-ceilinged dining room, with its progressive Art Nouveau inglenook. It was widely published and hailed as one of the most advanced houses in Europe. Like Broadleys and Moorcrag, it was a house for the summer with views over Lake Windermere, rather than a country house complete with estate. Nature Conservancy Council.

AA 1899; *AR* 7, 1900, 202, i; *B* 24 Feb 1900, i.

BRANCHES PARK, Suffolk

By George Hornblower for Gilbert Augustus Tonge. 1908.

A late eighteenth-century building enlarged into a big, Later Renaissance house with a water-tower at one end. Partly demolished about 1959.

BN 10 Feb 1905, i, p; *BN* 24 Dec 1909, 933, i.

BROADLEYS, Westmorland (Col. Pl. IX)

By C. F. A. Voysey for A. Currer Briggs, colliery owner. 1898.

This was one of Voysey's largest houses, built of rough-cast, stone and green slates. The plan is L-shaped, and there are three semi-circular window bays sharing the view west over Lake Windermere. The bays correspond to the principal rooms on the ground floor—the drawing room, hall and dining room. Voysey preferred to have a small number of relatively large rooms to a large number of small ones, so the hall is an ample living space, going up through two-storeys, being over-looked by a gallery, and containing a billiard table. Like Blackwell and Moorcrag, Broadleys was a house for the summer. Now motor boat club.

BJAR 16, 1902–3, 389, i, p; *BJAR* 17, 1903, 29, i, p; *S* 31, 1904, 127, i; *A* 27 Mar 1908, 208, i.

BROCKLESBY PARK, Lincolnshire

New east wing by Reginald Blomfield for the Earl of Yarborough. 1898.

An early example of Blomfield's Wren style, built of small red bricks and Ancaster stone. There is a vestibule paved in marble and lined with green Cippolino marble columns. Blomfield also designed the new terraces.

AR 11, 1902, 94–8, i; *CL* 24 Feb 1934, 192, 218, i.

BRYANSTON, Dorset (Pls. 4, 223)

By Richard Norman Shaw for Viscount Portman. 1889–94.

Enormous, symmetrically planned neo-Baroque house built with carte blanche as to cost. It prefigures much of the Classical domestic architecture of the 1890s and early 1900s, although generally the palatial interiors were admired more than the elevations. Now a school.

B 5 Aug 1899, 32, i.

BURDOCKS, Gloucestershire (now called Claremont) (Pl. 103)

By E. Guy Dawber for J. Read. 1911.

A beautifully proportioned smaller country house, almost a replica of an eighteenth-century stone-built manor house, with the service court making an L and creating a picturesque effect. Inside, the low ceilings and tall sashes are less happy. The main room is the parlour, the other rooms being the morning room, dining room and entrance hall.

AR 53, 1923, 160–5, i, p; *B* 7 Jul 1911, 12, i; *BN* 23 Jun 1911, 873, i.

BURGH HEATH, Surrey

By Ernest Newton for Gordon Colman. 1912. Neo-Georgian.

B 7 May 1920, 549, i; *BN* 18 Jul 1913, 79, i, p.

BURROUGH COURT, Leicestershire

By W. H. Brierley for H. C. Allfrey. 1906.

A hunting lodge 'in the quiet and unpretending architectural style which, in a country house of this kind, is often more satisfying than any assumption of architectural style and dignity'. Although the house is small, it has a fully developed service wing.

AR 19, 1906, 235, i, p; *B* 6 Apr 1907, 426, i, p; *BN* 7 Jul 1906, 13, i, p.

BURTON COURT, Dorset

By M. H. Baillie Scott for E. W. Bartlett, solicitor. 1908–10.
See pp. 160–1.
A 27 Jul 1923, 65, i; *AJ* 7 Jan 1925, 70, i, p; *BA* 7 May 1909.

BURTON MANOR, Cheshire

Remodelled and extended by Nicholson and Corlette for Henry Neville Gladstone, son of W. E. Gladstone. 1904.
The house was refaced in red sandstone and greatly enlarged by adding two new ranges to the existing L-shaped house, creating a courtyard. H. N. Gladstone had worked in Calcutta and married Maud Rendel, daughter of the armaments manufacturer Lord Rendel. Garden by Mawson.
CL 12 Oct 1912, 490, i, p.

THE BURY, KINGS WALDEN, Hertfordshire (Kings Walden Bury)

By Beeston and Burmester for T. F. Harrison. 1894.
Big, amorphous Elizabethan style house, principally of interest as having been replaced by a handsome brick Palladian house, built by Raymond Erith and Quinlan Terry in 1971 (see *CL* 27 Sept and 4 Oct 1973, 858, 970, i).
AA 1893, 42; *B* 10 Feb 1894, i, p.

BUSBRIDGE HALL, Surrey

By George and Yeates for Percy N. Graham. 1906.
Picturesque house in an Elizabethan-cum-Dutch style, with a loggia.
AR 22, 1907, 217, i; *B* 19 May 1906, 556, i, p.

CARLEKEMP, East Lothian

By John Kinross for James Craig, a paper manufacturer. 1898.
Large, neo-Tudor building, with palatial interiors. Now a school.

CASTLE DROGO, Devon (Col. Pls. XIII, XXII–XXIII, Pls. 64, 128)

By Edwin Lutyens for Julius Drewe, co-founder of the Home and Colonial Stores. 1910–30.
See pp. 183, 188–9. National Trust.
B 9 and 16 May 1924, 755, 791, i; *CL* 3 and 10 Aug 1945, 200, 244, i, p.

CAVENHAM HALL, Suffolk

By A. N. Prentice for H. E. M. Davies, who had money in gold. 1899.
A very big but finely proportioned Later Renaissance house on a large shooting estate. Built of dark red narrow bricks with stone dressings. The old hall to the south-west of the new building was pulled down. A strikingly free and opulent plan (Fig. 3). Demolished.

224. Chequers Court, Buckinghamshire: the hall

AA 1899(1), 44–5, i; *AA* 1899(2), 16–17, i; *AR* 6, 1899, i; *B* 17 Jun 1899, 596, i; *B* 18 May 1901, 491, i; *B* 1 Jun 1901, 536, i.

CAYTHORPE COURT, Lincolnshire

By Reginald Blomfield for Edgar Lubbock, brewer and banker. 1901.
At the client's request the house was based on the plain seventeenth-century work practised in Lincolnshire; consequently it is Early rather than Later Renaissance. Now an agricultural college.
B 14 Nov 1903, 492–3, i, p; *B* 28 Nov 1903, 550, i, p.

CEANNACROC, Inverness-shire

By J. K. Hunter for C. L. Orr-Ewing, M.P. 1900.
A shooting lodge, with electric light provided by turbine-driven dynamo.
B 31 Mar 1900, 320, i, p.

CHARTERS, Surrey (Col. Pl. XIV, Pls. 53, 74, 201–2)

By Adie and Button for Frank Parkinson, electrical goods manufacturer. 1938.
Stunning, apparently Modern Movement house, complete with home farm. On closer inspection, what looks like concrete turns out to be Portland stone, and the interior was decorated with antiques and frilly lace curtains. It contains probably the most enviable bathroom in Britain. Now owned by De Beers.
CL 24 Nov, 1 and 8 Dec 1944, 904, 948, 992, i, p.

CHELWOOD MANOR, Sussex

By A. N. Prentice for Lady Brassey, widow of Lord Brassey, railway contractor. 1904.
Lush half-timbering.
AA 1904(1), 50–1, i, p.

CHEQUERS COURT, Buckinghamshire (Pl. 224)

Remodelling by Reginald Blomfield for Arthur Lee, M.P. (later Lord Lee of Fareham). 1909–12.
The interior of this seventeenth-century house was partly reconstructed, and the courtyard was covered over to form a two-storey hall.
B 29 Jul 1911, 95, i; *CL* 31 Dec 1910, 970, i, p; *CL* 6, 13 and 20 Oct 1917, 324, 348, 372, i, p.

CHESTERS, Northumberland

Almost complete remodelling by Richard Norman Shaw for Nathaniel Clayton. 1891–4.
Absurdly extravagant plan, with the dining room, drawing room and billiard room set at angles to the main house, and a sweeping colonnade on the east front. It originated the butterfly or sun-trap plan (Fig. 5).
ABJ 27 Jul 1910, 100, p; *CL* 17 Feb 1912, 244; *CL* 17 Feb 1912, 244 i, p.

CLAUGHTON HALL, Lancashire

Removed by Henry F. Fairhurst of Manchester for Esmond Morse. 1932–5.
A sixteenth and early seventeenth-century stone house was moved to a more dramatic, hilltop position, re-oriented and added to at either end, the additions including a squash court.
CL 14 Dec 1940, 520, i.

THE CLOCK HOUSE, Sussex

By Barry Parker for Laurence Currie, a partner in Glyn Mills' bank. 1913–14.
This house comprises an old, half-timbered house, which was transported several fields to the present location. A barn was cut in half and added to each end to form wings.
AR 57, 1925, 106–11, i, p.

COLDHARBOUR WOOD, Hampshire

By T. E. Collcutt for Sir Thomas Sutherland, chairman of P & O. 1889–96.
Spreading, half-timbered house, Collcutt also designed interiors for P & O liners.
BN 3 Jan 1896, 45, i.

COLDICOTE, Gloucestershire

By E. Guy Dawber. 1905.
A smaller country house, built out of roughly dressed Cotswold stone. The main rooms, except the billiard room, face south. There is a squash court on the north side of the stable court.
AA 1904(2), 50, i; *AR* 26, 1909, 197, i, p; *BN* 13 Jan 1905, i, p.

COLETON FISHACRE, Devon

By Oswald P. Milne for Rupert d'Oyly Carte. 1925–6.
Substantial, stone-built house on the coast. As well as a sitting room, there was a big room set at an angle—perhaps to catch the evening sun, since it was presumably intended for entertaining. Milne had been apprenticed to Lutyens.
B 17 Jun 1927, 966, i, p; *CL* 31 May 1930, 782–9, i, p.

COUR, Argyllshire (Pl. 59)

By Oliver Hill for (?) J. B. Bray. 1920.
Wildly romantic, rather Expressionist house, rooted in the soil, with battered chimneys and banks of round-headed mullion windows. The walls are local whinstone, quarried on site, and have a quartz sparkle.
AA 1922, 49–63; *AJ* 64, 1926, 264–5, i, p; *AR* 63, 1928, 314–15, i, p.

CRAIG-Y-PARC, Glamorgan

By C. E. Mallows for Thomas Evans, colliery owner. 1913.
Enchanting smaller country house, with an 'atrium' (a square formed by the two projecting wings, closed by a screen of columns) on the garden front. The site falls abruptly to the south, so the garden was designed on four levels. Now a school.
BN 19 Sept 1913, 400–1, i, p.

CRATHORNE HALL, Yorkshire (Pl. 225)

By George and Yeates for Lionel Dugdale. 1903–5.
Large house in cream-coloured stone, with an uncharacteristically Palladian garden front but the expected Jacobean entrance elevation. Now an hotel.
BN 15 May 1903, 681, i, p; *BN* 9 Jan 1905, 821, i, p; *CL* 29 Apr 1911, 598, i, p.

CROOKSBURY, Surrey

By Edwin Lutyens for Arthur Chapman, who had made his money in Calcutta. 1889; 1898.
An early, vernacular house by Lutyens, remarkable for the new east wing he added in 1898. The latter is Wrenaissance in everything but symmetry, having the Baroque door-case placed purposefully off-centre.
CL 15 Sept 1900, 336, i; *CL* 6 and 13 Oct 1944, 596, 640.

CROWHURST PLACE, Surrey (Pls. 111–12)

'Restored' by George Crawley for himself, then Consuelo Vanderbilt, Duchess of Marlborough. 1909–15.
See pp. 162–4.
CL 20 Aug 1908, 286, i; *CL* 5 and 12 Jul 1919, 12, 44, i, p.

225. Crathorne Hall, Yorkshire

226. Culford Hall, Suffolk

CULFORD HALL, Suffolk (Pls. 182, 226)

Very large additions by William Young for the Earl of
  Cadogan. 1894.
Constructed of special bricks made to look like stone. Now
  a school.
BN 8 Jun 1894, 779, i, p.

DANESFIELD, Buckinghamshire

By W. H. Romaine-Walker for Robert Hudson, the soap
  manufacturer who also built Bidston Court (q.v.).
  1899–1901.
Luxurious Elizabethan, stone-built house by an elusive
  and intriguing architect. Now owned by Carnation
  Foods.
A 16 Jan 1903, 48, i; *A* 13 Mar 1903, 176, i.

DEANERY GARDEN, Berkshire (now called The
  Deanery) (Pl. 25)

By Edwin Lutyens for Edward Hudson. 1899–1902.
Built around a fountain court with chalk-vaulted cloisters
  on three sides. As Christopher Hussey remarked, it is an
  architectural sonnet on the theme of a romantic
  bachelor's idyllic afternoons beside a Thames back-
  water. In the village of Sonning.
CL 9 May 1903, 602, i.

DITTON PLACE, Sussex (Pl. 91)

By Smith and Brewer for A. B. Horne, solicitor. 1904.
Later English Renaissance, with an eccentric curved

gable to both the entrance and garden elevations. Built
  of red Wrotham bricks with Portland stone dressings.
  Now a school.
AR 22, 1907, 187–97, i, p; *AR* 27, 1910, 328, 334, i, p; *CL* 1
  Jul 1911, 18, i, p.

EASTWELL PARK, Kent (Col. Pl. xx, Pls. 9, 227–8)

By William Wallace for Lord Gerard. 1894.
The old mansion was virtually rebuilt, with a large winter
  garden, conservatory and stabling for forty horses. This
  house was in turn romanticised by Sir John de Fonblaque Pennefather in 1926–7. Now an hotel. See pp.
  168–71.
B 30 Mar 1895, 243, i, p; *CL* 10 Apr 1897, 379.

EDNASTON MANOR, Derbyshire

By Edwin Lutyens for W. G. Player, chairman of the
  Imperial Tobacco Co. 1912–14.
Lutyens looked back on it as a 'dear little Queen Anne
  house', much to be preferred as a commission to Castle
  Drogo. It did not become the Players' family home
  until the Second World War.
CL 24 Mar 1923, 398, i, p.

ELTHAM PALACE, Kent (Pls. 57, 75, 200)

Addition by Seely and Paget for Sir Stephen Courtauld,
  of the textiles firm. 1933–5.
Very large wing, virtually a new house, added to the
  fourteenth-century great hall. It is French Renaissance

315

227–8. Eastwell Park, Kent: the old mansion as altered by William Wallace in 1894, and as rebuilt for Sir John de Fonblaque Pennefather

229. Eridge Park, Sussex

in style outside, Art Deco within. The technology included underfloor heating and a Tannoy system, and there was gold-plate and onyx in the bathrooms. Although only half a dozen miles from Westminster, it was conceived as a country house and had its own farm. Now owned by the Ministry of Defence.
CL 15, 22 and 29 May 1937, 534, 568, 594, i, p.

ELVEDEN HALL, Suffolk (Pl. 34)

Enlarged by William and Clyde Young for Lord Iveagh, the Guinness brewery king. 1899–1903.
See pp. 56, 62. Now used as furniture store.
B 19 Mar 1904, 314, i; *BN* 6 Nov 1903, 617, i; *BN* 10 Jun 1904, 833, i.

ENCOMBE, Kent (Pls. 47–8)

By Basil Ionides for Ralph H. Philipson. 1923.
A very big seaside villa, Spanish in style. It replaced a house by George and Yeates. All the antique furniture was stripped of varnish and wax and bleached fawn-colour. As a labour-saving device, the bathroom had porcelain taps which did not need cleaning. There was an Italianate lily garden.
CL 20 and 27 Dec 1924, 992, 1032, i.

ERIDGE PARK, Sussex (Pl. 229)

Very substantial rebuilding by John Denman for the Marquess of Abergavenny. 1938–9.
An austere neo-Georgian house replaced one which was genuinely Georgian, but in the castellated Gothick style. About half was demolished in 1958.
CL 23 and 30 Sept 1965, 750, 818, i.

ESHER PLACE, Surrey

By G. T. Robinson and Duchêne for Sir Edgar Vincent (later Lord d'Abernon), an expert on Indian law, friend of Edward VII and member of the Souls. 1895–8.
Very large addition to an early nineteenth-century house,

French Renaissance in style. Practically in the town of Esher, but convenient for Sandown Park Racecourse. Lutyens designed the sunken garden. Lady Vincent was a great Edwardian beauty. Duchêne was the Duke of Marlborough's architect at Blenheim. Now owned by the Electricians' Union.
CL 6 Jan 1900, 17–21, i.

EWELME PARK, Oxfordshire

By Stanley Crosbie. 1914.
House on a spreading plan to allow for enclosed terraces and the collection of rainwater from the roof. It was praised by the *Builder* as 'excellent', although it is not immediately obvious why.
B 17 Apr 1914, 470, i; *B* 24 Apr 1914, 494–5, i, p.

EYFORD PARK, Gloucestershire

By E. Guy Dawber. 1910.
Smaller country house on the site of an older house, with an Arts and Crafts garden. Georgian in style, with an Ionic order on the garden elevation. It shows Dawber's 'simple and quiet manner' at its best. Remodelled in 1962.
AR 47, 1920, 11–13, i; *BN* 2 Jun 1911, 769, i, p; *BN* 4 Mar 1913, i.

EYNSHAM HALL, Oxfordshire (Pl. 92)

By George and Yeates for James Francis Mason, M.P. 1904–7.
A Georgian house, bought by J. F. Mason's father, James Mason, was demolished at the request of the owner's wife. The present building was inspired by Burton Constable Hall, outside Hull. Now a police training college.
AA 1904(1), 45, i.

FANHAMS HALL, Hertfordshire

By W. Wood Bethell for Captain Richard Page Croft. 1900–1.
Almost complete rebuilding in a bleak, Elizabethan style, with great banks of mullioned windows. The house still possesses the main lines of an outstanding garden (see p. 298). Now headquarters of Building Societies Association.
AR 18, 1905, 270, i, p.

FLINT HOUSE, Oxfordshire

By Ernest Newton for F. N. Garrard, wholesale grocer. 1913.
It was unfortunate that the Arts and Crafts desire for local materials dictated unknapped flints. They give the house a grim look, and were in any case only a facing, because the structure beneath was stone.
AR 51, 1922, 140–3, i, p; *B* 7 May 1920, 549, i; *B* 14 May 1920, i.

FORTHAMPTON COURT, Gloucestershire (Pl. 184)

Restored by Philip Webb for John Reginald Yorke. 1889–91; 1913.

This fascinating house is of immense interest as showing how Philip Webb, the secretary of the SPAB, himself put SPAB principles into action. The work was both radical and sensitive, at least to the surviving medieval fabric. The house was re-oriented, and a new wing was built that was uncompromisingly Webb. Typically, Webb baulked at the use of the word 'restituendas', meaning restored, in a Latin inscription the learned owner proposed putting over a fireplace, although for once he was overruled. The house was further modified by F. S. Chesterton in 1913, and R. Blenman-Bull in 1958.
CL 27 Sept and 11 Oct 1979, 938, 1166, i.

FRAMINGHAM HALL, Norfolk

By George Skipper of Norwich for Charles Edward Butler. 1930.
Originally a simple Queen Anne building, which was much enlarged and redesigned, with two bows, a screen of Ionic columns and an orangery on the garden front.
B 20 Jun 1930, 1179, i.

FRIAR PARK, Oxfordshire (Pls. 210–11)

For Sir Frank Crisp, baronet, a London solicitor, by Crisp himself with M. Clarke Edwards. 1896.
See pp. 297–8.
CL 13 Jun 1903, 773; *CL* 5 Aug 1905, 162; *CL* 3 May 1913, 641.

FRITHWOOD HOUSE, Hertfordshire

By Mervyn Macartney for E. J. van Wisselings. 1900.
'The house is designed in a domestic type of Renaissance, with an aim at simplicity and comfort.' A smaller country house, and one of the first strictly in the eighteenth rather than seventeenth-century Classical tradition, in other words neo-Georgian. The drawing-room ceiling was modelled on Het Huys ten Bosch, in The Hague.
AR 7, 1900, 204, i; *AR* 8, 1900, 235–6, i, p; *BN* 14 Sept 1900, 159, i, p.

FULBROOK HOUSE, Surrey

By Edwin Lutyens for A. Streatfield. 1897.
This house forms an instructive contrast with Norman Shaw's Surrey vernacular manner, because the client had married the daughter of Richard Combe, for whom Shaw built Pierrepoint. It has an intimacy of scale and touch of whimsy which Shaw neither sought nor achieved. A new wing containing a swimming pool was added impeccably in the Lutyens idiom by Roderick Gradidge in 1975.
CL 31 Jan 1903, 145.

GALTEE CASTLE, Co. Cork

By Darbyshire and Smith of Manchester for Abel Buckley, M.P. 1895.
Built of red rubble stone with limestone dressings. The style was French Renaissance. Electricity was generated by water power. Demolished *c.* 1940.
AA 1895, 39, i; *B* 14 Sept 1895, 188, i, p.

GARGRAVE HOUSE, Yorkshire

By J. B. Dunn for J. W. Coulhurst. 1917.
Eighteenth-century style mansion house, with extensive
formal garden. Dunn was an expert on drains.
AR 41, 1918, 57–9, i, p; *B* 27 Apr 1917, 268, i, p.

GLEBELANDS, Wokingham

By Ernest Newton for A. J. Nicholson. 1897.
Like many Arts and Crafts architects in the 1890s,
Newton liked to combine motifs from different styles
within the same building. This house has mullioned
windows and a Classical cornice.
B 27 Aug 1898, 192, i, p; *B* 14 Sept 1901, 232, i.

GLEDSTONE HALL, Yorkshire (Pl. 95)

By Edwin Lutyens for Sir Amos Nelson, cotton broker.
1923.
Very handsome, ashlar-faced Palladian house, with a
giant *porte-cochère* on the entrance front. It was designed
in collaboration with a local architect, Richard Jaques.
Although atypically extravagant for the post–First
World War years, it had only seven bedrooms, even if
each of these possessed its own bathroom. One of the
symmetrical wings of the forecourt contains a large
garage and service courtyard for the motor cars.
CL 13 and 20 Apr 1935, 374, 400.

GOSFORD HOUSE, East Lothian

Large additions by William Young for Lord Wemyss.
Late 1880s and early 1890s.
Work included a vast and opulent marble staircase hall,
dangerously akin to that which the architect executed
about the same time for Glasgow town hall. Lutyens,
surprisingly, rather liked it, although he thought the
effect comparable to a vigorous rendition of God Save
the King sung flat.
A 29 Mar 1895, 209, i; *A* 5 Apr 1895, 225, i; *A* 26 Apr
1895, 273, i; *BN* 3 Apr 1891, 489, p; *BN* 9 Sept 1892,
345, i, p; *CL* 2 Sept 1911, 342, i.

THE GRANGE, West Lothian

By J. N. Scott and A. Lorne Campbell for Henry Cadell, a
geologist at Edinburgh University. 1904.
A Baronial house on a hill top, planned around a square
tower four storeys tall. Formal garden. There were two
kitchens, one for the servants, another with access from
the main part of the house for the owner's seven
daughters.

GREAT DIXTER, Sussex (Pl. 110)

Enlargement of a fifteenth-century manor house by
Edwin Lutyens for Nathaniel Lloyd, managing direc-
tor of the Star Bleaching Company.
See p. 159
CL 4 Jan 1913, 18, i, p.

GREAT MAYTHAM, Kent

By Edwin Lutyens for H. J. Tennant, son of Sir Charles

Tennant, chemical manufacturer. 1907–9.
Huge Wrenaissance house of blue-grey bricks with red
dressings, it shows the unexciting qualities Blomfield so
much admired in seventeenth-century architecture. An
older house on the site was incorporated and Hudson
thought the result 'most extraordinarily cheap'.
Tennant also employed Lorimer at Lympne Castle.
BN 24 Feb 1911, 279, i, p; *CL* 30 Nov 1912, 746, i, p.

GREYFRIARS, Surrey

By C. F. A. Voysey for Julian Sturgis, dramatist. 1897.
Exaggerately long and low house, stretched out along a
ridge of the Hog's Back in Surrey. It only has four main
rooms, including the stair hall; all face due south and
have magnificent views. Herbert Baker made additions
to the entrance front in 1914, among which was a
squash court.
AA 12, 1897, 37; *AR* 1, 1897, 327, i, p; *B* 1900, 192, i; *BA*
1898, 292.

GREY WALLS, East Lothian (originally High Walls)
(Pl. 37)

By Edwin Lutyens for Alfred Lyttleton, barrister and
M.P. 1901.
A golf box on the edge of the Muirfield Links. The client
asked for a house with plenty of bedrooms and little
else, so the main rooms are intimate in scale. Nevertheless, the plan, with the entrance set in the rounded angle
of the L-shaped courtyard, is one of Lutyens's most
sophisticated, and local character, local style and
masterly sense of architectural form are combined with
infinite subtlety.
AR 53, 1923, 138, i; *CL* 9 Sept 1911, 374, i, p.

GRIMSTON COURT, Yorkshire

By W. H. Brierley for J. J. Hunt. 1901.
Sizeable Tudor style house, built of brick and half-
timbering and grouped in the picturesque manner
Brierley later abandoned for Thorpe Underwood and
Sion Hill.
AA 1901(2), 46, i; *B* 14 Sept 1901, 232, i, p.

HAGGERSTON CASTLE, Northumberland

Monumental remodelling by Richard Norman Shaw for
C. J. Leyland, director of turbine and shipbuilding
companies. 1892–7.
Bleak, very large Classical house, with swaggering
interiors. A large part was destroyed by fire in 1911,
and rebuilt on an even bigger scale by J. B. Dunn of
Edinburgh. This house was completed in 1915 and
probably had the shortest life of any house of the period.
Leyland died in 1926. In 1930 it was advertised,
desperately, as being 'extremely well adapted for any
institutional or scholastic purpose, or as a high-class
hotel, hydro, or country club'. Nearly everything
except Shaw's tall water-tower was demolished in 1931.
Now a caravan site.
B 23 Jul 1915, 68, 79, i, p.

THE HALLAMS, Surrey

By Richard Norman Shaw for Charles Durant Hodgson, who had inherited brewing money. 1894.
Late flowering of Shaw's Old English style of the 1860s and 1870s.
BN 3 Jan 1896, 45, i, p.

HALNAKER PARK, Sussex

By Edwin Lutyens and L. M. Gotch for Reginald McKenna, chairman of the Midland Bank and M.P. 1938.
Lutyens collaborated with the Midland Bank's architect for this late, somewhat unexciting house.

HAMPTWORTH LODGE, Wiltshire

By E. Guy Dawber. 1910–12.
Big half-timbered house on the edge of the New Forest. The style was apparently chosen to suit the owner's collection of oak furniture. True to Arts and Crafts principles, not a single piece of timber was worked away from the site, and the lead rainwater heads, downpipes and gutters were cast on the grounds. As far as possible, everything was made within sight of the house. Some old overmantels came from Goodrich Court, in Herefordshire.
B 16 May 1913, 566, i, p; *BN* 13 Jun 1913, 821, i, p.

HAPPISBURGH MANOR, Norfolk (now St Mary's)

By Detmar Blow for Albemarle Cator. 1900.
Sun-trap house used 'as a seaside residence, and planned to give shelter from the wind in the gardens'. Entirely constructed of local materials: beach shingle and flints bonded with bricks, with a roof of reeds grown on the estate. Only some wood and the glass came from outside. Now a country club.
AA 1909(1), 62, i; *AR* 15, 1904, 214, 219–22, i, p.

HARCOMBE CHUDLEIGH, Devon

By J. Archibald Lucas of Exeter for Sir Edward Wills, baronet, of W. D. and H. O. Wills, the tobacco manufacturers. 1913.
Irregular, low, stone-built house in the Elizabethan style, with a long verandah on the south side. Now an hotel.
BN 15 Aug 1913, 222–3, i, p.

HEATHCOTE, Yorkshire

By Edwin Lutyens for J. T. Hemingway, cotton broker. 1906.
Lutyens's most triumphantly classical house, although, ironically, by no means one of his largest: it is a villa on the outskirts of Ilkley. Now offices.
B 1 Feb 1918, 82, i; *BN* 24 Sept 1909, 455, i, p; *CL* 9 Jul 1910, 54, i, p.

HEATHFIELD PARK, Sussex

Major alterations, including new elevations, by Reginald Blomfield for W. C. Alexander. 1896–7.
Blomfield turned the house round, stripped it of its stucco, added a new attic storey, and made it, according to his *Memoirs*, into a 'normal Georgian house'.
B 16 Feb 1898, 108–9, i, p.

HEVER CASTLE, Kent (Col. Pl. xxiv, Pls. 134–8, 214–15)

Tudor castle bought, restored and enlarged by Frank Pearson for William Waldorf Astor. 1903–6.
See pp. 190–8. Presently on the market.
B 5 Dec 1908, 622, i, p; *BN* 2 Oct 1908, 473, i, p; *BN* 16 Oct 1908, 509, i; *CL* 12 and 19 Oct 1907, 522, 558, i; *CL* 12 and 19 Oct 1917, 522, 558; *CL* 1 and 8 Jan 1981, 18, 66, i.

HIGHFIELDS, Buckinghamshire

By Lionel Crane for A. L. Griffith-Williams. 1910.
It had a lounge hall, which formed an enfilade with the drawing room and dining room, making plenty of room for parties and dances. Generally, the architect aimed at 'an old world feeling'.
BN 30 Dec 1910, 939, i, p.

HILDON HALL, Hampshire

By Aston Webb for Sir Augustus Webster, eighth baronet. 1898.
Large Elizabethan style house, with the wings of the entrance courtyard set at an angle. Only the water-tower survives.
AA 1898 (1), 30–2, i, p; *B* 18 Jun 1898, 590, i, p.

HILLES, Gloucestershire (Pls. 1, 174–7)

By Detmar Blow for himself. Begun 1914; unfinished at Blow's death in 1939.
See pp. 244–50.
CL 7 and 14 Sept 1940, 212, 234, i.

THE HILL HOUSE, Dumbartonshire

By C. R. Mackintosh for W. W. Blackie, publisher. 1902–4.
Large and advanced Art Nouveau villa in the suburbs of Helensburgh. Outside, although there is a strong sense of 'abstract' massing, especially in the entrance front, the house belongs to the Scottish Baronial tradition. The client specified harling and slates. But the interior is far more original, whether in the pronounced vertical lines of the entrance hall, the black ceiling of the drawing room, or the weird and wonderful tulip motifs on the doors of the built-in cupboards in the bedroom. Mackintosh designed much of the furniture in his famous etiolated style, and also the light fittings. The most remarkable look like box-kites and brought a taste of Japan to the banks of the Clyde. National Trust for Scotland.

HOLLINGTON HOUSE, Hampshire

By A. C. Blomfield for F. Festus Kelly, owner of Kelly's Directories. 1904.
Rambling Elizabethan style house on L-shaped plan, in brick, stone, half-timber and rough-cast.
AR 22, 1907, 243–50; *B* 12 Mar 1904, 286–7, i, p; *B* 11 Jun 1904, 637, i.

230. Houndsell Place, Sussex

231. Ivorys, Sussex

HOME PLACE, Norfolk (originally Voewood, then Kelling Place) (Pl. 151)

By E. S. Prior for the Rev. Percy Lloyd. 1904–6.

This extreme Arts and Crafts sun-trap house was built as much as possible from local materials, including pebbles and sand dug out from an acre of land excavated to a depth of six feet in front of the house, which became the sunken garden. No general contractor; building was supervised by Randall Wells. The grounds were seven acres. Now a hospital.

AR 19, 1906, 70–80, 82, i, p; *CL* 6 Nov 1909, 634, i, p.

HORWOOD HOUSE, Buckinghamshire

By Detmar Blow for Frederick Denny. 1912.

Red brick house, gabled and mullioned, with thatched stable court and a particularly good Jekyllesque formal garden, complete with *étang* or pond. Now owned by British Telecom.

CL 10 Nov 1923, 644, i, p.

HOUNDSELL PLACE, Sussex (formerly Houndstall House) (Pls. 94, 230)

By Alwyn Ball for Arnold Ball. 1912–16.

Reticent, finely proportioned, although in places mannered, house, neo-Georgian in style. Attenuated doorcase on the garden elevation, and very tall windows to the staircase. A hall rising through two storeys. Alwyn Ball, formerly an assistant to Smith and Brewer, was killed on the Western Front in November 1916.

AR 53, 1923, 140, i; *CL* 2 Feb 1918, 108, i, p; *CL* 17 Jul 1958, 126, i, p.

HOUSE OF CROMAR, Aberdeenshire

By Arnold Mitchell for the Marquess of Aberdeen. 1902.
Substantial Baronial house used as a retreat from Haddo Hall.

HUNTERCOMBE PLACE, Oxfordshire

By Oswald P. Milne for W. B. Close. 1911.
A brick and half-timber house with a large tower, necessary to hold water which had to be pumped from a deep well. Milne was a pupil of Lutyens.

AR 33, 1913, 42, i, p.

HURSLEY PARK, Hampshire (Pl. 5)

Reconstruction of an eighteenth-century house by A. Marshall Mackenzie for G. A. (later Sir George) Cooper. 1902.

Redecorated with elaborate French, Jacobean and Caroline style interiors. Now IBM Laboratories.

CL 23 and 30 Oct 1909, 562, 598, i.

HURSTBOURNE PARK, Hampshire

By Beeston and Burmester for the Earl of Portsmouth. 1893–4.

The previous mansion was gutted by fire, and Lord Portsmouth took a hand in designing the new one, which had a curving wing on the garden front. Direct labour was employed. Demolished 1965.

B 11 Nov 1893, 358–9, i, p; *B* 27 Jan 1894, 72, i; *B* 13 Oct 1894, 260, i.

IVORYS, Sussex (Pl. 231)

By Walter Brierley. 1922.

One of Brierley's rare forays into the Home Counties, it is in a faultless neo-Georgian which could easily be mistaken for the real thing. As with many buildings of this size and type, the interior is rather cramped.

JARDINE HALL, Dumfriesshire

By E. J. May for D. J. Jardine, big-game hunter. 1894–7.
Sumptuous Classical remodelling of an eighteenth-century house, with new wings and grand flight of stairs leading up from the entrance door to the hall. Demolished.
AA 1898 (1), 34–7; *AR* 11, 1902, 104–6, i, p; *B* 12 May 1894, 370, i, p; *B* 4 Jun 1898, 546, i, p.

JOLDWYNDS, Surrey

By Oliver Hill for Wilfred (later Lord) Greene, barrister and Master of the Rolls. 1930–2.
The most famous of Hill's Modern Movement houses, stark but stylish. Unfortunately it took the place of a house by Philip Webb, although this had the advantage that the planting of the park was already mature: the dark green of the conifers was an effective contrast to the pink-washed walls of the house. This was much praised, although other Modern Movement houses were, by their low lines, held to complement their landscape settings—you could win either way. Structurally the house was not a success. Only seven years after it was finished, the Tecton partnership in the form of Margaret Lubetkin was called in to advise on repairs. It was felt that a completely new house could be built for the same money. The result is a committed Modern Movement building, but with a pitched roof.
CL 15 Sept 1934, 276, i, p.

KELLING HALL, Norfolk (Pl. 49)

By Edward Maufe for H. W. Deterding, director general of Royal Dutch Petroleum. 1912–13.
Late Arts and Crafts sun-trap house, by the future architect of Guildford Cathedral.
AA 1912 (2), 59.

KILDONAN HOUSE, Ayrshire (Col. Pl. v)

By James Miller for Captain the Rt Hon. Euan Wallace, P.C., M.P. 1914–15.
Wallace inherited 30,000 acres from an uncle, who had requested he make Kildonan his home. The new house, built of creamy white Northumberland sandstone, with a deep entrance courtyard, was perhaps the last great house in the Gothic Revival tradition, indicated by the different heights of roofs for the different departments of the structure. Captain Wallace married Barbara Lutyens in 1920. Even by then it seemed far too big and was never properly finished inside, which is why the *Architectural Review* thought the interior verged on 'monastic *baldness*'. Soon to be turned into flats.
AR 63, 1928, 124–9, i; *B* 15 Jun 1923, 966–7, 970, i, p; *B* 20 Jun 1924, 981, i.

KILTERAGH, Co. Dublin

By W. D. Caröe for Sir Horace Plunkett. 1905.
Built of local granite faced with rough-cast. Plunkett's study, the only room free from Lady Fingall's influence, was on the first floor. Destroyed by fire. See pp. 73–4.
AA 1905 (1), 48–9, i, p; *B* 23 Sept 1905, 322, i, p.

KINCARDINE HOUSE, Deeside

By Niven and Wigglesworth. 1895–6.
Baronial; rough-cast with red granite dressings.
AA 1895, 79, i; *AA* 1897 (1), 13, 90, i, p; *B* 6 Jul 1895, 13, i, p; *B* 29 May 1897, 484, i.

KINLOCH CASTLE, Isle of Rhum (Pl. 131)

By Leeming and Leeming for Sir George Bullough. 1901.
See p. 185. Nature Conservancy Council.

LAMBAY CASTLE, Co. Dublin

By Edwin Lutyens for the Hon. Cecil Baring. 1907–8.
In 1902 Baring ran off with the wife of his New York banking partner, married her, and five years later employed Lutyens to remodel this small castle, where they lived in surroundings that could alternatively be described as Spartan or Arcadian. A soft grey building, reflecting the colours of the sea, the mist and the garden.
CL 4 May 1912, 650, i, p; *CL* 20 and 27 Jul 1929, 86, 120, i.

LANGOED CASTLE, Breconshire

By Clough Williams-Ellis for Archibald Christy. 1912.
A stone-built, seventeenth-century style house. The architect got the commission through a chance meeting with the client on a train. Now empty and under threat of demolition.

LINDISFARNE CASTLE, Northumberland (Col. Pl. II, Pls. 27–30)

Reconstruction by Edwin Lutyens for Edward Hudson, proprietor of *Country Life*. 1902.
See pp. 38, 45. National Trust.
CL 7 Jun 1913, 830, i, p.

LITTLE MASSINGHAM HOUSE, Norfolk

By Wimperis and Best for Mrs Birkbeck, widow of a banker. 1906.
B 1906, 146.

LITTLE RIDGE, Wiltshire

By Detmar Blow for Hugh Morrison (later Lord Margadale). 1904.
Mellow, gabled house built of Cotswold stone. The entrance façade incorporated the seventeenth-century front of the manor house at Berwick St Leonards, moved from elsewhere on the estate. The house is near the site of William Beckford's Fonthill Splendens. Little Ridge, now demolished, was outstanding for its Elizabethan style plasterwork.
B 14 Aug 1925, 246, i; *CL* 26 Oct 1912, 566, i, p.

LODGE STYLE, Bath, Somerset (Pl. 232)

By C. F. A. Voysey for T. S. Cotterell, general manager of Bath and Portland Stone Companies. 1909.
A charming but eccentric castellated bungalow, too small to be called a country house, too curious to leave out.
B 1910, 264, i, p.

LUCKLEY, Berkshire (Pl. 233)

By Ernest Newton for E. D. Mansfield. 1907.
Elizabethan in the suggestion of an E-shaped plan, neo-
Georgian in detailing. Typical of Newton's quiet
strengths.
B 17 Jul 1909, 72–3, i, p.

LUTON HOO, Bedfordshire (Pl. 190)

Adam mansion remodelled by Mewès and Davis for Sir
Julius Wernher, diamond millionaire. 1903.
Mewès and Davis built the two pavilions to the garden
front, added the French-style mansard roof (as at the
Ritz), and remodelled the interior, creating an elegant
neo-Classical staircase hall and a very opulent dining
room, where Beauvais tapestries hung against marble
walls. Wernher himself was rather retiring and had
advanced social ideas; it was his wife who provided the
social ambition. The house now contains Wernher's
magnificent art collection, part of which was originally
housed in his house in Park Lane.
CL 5 May 1950, 1282.

MADRESFIELD COURT, Worcestershire (Col. Pls. XXVII–XXIX, Pls. 40, 178–81)

Decoration of the staircase hall, library and chapel for
Lord and Lady Beauchamp. 1902 onwards.
Madresfield has been the home of the Lygon family since
the 1450s, although only part of the entrance front
survives from the Tudor period. Most of the rest of the
house is the work of P. C. Hardwick, who 'restored' the
house in 1863–88. The Beauchamps' work involved
little structural alteration, beyond knocking four rooms
into one to form the staircase hall, but the library and
chapel are, perhaps, the most beautiful and touching of
all Arts and Crafts interiors. See pp. 250–5.
CL 30 Mar 1907, 450; *CL* 16, 23 and 30 Oct 1980, 1338,
1458, 1551.

MAESYCRUGIAU MANOR, Dyfed

By Arnold Mitchell for Sir Courtenay Mansel, baronet.
1902.
Begun as a large stone house, although only the service
court and tower were built. Stones left jutting out of the
side wall and the staircase inside leading nowhere are
evidence of the intention to continue. The halt may
have been connected with Sir Courtenay's mysterious
decision to resign his baronetcy in favour of his uncle,
Sir Edward, in 1903, to resume it on the latter's death
five years later. Now an hotel.

AA 1903 (2), 16, i; *AA* 1905 (1), 58, i; *B* 3 Dec 1903, 580, i,
p.

MANCROFT TOWERS, Suffolk

By G. J. Skipper, 1898.
Elizabethan style house with enormous tower.

MANDERSTON, Berwickshire (Col. Pl. x, Pls. 6, 35, 84–9, 191–3)

232. Lodge Style, Bath, Somerset

By John Kinross for Sir James Miller. 1894–1905.
See pp. 121–7.
CL 15 and 22 Feb, 1 Mar 1979, 390, 466, 542.

MANOIR DE LA TRINITÉ, Jersey (Pl. 234)

Restoration by Reginald Blomfield for Athelstan Riley.
1909–12.
Blomfield was a thorough-going professional and not
wholly sympathetic to the SPAB. Consequently the old
manor was gutted and given the present very high roof,
which determines its character. Originally a low roof
was intended, and the present one follows mainland
rather than Jersiaise precedent. Nevertheless, the house
is one of Blomfield's most successful, partly because of
his detailed scholarly knowledge of French architecture.
BN 3 May 1912, 631, i, p.

MAR LODGE, Aberdeenshire (Pl. 2)

By A. Marshall Mackenzie for the Duke of Fife, son-
in-law of Edward VII. 1896.
Although only a shooting lodge, it had twenty-six bedrooms for the family and guests, as well as sufficient
bedrooms for twenty-five menservants and forty maids.
The house previously on the site had been destroyed by
fire, so the new one had special fireproof ceilings, which
were also watertight: if there was a fire, water could be
turned on to stand eight inches deep in all the rooms,
providing insulation between the storeys. Now an hotel.
B 23 Jan 1897, 80, i, p; *BN* 29 Jan 1897, 80, i, p; *CL* 17 Jul
1937, 64, i.

MARSH COURT, Hampshire

By Edwin Lutyens for Herbert Johnston, stockbroker.
1901.
Spectacular large house built of chalk clunch, and
consequently mottled white in colour. The style derives
from great Elizabethan houses such as Haddon Hall,
although historical reference is subordinate to the
vigorous use of native materials. The interiors are
Classical. Now a school.
CL 1 Sept 1906, 306, i.

MARYLAND, Surrey (Pl. 235)

By Oliver Hill for M. C. Warner. 1929.
Spanish style house, built out of local sandstone with
glazed green tiles for the roof. Extraordinary, fort-like
interior, more suggestive of the Sierras than Surrey.
CL 24 Oct 1931, 452, i, p.

MELSETTER HOUSE, The Orkneys (Pls. 152–6)

An eighteenth and nineteenth-century building enlarged
by W. R. Lethaby for the Birmingham industrialist
Thomas Middlemore. 1898.
See pp. 217–24.
CL 13 Aug 1981, 566, i.

MIDDLEFIELD, Cambridgeshire

By Edwin Lutyens, for Henry Bond, law fellow at Trinity
Hall, Cambridge. 1908.
Smaller country house, Georgian vernacular: there is a
pronounced sense of geometry in the low roofs.

MIDDLETON PARK, Oxfordshire (Pl. 236)

By Edwin Lutyens for the seventh Earl of Jersey. 1938.
Very large, rather French house, designed with his son
Robert. The entrance hall uses the Order Lutyens had
devised for New Delhi. Although this is one of Lutyens's
two last houses, and one of the last great houses in
Britain, it is the only one he built as an aristocrat's seat.
Now flats.
CL 5 and 12 July 1946, 28, 74.

MINTERNE MAGNA, Dorset (Pls. 105–6, 237)

By Leonard Stokes for Lord Digby. 1903–7.
See pp. 146–53.
AA 1904 (2), 48–9, i, p; *AA* 1905 (1), 37, i; *ABJ* 27 Jul
1910, 84, 87–91, i, p; *AR* 25, 1909 (1), 143–50, i, p; *CL* 21
and 28 Feb 1980, 498, 574, i.

MONKTON, Sussex (Col. Pls. XII, XXXIII, Pl. 31)

By Edwin Lutyens for William Dodge James. 1902.
Remodelled by Kit Nicholson and Hugh Casson with
the help of Salvador Dali. 1930s.
Summer retreat built for the Jameses on the West Dean
estate. See p. 47.

MOORCRAG, Westmorland

By C. F. A. Voysey for J. W. Buckley. 1899.
Originally designed on an L-shaped plan similar to
Broadleys, it was built in a long block, with a very low,
sweeping roof over the service end. There were only
three main rooms (living, drawing and dining rooms),
and Voysey, true to his radical principles, hoped to save
space by doing away with the back stairs for the
servants. He was evidently overruled by the Buckleys.
A 88, 1907, 296, i; *BJAR* 16, 1903–4, 176–7, i, p; *S* 21,
1904, 128, i.

233. Luckley, Berkshire

234. Manoir de la Trinité, Jersey

235. Maryland, Surrey

236. Middleton Park, Oxfordshire

237. Minterne Magna, Dorset

238. Moundsmere Manor, Hampshire

324

MOTCOMBE MANOR, Dorset (Pl. 58)

By George and Peto for Richard Grosvenor, Lord
    Stalbridge, railway magnate. 1893.
Built to rival Lord Portman's Bryanston. 'A house of the
    Tudor type,' wrote the *Building News*, 'studiedly simple
    and dignified'. It is built of brick with Ham Hill stone
    mullions and dressings. Now a school.
AA 1894, 28–9; *B* 5 Aug 1899, 132, i, p; *BN* 19 May 1893,
    667, i, p.

MOUNDSMERE MANOR, Hampshire (Pls. 102, 238)

By Reginald Blomfield for Wilfred Buckley, an authority
    on dairy farming and old glass. 1908–9.
Large house in the style of Wren.
B 3 Oct 1908, 352, i, p; *B* 28 Jul 1911, 102, i; *CL* 12 Mar
    1910, 378, i, p.

MUNSTEAD WOOD, Surrey

By Edwin Lutyens for Gertrude Jekyll. 1896.
Rightly hailed as the key house of Lutyens's early archi-
    tectural development, although, like most of his build-
    ings of the 1890s, a house in the country rather than a
    country house. Largely from Miss Jekyll came the Arts
    and Crafts feeling for local materials and solid, un-
    adorned hand-work. It does not have the sense of form,
    space or cleverness that arrived quickly with Orchards.
CL 8 Dec 1900, 730, i.

NASHDOM, Buckinghamshire (Col. Pl. III, Pl. 26)

By Edwin Lutyens for Princess Alexis Dolgorouki.
    1905–8.
See p. 40. Now a monastery.
CL 31 Aug 1912, 292, i, p.

NETHER SWELL MANOR, Gloucestershire

By E. Guy Dawber for Sir John Murray Scott. 1903; 1909.
Sir John, a man of 25 stone and 'rich human juices'
    according to *Vanity Fair*, was the son of a doctor born in
    Boulogne. He became virtually adopted by Sir Richard
    Wallace, illegitimate son of the Marquess of Hertford.
    It was largely his doing that Sir Richard's widow left
    the Wallace Collection to the nation, although he
    himself fell under the influence of Lady Sackville and
    left her, in a famous will contested by his brothers and
    sisters, nearly a million pounds' worth of works of art,
    which were sold to keep up the Knole. Built in 1903,
    Nether Swell Manor was almost completely remodelled
    in 1909, when a concert room was added for perfor-
    mances by the tenor John McCormack, a friend of Sir
    John's. Although Dawber's house is Early Renaissance
    in style, it was decorated by Marcel Boulanger of Paris
    to form a setting for the French furniture Sir John had
    been left. Hals's *Laughing Cavalier* was hung in the
    house. Now a school.
AA 1909 (1), 51, i; *AR* 19, 1906, 22–9, i, p; *B* 15 Aug 1903,
    184, i, p; *B* 15 May 1909, 587–8, i; *B* 9 May 1919, 454,
    i; *B* 16 Jun 1925, i; *CL* 26 Nov 1910, 754, i, p.

NEW PLACE, Hampshire

By Edwin Lutyens for Mrs A. S. Franklyn. 1906.
Rather a bleak, Elizabethan style house in brick, incorporating two panelled rooms and the staircase from an early seventeenth-century house in Bristol. Now a conference centre.
CL 9 Apr 1910, 522, i, p.

NEW PLACE, Surrey

By C. F. A. Voysey for A. M. M. Stedman (later Sir Algernon Methuen), publisher. 1897–1901.
Many of Voysey's houses are mannered, but usually for the sake of calmness and repose rather than complexity. This, with its clash of gables and projecting bays on the entrance front, is the exception. In an early attempt to cope with the motor car, a 'motor stables' is marked on the plan.
S 21, 1901, 242–3, i, p.

NEWTON HALL, Cambridgeshire

By F. Foster for the distinguished classical scholar and archaeologist Sir Charles Waldstein. 1909.
This house, in the Later Renaissance style, encases a Victorian one. The garden front is symmetrical, although the entrance front is irregular. Foster made use of an unusual order, apparently excavated by the client. The parish churchyard contains the Waldstein mausoleum, a Beaux-Arts structure designed by Sir Ambrose Poynter in 1922.

NORTH BOVEY MANOR, Devon

By Detmar Blow, for the second Viscount Hambleden, son of W. H. Smith II, politician and newsagent. Completed 1907.
Large Early Renaissance house, with a Jacobean great hall and 'Adams' drawing room. Unexpectedly conventional for the architect. Now an hotel.

NORTH FORELAND LODGE, Hampshire (originally Sherfield Manor)

By Fairfax B. Wade for James B. Talor. 1898.
Combined Classical and Arts and Crafts features. The architect was paralysed by a fall from a dog cart in the early 1890s and had to work with partners to supervise his commissions, in this case C. Frankriss. (Information Andrew Saint.) Now a school.

NUTLEY DOWN, Hampshire

By E. Guy Dawber. 1913.
A big neo-Georgian house with a forecourt.
BN 9 and 16 May 1913, 638, 677.

NYMANS, Sussex (Col. Pl. XIX, Pl. 117)

A Victorian house transformed into a medieval romance, by Norman Evill and Walter Tapper for Lieutenant-Colonel and Mrs Leonard Messel, the parents of the decorator Oliver Messel. 1925–30.
National Trust.
CL 10, 17 and 24 Sept 1932, 292, 320, 346, i, p.

OKEWOOD, Sussex

By George and Yeates for the Duchess of Santo Teodoro. 1898.
AA 1898 (1), 14, i.

OLDCASTLE, Sussex

By Ernest Newton for Lord Wrenbury. 1910.
A lyrical Tudor house, unexpected from an architect who, in his earlier work, seemed to share Lethaby's 'rationalist' beliefs.
AR 51, 1922, 135, i; *B* 21 Jun 1912, 725–6, i, p.

OLD SURREY HALL, Surrey (Pls. 113–14)

A fifteenth-century house restored and greatly enlarged by George Crawley for the Hon. Mrs George Napier in 1922. A further range was built by Walter Godfrey in 1937.
CL 14 Sept 1929, 352, i, p; *CL* 15 and 22 Oct 1959, 554, 654, i, p.

ORCHARDS, Surrey

By Edwin Lutyens for Sir William Chance, banker. 1897.
Such was the leisurely craftsmanship of this most poetic of Lutyens's Surrey vernacular houses (and not an especially large one at that) that it took three years to build. As Christopher Hussey remarked, it was created by an artist for artists, witness the studio on the right of the entrance arch. The house is loosely planned around a courtyard, with a cloister on the west side; the courtyard theme was to be developed at Deanery Garden, Overstrand Hall and other Arts and Crafts houses.
CL 31 Aug 1901, 272, i.

OTTERSHAW PARK, Surrey

Very opulent remodelling and enlargement by Niven and Wigglesworth for Friedrich Eckstein, a partner in the diamond firm Wernher Beit and Co. 1910.
Sir Robert Taylor's house of 1761 was engulfed in stone, raised a storey and given new wings. The new accommodation included a sculpture gallery, winter garden and swimming pool. Now a school.

OVERSTRAND HALL, Norfolk

By Edwin Lutyens for Lord Hillingdon, banker. 1899–1901.
A courtyard house in the Arts and Crafts style popular on this section of the Norfolk coast. Now a hospital.

PADDOCKHURST, Sussex (Pls. 32, 67–8)

Additions by Aston Webb for Sir Weetman Pearson (later Lord Cowdray), government contractor. 1897.
The work included a new dining room and a conservatory-cum-bowling alley. The dining room has a plasterwork frieze by Walter Crane illustrating the growth and history of locomotion. Now a school.
B 11 Sept 1897, 204, i, p; *B* 12 Nov 1898, 433, i; *BN* 10 Sept 1897, 365, i.

239. The Peel, Clovenfords

PANGBOURNE TOWER, Berkshire

By John Belcher for John Donaldson, shipbuilder. 1898.
Eccentrically, a tower in the style of a Henry II hunting lodge thought to have once stood on the site was combined with a Later Renaissance mansion, with a symmetrical garden front. Now a college.
A 1900, 200, 216; *AA* 1898 (1), 27, i; *AA* 1898 (2), 32, i, p; *AR* 4, 1898, 272, i, p; *B* 26 Nov 1898, 484, i, p; *B* 13 Jan 1900, 38, i, p.

PAPILLON HALL, Leicestershire

By Edwin Lutyens for Frank Belville, maker of Robinson's Barley Water. 1903–4.
Remodelling of earlier house built by the seventeenth-century military engineer David Papillon. The butterfly-plan, inspired by Norman Shaw's Chesters, is of course a pun, because *papillon* means butterfly in French. Demolished.

PEASMARSH PLACE, Sussex

By Sir Edwin Cooper for Lord Devonport. 1937.
The second Lord Devonport did not like the climate in the Thames valley, so sold Whittington (q.v.), bought this house, and had it remodelled in a rather bleak and unfeeling neo-Georgian. Cooper had been associated with the Devonports through the Port of London Authority. Now a rest home.
B 1939, 63–6, i, p.

THE PEEL, Clovenfords (Pl. 239)

By John Kinross for W. R. Ovens, a baker. 1899.
Baronial, with Classical interiors.

PICKENHAM HALL, Norfolk

By R. Weir Schultz for George W. Taylor, a banker who inherited a fortune from button-making. 1902–5.
Long, Later Renaissance house, incorporating an early nineteenth-century one by Donthorn. The architect's instructions were 'to save as much of the house as was reasonably possible, and to incorporate it into a larger house to be built of red brick with white cornice and good chimneys'.
AR 21, 1907, 101–8, i, p; *BN* 19 Jan 1906, 97, i, p.

THE PLEASAUNCE, Norfolk

By Edwin Lutyens for Lord Battersea. 1897.
Lutyens's most eccentric house and not on the whole one he was proud of. At the client's insistence, it was created out of two villas, and grew piecemeal. Nevertheless, there are some touches of originality, notably in the rough-cast, battered tower to the stable court and the equally striking garden cloister, with its low, sweeping roof.

PLUMPTON PLACE, Sussex (Col. Pl. xxxiv)

By Edwin Lutyens for Edward Hudson, proprietor of *Country Life*. 1928.
This was the last of Hudson's places in the country, and it is Lutyens's most romantic idyll on a vernacular theme. The principal building when Hudson bought the sixty-four acre site was a derelict manor house, which Lutyens restored with the addition of a big, oak-mullioned bay like that at Deanery Garden. It is reached through an arch set between weather-boarded cottages. Hudson did not live in the manor house, but in the mill house which Lutyens also restored. Lutyens also created the setting of a garden and three lakes.
CL 20 May 1933, 522, i.

POLESDEN LACEY, Surrey (Pls. 11, 36, 42–4)

By Sir Ambrose Poynter for Sir Clinton Dawkins, an Indian civil servant who married an heiress; it was partly remodelled and redecorated by White Allom and Mewès and Davis for Captain R. Greville. 1905.
See pp. 66–71. National Trust.
AR 51, 1922, 202–3, i, p; *CL* 12 and 19 Feb 1981, 378, 442.

PORT LYMPNE, Kent (Col. Pl. vi, Pls. 51, 198, 217, 240)

By Herbert Baker for Sir Philip Sassoon. About 1912. Additions and garden by Philip Tilden. 1918–21.
Baker's house was brick-built in the Cape Dutch style; Tilden added a Moorish courtyard, a superb Roman swimming pool, and a monumental staircase 17 ft wide, flanked by temples and pylons. There were mural paintings by Michel Sert, Rex Whistler and others. Now a wildlife reserve.
AR 52, 1922, 90–5, i, p; *AR* 52, 1923, 137, i; *BN* 1 Jul 1921, 14, i; *CL* 19 and 26 May 1923, 678, 714, i, p; *CL* 4 Feb 1933, 116, i; *CL* 19 Oct 1929, 513, i; *CL* 10 Sept 1932, 285, i; *CL* 14 Mar 1936, 276, i.

PUTTERIDGE BURY, Hertfordshire

By George and Yeates for T. M. Clutterbuck. 1908.
George and Yeates's last large house, in the Elizabethan style. Even at this date, it contained a ballroom, library, boudoir, hall, billiard room, business room, dining room and gun room, although there was no drawing room: its function had been taken over by the hall. Now a college.

240. Port Lympne, Kent: the tent room

AA 1909 (1), 45, i; *B* 20 Mar 1909, 346, i, p; *BN* 22 May 1908, 741, i, p; *BN* 7 May 1909, 679, i.

PYRFORD COURT, Surrey

The original house by Clyde Young for the second Lord Iveagh. About 1910. Wings and other additions by J. A. Hale of Woking, working closely with the owner. 1920–9.

Stylish neo-Georgian. The land was sold by Lord Onslow, Iveagh's father-in-law and owner of Clandon Park, and the two houses are visible to each other from the tops of their respective hills. On the ground floor was a laboratory for Lord Iveagh's scientific experiments. It communicated with his bedroom above it by a staircase concealed in the panelling. Clyde Young had worked at Elveden (q.v.). Now a rest home.

CL 7 May 1964, 1118, i.

REDCOURT, Surrey

By Ernest Newton. 1894.

This house is in Newton's free Georgian style, with triangular Tudor gables. The beauty lies in the craftsmanship, for instance the cast-lead flashing to the oriel-like bay on the garden elevation, handmade tiles, diaper pattern brickwork. Newton said he preferred plainness when funds were limited, as they were here; the *Builder* thought this could be overdone.

B 14 Nov 1896, 404, i.

THE RED HOUSE, Yorkshire

By W. Bedford and Sydney Kitson. 1904.

This small house is of interest because of the very large central hall, which was top-lit and specially needed for the owner's collection of prints. There was a gallery at first-floor level, although the architects were at pains to ensure that neither bathrooms nor bedrooms opened directly off it.

AR 16, 1904, 216, 219–22, i, p.

THE RETREAT, Suffolk (Col. Pl. VIII)

By A. N. Prentice.

A small country house in local building materials.

AA 1900 (1), 56, i; *AR* 7, 1900, 212, i; *AR* 8, 1900, 146, i.

RODMARTON MANOR, Gloucestershire (Col. Pls. XXV–XXVI, Pls. 7, 157, 162–9, 209)

By Ernest Barnsley for the Hon. Claud Biddulph, banker. 1909–26.

See pp. 225–36.

CL 19 and 26 Oct 1978, 1178, 1298, i.

ROSEHAUGH HOUSE, Ross and Cromarty (Pl. 219)

By William Flockhart for Douglas Fletcher, the millionaire chairman of the Highland Railway. 1893–1903.

Designed in the French Renaissance style, it was fitted up with several chimneypieces and doorcases from other houses, as well as other works of art—so much so that it became 'largely a museum of antiquities'. Stanley Adshead was clerk of works. He remembered that Flockhart, a Glaswegian who practised in London, would come up for a few days every month, when everything stopped and the house was redesigned on the spot. 'He could not stand anything plain.' Demolished 1959.

AA 1903 (1), 70, i; *AA* 1904 (2), 30–5, i; *B* 9 Sept 1893, 192, i, p; *BN* 11 Dec 1903, 793, i, p; *BN* 1 Jan 1904, 7, i, p; *BN* 29 Jan 1904, 163, i.

ROWALLAN, Ayrshire

By R. S. Lorimer for A. Cameron Corbett (later Lord Rowallan), Glasgow land developer and M.P. 1903–6.

A substantial Baronial house which would have been much larger had not Mrs Corbett died shortly after the first plans were drawn. It was intended for the political parties Corbett felt it necessary to hold as M.P.

AR 29, 1911, 334, i, p; *CL* 27 Sept 1913, 420, i, p; *CL* 21 and 28 Dec 1978, 2142, 2210, i.

RUCKLEY GRANGE, Shropshire

By George and Yeates for J. Reid-Walker. 1904.

Big Elizabethan style house.

AA 1904 (1), 44, i.

ST ANNE'S HILL, Surrey

By Raymond McGrath for Christopher Tunnard, landscape gardener. 1938.

Modern Movement house in an eighteenth-century landscape park. The main rooms on the ground and first floors are circular; there is a billiard room and roof terrace on the second.

AR Oct 1937, 117–22.

ST DONAT'S CASTLE, Glamorgan (Pls. 139–45, 147–8)

This fourteenth and sixteenth-century castle was restored by Thomas Garner and G. F. Bodley in 1901–7 for Morgan Stuart Williams, who had found coal on the family estates. The elaborate terraced garden was laid out at this time. In 1925 St Donat's was bought by the newspaper tycoon William Randolph Hearst and modernised by Sir Charles Allom.

See pp. 199–212. Now United World College of the Atlantic.
CL 24 and 31 Aug 1907, 270, 306, i; *CL* 18 Sept 1980, 942, i.

THE SALUTATION, Kent

By Edwin Lutyens for Gaspard Farrer. 1911.
Perfect 'Georgian' house in Sandwich, with no land.
CL 27 Mar 1969, 701, i.

SAUCHIEBURN CASTLE, Stirlingshire (Pl. 129)

By Sydney Mitchell and Wilson for Sir James Maitland, baronet, coal owner. 1890.
Enormous Baronial house of which nothing now remains.
BN 31 Oct 1890, 608, i.

SENNOWE PARK, Norfolk (Col. Pls. XVI–XVII, XXXV, Pls. 3, 69, 77, 96–101, 213)

By George J. and F. W. Skipper of Norwich for Thomas Cook, grandson of the travel agent. 1905–7.
See pp. 134–40.
B 5 May 1915, Royal Academy supplement, i; *BN* 25 Aug 1911, 259, i, p; *CL* 24 and 31 Dec 1981, 2242, 2298, i.

SION HILL, Yorkshire

By W. H. Brierley for Percy Stancliffe. 1912.
Substantial neo-Georgian house, planned to let the maximum sunlight into the rooms and to take advantage of the views.
B 2 Jan 1920, 16–18, i; *BN* 10 May 1912, 666, i, p; *CL* 16 Dec 1922, 830, i.

SIZEWELL HALL, Suffolk

By W. Gilmour Wilson for G. S. Ogilvie, the founder of Thorpeness. 1921.
The half-timbered Elizabethan mansion was burnt and rebuilt in the same style, although the structure, like many of the fanciful buildings in the holiday village of Thorpeness, was concrete.

SKIBO CASTLE, Sutherland (Pls. 132–3)

By Ross and Macbeth for Andrew Carnegie, Scottish-American steel millionaire. 1899–1903.
Remodelling of eighteenth and nineteenth-century castle on a massive scale. Now on the market. See pp. 185–9.
BN 20 Mar 1903, 400–1, i, p.

SLEDMERE HOUSE, Yorkshire (Col. Pl. xv)

Restoration and remodelling by W. H. Brierley for Sir Tatton Sykes, baronet. 1911.
After a fire, Brierley rebuilt this outstanding house in the style of Wyatt. His work included taking down several internal walls and opening up a staircase hall that runs the full depth of the building. It thus offers a pregnant contrast between an eighteenth and an early twentieth-century Classicist's sense of space.
B 17 May 1918, 300, i.

241. South Lytchett Manor, Dorset

SNOWSHILL MANOR, Gloucestershire

Reconstructed by Charles Wade for himself. From 1919.
Snowshill is a sixteenth-century Cotswold manor house with an early eighteenth-century front. Wade, an architect with the LCC who had private means, bought it and filled it with an extraordinary collection of curios and *objets d'art*: Jacobean furniture, suits of Samurai armour, narwhal tusks, hour-glasses, glass demi-johns, a Bowstreet runner's tipstaff and so on. There is also, significantly, a wide collection of craft tools. The extreme romance of it reflects the tastes and values associated with 1920s Tudor. Wade lived the part, refusing electric light, eating in an old world kitchen, sleeping in an equally old world Tudor cupboard bed, labouring at a forge and using part of his collection of old tools in his workshop. Eventually the house became so full of memorabilia that he was driven out altogether, and made his home in an outbuilding. The garden was designed by Baillie Scott. National Trust.
CL 1 Oct 1927, 470, i, p.

SOUTH LYTCHETT MANOR, Dorset (Pl. 241)

By W. D. Caröe for Sir Eliott Lees, baronet, formerly M.P. for Oldham. 1892; 1900–4.
Substantial remodelling of an early nineteenth-century house. The first campaign created a living hall, the second gave rise to the present external appearance of the house, with its giant niche combined with a gable on the entrance front. Ham Hill stone was used. Now a school.
AA 1892, 59; *AA* 1900 (1), 17, i; *B* 24 Sept 1892, 244, i; *B* 26 May 1900, 518, i, p.

SPIDDAL HOUSE, Co. Galway

By William Ascott for the second Baron Killanin, barrister. 1910.
In the Romanesque style. The house was rebuilt in 1931 following a fire.

242. Thurston Hall, Berwickshire

243. Tirley Garth, Cheshire

STANDEN, Sussex (Pl. 12)

By Philip Webb for J. S. Beale, a London solicitor. 1892–4.

Webb insisted that the building already on site, Holly-bush Farm, was retained and it became part of the stable court, setting the scale for the rest of the building. The house is comfortable and homely and spacious and light, but perhaps also slightly awkward, like Webb himself. National Trust.

CL 7 May 1910, 666, i, p; *CL* 26 Feb and 5 Mar 1970, 494, 554, i, p.

STOWELL HILL, Somerset

By E. Guy Dawber for Lord Vestey, meat importer. 1927.

Comparatively modest, stone-built house, constructed soon after the Vesteys had established their off-shore tax avoidance trust. It has a shingle-clad water-tower and, as in most of Dawber's houses, the main living room is called the parlour. The architect disowned the iron gates and vases on top of the gatepiers the client added to the entrance front; wood gates, he said, would have been more appropriate to the house he designed.

AR 61, 1927, 25–7, i, p; *B* 29 Apr 1927, 683, i.

TEMPLE DINSLEY, Hertfordshire

Large additions by Edwin Lutyens for H. G. Fenwick. 1908.

The size of the existing house, a Queen Anne mansion, was increased by three or four times by the addition of cross-wings at either end. In part, this arrangement was adopted because the entrance had to be on the south side, a disposition that no Edwardian architect liked because it squandered the sun.

AA 1909 (1), 55, i; *BN* 12 Nov 1909, 717, i; *CL* 22 Apr 1911, 562, i, p.

TETTON HOUSE, Devon

Remodelled by H. S. Goodhart-Rendel for the Hon.

Mervyn Herbert, son of the fourth Earl of Caernarvon. 1926.

A house of about 1800 was remodelled in a Soane-like manner and covered in bright apricot-coloured plaster.

B 4 Jun 1926, 906, i.

THANET PLACE, Kent

By Edgar Ranger, in collaboration with Sir Charles Allom for Sir Edmund Vestey, director of the Union Cold Storage Co. and joint head of the Blue Star Line of steamers. 1929.

Big house on the coast, with Tuscan colonnades and spreading, pantiled roofs. It had a lounge hall and double-glazing and was regarded as one of the largest houses built since the war.

B 11 Nov 1929, 94–8, 105, 107, i, p.

THORNTON MANOR, Cheshire (Pls. 23, 46, 194–5)

By various architects for Lord Leverhulme, soap manu-facturer. 1888–1914.

In 1888 Leverhulme first rented the house. By the time he bought it outright in 1891 it had already been altered by William Owen and Jonathan Simpson. However, it was completely remodelled by Douglas and Fordham in 1896–7, then again by J. Lomax Simpson in 1912–14. Other alterations in the meantime included the huge music room modelled on Dawpool, Cheshire, by J. J. Talbot in 1902. Lomax-Simpson built the half-timbered gatehouse in 1910. The result is a red sandstone, Elizabethan style house, attractively pictur-esque on the entrance elevation, imposingly plain to the south. Gardens by Mawson.

BN 10 Apr 1896, 525, i, p.

THORPE UNDERWOOD HALL, Yorkshire

By W. H. Brierley for F. W. Slingsby. 1903.
Low and symmetrical Jacobean building, constructed

from two-inch handmade bricks with Hollington stone dressings.
BN 8 May 1903, 647, i.

THURSTON HALL, Berwickshire (Pl. 242)

By John Kinross for Mrs Hunter, the sister of Sir James Miller of Manderston. Mid-1890s.
Neo-Baroque remodelling of a Palladian villa.

TIGBOURNE COURT, Surrey

By Edwin Lutyens for Edgar Horne, chairman of the Prudential Assurance Co. 1899.
A house in the country famous for its colourful entrance elevation, which is visible from the Petworth Road. The dramatic sweep of the wings, ending in tall chimneys, can be overemphasised in photographs. When you see the house, it is equally striking for the use of tawny Bargate stone with galletting joints—that is, joints with pebbles and chips of flint set into the mortar.
CL 23 Sept 1905, 414, i.

TIRLEY GARTH, Cheshire (Pl. 243)

By C. E. Mallows, begun for B. Leesmith, a director of the chemicals firm of Brunner Mond, and finished for R. H. Prestwich, mill owner and future chairman of Burberrys. 1906–12.
Built around a cloister garth, the cloisters also serving as a terrace for the first-floor corridor. The site was forty acres. It seems from drawings at the RIBA drawings collection that the original scheme grew bigger and bigger until the first client was unable to finish it. Now owned by Moral Re-armament.
B 29 Nov 1908, 591, i; *BN* 17 Jan 1908, 103, i, p; *BN* 31 Jan 1908, 174, i; *CL* 18 Mar 1982, 702, i, p.

TUESLEY COURT, Surrey

By E. Guy Dawber for Major-General D. A. Scott, C.B.
Largish house in Lutyens rather than Dawber country.
AA 1909 (1), 54, i; *AR* 33, 1913, 22, i, p; *B* 16 Apr 1910, 436, i.

TYLNEY HALL, Hampshire (Col. Pl. IV)

By R. S. Wornum for Sir Lionel Phillips, partner in Wernher Beit and Co. 1898–1902.
Ostentatiously large house, not especially original but with a pleasingly boisterous water-tower, and a heady sense of sheer extent. Some internal walls survived from an earlier house. The gardens were by R. Weir Schultz, who lived nearby. Now a borstal.
AA 1904 (1), 46–7, 49, i, p; *AR* 16, 1904, 80–5, 117, 122–5, i, p; *BN* 9 Dec 1904, 829, i, p.

WALDERSHARE PARK, Kent

By Reginald Blomfield for the Earl of Guilford. 1912–14.
Almost total rebuilding after destruction by fire.

WELBECK ABBEY, Nottinghamshire

Rebuilding of the Oxford wing by George and Yeates for the Duke of Portland. 1902–5.

The early eighteenth-century structure had been damaged by fire and even more by the water used to put it out. The rebuilding included a Palladian, ashlar-faced exterior, a barrel-vaulted dining room, and a French style drawing room, all very smart. Now occupied by the Ministry of Defence.
AA 1902 (1), 37, i; *AR* 16, 1904, 18–19, 24–9, i; *B* 23 Sept 1893, 226, i; *B* 24 May 1902, 522, i; *BN* 9 Jun 1905, 821, i.

WELBURN HALL, Yorkshire

By W. H. Brierley. 1892.
Brierley's work represents the restoration of an early seventeenth-century building that had been used as a cattle shed for the last eighty years, and the addition of a large new wing in the same style.
AA 1901 (2), 47–8, i; *AR* 14, 1903, 146, 158–64, i, p; *B* 18 May 1901, 491, i, p; *BN* 2 Sept 1892, 315, i.

WERNFAWR HALL, near Harlech

By George Walton for George Davison, a director of Kodak. 1907–10.
Set on only eleven acres, this was nevertheless the largest house designed by the Glasgow Art Nouveau architect and decorator George Walton: an uncompromisingly four-square building constructed out of rough masonry, with broad triangular pediments on each elevation, and views towards Snowdon. There is a big music room, but fewer of the Art Nouveau details than one might have expected. Walton also designed shops for Kodak, and built the Leys, Elstree, in Hertfordshire, for the first manager of the Kodak works at Harrow, J. B. B. Wellington. Now a college.

WEST DEAN PARK, Sussex (Pls. 13–21)

Remodelled and enlarged by George and Peto for William Dodge James. 1891–3.
See pp. 17–27. Now a crafts college.
A 19 Jun 1896, 394, i; *AA* 1893, 27, i; *AA* 1905 (1), 36, i; *BM* 19 May 1893, 667, i; *BN* 9 Jun 1905, 821, i; *CL* 22 and 29 Oct 1981, 1378, 1462, i.

WHITTINGTON, Buckinghamshire (also spelt Wittington)

By Reginald Blomfield for Hudson Kearley (later Lord Devonport), founder of the International Stores and first chairman of the Port of London Authority. 1904; 1909.
Smaller than some of Blomfield's houses, and so less overbearing in its Wrenaissance. The present house is an almost complete rebuilding of one Blomfield had built for the same client only five years previously. Now offices.
AA 1902 (1), 52–3, i; *AA* 1910 (2), 50; *B* 20 and 27 Feb 1904, 198, 223, i, p; *B* 1 May 1909, 524, i, p; *BN* 24 Jun 1898, 887, i.

WICKHAM HALL, Kent (Pls. 24, 183)

By Walter Millard for Gustav Mellin, food manufacturer and importer. 1895.

244. Woodfalls, Melchet Park, Hampshire

Pompous *nouveau riche* remodelling, with billiard room on a curve to allow room for kitchen wing behind. Interiors all in execrable taste, except for the nursery. There was a telescope in the tower. Demolished.
AR 11, 182–4, 187–8, i, p.

WILSFORD MANOR, Wiltshire (Pl. 173)

By Blow and Billery for Sir Edward Tennant, son of Sir Charles Tennant, the chemical manufacturer. 1904–6.
Magnificent gabled house with walls in a chequerwork of stone and flint and a thatched kitchen court.
CL 29 Sept 1906, 450, i.

WITLEY PARK, Surrey (originally known as Lea Park)

By H. Paxton Watson for Whitaker Wright, financier. About 1890.
A big neo-Tudor house, which included a billiard room with a glass ceiling constructed under the lake. There was also a bathing pavilion and boat house by Lutyens. Demolished.
CL 27 Dec 1973, 2190.

WITTERSHAM HOUSE, Kent

By Edwin Lutyens for the Hon. Alfred Lyttelton, builder of Grey Walls (q.v.). 1907–8.
Sophisticated and finely proportioned neo-Georgian house, almost in the village of Wittersham. Lyttelton sold Grey Walls to Willie James of West Dean when it was built.

WOODFALLS, Melchet Park, Hampshire (Pls. 50, 244)

By Darcy Braddell and Humphrey Deane for the Hon. Henry Mond (later second Baron Melchett), of ICI. 1930.
Originally a low vernacular building intended as a nursery bungalow for the children. Mr Mond used it to recuperate after an illness, liked it, and converted it into his country home, adding a bedroom, guest bedroom, living room, study and swimming pool. The new work was heavily influenced by the Cape Dutch style of South Africa, but also showed more than a hint of

Hollywood Spanish. It is in the grounds of Melchet Court, which Braddell had altered shortly before the First World War.
CL 4 Oct 1930, 412, i, p.

WRETHAM HALL, Norfolk

By Reginald Blomfield for Sir Saxton Noble, son of Sir Andrew Noble of Ardkinglas (q.v.). 1913.
In the same style as Moundsmere (q.v.). Blomfield commented that the commission gave him the 'best shooting I ever had'. Demolished.
B 10 Oct 1913, 370, i, p.

WYKE MANOR, Worcestershire (Pl. 108)

Remodelling by Cecil G. Hare. 1924.
See p. 156.
B 4 Dec 1925, 804, i, p.

YEATTON PEVEREY HOUSE, Shropshire

By Aston Webb for Sir Offley Wakeman, baronet. 1890.
Long, low Elizabethan style house built of local red sandstone, with a large living hall.
BA 1899, 312, i; *BN* 16 May 1890, 686, i.

COUNTRY HOUSES BUILT BY BRITISH ARCHITECTS ABROAD

ROYAL VILLA AND GOLD PAVILION, Coq-sur-Mer, Belgium

By Arnold Mitchell for the King of the Belgians. 1903.
This resort was under the special care of the King. As well as a golf links he also built a racing-car circuit. The villa itself was in the unexpectedly old-fashioned Queen Anne Revival style, perhaps still thought of as right for the seaside
B 28 Mar 1903, 338, i, p.

CHATEAU COURTEUIL, near Chantilly, France

By Stanley Hamp of Collcutt and Hamp for the Duc Decazes. 1913.
The building replaced the old chateau which had to be demolished. It has a two-storey living hall, and a racing stable for thirty-six horses.
BN 4 Jul 1913, 14, i, p.

CHATEAU MAURICIEN, Wimereux, France

By John Belcher for M. Ulcoq. 1900.
This was virtually a complete rebuilding in the Empire manner of the house previously on site. It is revealing to discover that Belcher found that the local craftsmen were showing an interest in their work 'such as may be looked for in vain from the British workman'.
AA 1900 (1), 54, i; *AA* 1901 (1), opp. 52, i; *AR* 7, 1900, 204, i; *B* 15 Sept 1900, 235, i, p.

LE BOIS DES MOUTIERS, Normandy

Remodelling by Edwin Lutyens for Guillaume Mallet, who came from a Protestant banking family. 1898.

The long thin oriels over the porch (described by Jean Cocteau in *Le Potomac*) and the extraordinarily mannered west elevation show Lutyens toying with Art Nouveau, although in a way that really prefigured his games with three dimensional geometry in the next decade. It was here that Lady Emily was introduced to Theosophy.

CL 21 and 28 May 1981, 1418, 1494, i.

HOUSE AT CAP D'AGLIO, Monaco

By Giles and Trollope for the Rt Hon. Sir E. Mallet. 1894.

The house was largely built to contain Mallet's superb collection of art treasures, for which a top-lit central hall was constructed. Externally, the house was French Renaissance, with a tall cupola over the concave entrance front; inside, the style was Rococo. The central hall had a ceiling based on Tiepolo. All the rooms had the comfort of open fireplaces although there was also a central heating system: something of an extravagance, one would have thought, in view of the sunny clime.

BN 7 Dec 1894, 783, i, p.

HOUSE NEAR LASKOWICZE, Russia

By M. H. Baillie Scott for Count M. W. Chludzinski. 1912–13.

The house developed the courtyard theme popular with Arts and Crafts architects, although in this case it was regarded as the outcome of the feudal conditions of the area. The Count, who never paid Scott for his work, stipulated that the building had to be defensible against bands of robbers. The original scheme was for an imaginative white-stucco, rather Byzantine structure; the final one was more Surrey vernacular.

A 13 Nov 1914, 413, i; *AA* 1923; *B* 30 Jan 1914, 314, i, p; *S* Jul 1912; *S* Sept 1913.

GROOTE SCHUUR, near Cape Town, South Africa

By Herbert Baker for Cecil Rhodes. 1893–6.

It was Rhodes's wish for the rebuilding of this house that the resources of the colony should be encouraged and developed. This accorded with Baker's Arts and Crafts sympathies. The woodwork, bronze casting and smiths' work were all done locally. The stoep or verandah on the garden front was widely influential back home.

AR 30, 1911, 133ff, i, p; *B* 24 Mar 1900, 294, i, p.

VILLA ARCADIA, Johannesburg, South Africa

By Herbert Baker and Fleming for Sir Lionel Phillips (see Tylney Hall). 1915.

A long, narrow house built on a mountainside ledge to take advantage of more than usually magnificent Transvaal views. The house was faced in plaster and had a loggia or stoep. Like Cecil Rhodes and other men in South Africa, Phillips believed in encouraging local crafts and industries and building in a local style. Consequently, the overhanging pantile roof was the first of its kind in the country, and there were fine wrought-iron screens to the balconies.

B 24 Sept 1915, 223–5, i, p; *CL* 21 Jan 1922, 93, i.

HOUSE AT LAS ARENAS, Bilbao, Spain

By Chatterton and Couch for Don Ramon de la Sota. 1909.

'On the particular instructions of the client it was designed in the English tradition, both as regards plan and elevation.'

BN 27 Aug 1909, 306, i, p.

LAS FRACOAS, Santander, Spain

By Ralph Selden Wornum for the Duke of Santo Mauro. 1899.

'He wished it to look quiet, and as much like an English house as possible.' Rough masonry with ashlar dressings was used for the main house, red brick and half-timber for the offices and stables.

BN 29 Sept 1899, 405, i, p.

MIRAMAR PALACE, San Sebastian, Spain

By Ralph Selden Wornum for the Queen Regent of Spain. 1892.

The Queen Regent used this house as a summer palace, and it has a broad verandah, balcony and tower. It was the first of several commissions Wornum received from the aristocracy of the Iberian peninsula.

B 17 Dec 1892, 480, i.

DAS LANDHAUS WALDBÜHL, near Bern, Switzerland

By M. H. Baillie Scott for Dr Rolf Bühler. 1909–11.

Scott designed the house, the furniture and the garden, although of these the house was probably the least exciting of the three. See Katharina Medici-Mall, *Das Landhaus Waldbühl* (Bern, 1979).

Notes to the Text

Unless otherwise indicated, place of publication London
Lutyens RIBA: Lutyens manuscript letters at the Royal Institute of British Architects' Library (British Architectural Library), London

1. The Smart Set and the Romantics

1. Simon Nowell-Smith (ed.), *Edwardian England, 1901–1914*, Oxford, 1964, 107.
2. George Smalley, *Anglo-American Memories*, 2nd series, 1912, 241.
3. E. F. Benson, *As We Are*, 1932, 240.
4. A. L. Bowley, *The Change in the Distribution of the National Income, 1880–1913*, 1920, 20.
5. *The Studio Yearbook of Decorative Art*, 1908, xi–xii.
6. E.g. Witley Park, Arundel Castle, Kings Walden Bury, Stratton Park.
7. Barbara Lutyens, who married Captain Wallace of Kildonan, remembered that the house, built in 1915, was already regarded as a mistake in 1920; the family left it after the Second World War. Even shorter was the time Haggerston Castle spent in family occupation after its rebuilding in 1915; it was demolished in 1931.
8. Gabriel Tschumi, *Royal Chef: Recollections of Life in Royal Households from Queen Victoria to Queen Mary*, 1954, 101.
9. Such was Lord Iveagh's lunch tent at Elveden.
10. Neville Lytton, *The English Country Gentleman*, 1925, 28.
11. Mark Girouard, *The Victorian Country House*, Oxford, 1971, 168–71.
12. T. H. Escott, *Society in the Country House*, 1907, 96. For West Dean, see *Country Life*, 22 and 29 October 1981, 1378, 1462.
13. T. H. S. Escott, *Society in the New Reign, by a Foreign Resident*, 1904, 89.
14. Jamie Camplin, *The Rise of the Plutocrats*, 1978, 103.
15. Ibid.
16. See for instance the *Ladies Pictorial*, 9 March 1889.
17. Sir Almeric Fitzroy, *Memoirs*, 1925, 73.
18. 29 April 1897.
19. Lutyens RIBA, 15 March 1902.
20. See *Notes and Queries*, 10 August 1935, 92–4.
21. From one of the Jameses' newspaper cuttings scrapbooks at West Dean.
22. Ibid.
23. Darcy Braddell, *Builder*, 12 January 1945, 27–9.
24. Quoted by Nicholas Cooper in *The Opulent Eye*, 1976, 32.
25. G. M. Cornwallis-West, *Edwardian Hey-Days*, 1930, 177.
26. 21 October 1909.
27. There is an account of Culford by Gertrude Storey in *People and Places: An East Anglian Miscellany*, Lavenham, 1973. See also T. H. Escott, *King Edward and His Court*, 1903, 50, and *Society in the New Reign*, 136.
28. Ruth Brandon, *The Dollar Princesses*, 1980, 5.
29. Lord Bryce, *The American Commonwealth*, 1888, vol. 3, 532.
30. Escott, *King*, 190.
31. John Buchan, *Prester John*, 1910 (1922 ed.), 27.
32. He gave an account of his life in *Some Reminiscences*, 1924. I am grateful to Dr Andrew Saint for information on Tylney.
33. Beatrice Webb, *Our Partnership*, 1948, 412–13. Proximity to the squalors of Luton spoiled their enjoyment of 'close contact with an expenditure of £30,000 a year on a country house alone'.
34. See the entry in John Grant (ed.), *Surrey: Historical, Biographical and Pictorial*, c. 1911.
35. Whitaker Wright of Witley Park made his first fortune in West Australia.
36. W. D. Rubinstein, 'British Millionaires, 1809–1949', *Bulletin of the Institute of Historical Research*, vol. 47, 202.
37. By Kennedy Jones, Lord Northcliffe's right-hand man. See Camplin, *Plutocrats*, 9.
38. See also Lutyens's Whalton Manor, built for the widow of the shipbuilder Eustace Smith.
39. Irene Prestwich, *Irene Prestwich of Tirley Garth: A Personal Memoir*, Liverpool, 1974, 4–5. See also *Country Life*, 18 March 1982, 702.
40. Osbert Sitwell, *Great Morning*, 1948, 24–5.
41. Peter Savage, *Lorimer and the Edinburgh Craft Designers*, 1979, 25.
42. Lutyens RIBA, 22 July 1905.
43. Quoted by Christopher Hussey in *The Life of Sir Edwin Lutyens*, 1950, 218.
44. Lutyens RIBA, 22 August 1910.
45. Ibid.
46. I am grateful to Mr Noel Carrington, who knew Hudson through working in the books section of *Country Life* in the 1930s, for showing me the unpublished typescript of a memoir of Hudson.
47. Lord Riddell, *More Pages from My Diary*, 1934, 15.
48. Marjorie Noble, *Marc Noble*, 1918, 51.
49. Lady Emily Lutyens, *Candles in the Sun*, 1957, 80.
50. Lutyens RIBA, 22 April 1911.
51. Ibid., 24 April 1911.
52. Hussey, *Life*, 100, 106.
53. This was Mr Basil Drewe's memory (see the National Trust's guidebook to Castle Drogo by Michael Trinick).

2. Changes in the Country House

1. Kenneth Graham, *The Wind in the Willows*, 1909, 41.

2. C. F. G. Masterman, *The Condition of England*, 1909, 65. 'A few motor-cars can in a week give evidence of wasteful and arrogant expenditure over several counties, while an equal sum spent on carriages would have a much more limited effect,' wrote A. L. Bowley (*Change*, 20).

3. Masterman thought that the atmosphere in 1914 was similar to that preceeding the French Revolution (Riddell, *More*, 213).

4. *Punch*, 19 June 1907, 442.

5. Lord Ernest Hamilton, *The Halcyon Era*, 1933, 23.

6. Cornwallis-West, *Edwardian*, 47.

7. C. W. Stamper, *What I Know*, 1913, 105.

8. Hamilton, *Halcyon*, 21.

9. See David Kerr and Bryan Morgan, *Golden Milestone : Fifty Years of the A.A.*, 1955.

10. Stamper was particular about not being a chauffeur, let alone a footman, although, since he occupied the seat next to the driver, there was not room for one and he had to open the door for the King.

11. Tschumi, *Royal*, 104.

12. 'Imagine the chance of being able to drive the Queen back to the palace in your own car,' gasped Mabel C. Carey in *The King's Service* as late as 1935.

13. Rhoda Broughton, *A Waif's Progress*, 1905, 160.

14. Sir L. Jones, *An Edwardian Youth*, 1956, 229–31.

15. The Duke of Portland, *Men, Women and Things*, 1937, 316.

16. I am grateful to Mr John Kinross, son of the architect, for this recollection. By 1911 Banister Fletcher considered a pit for working beneath the car to be no longer essential, although advisable (*The English Home*, 1911, 372–3).

17. As at Old Surrey Hall.

18. P. A. Barron, *The House Desirable*, 1929, 201.

19. See *Country Life*, 21 and 28 February 1980, 498, 574.

20. MS journal at Minterne Magna.

21. Ralph Nevill (ed.), *Leaves from the Note-Books of Lady Dorothy Nevill*, 1907, 44.

22. Quoted by F. M. L. Thompson in *English Landed Society in the Nineteenth Century*, 1963, 240.

23. See S. B. Saul, *The Myth of the Great Depression, 1873–1896*, 1969.

24. Wickham Hall and Stowell Park. For the Vesteys, see the *Sunday Times*, 5, 12 and 19 October 1980.

25. Price Collier, *England and the English from an American Point of View*, 1909, 56.

26. Subsequent supporters have been more prosaic. In 1950 Lord Hives, managing director of Rolls-Royce, chose a mechanic in overalls and a white-coated laboratory technician.

27. Camplin, *Plutocrats*, 96.

28. 17 December 1910. Quoted in Thompson, *English*, 324.

29. 16 December 1911.

30. For peers with directorships, see G. E. Cockrayne, *The Complete Peerage*, 1926, vol. 5, Appendix C.

31. E. F. Benson, *Mammon and Co.*, 1899.

32. Cornwallis-West, *Edwardian*, 122–5.

33. Even P. G. Wodehouse's old Etonian hero Psmith went into a bank, albeit briefly (*Psmith in the City*, 1910). Remarkably, only thirty-five younger sons of peers were in holy orders in 1899 (Helen Bosanquet, *The Family*, 1906, 185–6).

34. Giles St Aubyn, *Edward VII Prince and King*, 1979, 418.

35. By Lloyd George in a speech to a Newcastle audience on 9 October 1909.

36. Thompson, *English*, 333.

37. Nevill, *Leaves*, 43–4.

38. Ibid.

39. *Country Life*, 6 October 1917, 328.

40. See Loelia (Ponsonby), Duchess of Westminster, *Grace and Favour*, 1961, 90.

41. Cornwallis-West, *Edwardian*, 174.

42. Escott, *Society*, 95. I use the *Survey of London* spelling of Murrietta.

43. Ouida, *A House Party*, 1887, 71.

44. G. G. Scott, *Remarks on Secular and Domestic Architecture, Present and Future*, 1857, 152.

45. Hugh Montgomery Massingberd and David Watkin, *The London Ritz*, 1980, 68.

46. See Kelling Hall (Plate 49).

47. Walter Shaw Sparrow (ed.), *The British Home of Today*, 1904, Ev.

48. C. R. Ashbee MS journal at King's College, Cambridge, 22 April 1913. I am grateful to Alan Crawford for drawing my attention to this quotation.

49. Sparrow, *British*, Ev.

50. See the *Architectural Review*, 16, 1904, 216, 219–22.

51. *Country Life*, 16, 23 and 30 October 1980, 1338, 1458, 1551.

52. A. G. C. Liddell, *Notes from the Life of an Ordinary Mortal*, 1911, 116–17.

53. By Lady Diana Cooper and her friends.

54. Permission to photograph this room was refused.

55. The Countess of Fingall, *Seventy Years Young*, as told to Pamela Hinkson, 1937, 296.

56. Photographs from the trip are at Elveden.

57. Stamper, *What*, 13. For Elveden, see also George Martelli, *The Elveden Enterprise*, 1952.

58. Osbert Lancaster, *Home Sweet Homes*, 1939, 68–9.

59. Ben Travers, *Rookery Nook*, 1933, 50.

60. *Country Life*, 12 and 19 February 1981, 378, 442.

61. E.g. Osbert Sitwell, who described the house and its hostess in *Laughter in the Next Room*, 1944, 43–5, 155–7.

62. *Architectural Review*, 51, 1922, 202–7.

63. Escott, *Society*, 143–4.

64. There are pre-alteration photographs at the house.

65. According to Captain Greville's obituary in *The Times* (6 April 1908), she was married as Margaret Helen Anderson.

66. See Sonia Keppel, *Edwardian Daughter*, 1958, 23.

67. Sitwell, *Laughter*, 43.

68. Keppel, *Edwardian Daughter*, 170.

69. Cornwallis-West, *Edwardian*, 136–7.

70. Rubinstein, *British Millionaires*. Millionaires were distinctly uncommon; only six others died that year.

71. Cornwallis-West, *Edwardian*, 137.

72. The library was also sometimes used as a second drawing room.

73. The remainder is still in the basement.

74. Of 1906.

75. For Edwardian eating patterns, see John Burnett, *Plenty and Want : A Social History of Diet in England from 1915 to the Present Day*, 1966.

76. Consuelo Vanderbilt, *The Glitter and the Gold*, 1952, 62.

77. Mrs Hwfa Williams, *It was Such Fun*, 1935, 34–5.

78. See Jeune, *Lesser*, 61–74.

79. MS at Polesden.

80. E. F. Benson, *The Climber*, 1908, 170–1.

81. Ladies' maids, consequently, were invaluable, and their services increasingly expensive, according to Lady Jeune.

82. Lady Jeune, *Lesser Questions*, 1894, 133–4.

83. Jonathan Garnier Ruffer, *The Big Shots*, 1977, 24.

84. Anita Leslie, *Edwardians in Love*, 1972, 16.

85. E. F. Benson, *Mammon and Co.*, 1899, 68.

86. *Builder*, 101, 27 July 1911, 95.

87. Sir Frederick Ponsonby, *Recollections of Three Reigns*, 1951, 135.

88. *Building News*.

89. For Edwardian Fashions, see C. W. Cunnington, *English Women's Clothing in the Present Century*, 1952.

90. *Lady*, 15 June 1911, 1189.
91. *Country Life*, 8 January 1910, 71.
92. Fingall, *Seventy*, 312–17.
93. Ibid. Roderick Gradidge describes Groote Schuur in *Dream Houses*, 1980, 131–40.
94. Sparrow, *British*, Av.
95. See Jill Frankling, 'Edwardian Butterfly Houses', *Architectural Review*, 157, 1975, 220–5.
96. Benson, *Mammon*, 18.
97. On the other hand, the shortage of real cottages for the agricultural labourer was regarded as a genuine social problem and had its own extensive literature.
98. Constance Battersea, *Reminiscences*, 41.
99. Girouard, *Victorian*, 174–5.
100. 'Quite the most ornamental in every way of Anglo-Saxon semites,' commented Escott (*Society*, 90), with typical prejudice.
101. Battersea, *Reminiscences*, 329.
102. Lutyens RIBA.
103. C. F. G. Masterman, *England After the War*, 1922.
104. Reginald Blomfield, *Memoirs of an Architect*, 1932, 81.
105. Ponsonby, *Recollections*, 16.
106. Nevill, *Leaves*, 137–8.
107. See *Architectural Review*, 82, 1937, 117–22.
108. By Henry W. Binns.
109. *The Studio Yearbook of Decorative Art*, 1926, 5.
110. P. A. Barron, *The House Desirable*, 1929, 2.
111. Ralph Nevill, *The English Country House*, 1925, 3.
112. I am grateful to the dowager Lady Cholmondeley for conversation about Port Lympne.
113. See catalogue.
114. Whiteladies House is in the Bethnal Green Museum of Childhood.
115. Jeremy Gould, *Modern Houses in Britain*, 1977.
116. Lancaster, *Home*, 76.
117. Bridget Clark, 'Charters, Berkshire', *Thirties Society Journal*, No. 2, 1982, 35–40.

3. The Servant Question

1. Alice Ravenhill and Catherine Schiff (ed.), *Household Administration*, 1910, 183.
2. J. H. Elder Duncan, *Country Cottages and Week-End Homes*, 1912, 44.
3. Katharina Medici-Mall, *Das Landhaus Waldbühl von Baillie Scott*, Bern, 1979, 81n.
4. Mrs I. Beeton, *Book of Household Management*, 1915, preface, vi.
5. Ibid., 1923, 9.
6. Clark, 'Charters', 39.
7. J. H. Elder Duncan, *Country Cottages*, 44.
8. Quentin Crewe, *The Frontiers of Privilege: A Century of Social Conflict as Reflected in The Queen*, 1961, 168.
9. This was the regime at Nether Swell Manor, according to the second housekeeper there in 1921–31, Mrs Muriel Hooper (MS recollections at the house).
10. William Lanceley, *From Hall-Boy to House Steward*, 1925, 25.
11. Charles W. Cooper, *Town and Country, or Forty Years Service with the Aristocracy*, 1937, 27.
12. Westminster, *Grace*, 40.
13. Arthur Martin, *The Small House: Its Architecture and Surrounds*, 88.
14. Hermann Muthesius, *Das Englische Haus*, Berlin, 1904–5 (translated, *The English House*, ed. Dennis Sharp, 1979), 149.
15. Beeton, *Household*, 1892, 96.
16. Lawrence Weaver (ed.), *The House and its Equipment*, 1911, 89–90.
17. See catalogue.
18. The Duke of Fife was one of the few men who made an improper suggestion to his mother-in-law, Queen Victoria. He not only suggested that the old lady should dance a reel with him, but chose one that was associated with sweethearts, a fact, of course, of which the Queen was wholly ignorant.
19. Fingall, *Seventy*, 337.
20. Sparrow, *British*, File 4.
21. Lady Jeune, *Lesser Questions*, 1894, 269–70.
22. Tschumi, *Royal Chef*, 138.
23. Jeune, *Lesser*, 264.
24. John, Duke of Bedford, *A Silver-plated Spoon*, 1959, 20.
25. Burnett, *Plenty*, 224.
26. J. E. Panton, *From Kitchen to Garret*, 1888, 152.
27. Quoted by Jill Franklin in *The Gentleman's Country House and its Plan, 1835–1914*, 1981, 103.
28. Martin, *Small House*, 88.
29. 27 February 1919, 196.
30. Lanceley, *Hall-Boy*, 157.
31. Life below stairs at Longleat was engagingly described by the Marchioness of Bath in *Before the Sunset Fades*, 1951. At Petworth the butler insisted that the valets dine in evening dress (Westminster, *Grace*, 43).
32. Vanderbilt, *Glitter*, 57.
33. Lanceley, *Hall-Boy*, 175.
34. Lytton, *English Country Gentleman*, 35.
35. Lucy Maynard Salmon, *Domestic Service*, New York, 1901, 301.
36. A view shared by Lady Jeune, *Lesser*, 263.
37. Ravenhill, *Household*, 187.
38. Lord and Lady Aberdeen, '*We Twa*', 1925, vol. 2, 4ff.
39. Hooper MS recollections, Nether Swell Manor.
40. Jeune, *Questions*, 263.
41. Fingall, *Seventy*, 303.
42. Beeton, *Book*, 1915, 15.
43. Arthur Ponsonby, *The Camel and the Needle's Eye*, 1910, 55–6.
44. Rosina Harrison, *Rose: My Life in Service*, 1975 (paperback edition 1977), 126.
45. Lady Mary Clive, *Brought Up and Brought Out*, 1938, 140ff.
46. *The Cheltenham Looker-On*, 31 August 1901, 829–30.
47. Ernestine Mills, *The Domestic Problem*, 1925, 2.
48. See Weaver, *Equipment*, 113–15.
49. Hamilton, *Old Days*, 91.
50. See Lesley Lewis, *The Private Life of a Country House, 1912–39*, 1980, 80.
51. Salmon, *Domestic*, 295n.
52. *Country Life*, 12 June 1920, 864.
53. Harrison, *Life*, 158–9.
54. Brierley papers, York City Library.
55. *Country Life*, 12 April 1913, supplement 8–12.
56. *Country Life*, 27 December 1913, supplement 7–11.
57. Clive, *Brought Up*, 144–5.
58. MS journal at Minterne.
59. Hooper MS recollections, Nether Swell Manor.
60. Brierley papers, York City Library.
61. Hamilton, *Old Days*, 87–8. Consuelo Vanderbilt remembered how, in view of the shortage of bathrooms at Blenheim, visiting ladies' maids had battled to secure ones for their mistresses (*Glitter*, 81).
62. Quoted in Franklin, *Gentleman's*, 112.
63. Muthesius, *English House*, 237.
64. Elder Duncan, *Country Cottages*, 42.
65. Northamptonshire Record Office.
66. *Country Life*, 21 March 1931, 368–9.
67. *Lady*, 30 January 1930, 141.
68. See the section on 'Labour-Saving in the Home' in Beeton, *Book*, 1923, 69–78.

69. Mills, *Domestic*, 52.

Alyosius Scott Stokes', Nottingham University, 1972.

4. The History Men

1. T. H. Mawson, *The Life and Work of an English Landscape Architect*, 1927, 79.
2. Reginald Blomfield, *History of Renaissance Architecture in England, 1500–1800*, 1897.
3. See the obituary in the Council of the Royal Scottish Academy's annual report for 1931, 14–16.
4. I am grateful to Mr John Kinross, son of the architect, for showing me the typescript draft of his memoir, 'Fifty Years in the City', to be published in 1982, and for other information on his father.
5. 'Remarks by Mr John Kinross, R.S.A., on Statement by Vice-Chairman on Teaching and Design', typescript, Edinburgh College of Art, 1918.
6. For Manderston, see *Country Life*, 15 and 22 February, 1 March 1979, 390, 466, 542.
7. Information Mr John Kinross.
8. Peter Quennell, *The Marble Foot*, 1976, 49.
9. *Vanity Fair*, 6 September 1890.
10. For the history of architectural publishing in England, see David Watkin, *The Rise of Architectural History*, 1980.
11. Quoted Hussey, *Life*, 17.
12. See *Country Life*, 11, 18 and 25 February 1982, 346, 410, 478.
13. See *Country Life*, 24 and 31 December 1981, 2242, 2298.
14. See John Pudney, *The Thomas Cook Story*, 1953.
15. See David Jolley's catalogue to the exhibition, 'Architect Exuberant: George Skipper, 1856–1948', Norwich School of Art, 1975.
16. Ibid., 14.
17. Sketchbook at the RIBA drawings collection.
18. However, the Italians were, sadly, confined to the more routine work. E. W. D. Potter of Norwich, Farmer and Brindley of Westminster, and H. Fehr of the Fulham Road executed the major pieces of sculpture (*Builder*, 22 September 1911, 329).
19. Blomfield, *Renaissance*, vol. 2, 402.
20. See catalogue.
21. Reginald Blomfield, *Memoirs of an Architect*, 1932, 94–5. It was characteristic that, on one occasion, Blomfield and horse nearly landed on top of him when jumping a fence on the other side of which James was sitting.
22. *Arts and Crafts Essays by Members of the Arts and Crafts Exhibition Society*, 3rd ed., 1901, 296.
23. Blomfield, *Renaissance*, vol. 2, 202.
24. John Buchan, *A Lodge in the Wilderness*, 1906, 258.
25. W. R. Lethaby, *Form in Civilization*, 2nd ed., Oxford, 1957, 17.
26. W. R. Lethaby, *Philip Webb and his Work*, Oxford, 1935 (reprinted 1979), 156.
27. *Architectural Association Notes*, 19, 1899, 130.
28. Lethaby, *Webb*, 136.
29. See Jill Franklin, 'The Planning of the Victorian Country House', Ph.D. thesis, London University, 1973, 35; although there were other exceptions, see catalogue.
30. W. G. Newton, *The Work of Ernest Newton*, 1925, 4.
31. As well as strict neo-Georgian at Burgh Heath and Luckley.
32. Quoted in Charles McKean and Robert Rogerson's guide to The Hill House, 1981.
33. Peter Ferriday (ed.), *Victorian Architecture*, 1963, 83.
34. The Bath City Archivist holds obituaries for T. S. Cotterell, who died February 1950.
35. See *Country Life*, 21 and 28 February 1980, 489, 574.
36. Comment on lecture at the Architectural Association, 1893. Quoted by T. Rory Spence in his B.A. Dissertation 'Leonard

5. The Tudor Taste

1. The reaction, perhaps, to the dislocation described in George Dangerfield's *The Strange Death of Liberal England*, 1966.
2. Marjorie Noble, *Marc Noble*, 1918, 51.
3. Sir Gordon Russell, *Designer's Trade*, 1968, 78.
4. I am grateful to Mr Charles Hudson for information on Wyke Manor. See the *Builder*, 4 December 1925, 805.
5. See *Country Life*.
6. Savage, *Lorimer*, 25.
7. Lutyens RIBA, 17 August 1921.
8. Ibid., 4 August 1904.
9. T. Garner and A. Stratton, *The Domestic Architecture of England During the Tudor Period*, 1908–11, preface v.
10. Lutyens RIBA, 26 August 1909.
11. Gill and Reigate.
12. There are drawings and letters in Northamptonshire Record Office.
13. That of course was the date of the People's Budget.
14. The *British Architect*, 7 May 1909, 329. The published designs were modified.
15. See James D. Kornwolf, *M. H. Baillie Scott and the Arts and Crafts Movement*, Baltimore, 1972, 410–15.
16. M. H. Baillie Scott, *Houses and Gardens*, 1933, 155.
17. 1864–1926. See Cuthbert Headlam, *George Abraham Crawley: A Short Memoir*, 1919.
18. See John Cornforth's articles on Castle Fraser, *Country Life*, 17 August 1978, 444–5.
19. Ian Nairn and Nikolaus Pevsner, *The Buildings of England, Surrey* (2nd ed.), 1971, 396.
20. Crawley had thought of buying Crowhurst when it came on the market some years earlier; it was in fact bought by a Mr Gainsford, a descendant of the family that built it, and he gave Crawley, and later Consuelo Vanderbilt, a lease that permitted repair work and additions.
21. The date given on a plan prepared by Crawley that is still at the house, and was illustrated in *Country Life*, 12 July 1919, 51.
22. Née Vanderbilt. See her book *The Glitter and the Gold*, from which the succeeding quotations are taken.
23. *Architects' Journal*, 4 August 1926, 158.
24. Headlam, *Crawley*, 50.
25. *Country Life*, 14 September 1929, 352; *Country Life*, 15 and 22 October 1959, 554, 654.
26. Widow of Lieutenant-Colonel the Hon. George Campbell Napier, twin brother of the second Baron Napier of Magdala.
27. A member of the stock exchange for thirty-three years, a director of Brewerley Mines Ltd and of the British Syphon Company Ltd.
28. Of 1935.
29. *Country Life*.
30. I am grateful to Emil Godfrey for information on his father's work.
31. Barron, *House Desirable*, 168–75.
32. See catalogue.
33. *Country Life*, 10 September 1932, 292.
34. Philip Tilden, *True Remembrances*, 1954, 33 and 60.
35. For instance, the Clock House, West Grinstead (see catalogue and the *Architectural Review*, 17, 1925, 106). The idea was also seen in church architecture. *New Churches Illustrated*, published by the Incorporated Church Building Society (London), 1936, gives details of the St Philip, North Sheen, erected in 1928–9 to the designs of Edward A. Swan. The

interior consists of a timber-frame barn from Oxted. At £6,750 the cost was less than most churches in the book, so it is perhaps surprising that the solution was not adopted more often.

36. Small Downs House, Sandwich, by G. H. Biddulph-Pinchard for Mrs Leverton Harris, 1914. Even the glass was old and 'slightly golden in tint', according to the *Architectural Review*, 60, 1926, 24.
37. *Country Life*, 1924.
38. Ivor Stewart-Liberty, *Liberty's Tudor Shop*, 1924.
39. *Building News*, 11 July 1924, 34–6.
40. *Builder*, 9 August 1929, 218. See also *Cheshire Life*, December 1975.
41. It includes a section giving plans and elevations of the houses discussed.
42. Major and Mrs P. A. Brooke, the clients of Smuggler's Way, came into contact with Shadbolt through seeing his work at the Ideal Home exhibition. The site was ten acres. I am grateful to Mr Gurth R. E. Brooke for information on the house.
43. 1891–1962. I am grateful to his widow, Mrs A. Phillips, for information on her husband's career.
44. Lady Diana Mosley, *A Life of Contrasts*, 1977, 65–6.
45. Besford, *Spoon*, 65.
46. E. F. Benson, *Queen Lucia*, 1920, 12.
47. Walter Guinness (1880–1944), the third son of the first Earl of Iveagh, created Baron Moyne in 1932, having been M.P. for Bury St Edmunds since 1907. He was Under Secretary for War in 1922, Financial Secretary to the Treasury in 1923–4 and Minister of Agriculture and Fisheries in 1925–9. He travelled widely on his yacht and published travel books. He was appointed Resident Minister in the Middle East in January 1944 and was assassinated on 6 November the same year, having refused a police escort. Lady Moyne, whom he married in 1903, was Lady Evelyn Erskine, daughter of the fourteenth Earl of Buchan.
48. Mosley, *Contrasts*, 61.
49. There is a description of Bailiffscourt in *The Cottage in the Fields*, by Gerard Young, 1945.
50. Phillips wrote a detailed dissertation on the history and restoration of the chapel. I am grateful to Mrs Phillips for showing me the typescript.
51. Undated but probably produced in the 1950s. The idea of the Manor House, Hitchin, where Phillips's business was located, was that Georgian antiques could be displayed in period Georgian rooms. Phillips's personal preference was for Georgian rather than medieval furniture.
52. Many were still at the house when I visited in 1979 and 1980, although it has since changed hands more than once.
53. Robert Rhodes James (ed.), *Chips: The Diaries of Sir Henry Channon*, 1967, 13 August 1934.
54. See note 50.
55. Bedford, *Spoon*, 65.
56. Mosley, *Contrasts*, 62.

6. Castles of Comfort

1. Hussey, *Life*, 218.
2. *Building News*, 31 October 1890, 608.
3. Savage, *Lorimer*, 98.
4. Ibid., 126.
5. John Betjeman, 'Kinloch Castle', *Scotland's Magazine*, December 1959, 17–21.
6. Smalley, *Anglo-American*, 258–9.
7. Carnegie mentioned Skibo and his reasons for building it in his *Autobiography* (1920, 217). The brevity of this account suggests that he was not deeply interested in the architecture.

8. His partner was presumably the R. J. Macbeth who designed the Masonic Hall, Portree, Skye, in 1912.
9. See Carnegie's Autobiography and Burton J. Hendrick, *Life of Andrew Carnegie*, 1932.
10. William Calden, *The Estate and Castle of Skibo*, 1949, 38. For Skibo, see also Peter Gray, *Skibo: Its Lairds and History*, 1906.
11. M. H. Baillie Scott, *Houses and Gardens*, 1933, 240.
12. *Country Life*, 8 and 15 January 1981, 18, 66.
13. T. H. S. Escott, *Personal Forces of the Period*, 1898, 318.
14. Astor's son, Waldorf, was not so self-important; see Dangerfield, *Strange Death*, 48.
15. See Virginia Cowles, *The Astors*, 1979, and others.
16. Cowles, *Astors*, 153.
17. William Waldorf Astor, *Silhouettes, 1855–1885*, 1917, 11.
18. Ibid., 60.
19. The Countess of Warwick, *Afterthoughts*, 1931, 114.
20. For the Pearsons, see Anthony Quiney, *John Loughborough Pearson*, London and New Haven, 1979.
21. Tilden, *True Remembrances*, 114.
22. The Hearst papers relating to St Donat's are in the library of the National Magazine Company, London. I am grateful to Susanna van Langenberg, library and syndication manager, for giving me access to what consists literally of crateloads of archival material.
23. 12 August 1925.
24. W. A. Swanberg, *Citizen Hearst*, 1961, 408.
25. Sir Charles Allom (1865–1947) was knighted in 1913 for his work at Buckingham Palace. *Times* obituary, 5 June 1947.
26. Swanberg, *Citizen*, 486.
27. Ibid., 324.
28. There is no mention of the fate of the old roof in the plans for the restoration filed with the Diocesan Registry.
29. Alice M. Head, *It Could Never Have Happened*, 1939, 124. Unfortunately it escaped the *Hansard* index.
30. *Times*, 13 May 1929.
31. Ibid., 4 October 1930.
32. Swanberg, *Citizen*, 280.
33. *Wiltshire Gazette*, 18 September 1930. 'I sometimes think,' said Sir Charles, 'that what I know about Mr Hearst's plans and dreams are a fairy tale, but they are happily true.'
34. National Magazine Company inventory.
35. Swanberg, *Citizen*.
36. An account of Lord Conway's career is given in *Country Life*, June and July 1932. See also *Country Life*, 20, 27 April and 4 May 1918, 386, 404, 424.
37. *Country Life*, 2, 9 and 16 March 1918, 214, 242, 270; *Country Life*, 30 November, 7 and 14 December 1935, 566, 606, 630.
38. Marquess Curzon, *Bodiam Castle*, 1926, xiii.
39. Ibid., 11 February 1914.
40. Ibid., letter from Weir, 17 July 1919.
41. Tilden, *True Remembrances*, 51–9.

7. The Country House as Cottage

1. Charles Holme (ed.), *Modern British Domestic Architecture and Decoration*, 1901, 13.
2. David Ottewill, 'Robert Weir Schultz (1860–1951): 'An Arts and Crafts Architect', *Architectural History*, 22, 1979, 88.
3. See J. H. Elder Duncan, *Country Cottages*, 1912, 27, and Barron, *House Desirable*, 33–5.
4. See e.g. Peter Davey, *Arts and Crafts Architecture*, 1980, and Lionel Lambourne, *Utopian Craftsmen*, 1981.
5. *Royal Institute of British Architects' Journal*, 39, 1932, 303. For Melsetter, see John Brandon Jones, *Architectural Association Journal*, March 1949, 167–71; and *Country Life*, 13 August 1981, 566. I am grateful to Mr Brandon Jones for discussing

the house with me.

6. I am grateful to Alan Crawford for information on the Birmingham connection

7. Entry in the Morris and Co. order book for 1893.

8. W. R. Lethaby, 'What shall we call beautiful?' originally published in *Hibbert Journal*, 1918; reprinted in *Form in Civilization*, Oxford, 1957, 121.

9. W. R. Lethaby, *Ernest Gimson*, 1924, 3–4.

10. Margot Asquith, *Autobiography*, 1920, 155 et passim.

11. *Royal Institute of British Architects' Journal*, 39, 1932.

12. Quoted by Peter Savage in his Ph.D. thesis at Edinburgh University, 'An Examination of the Work of Sir Robert Lorimer', 1973.

13. *Architecture*, 1912, 14.

14. A copy is in the possession of Mr John Brandon Jones.

15. See Alan Crawford, *Country Life*, 24 and 31 January 1980, 252, 308.

16. Ibid.

17. C. R. Ashbee journal, 14 October 1914 (MS in King's College, Cambridge).

18. Norman Jewson, *By Chance I Did Rove*, 1952.

19. Letter to Philip Webb, 6 July 1902. In the possession of Mr Edward Barnsley, to whom I am grateful for his recollections of the Sapperton community.

20. Ibid., 1 May 1904.

21. Preface to the 'Ernest Gimson' exhibition at Leicester Museums and Art Gallery, 1969.

22. Drawing at Cheltenham City Art Gallery and Museum, dated 27 September 1907.

23. *Builder*, 113, 6 July 1917, 3.

24. John Rothenstein, *Summer's Lease*, 1965, 50.

25. Ashbee journal, 14 October 1914.

26. The two-man saw is in Arlington Mill museum, Gloucestershire.

27. Cheltenham City Art Gallery and Museum.

28. 30 June 1901.

29. Lutyens RIBA, 6 May 1906.

30. This is Mr Edward Barnsley's interpretation.

31. George Sturt (George Bourne), *Change in the Village*, 1912, 111.

32. William Rothenstein, *Men and Memories*, 1932, 275.

33. Conversation with Edward Barnsley.

34. See Nicholas Pevsner and Enid Radcliffe, 'Randall Wells', *Architectural Review*, 136, 1964, 336–8.

35. See *Country Life*, 7 and 14 September 1940, 212, 234.

36. Quoted by Roderick Gradidge in *Dream Houses*, 1980, 165.

37. Sydney Blow, *The Ghost Walks On Fridays*, 1935, 15.

38. Neville Lytton, *The English Country Gentleman*, 1925, 27–39.

39. *Building News*, 11 July 1913, 46.

40. 'Remarks by John Kinross, R.S.A., on Statement by Vice-Chairman on Teaching and Design', typescript, Edinburgh College of Art, 1918.

41. Lutyens RIBA, 24 August 1917.

42. See Westminster, *Grace*, 183–5.

43. Michael Davie (ed.), *The Diaries of Evelyn Waugh*, 1976, 802.

44. Letter from Will Hart to C. R. Ashbee, 3 March 1905. I am grateful to Alan Crawford for this and other references to Ashbee MSS.

45. Ashbee journal, March 1902.

46. See *Country Life*, 16, 23 and 30 October 1980, 1338, 1458, and 1551.

47. I have not found documentary evidence for the work in the library.

48. H. Massé, *The Art Workers' Guild*, 1935.

49. I am grateful to Alan Crawford and George Breeze for showing me the typescript of the chapter on decorative painting 'For the Common Good and Beauty of Our Towns' in the forthcoming book, *By Hammer and Hand*.

50. See Christopher Sykes, *Evelyn Waugh*, 1975, 114–15, 168–9.

8. The Road to Good Taste

1. Walter Shaw Sparrow (ed.), *The Modern Home*, n.d., 102–3.

2. J. H. Elder Duncan, *The House Beautiful*, 1907, 21–2.

3. See Girouard, *Victorian*, 168–71.

4. See *Country Life*, 27 September and 4 October 1979, 938, 1166.

5. Letter in the possession of Mr G. J. Yorke, to whom I am grateful. Helen Smith discusses Webb's correspondence with Reginald Yorke in *Architectural History*, 24, 1981, 92–102.

6. Sparrow, *British*, Ci.

7. Joseph Crouch and Edmund Butler, *The Apartments of the House*, 1900, 74, 77.

8. Lutyens RIBA, 24 July 1904.

9. Muthesius, *English House*, 195.

10. As Brierley was called the Lutyens of the North.

11. Savage, *Lorimer*, 65.

12. *Magazine of Art*, new series, 2, 1903, 210.

13. Kornwolf, *Baillie Scott*, 173–81.

14. Illustrated in Alexander Koch, *Meister Der Innenkunst*, Darmstadt, 1902.

15. See Simon Jervis, 'Holland and Sons, and the Furnishing of the Atheneum', *Furniture History*, 6, 1970, 43–7, 54.

16. Mrs Haweis, *The Art of Decoration*, 1881, 29–31.

17. *Lady*, 8 April 1897, 464.

18. Ibid.

19. Ibid., 470.

20. For a full discussion of the French taste, see Nicholas Cooper, *The Opulent Eye*, 1976.

21. Nevill, *Leaves*, 107.

22. For instance, Marcel Boulanger, C. J. Corblet, P. Turpin and Co., René Sergent. See *The Survey of London* volumes for the Grosvenor Estate.

23. See *Country Life*, 13 and 20 January 1934, 38, 66; *Country Life*, 12 November 1981, 1622.

24. Information Furniture and Woodwork Department, Victoria and Albert Museum. However, it was Mellier and Co. who decorated the oak hall for George and Peto in the early 1890s.

25. Account taken from newspaper cuttings (dated 7 November 1905) in an album in the house.

26. Clive Wainwright, 'The Dark Ages of Art Revived', *Connoisseur*, June 1978, 95.

27. *Furniture Gazette*, 15 June 1890, 160.

28. Muthesius, *English House*, 195.

29. H. J. Jennings, *Our Homes and How to Beautify Them*, 1902, 73–4.

30. Aldous Huxley, *Crome Yellow*, 1921, 7–8.

31. I am grateful to Michael Pick for this information.

32. See Wainwright, 'The Dark Ages'.

33. Ibid.

34. Lewis, *Private Life*, 58–9.

35. Elder Duncan, *House Beautiful*, 101.

36. Inventory of 1912 at West Sussex Record Office.

37. Elder Duncan, *House Beautiful*, 136.

38. Muthesius, *English House*, 211.

39. Elder Duncan, *House Beautiful*, 139.

40. Muthesius, *English House*, 205.

41. By J. H. Elder Duncan, 1907.

42. But Edis was best known for his hotels (Claridges) and clubs (the Constitution Club).

43. *Country Life*, 12 March 1910, 378.

44. *Country Life*, 19 and 26 March 1923, 678, 714.

45. *Country Life*, 17 January 1931, 66–7.

46. Westminster, *Grace*, 100.
47. Simon Houfe, *Sir Albert Richardson, the Professor*, Luton, 1980, 148.
48. Westminster, *Grace*, 100.
49. *Country Life*, 23 May 1929, 423.
50. Evelyn Waugh, *A Handful of Dust*, 1934.
51. *Country Life*, 6 December 1930, 741.
52. Ibid., 14 February 1931, 200.
53. Ibid., 6 December 1930, 741.
54. Ibid., 743.

9. Postscript: The Edwardian Garden

1. See Mark Girouard, *Sweetness and Light*, Oxford, 1977, 152–9.
2. William Morris, *Hopes and Fears for Art*, 1882, 128.
3. J. D. Sedding, *Garden-Craft Old and New*, 1891, 130.
4. Reginald Blomfield and F. Inigo Thomas, *The Formal Garden in England*, 1892, 19.
5. William Robinson, *The Wild Garden*, 1870 (reprinted from the fourth edition 1979), B2.
6. Countess von Arnim, *Elizabeth and her German Garden*, 1898, 8.
7. *Edinburgh Review*, 184, July 1896, 161–84.
8. Quoted from 'The Influence of Gertrude Jekyll in the Use of Roses in Gardens and Garden Design', *Garden History*, V, I, 1977, 53.
9. *Country Life*, 10 october 1908, 493.
10. T. H. Mawson, *The Life and Work of an English Landscape Architect*, 1927, 123.
11. Gertrude Jekyll, *Garden Ornament*, 1918, 73.
12. Sir Lawrence Weaver, *Report of the Conference on Garden Planning*, Royal Horticultural Society, 1928, 37.
13. Anonymous, *The Chapel, Madresfield Court*, n.d.
14. Muthesius, *English House*, 107.
15. See *Country Life*, 5 August 1905, 162.
16. Sir Frank Crisp, *Guidebook to Friar Park* (abridged from the fourth edition), 1914 (Royal Horticultural Society library).
17. *Country Life*, 4 July 1903, 18.
18. See Mea Allan, *E. A. Bowles and his Garden at Myddleton House*, 1865–1954, 1973.
19. Described by Lord Devonport in *The Travelled Road*, 1934, 232ff.
20. Gertrude Jekyll, *Colour in the Flower Garden*, 1908, 89–105.
21. Alice Martineau, *The Herbaceous Garden*, 1913, 140.
22. The Countess of Warwick, *An Old English Herb Garden*, passim.
23. *Country Life*, 4 May 1901, 560.
24. Interestingly, this was republished with other plates by the architect William Young in 1900.
25. *Country Life*, 2 September 1922, 272.
26. Ibid., 277.

Index

343